THE GREEKS
AND THEIR HERITAGES

The Greeks

AND THEIR HERITAGES

ARNOLD TOYNBEE

Oxford New York Toronto Melbourne

OXFORD UNIVERSITY PRESS

1981

Oxford University Press, Walton Street, Oxford OX2 6DP

London Glasgow New York Toronto
Delhi Bombay Calcutta Madras Karachi
Kuala Lumpur Singapore Hong Kong Tokyo
Nairobi Dar es Salaam Cape Town
Melbourne Auckland
and associate companies in
Beirut Berlin Ibadan Mexico City

British Library Cataloguing in Publication Data
Toynbee, Arnold
    The Greeks and their heritages
    1. Civilization, Greek
    2. Greece, Modern – Civilization
    I. Title
    938   DF77   80-41711
    ISBN 0-19-215256-4

Printed in the United States of America

NOTE ON SPELLING

SEVERAL reviewers of my book *Constantine Porphyrogenitus and his World* criticized my phonetic transliteration of Byzantine Greek personal names and place-names. It is true that, in English books, Greek proper names are usually written as if they were Latin for all periods down to the reign of the Ottoman Emperor Mehmet II (1451–81), and for convenience of reference, I have followed this usual practice myself, with only one exception, in citing the works of Byzantine authors.

Latinization (e.g. 'Plato') or Anglicization (e.g. 'Aristotle') is so well established for Greek proper names dating from the pre-Byzantine Age that it would be pedantic to depart from this practice, but it is not easy to choose a date at which Latinization shall stop and phonetic transliteration begin. It would be absurd, in a book written in English, to write 'Platon' and 'Aristoteles', but it would also be absurd to Latinize Mavrokordháto into 'Maurocordatus' or Venezélos into 'Benizelus'. It would be equally absurd to Latinize the place-name Kydhoniés as 'Cydoniae', or Mesolónghi as 'Mesolongium'.

We now have written specimens of the Greek language that are perhaps as early as *circa* 1400 B.C., and are certainly as early as *circa* 1200 B.C. Since then, the pronunciation of Greek has changed. The prosody of Hellenic-Age Greek poetry is based on a distinction between long and short syllables. In that age, the accent on Greek words appears to have been a tone-accent, and, in Hellenic metres, no account is taken of it. Since then, the accent has become a stress-accent. The prosody of some Byzantine-Age Greek poetry, and of all subsequent Greek poetry, is based on the stress-accent, like the prosody of English poetry. A foreigner who ignored the stress-accent in trying to speak Greek to a present-day Greek would be unintelligible. There have also been changes in the pronunciation of some of the letters of the Greek alphabet: e.g. β is now pronounced as English 'v', not as English 'b'; η and υ are now pronounced like the 'i' in the English word 'machine'. No doubt these changes took place gradually, but the Hellenic pronunciation had been replaced by the modern pronunciation at least as early as the seventh century of the Christian Era.

In the present book, no accents or marks distinguishing long vowels are placed on Hellenic-Age Greek words. The names of Greek authors, down to those who wrote in the Ottoman Emperor Mehmet II's reign, are cited in the conventional Latinized form. But, in the text, Byzantine-Age and Modern-Age Greek proper nouns and other words are transliterated into English phonetically, except for a few place-names (e.g. Constantinople, Athens) and many Christian names (e.g. George, Constantine) that are current in English and have a well-established English spelling.

PREFACE

POSTERITY's view of the so-called 'classical' age of Greek history is still being influenced, to a surprising and unfortunate degree, by the outlook of a clique of Greek pedants who lived under Roman rule during the reign of the first Roman Emperor, Augustus (31 B.C.–A.D. 14). These pedants were the neo-Atticists. They set out to revive the form of the Attic dialect of the Greek language that had been current in the fifth and fourth centuries B.C. They held that, if contemporary Greeks took to speaking and writing the language of the Athenians of that past age, they would recapture that age's lost 'greatness'.

The neo-Atticists' thesis is invalidated by at least two fallacies. The first fallacy is that the language in which a great literature has been written is itself intrinsically 'great' and 'pure' and 'sublime'. Every language is always in process of change. No particular phase of any language is more permanent or more 'pure' than any other. In any phase, any language may become the vehicle of a great literature. This depends, not on the structure of the language itself, but on the calibre of the poets and philosophers whose mother-tongue this language happens to be. The Attic dialect of the Greek language in the fifth and fourth centuries B.C. had the good fortune to be used by great writers; but, before that, a different dialect of Greek had been the vehicle of the Homeric epic, and, within the last 150 years, Modern Greek has provided a vehicle for poets who have been great enough to be able to look their famous Hellenic predecessors in the face without being abashed.

A second fallacy in the neo-Atticists' thesis is that literature can serve as a criterion for assessing the value of the sum total of human activities. Man may be the measure of all things, but literature certainly is not. The Attic literature of the fifth and fourth centuries B.C. was unquestionably great, and so was contemporary Attic philosophy and visual art and architecture. On the other hand, the years 478–338 B.C. were the political nadir of Attic history and of the history of the Hellenic World as a whole. This cultural golden age of Hellenism was disgraced by political factiousness and by fratricidal wars. The Greeks of the Augustan Age ought to have looked back to their ancestors' political performance in the Periclean age, not with nostalgia, but with aversion and contrition. If they had really been able to conjure the Periclean Age back into life again by reviving a transitory form of one of its dialects, they would soon have found themselves longing for the Roman Peace that they had been the first generation of Greeks to enjoy.

These fallacies seem obvious, yet, in spite of them, the neo-Atticists' thesis has governed the subsequent view of Greek history that has been taken by later generations of Greeks and by the Greeks' foreign admirers. For instance, in this conventional presentation, the curtain is often rung down on the performance at the year 338 B.C., in which a great Greek statesman, King Philip II of Macedon, imposed peace on all the warring states of Greece. This had never been achieved before, except possibly by some ruler of Mycenae in the thirteenth century B.C.

King Philip also made the fortune of the Attic dialect of Greek by adopting it, and not his native Macedonian dialect, as the official language of his kingdom. Thanks to Philip's historic decision, Attic Greek had become, by the neo-Atticists' time, the lingua franca of the western end of the Old World all the way from India to the hinterland of Marseilles. As a result of this enormous spread in the course of three centuries, the Attic dialect had undergone changes, and this was natural and healthy. If the neo-Atticists had succeeded in substituting for the contemporary Attic *koine* the archaic Attic of the fifth and fourth centuries B.C., the result would have been a shrinkage of the 'vulgar' *koine*'s currency. The neo-Atticists failed, and today the *koine* is still the liturgical language of the Greek-speaking Christian churches of the Eastern Orthodox communion.

Greek history of periods earlier than the year 338 B.C. is certainly interesting and instructive, but so too is Greek history from 338 B.C. onwards down to the present day. The post-Hellenic Greeks have had no need to be overawed by their ancestors' achievements in the Hellenic phase of Greek history. The Byzantine Greeks' achievements in architecture and in visual art are likewise both distinctive and great. The Modern Greeks have not only produced great poets; in their war of independence and in their recent resistance-movements to foreign invaders, they have performed feats of heroism that are as fine as their ancestors' feats at Marathon and at Thermopylae, while, on a more mundane plane, they have played a highly successful part in the Modern World's commercial life.

Nevertheless, the Modern Greeks have not yet overcome their awe of their 'classical' predecessors, and this excessive reverence for a particular phase of their past history is still hampering them. The Hellenic-Age Greeks did not feel this undue piety towards their Mycenaean predecessors. They made use of their memories of the Mycenaean Age, not for canonizing the Mycenaean Greeks' achievements, but as mental raw material for the creation of their own great poetry. Why have the Greeks' reactions to their heritages differed so greatly at different stages of Greek history? This question is the theme of the present book.

CONTENTS

I

THE INFLUENCE OF
HERITAGES FROM THE PAST

ALL human beings now alive have a heritage of equal length. Our coeval common heritage can be traced back in time beyond the date of the genesis of human nature and the far earlier date of the genesis of life on this planet. The heritage dates from the genesis of the Universe itself, supposing that the Universe had a beginning—and this is a hotly debated question which seems unlikely to be answered conclusively. Even if the physical facet of the Universe could be demonstrated to have originated *ex nihilo* (in the physical sense of the word *nihil*) at some ascertainable initial date/location of time/space, this would not prove that the spiritual presence in and behind the Universe is not eternal.

Thus the heritage of the present generation of mankind is at least as old as the Universe, and the age of the Universe may be infinite. This holds true for all present-day human societies. Societies are realities of a different order from human beings. They are networks of relations between human beings; and a social network is neither an organism nor a person; it is an institution. If we picture a society mentally in organic or personal imagery, we are succumbing to the fallacy of anthropomorphism; and this is a delusion which is misleading both intellectually and morally. However, human societies do share with human beings the characteristic of having a heritage from the past. Living human societies, like living human beings, have a heritage of a uniform length which may be infinite. Our societies probably have a longer history than we human beings have; for our ancestors could hardly have become human if they had not succeeded previously in becoming social animals.

Heritage is karma. This is a Sanskrit word whose literal meaning is simply 'action', but which is used technically, in the vocabulary of Buddhism, to mean the influence of the momentum of past action on present action. Karma, in this technical sense of the word, can be either an asset or a liability. It is neither the one nor the other unalterably; for karma is a current account which is constantly receiving credits and debits. Karma is being changed, either for better or for worse, by continual further action; and action will continue for so long as the human race survives. To believe this, it is not necessary also to accept the Buddhist hypothesis that human beings are reincarnated in a cycle of rebirths which recurs unless and until the revenant's whole heritage of karma has been dissipated. Even if we believe that death spells spiritual as well as physical annihilation for each individual, we must concede that karma will be transmitted either physically through genes or culturally through the transmission of a social heritage by education in the broadest meaning of this word.

Karma is at work even if we have no conscious memory of our own past acts or of the acts of previous incarnations of ourselves or of our ancestors or of other deceased members of the human society to which we are parties. This is one of the senses in which 'all history is contemporary history'. (The aphorism is Croce's,[1] though this interpretation of it is not what Croce meant by it.) The whole of the past is always alive and at work in the present, even if we are now oblivious of it. If, however, we do consciously remember the past, this is likely to have an effect on our reaction to karma. The recognition of our karma may stimulate us to try to modify it by further action on lines that we choose. On the other hand, awareness may intimidate us into passively permitting karma to take its course. We may dislike our karma, yet may feel it to be too potent for us to have any power to change it for the better. Alternatively, we may idealize it, and may therefore feel that any attempt to change it would be sacrilegious.

Among all the peoples that exist in the present-day world, the three that have the longest memories of their pasts are the Chinese, the Jews, and the Greeks. The memories of each of these three peoples reach back to the thirteenth century B.C. The history of literate civilization in 'Iraq and Egypt is nearly 2,000 years older. It begins about 3000 B.C. This is, however, a discovery that has been made by modern Western archaeologists who have found out the dates and purposes of ancient monuments and have deciphered disused scripts conveying extinct languages. The memory of present-day 'Iraqis and Egyptians is considerably shorter than the memory of present-day Chinese and Jews and Greeks. It does not reach back beyond the successive conversions of the 'Iraqis' and Egyptians' ancestors first to Christianity and then to Islam. Present-day Egyptians have no memory of Pharaonic Egypt, and present-day 'Iraqis none of the first dynasty of Ur, or even of the last dynasty of Babylon.

Memory is, of course, fallible. It is well known that memoirs, written late in life, sometimes give retrospective accounts of events that differ markedly from contemporary accounts of the same events in a diary

---

[1] Croce, Benedetto: 'Ogni vera storia è storia contemporanea', in *Teoria e storia della storiografia* (Bari 1917), p. 4 of 2nd edn. (1920).

written by the same hand. Such discrepancies indicate that memory is an imperfect intellectual instrument. Moreover, remembering is not in all cases a purely intellectual activity. Memories may be evoked by emotions, conscious or unconscious, and, conversely, emotions may be aroused by memories, even if the memories have been purely intellectual events to start with. The interplay between memory and emotion may distort to a further degree the, at best, imperfect image of the past that the memory presents. I may believe, in all good faith, that my memory has preserved an accurate record of the truth; yet my feelings may have led my memory to play me false. They may have led it to present the past, not as this truly was, but as I should like it to have been. This disturbing effect of my feelings and my wishes may be obvious to someone else who, unlike me, is not involved emotionally and who has independent first-hand or second-hand information of his own about the same past events.

This happens not only with our memories of past events in our own lives, but also with the memories that we possess as participants in some network of social relations—our family or our political or ecclesiastical community or some other institution in which we are implicated. A people's sentimental picture of its own history may differ very widely indeed from the picture of the same people's history that is reconstructed by the professional operations of emotionally uninvolved archaeologists and 'higher critics'.

For instance, the normal political condition of China from 221 B.C. to A.D. 1911 was political unity, interrupted by occasional bouts of disunity that proved, each time, to be only temporary departures from the norm. The Chinese records of China's history during these twenty-one centuries are good, and they have not been challenged except, perhaps, over some minor details here and there. However, the Chinese tradition has created a picture of pre-221-B.C. Chinese history that is not accepted by critical modern scholars as being true to life. This traditional picture of pre-221-B.C. Chinese history is an unwarrantable extrapolation of the authentic configuration of post-221-B.C. Chinese history. It has prefaced the Ch'in dynasty and its successors by three previous dynasties that are deemed not only to have been historical but to have exercised an effective centralized authority of the kind that was actually exercised by the Ch'in dynasty after 221 B.C., by the Ch'ing dynasty before A.D. 1839, and by a number of other dynasties in between.

The traditional picture of this pre-221-B.C. period of Chinese history has been challenged. The archaeologists and the textual critics have confirmed the traditional belief in the authenticity of the Chou and the Shang dynasties, but they have not found evidence that these dynasties were in effective command of more than a patch of the China of 221 B.C.

As for the Hsia dynasty, which the Chinese tradition presents as having been the predecessor of the Shang, no archaeological or inscriptional evidence for its historicity has been discovered so far. The traditional Chinese picture of Chinese history before 221 B.C. is now believed by modern critical students, Chinese as well as foreign, to be a fiction, fabricated, in good faith, in response to a feeling that Chinese history 'must have' conformed from the outset to the post-221-B.C. configuration. This misrepresentation, in the tradition, of the true historical facts, had an emotional origin. The post-221-B.C. configuration became so sacrosanct in Chinese minds that they were unable to imagine that there could have been another configuration at an earlier date.

The Jewish tradition of the religious history of Israel and Judah has been shaped, like the Chinese tradition of China's history, by masterful emotion. No one disputes that the Jews have been monotheists since at least the date in the sixth century B.C. at which Deutero-Isaiah was writing. This sixth-century Jewish writer unquestionably believed that Yahweh, the god of Israel and Judah, was the only god who genuinely existed, and he also believed that, besides being the national god of the Jews, Yahweh was also the creator and the master of all mankind and of the whole Universe. This belief is true monotheism, and the Jews have been attached to it devotedly since then until the recent date at which some of them have become agnostics. Consequently, the Jewish tradition has extrapolated its post-sixth-century-B.C. monotheism into the pre-sixth-century-B.C. history of Israel and Judah. It has ascribed Deutero-Isaiah's conception of the Godhead to Moses, and to Abraham still further back in the past.

It seems likely that Jewish monotheism was the end-product of a long evolution in which monotheism had replaced a previous henotheism (the worship of a sole national, but not sole universal, god), and probably this henotheism had previously replaced polytheism. Though the Jewish scriptures have been sedulously re-edited to project post-sixth-century-B.C. Jewish monotheism backwards in time into the pre-sixth-century-B.C. age, the evidence in these scriptures for pre-monotheistic phases of Jewish religion has not been entirely eliminated. All the kings of Israel after Solomon, and all but two of the kings of Judah after Solomon, are condemned as evil-doers in the record as the Jewish tradition now presents it. We may guess that the rare kings who are certified to have been righteous were monotheist innovators who were controversial figures in their own age, and that the henotheism or polytheism of the retrospectively discredited kings was, in their age, the normal form of Israel's and Judah's religion. It is also significant that, in one of the sources of the Pentateuch, the Godhead is called, not Yahweh (a proper name in the singular) but Elohim (a common noun in the plural).

Like the Jews and the Chinese, the Greeks have made images of their own past that do not correspond to the picture seen by emotionally uninvolved archaeologists and historians. The Hellenic Greeks idealized the war-lords of the Mycenaean phase of Greek history. The Byzantine Greeks were adulators of the language and the style of Hellenic Greek literature from the Homeric poems to the fourth-century-B.C., Attic orators inclusive, and they admitted into this literary canon the neo-Atticists of the age of the Roman principate and the Atticizing Greek Christian Fathers. The Byzantine Greeks also treasured the East Roman Empire, an institution which was their ultimate political heritage from the Hellenic Age. The Modern Greeks have not only idolized the Hellenic 'classical' Greek literature; they have idealized the whole of the Hellenic Greek civilization in all its facets, and they have felt a nostalgia for this image of it which they have created. At the same time, the Modern Greeks have cherished—or did cherish until at least as recently as 1922—the ambition of resuscitating the East Roman Empire and making Constantinople its capital once again.

From the second half of the eleventh century onwards, the Greeks were under mounting pressure from Western Christians on one side and from Turkish Muslims on the other side. This dual pressure eventually became so severe that it produced an interregnum in Greek history.

A break in historical continuity is a tribulation, but it is also an opportunity. At this price, the momentum of karma is reduced to a minimum, and it becomes possible for a society that survives an interregnum to make, if it so chooses, a fresh start, unencumbered by tradition. This was the choice that the Hellenic Greeks had made when, in the eighth century B.C., they had at last recovered from the catastrophe of the downfall of the Mycenaean Greek civilization. Of course the Hellenic Greeks did not slough off their heritage from the past; the effects of the past can be mitigated or aggravated, but they cannot be escaped. However, the Hellenic Greeks did at least start their career without being overshadowed by an emotionally charged image of the foundered Mycenaean Greek World. The Hellenic Greeks were saved from this by oblivion. Their only tradition of the Mycenaean Age was the echo of this age in the Homeric epic; and, in this eighth-century-B.C. end-product of centuries of oral epic poetry, the image of the Mycenaean past had been assimilated progressively to an Hellenic present that was changing all the time and, at each successive change, was departing further and further from its Mycenaean heritage.

The Modern Greeks were less fortunate than the Hellenic Greeks. They suffered the tribulation of an interregnum in a more disagreeable and humiliating form than the chaos of the post-Mycenaean Age. The Modern Greeks' fate, during the post-Byzantine interregnum, was subjection to alien dominations; this subjection was cultural as well as political; and, even at this price, the Modern Greeks did not succeed in shaking off the incubus of their past. Both their Byzantine past and their Hellenic past continued to haunt them, and, when they recovered their independence, the energies that might have been spent by them more profitably on the Promethean enterprise of finding their feet in the modern world were partly diverted to the Epimethean exercise of debating whether to re-establish or to remould or to transcend their importunate Byzantine and Hellenic traditions.

This quest for an emotionally satisfying past has not been a peculiar idiosyncrasy of the Modern Greeks. Today the inhabited portion of the land-surface of this planet is partitioned politically into the domains of at least 140 states that are juridically sovereign and independent, and many of these states are multinational. All but a small minority of these present-day states have gained their independence since the beginning of the nineteenth century, and many of the nations that are incorporated in them are now in search of a past. They are not concerned with the objective past in the shape of karma—the inescapable and indisputable product of previous action and experience. What the recently emancipated peoples are seeking is an image of the past which may not correspond to the reality but which will provide them with a background, authentic or imaginary, for coping with the problems of their present-day life. This is what Croce did mean by his saying that 'all history is contemporary history'. He did not mean (though this, too, is true) that the past is at work in contemporary history through the operation of karma. Croce meant that our picture of the past is always seen from the present observer's standpoint and is always coloured by his present feelings and wishes and needs, even if he is sincerely doing his best to reconstruct the past *wie es eigentlich gewesen ist.*

The quest for a past is being pursued eagerly today by the non-white peoples of Africa, to the south of the Sahara, that have obtained their political independence since after the end of the Second World War. A paradoxical solution of this common problem has been sought by the intelligentsia in Mexico. This minority of the Mexican people has more European blood in its veins than the majority, and the Castilian language is its mother tongue; but a distinctively Mexican national past cannot be provided for Mexico by the Castilian language and literature or by the Spanish Empire, for these heritages are shared by Mexico with a score of other American countries and with Spain herself. If Mexico's past is to be distinctive, it must be a pre-Columbian meso-American past. Consequently the Mexican intellectuals have adopted an idealized image of the local pre-Columbian civilization as their national heritage, and they have denounced, as the ruffianly oppressors that they truly were, the Spanish conquistadores who are the present-day Mexican intellectuals' true spiritual precursors and are to some extent even their physical progenitors too. By contrast, the present-day Mexican peasantry have little or no European blood in their veins and speak Spanish, if at all, as a lingua franca supplementing their pre-Columbian mother-tongues. Yet the present-day Mexican peasants are as oblivious of Mexico's pre-Columbian past as the present-day Egyptian peasants are of Pharaonic Egypt. These Mexican peasants are hardly aware that their ancestors have not always been Roman Catholic Christians. They might be surprised and shocked if they were told that the pre-Christian beliefs and rites that they have innocently retained are not integral and original features of the Catholic Faith.

Images of the past, collective or individual, affect present action, and all present-day peoples and living individuals, all over the World, are having, today, to cope with one common paramount problem. We are all having to try to make life possible and endurable in the artificial man-made environment that has been substituted for our former natural environment by the astonishing modern advance of technology. The Western peoples are not exempt, though the West was the local workshop in which this modern advance of technology was carried out. The new environment that has been conjured up is so inhuman that even its own human makers are aliens in it; and the non-Western peoples are aliens here *a fortiori*.

The task of coping with this 'Brave New World' is common to all present-day peoples, but a people's prospects are affected by its image of its past, and in this point the present-day peoples are not all on a par with each other. Their actual pasts, and their images of their pasts, differ widely, and so do the dates at which the West impinged on them. The interior of Africa to the south of the Sahara did not receive the impact of the West before the nineteenth century. Even the west coast of trans-Saharan Africa did not receive this impact till the fifteenth century. The Americas did not receive it before 1492. Eastern Asia received it in the sixteenth century but warded it off in the seventeenth century and did not succumb to it till the nineteenth century. On the other hand, the impact of the West on the Greeks began in the eleventh century with the Norman conquest of South-Eastern Italy and Sicily. No other surviving non-Western people has had to contend with pressure from the West for as long a time as this.

The Modern Greeks' experience has also been unique—and uniquely interesting—in another respect. Their image of their past has been a dual image. The Modern Greeks have had both a Byzantine and an Hellenic past to digest, and the Byzantine and the Hellenic attitudes to life are not only different from each other; they are antithetical to each other. Were the Modern Greeks to feel and act as heirs of the Byzantines or as heirs of the Hellenes? Alternatively, were they to assert their spiritual independence against both these Greek pasts, as the Hellenes did assert their independence against the Mycenaeans? The hold of the past on the Modern Greeks has not been stronger than its hold on the Modern Jews or on the Modern Chinese, but, for the Greeks, the problem has been more complex. They will solve it only in so far as they succeed in confronting these potent pasts of theirs with self-assurance, and they will not feel sure of themselves until they have become convinced that they have emulated the Hellenes' and Byzantines' dazzling successes and have not repeated their dismal failures. I have been in touch with the Modern Greeks for sixty-three years by now, and I have watched them gradually gaining ground in their arduous struggle to master their heritages by digesting them and transcending them.

II

THE MYCENAEAN GREEKS'
SUCCESSES AND FAILURES

WHAT is the link between the present-day Greeks (the Modern Greeks) and the Byzantine, Hellenic, and Mycenaean Greeks? Why do we call them all Greeks, in spite of the striking differences between their respective civilizations and attitudes to life? Why do the Modern Greeks feel that they and the Byzantine Greeks and the Hellenic Greeks are the same people?

The answer that first suggests itself is that the link is the Greek language. Present-day Greek is manifestly a later phase of the language of the Homeric poems, and these are now believed to have arrived in the eighth century B.C. at the form in which we now have them. We also have documents, written in a Greek that is manifestly an earlier phase of the same language as Homeric Greek, from Pylos in the Pelopónnesos and from Knossos in Crete. The Pylos documents are dated *circa* 1200 B.C. and the Knossos documents *circa* 1400 B.C. by most scholars (though this dating of the Knossos documents has been challenged by a minority).

There is archaeological evidence for a cultural differentiation between Knossos and the rest of Crete *circa* 1480–1450 B.C.[1] The so-called Late Minoan II style (*circa* 1480/1450–1400 B.C.), is confined to Knossos. Since the discovery that the language of the Knossos tablets inscribed in the 'Linear B' script is Greek, it has been inferred that the Late Minoan II style at Knossos was the product of an occupation of Knossos by Greek-speaking invaders. These presumably came from Continental Greece, and Greek was being written there in the same script, not only at Pylos *circa* 1200 B.C., but also at Mycenae. The archaeological evidence indicates[2] that the most recent previous change of population in Continental Greece had occurred *circa* 1900 B.C., at the transition there from the Early to the Middle Helladic phase of the Bronze Age. There was widespread destruction on the mainland at that date, and a new

[1] See, for instance, Dow, S., 'The Greeks in the Bronze Age', in Kirk, G. S., *The Language and Background of Homer* (Cambridge 1964), pp. 149 and 154.

[2] See Taylour, Lord William, *The Mycenaeans* (London 1964), p. 22; Dow, 'The Greeks in the Bronze Age' in Kirk, op. cit., pp. 141 and 143; Vermeule, E., *Greece in the Bronze Age* (Chicago 1964), p. 66.

make of pottery (now misleadingly labelled 'Minyan') appears there simultaneously. It is inferred that this 'Minyan' ware was introduced by invaders; and it has been guessed that the invaders were Greek-speakers and that these were the first Greek-speakers to enter the country now called Greece.

This guess is supported by inscriptional evidence in Eastern Asia Minor for the presence there, since an early date in the second millennium B.C., of a people speaking languages—Luvian and Indo-European Hittite—which belong to the same set of Indo-European languages—the 'centum' set—as Greek. The arrival of a people speaking the Luvian and the Indo-European Hittite languages in Asia Minor by this date shows that, if there had originally been a unitary Indo-European *Ursprache*, this had, by then, already become differentiated, and that the speakers of the derivative languages were already moving far afield from the region, perhaps somewhere in eastern Europe, from which the languages of the Indo-European family had been disseminated.

Can we, then, define 'Greeks' as being the speakers of the language, still spoken today in its Modern Greek form, whose history can be traced back, by archaeological and philological clues, to a date at least as early as 2000 B.C. and to a location somewhere to the north of the Black Sea and the Danube? This definition turns out to be inadequate.

Within living memory there were Muslim Greek-speakers who felt themselves to be, not Greeks, but 'Osmanlis,[3] and there were Christian Turkish-speakers from Asia Minor who felt themselves to be Greeks and who wrote the Eastern Orthodox Christian liturgy in the Greek alphabet, though Turkish was the language that was conveyed by them in this Greek script. There is a story[4] that, for a short time at the turn of the nineteenth and twentieth centuries, the 'Turks' in the city of Antalya, on the south coast of Asia Minor, were Greek-speaking (they were Cretan Muslim refugees) and the 'Greek' inhabitants were Turkish-speaking (they were native Qāramānlis).

And can we deny the name 'Greeks' to the inhabitants of Greece who were there already before the earliest Greek-speakers arrived? By 1900 B.C. Greece had already lived through the first phase of its Bronze Age, Early Helladic I, and through a preceding Neolithic Age that had lasted for about 4,000 years.[5] The Neolithic site at Néa Nikomêdheia in Macedonia is dated 6218 ± 150 B.C.; the site at Drakhmáni (Eláteia) in

---

[3] Note contributed by Professor Robert Browning: 'There are still some Muslim Greek-speakers from Crete living at Side in Pamphylia, and Anthony Bryer tells me that there are several villages of Hellenophone Muslims in Pontus, from one of which sprang ex-president Sunay of Turkey, whose mother-tongue was Greek.'

[4] Told by G. D. Hogarth as an amusing tale. Hogarth did not go bail for its being true.

[5] Vermeule, op. cit., p. 22.

Central Greece is dated 5520 ± 70 B.C.[6] The 'Neolithic A' site at Sesklo in southern Thessaly is dated circa 4800 B.C.;[7] the adjacent 'Neolithic B' site at Dhimini is given an early date in the fourth millennium B.C.[8] Thus, by the time of the break, *circa* 1900 B.C., between the Early Helladic and the Middle Helladic Bronze Age, Greece had been inhabited for longer than 4,000 years by a settled agricultural population, and this had reached, at Lerna in the Argolid, the impressively high level of civilization that is represented by the Early Helladic strata there.[9] In the Bronze Age, Crete had forged ahead of Continental Greece, and the Cretan bronze-age civilization had perhaps almost as long a Neolithic pre-history behind it.[10]

We cannot guess what were the relative numbers of the supposedly Greek-speaking invaders of Continental Greece *circa* 1900 B.C. and the non-Greek-speaking population that was already established there. Nor do we know at what stage in the history of Asia Minor and South-Eastern Europe, including Greece, the place-names ending in -nth- and in -ass- were introduced there. Their provenance is obscure, but they are not Greek, and there is no evidence that they are relics of any non-Greek Indo-European language. We can merely guess that the population of Continental Greece was already multi-lingual and multi-racial before the first Greek-speakers arrived, and we know that here the races had mingled and the Greek language had become prevalent in the course of the 500 years that had elapsed between the appearance of 'Minyan' ware in Continental Greece and the generally accepted date of the earliest inscriptions in Greek in the 'Linear B' script.[11] This means that a large share of the credit or discredit for everything, good or bad, that has ever been written in the Greek language—and also for everything that has been done by Greek-speakers within the last 3,900 years—must be given to Greek-speakers who had in their veins little or none of the blood of the invaders of Continental Greece who brought the Greek language with them in the twentieth century B.C. The Greeks, then, must be defined as being the people who, since the twentieth century B.C., have been the makers of Greek visual art, architecture, literature, philosophy, theology, mysticism, politics, economics, and warfare. All these people have been Greeks, in the pertinent cultural meaning of the name, even

[6] Ibid., p. 7. (S. S. Weinburg, in *Cambridge Ancient History*, vol. i, 3rd edn., part i (1970), p. 570, holds that pottery was being made in the Aegean area by about 6000 B.C.)

[7] Ibid., p. 10.

[8] Ibid., p. 14.

[9] See Dow, in Kirk, op. cit., pp. 144–5; Vermeule, op. cit., pp. 29–30.

[10] See Schachermeyr, F., *Die ältesten Kulturen Griechenlands* (Stuttgart 1955), table on pp. 30–1; *eundem*, *Die minoische Kultur des alten Kreta* (Stuttgart 1964), pp. 16–18.

[11] 'We need not suppose that the Mycenaeans were a racial unity'—Desborough, V. R. d'A., *The Last Mycenaeans and their Successor: An Archaeological survey c. 1200–c. 1000 B.C.* (Oxford 1966), p. 242.

if their own, as well as their ancestors', mother-tongue has been some non-Greek language, and even if they have had no physical kinship whatsoever with the people who spoke the Indo-European *Ursprache* somewhere on the Eurasian steppe at some date in the third millennium B.C.

What were the Mycenaean Greeks' principal successes and failures? Their greatest achievement was that they gave cultural unity to the Aegean basin for the first time in this region's history.[12] In the course of Late Helladic (*alias* Mycenaean) phase III (*circa* 1400–1100 B.C.) the Mycenaean culture established itself all over the Aegean basin, except for its Asian coast and the adjacent islands between the Troad and Miletus, two points on the Asian mainland which were recipients of the Mycenaean culture. This cultural unification was something new. Originally the Aegean basin had been divided into a number of distinct cultural provinces.[13] These—apart from the Aegean's Asian coast— were the Troad, Continental Greece (the 'Helladic' area), the Aegean Archipelago, and Crete. The Neolithic cultures of the mainland, the Archipelago, and Crete were different from each other.[14] The Archipelago was uninhabited till almost the end of the Continental Neolithic Age in Thessaly.[15] In the Bronze Age, the successive phases of Early Helladic do not correspond in date with those of Early Minoan.[16] The first human settlements in the Cyclades may have been as late as *circa* 2500 B.C.—the date, on the mainland, of Early Helladic II.

Once installed in the Archipelago, the islanders took the first steps towards the cultural unification of the Aegean basin. They influenced the culture of the mainland,[17] and they travelled far afield. Cycladic artifacts have been found in Crete, Troy, Bulgaria, Dalmatia, Sicily,[18] and, on beyond, in the Lipari islands (a source of obsidian).[19] The islanders could not have occupied their islands if they had not previously made themselves at home on the sea, and, in fact, drawings of Early Cycladic ships survive.[20]

The Cycladic culture's penetration of the mainland in the Early Helladic Age, phase II, seems to have been peaceful,[21] and this is the first evidence of the mainlanders' receptivity. At the beginning of the Middle

---

[12] See Desborough, op. cit., pp. 1, 219, 242; Snodgrass, A. M., *The Dark Age of Greece* (Edinburgh 1971), p. 25.

[13] Vermeule, op. cit., p. 1.

[14] Dow, in Kirk, op. cit., pp. 143–4.

[15] Vermeule, op. cit., p. 12.

[16] Ibid., p. 28.

[17] Ibid., pp. 45 and 46.

[18] Ibid., p. 55.

[19] See Starr, C. G., *The Origins of Greek Civilization, 1100–650 B.C.* (New York 1961), pp. 49–50.

[20] Vermeule, op. cit., pp. 54–6.

[21] Ibid., p. 45.

Bronze Age, the 'Minyan' type of pottery and the horse were introduced simultaneously into Continental Greece and into the Troad.[22] But there is no archaeological evidence for the Troad's having had relations either with the Hittites[23] or with Minoan Crete.[24] The Bronze-Age civilization of the mainland, too, remained 'radically unlike' the Minoan throughout the Middle Helladic and the Middle Minoan Ages;[25] but *circa* 1600–1550 B.C., at the simultaneous beginnings of the Late Helladic (i.e. the Mycenaean) and the Late Minoan Age, the mainlanders adopted many elements of the Minoan civilization, and this was a veritable cultural revolution—a far more radical change than had been produced by the mainland's previous reception of Cycladic cultural influence. Cretan influence, when this in its turn invaded the mainland at last, swamped the older Continental styles of art.[26] There was nothing in the Continental culture of the Middle Helladic Age that portended the contents of the shaft-graves at Mycenae,[27] whose date is the transition from Middle Helladic III to Late Helladic I, at the beginning of the Minoan civilization's impact on the mainland. The mainlanders adopted the Cretan style of vase-painting (though not the Cretan shapes of the vases themselves),[28] and fresco painting.[29] They adopted the Minoan *grandes dames'* dress unchanged.[30] They also adopted at least some of the outward forms of Minoan religion.[31]

It would be hazardous, however, to infer from this that the Mycenaeans also adopted the Cretan religion's practices, beliefs, and spirit. For instance, there is no evidence for blood sacrifices in Crete, but they seem to have been practised on the mainland.[32] The mainlanders were not servile imitators.[33] The differences, as well as the likenesses, between the Mycenaean and the Minoan civilization are important.[34] Half of the weapons from the shaft-graves at Mycenae are of types not made in Crete.[35] When the Mycenaeans found that they needed, for

[22] Blegen, C. W., *Troy and the Trojans* (London 1963), pp. 111, 140, 145. Cp. Page, D. L., *History and the Homeric Iliad* (Berkeley and Los Angeles 1959), pp. 57–8; Starr, op. cit., pp. 30–6.

[23] Blegen, op. cit., p. 37. Cp. Page, op. cit., p. 66. This finding is provisional, pending further archaeological exploration in Asia Minor. This might also perhaps throw light on the question of where it was that the 'Minyan' type of pottery originated.

[24] Page, op. cit., p. 67; Vermeule, op. cit., p. 275.

[25] Ibid., p. 61.

[26] Ibid., p. 106. Cp. Starr, op. cit., pp. 57 and 105.

[27] Vermeule, op. cit., p. 81.

[28] Taylour, op. cit., p. 48.

[29] Ibid., p. 131.

[30] Ibid., p. 67.

[31] Ibid., pp. 60–1. For the Minoan-type sanctuary in the Mycenaean palace of Asine in the Argolid, see Desborough, op. cit., pp. 42, 83, 190.

[32] Vermeule, op. cit., pp. 283, 293, 295.

[33] Starr, op. cit., p. 56.

[34] See Vermeule, op. cit., pp. 136–7.

[35] Ibid., p. 98.

their own administrative purposes, a script for conveying their Greek language,[36] they did not take over the 'Linear A' script which the Minoans had devised for conveying their own non-Greek language. The Greeks created a new script, 'Linear B'. Possibly this was made for the fifteenth-century-B.C. Mycenaean Greek masters of Knossos by the local Minoan literati at their masters' command,[37] but the initiative must have been taken by the Knossian Mycenaean Greeks themselves. In vase-painting, which is the most precise of the indicators of cultural change, the Continental Mycenaeans were asserting their independence of the Minoan style as early as Late Helladic phase II. They were reverting from Cretan naturalism to the geometric style of Middle Helladic vase-painting—the native style that had been temporarily submerged by the sudden influx of Cretan culture.[38] One scholar has gone so far as to maintain that there is 'a formulaic quality in every field of Mycenaean art'.[39] Yet she also observes[40] that at Knossos, which was occupied by Mycenaean Greeks from *circa* 1480–1450 B.C. till its destruction *circa* 1400 B.C., 'Minoan traditions affected the Greeks in every field but warfare and language'.

This same scholar gives the Mycenaean Greeks high praise for their success in coping with the problem of receiving an alien culture that was higher than theirs. 'Perhaps there has never been so dramatic an influence from one culture upon another, corrupting neither and strengthening both.'[41]

The Helladic Greeks' appetite for alien cultures was as great as their capacity for adopting elements from them without entirely forfeiting their own cultural independence. Besides drawing on the Cycladic and the Cretan cultures, they drew on the Syrian culture as well. Already the niello technique of the inlaid dagger blades from the shaft-graves at Mycenae appears to be Syrian, though the treasure in the shaft-graves dates from the time of the first impact of Cretan culture on the mainland.[42]

The Mycenaean Greeks followed up their reception of the Minoan culture by outflanking the Minoans geographically. Westward, the earliest Late Helladic artifacts have been found in the Lipari Islands. (These had been reached already by Cycladic mariners in the Middle Cycladic Age.)[43] After the fall of Knossos *circa* 1400 B.C., the

---

[36] Vermeule, op. cit., p. 238.
[37] Dow, in Kirk, op. cit., p. 155.
[38] Taylour, op. cit., pp. 49–50, 127, 130; Vermeule, op. cit., p. 188.
[39] Vermeule, op. cit., p. 156.
[40] Ibid., p. 243.
[41] Ibid., p. 151.
[42] Ibid., pp. 98–100.
[43] See Starr, op. cit., pp. 49–50, cited on p. 12, n. 20.

Mycenaeans' trade with the Lipari Islands declined, and it has been guessed that they were now able to get obsidian (the Lipari Islands' most valuable product) from the island of Melos, from which the Cretans may, till then, have barred the Continental Mycenaeans.[44] However, the Mycenaeans' westward trade did not cease. Mycenaean potsherds of the Late Helladic III A phase have been found as far afield in the western Mediterranean basin as Ischia.[45] Already, in the fifteenth century B.C., the Mycenaeans had been trading direct with Egypt. The Aegean vases in fifteenth-century-B.C. Egyptian tombs are Mycenaean, not Minoan,[46] though the visitors from the Aegean who are depicted on the walls of the Egyptian sepulchral chambers are Minoans, not Mycenaeans.[47] The Mycenaeans may have reached Egypt via Miletus and Rhodes. Both places were colonized by Minoans and by Mycenaeans in succession. On Rhodes a Late Helladic II Mycenaean settlement existed for a time side by side with an older Minoan settlement, before the Minoan settlement faded out.[48] After the fall of Knossos *circa* 1400 B.C., there was a two-way trade between the Mycenaean World and Syria,[49] and in this period of Mycenaean Greek history—Late Helladic III (*alias* Mycenaean III)—the Mycenaeans borrowed more artistic *motifs* from Syria than from Crete.[50] This was the age in which the geographical range of the Mycenaean civilization was at its widest.[51]

The receptivity, which was so marked a characteristic of the Mycenaean Greeks, was a source of strength for them in so far as they applied themselves to the arts of peace. However, they were addicted to war and their cultural imports included a formidable armoury. They also imported a sophisticated system of bureaucratic government. These two imports, between them, may account for the catastrophe in which the Mycenaean Greek civilization ended.

The Mycenaean World's history can be reconstructed fragmentarily from the archaeological evidence, from the texts of the 'Linear B' tablets, from contemporary Hittite and Egyptian records, and from the retrospective glimpses of it in the Homeric poems (glimpses in which some patches of what may be historical reality can be discerned dimly and uncertainly through the mist of a centuries-long oral poetic tradition). The Mycenaean Greeks' receptivity has parallels, about

[44] See Taylour, op. cit., p. 149.
[45] Ibid., p. 152.
[46] Ibid., p. 156; Vermeule, op. cit., pp. 113–14.
[47] Ibid., p. 150.
[48] Taylour, op. cit., p. 156; Starr, op. cit., p. 52.
[49] Taylour, op. cit., pp. 158–9; Starr, op, cit., p. 51.
[50] Taylour, op. cit., p. 130. Cp. ibid., p. 159.
[51] Ibid., p. 170.

which we are better informed, in the receptivity of other warlike peoples, for instance the Japanese, the Normans, and the Normans' kinsmen and contemporaries the Scandinavian rulers of Kievan Russia.

Like the Mycenaean Greeks, the Normans and the Rhos extended their operations rapidly over enormous distances, and were ready either to raid or to trade, whichever way of making profits seemed the more promising in the situation of the moment. Their combination of a shrewd business sense with an uneconomic-minded passion for military adventures may seem incongruous to us, but it is a well authenticated fact, and the Mycenaean Greeks' attitude to life appears to have been similar. What may happen when a sophisticated system of government is imposed on a relatively backward warlike people is illustrated by the history of Japan after her adoption, in the seventh century of the Christian Era, of the contemporary Chinese system of administration. This exotic regime soon broke down in the unpropitious Japanese social environment into which it had been transplanted, and its breakdown there was followed by fratricidal warfare.

This happened in Japan in spite of the imported regime's being unitary—in reality during the short period for which it was effective, and still nominally thereafter. We do not know whether the Mycenaean Greek World had even a nominally unitary government at any stage of its history. The tablets reveal the existence of local principalities, and give us details of the domestic administration of one of them, the principality of Pylos, towards the close of the thirteenth century B.C. But the tablets throw no light on the relations of the Mycenaean Greek principalities to each other.

The Hittite records inform us that, *circa* 1300 B.C., a Hittite Emperor—either Mursiliš II (?1334–1306 B.C.) or Muwattalliš (?1306–1282 B.C.)—was in correspondence with a king of Ahhiyawā who possessed at least a beach-head on the mainland of Asia Minor.[52] The Hittites' Ahhiyawā must be the same ethnikon as the Homeric Ἀχαιοί, though the two words are not equivalent to each other philologically.[53] But the Hittite documents do not enable us to locate Ahhiyawā, or to discern whether this kingdom included the whole of the Achaean (i.e. the Mycenaean Greek) World or was merely one Achaean state among a number. A king of Ahhiyawā is mentioned by another Hittite Emperor, Tuthaliyas IV (?1250–1220 B.C.), together with the kings of Egypt, Babylonia, and Assyria, in the first draft of a list of kings who are the Hittite Emperor's equals. The original inclusion of the king of Ahhiyawā in this list is presumptive evidence that his kingdom was a great one and that it did include the whole of the Mycenaean Greek World. However,

---

[52] See Page, op. cit., p. 10.
[53] For the philological problem, see ibid., pp. 37–9.

the mention of the king of Ahhiyawā was erased from the tablet before the clay was dry, and this erasure makes this king's status dubious.[54]

In the *Iliad*, Agamemnon does seem to have the status of an overlord over all the other Achaean princes. One of his standing epithets is Ϝάναξἀνδρῶν, and this formula seems likely to be a heritage from the Mycenaean Age; for we know from the 'Linear B' tablets that the title of a ruler of a Mycenaean state was Ϝάναξ, and we also know that, in the Hellenic Age, this title was obsolete for human kings, and survived only for gods.[55] However, Agamemnon's status in the *Iliad* may be interpreted alternatively as being, not a permanent overlordship, but only an *ad hoc* commandership-in-chief of a coalition's joint expeditionary force; and, in any case, a poem which probably did not take its present shape until the eighth century B.C. is not good enough evidence by itself, without confirmation by Mycenaean-Age documentary evidence.

Whether or not the Mycenaean Greek World ever acknowledged a single overlord's authority over all its principalities, it is clear that these principalities were free, in practice, to make war both on aliens and on each other. It is also clear that, during Late Helladic (Mycenaean) III, Mycenaean Greek militarism worked up to a climax which precipitated a catastrophe. This crescendo movement can be observed in the development of both armaments and fortifications.

In Late Helladic III, that is, from the fourteenth century [B.C.] onwards, the whole Mycenaean armoury undergoes a change. Contacts with the East increase, and influences from that quarter are reflected in new styles of weapons both of offence and defence. The large body-shield, which figured prominently in single combat and in the chase, is now replaced by the small round shield that was better adapted to collective fighting.[56]

The change in the shape and size of the soldier's shield required additions to his body-armour. Besides a helmet, he now needed to wear a corslet and greaves. Both the ideograms and the words for corslet are

---

[54] See ibid., p. 6. At pp. 15–17, Page holds that the state called Ahhiyawā in the Hittite records was confined to Rhodes, and was not an empire embracing the whole cultural domain of the Mycenaean civilization. Vermeule, in op. cit., pp. 236–7, 265, 268, holds that the Mycenaean World was not politically united in the fourteenth and thirteenth centuries B.C. She does not deny that Mycenae was the cultural capital of the Mycenaean World, but she does not consider that this is adequate evidence for its having been the political capital as well. On the other hand, Desborough, *The Last Mycenaeans*, p. 242, holds that the cultural uniformity of the Mycenaean World, before the catastrophe at the close of the Late Helladic III B period, was 'due to the existence of a single closely united ruling caste, probably acknowledging one overlord, whose seat was at Mycenae.' Cp. ibid., pp. 4 and 218–19. Desborough reaffirms his belief in the political unity of the Mycenaean World in *The Greek Dark Ages* (London 1972), pp. 17–18. The archaeological evidence that has come to light so far is inconclusive, as Desborough points out, and the controversy seems unlikely to be settled unless and until some further relevant Hittite or Egyptian archives are discovered.

[55] See Page, op. cit., pp. 183 and 187–8.

[56] Taylour, op. cit., pp. 142–3.

different at Late Minoan II Knossos and at Late Helladic III Pylos. The Knossos type of corslet is stated, on the tablets, to be made of bronze, and a bronze corslet, of slightly earlier date than the Knossos tablets, has been found in a chamber-tomb at Dhéndra (Midea) in the Argolid.[57] The Pylos type of corslet has some resemblance to the type depicted on the Warrior Vase. This appears to be made, not of metal, but of leather. The Warrior Vase was painted in the last days of the Mycenaean Age, after Mycenae had already been sacked; and, by this time, impoverishment may have necessitated the use of cheaper materials for military equipment.

The fortification of palaces on the mainland was the rule on the east coast. There was a concentration of fortified palaces in the Argolid : Mycenae, Tiryns, Midea, Asine. In Central Greece the only strong Mycenaean-Age fortress besides the acropolis of Athens was Gla, the island in Lake Kopais.[58] The fortifications of the palace at Pylos, on the west coast of the Pelopónnêsos, were slight, and so were those of Thebes in Central Greece and of Iolkos in southern Thessaly.[59] Mycenaean Miletus was fortified in the thirteenth century B.C., during the Late Helladic III B period.[60] Towards the end of the thirteenth century the *enceinte* of Mycenae was extended to include within the walls a cistern, fed by a hidden channel from the Perseia spring, outside the fortress, on which Mycenae had always depended for its water-supply.[61] The houses outside the wall had been sacked *circa* 1250 B.C. and had been left derelict.[62] At Athens a new well was opened up below the summit of the acropolis but accessible from it, and, at the end of Late Helladic (Mycenaean) III B, i.e. *circa* 1200 B.C., the houses on the slopes of the acropolis, outside the wall, were evacuated.[63] The *enceinte* of Tiryns was enlarged at about the same date as the *enceinte* of Mycenae.[64] It is significant that arrangements for providing a water-supply inside the *enceinte* were made at Tiryns, at Mycenae, and at Athens contemporaneously.[65]

[57] See Taylour, op. cit., pp. 141–2, with plate 65 and n. on p. 233; Vermeule, op. cit., p. 135.

[58] The *enceintes* of the Mycenaean fortresses to the north-west of Attica embrace large areas (Desborough, *The Last Mycenaeans*, pp. 30 and 221). They must have been designed to serve as cities of refuge for the rural population with its flocks and herds.

[59] Taylour, op. cit., pp. 90 and 108–19; Vermeule, op. cit., pp. 165 and 264.

[60] Desborough, *The Last Mycenaean*, p. 162, and *The Greek Dark Ages*, p. 19; Vermeule, op. cit., p. 264. Starr, op. cit., p. 60, footnote 3, appears to be mistaken in stating that the date of the earliest Mycenaean fortifications at Miletus is the fourteenth century B.C.

[61] See Taylour, op. cit., pp. 107–18. Cp. Starr, op. cit., p. 60.

[62] Starr, op. cit., pp. 60–1; Taylour, op. cit., pp. 171–2; Desborough, *The Last Mycenaeans*, pp. 74 and 221.

[63] Taylour, op. cit., pp. 108 and 176; Starr, op. cit., p. 68. Vermeule, op. cit., p. 268; Desborough, *The Last Mycenaeans*, p. 221.

[64] Starr, op. cit., p. 61.

[65] Vermeule, op. cit., p. 268.

Troy had been fortified from the start,[66] but Troy's *enceinte*, too, was repeatedly extended and strengthened. The precautionary measure of including a water-supply within the fortifications was taken at Troy before the end of Troy VI. A well-cistern, hewn into the bedrock, was enclosed within the tower at the north-east corner of Troy VI's defences.[67] After Troy VI had been wrecked—apparently by an earthquake[68]—*circa* 1300 B.C.,[69] its massive walls were patched up—and were even extended in places—by the squatters in Troy VIIa.[70] The lay-out of the houses in Troy VIIa suggests that here, in the early years of the thirteenth century B.C., as at Athens later in the same century, people who had previously lived outside the walls of the citadel took refuge inside the *enceinte*. In Troy VIIa the housing was poor by comparison with what it had been in Troy VI.[71] There is evidence of overcrowding at this stage.[72] There is evidence, at the same stage, for arrangements for storing provisions, presumably for fear of a siege. In the houses of Troy VIIa, *pithoi* were buried under the floors, with their lips at floor level and with stone lids, flush with the floor.[73] This was a device for providing storage-space without diminishing living-space. Here, again, the Trojans anticipated the Mycenaeans. At Mycenae, basement store-rooms were constructed at the same time as the cistern fed from the Perseia spring.[74]

These are clear indications of the intensification of militarism in the Mycenaean World in the course of Late Helladic (Mycenaean) III. However, war was not invariably the means by which the Mycenaean Greek World achieved its wide expansion. We do not know whether the Mycenaean Greek occupation of Knossos in the fifteenth century B.C. was accomplished peacefully or by force, but we do know[75] that the 'Mycenaeanization' of Knossos was a local event. Whatever may have been the political relation of Mycenaean Knossos, during the short life of the Mycenaean regime there, to the other palaces in Crete, the Minoan culture and way of life continued, in these other palaces, undisturbed. 'Late Minoan II is an expression of the Greek influence at Knossos rather than a chronological phase.'[76] We also know that, on the island of

---

[66] See Blegen, op. cit., p. 43. Cp. Page, op. cit., p. 42.
[67] Blegen, op. cit., p. 119.
[68] See ibid., pp. 143–4.
[69] See ibid., pp. 160 and 174.
[70] Taylour, op. cit., p. 172; Page, op. cit., pp. 71–2; Vermeule, op. cit., p. 276.
[71] Blegen, op. cit., pp. 150–1
[72] Ibid., p. 152.
[73] Ibid., pp. 154–6.
[74] Starr, op. cit., p. 60.
[75] See Vermeule, op. cit., pp. 137 and 146–7.
[76] Ibid., p. 146.

Rhodes, a Mycenaean settlement coexisted with an older Minoan settlement peacefully.[77]

On the other hand, war seems more likely than an earthquake or a volcanic eruption to have been the cause of the destruction of Knossos *circa* 1400 B.C. and of the simultaneous destruction[78] of Phaistos, Ayía Triádha, Mállia, Gourniá, and Zákro in Crete, Ayía Eirênê on Keos, and Triánda on Rhodes. The most likely perpetrators of this destruction would be another band of Continental Mycenaean Greeks, following at the heels of the band that had occupied Knossos some fifty or eighty years earlier. In that case, the destruction of Knossos *circa* 1400 B.C. would have been caused by a fratricidal war between two powers that were both Greek. It can hardly be a mere coincidence that 'the ruin of the island palaces is immediately followed by the rise of several on the mainland',[79] and that the immediately following period, Late Helladic (Mycenaean) III, was the one in which the geographical expansion of the Mycenaean Greeks' activities attained its maximum extent.

During this same period the Mycenaeans repeatedly went to war both at home and abroad. Both these ways of indulging in militarism were exhausting, but, of the two, we may guess that the fratricidal warfare was the principal cause of the Mycenaean Greek civilization's downfall.

The Achaean exploit abroad that has become most famous is the expedition against Troy that is the setting of the plot of the *Iliad*. The authenticity of the Hellenic tradition is attested, in this case, by archaeological evidence. Troy VIIa was destroyed by violence at a date about half way through the thirteenth century B.C.[80] Blegen's dating is *circa* 1260 B.C.[81] Desborough's is between 1250 and 1230 B.C. *Circa* 1230 B.C., in the fifth year of the reign of the Pharaoh Merneptah (he reigned *circa* 1235–1224 B.C.[83]), Egypt was attacked by a coalition of peoples, one of which was the Aqiyawasa, and this, like the Hittite Ahhiyawā, looks as if it is a rendering of the Greek Ἀχαιοί or Ἀχαῖα. In an indictment of a man named Madduwattaš by the last of the Hittite Emperors, Arnuwandaš IV (?1220–1200 B.C.), it is recorded that 'the man from Ahiiā, Attarssiyaš', drove Madduwattaš out of Madduwattaš's principality, Zippaslā, pursued him into the interior of Asia Minor, and was eventually defeated and driven off by a Hittite army that had come to

---

[77] Taylour, op. cit., p. 156, cited already on p. 15, n. 48.

[78] For this, see Vermeule, op. cit., p. 151. Cp. Dow, in Kirk, op cit., pp. 155 and 156.

[79] Vermeule, op. cit., p. 155.

[80] See Taylour, op. cit., pp. 59, 173, 175; Dow, in Kirk, op. cit., p. 163; Page, op. cit., pp. 1, 73–4 and 95.

[81] Blegen, op. cit., pp. 163 and 174. Cp. Forsdyke, J., *The Greeks before Homer* (London 1956), p. 62.

[82] Desborough, *The Last Mycenaeans*, pp. 164, 220, and 249.

[83] See Pirenne, J., *Histoire de la civilisation de l'Égypte Ancienne*, vol. ii (Neuchâtel 1962), pp. 461–2.

Madduwattaš's rescue.[84] Later on, according to the same document, Madduwattaš and Attarssiyaš joined forces in an invasion of Alasiya (Cyprus).[85] The dates of these military operations of Attarssiyaš must have been near the end of the thirteenth century B.C. Arnuwandaš IV's description of him does not make it clear whether he was a private adventurer or was a ruler of all the Akhaioi or was only the ruler of one out of a number of Achaean principalities. A people called Denyen is mentioned in the fourteenth century B.C. in the Tell-el-'Amarnah correspondence, and it also took part in the Sea Peoples' attacks on Egypt in the eighth year of the reign of Ramses III (?1198–1166 B.C.)[86] Denyen looks like a rendering of the Greek 'Danaoi', which, together with 'Akhaioi' and 'Argeioi', is one of the three names that are used in the *Iliad* synonymously as comprehensive appellations for the Greek expeditionary force that was besieging Troy.

The dates of the destruction of the Mycenaean Greek palaces and colonial outposts can be ascertained approximately from the archaeological evidence. Knossos, as has been noted already, was destroyed *circa* 1400 B.C. and Thebes soon after.[87] At Mycenae, the houses outside the walls were sacked *circa* 1250.[88] *Circa* 1200, all the mainland palace-fortresses except the acropolis of Athens were sacked, and Mycenae alone was re-occupied, though this on a reduced scale.[89] Cyprus was devastated for the second time at some date earlier than 1100 B.C.[90] The date of the final fall of the Mycenaean Greek civilization is obscure; for the finds of pottery of the Late Helladic C III period have been meagre,[91] and pottery is the key to the chronology for periods for which there is no evidence in the form of documents in writing. The final destruction of Mycenae and Iolkos and Mycenaean Miletus is dated by Taylour tentatively *circa* 1100 B.C.[92]

Who did it? Stones do not cry out in real life, and the 'Linear B' tablets give us no internal information. The Hellenic tradition about the fall of the Mycenaean Greek civilization would be invalidated if it were contradicted by the archaeological evidence, but actually this

---

[84] Page, op. cit., p. 98.

[85] Ibid., p. 100.

[86] This dating of Ramses III's reign may be too high. The right dating may be 1180–1148 B.C., but, alternatively, it may be 1205–1173 B.C. (see Snodgrass, op. cit., p. 109).

[87] Taylour, op. cit., p. 169. Cp. Starr, op. cit., p. 60.

[88] Taylour, op. cit., p. 171; Desborough, *The Last Mycenaeans*, pp. 74 and 221.

[89] Taylour, op. cit., p. 177; Desborough, *The Last Mycenaeans*, locc. citt., and *The Greek Dark Ages*, p. 19. Cp. Blegen, op. cit., p. 163.

[90] Taylour, op. cit., p. 177; Desborough, *The Last Mycenaeans*, pp. 25, 205, and 236, and *The Greek Dark Ages*, pp. 49–57; Snodgrass, op. cit., p. 365.

[91] Taylour, op. cit., p. 59.

[92] Ibid., p. 177. See also Desborough, *The Last Mycenaeans*, pp. 75 and 225–6, for Mycenae. In *The Greek Dark Ages*, Desborough dates the last agonies of the Mycenaean civilization *c.* 1125 B.C. (p. 11) or *c.* 1125–*c.* 1100 B.C. (p. 289).

neither impugns the tradition nor confirms it. According to the Hellenic tradition, the Mycenaean Greeks wrecked their world by foreign adventures and by domestic strife, and thus created a vacuum that was then occupied by North-West-Greek-speaking barbarians from beyond the Mycenaean Greek civilization's pale. According to the Hellenic tradition, Cadmean Thebes had been ruined by a feud between members of the Theban royal house in which the rulers of other contemporary principalities had intervened. The Greeks' siege of Troy was reputed to have lasted for ten years; some of the contingents of the Greek expeditionary force never found their way back home; Odysseus's wanderings were protracted; Agamemnon returned to Mycenae, only to be murdered by his wife and her paramour, Agamemnon's kinsman Aigisthos. According to the tradition, this was neither the first nor the last atrocity in the grim history of the House of Atreus.

As for the Akhaioi—the people whose name is used in the *Iliad* as one of its three alternative collective names for the participants in the Greek expedition against Troy—they may have been, like the medieval Rhos, a ruling class which differed in nationality from the mass of their subjects. The 'Linear B' tablets have shown that the Mycenaean Greeks—at least those in the Pelopónnêsos and at Knossos—spoke a Greek dialect that was the ancestor of the Hellenic-Age Arcado-Cyprian dialect, and perhaps of the Ionic dialect too.[93] On the other hand, the two peoples in Continental European Greece who bore the name Akhaioi in the Hellenic Age are proved, by inscriptional evidence, to have spoken neither Arcado-Cyprian nor Ionic but North-West Greek. The bearing of the same tribal name is not cogent evidence that all the bearers of it were members of an identical linguistic and ethnic group; yet, subject to this reservation, it is conceivable that the Akhaioi of the Homeric poems and of the Mycenaean-Age Hittite and Egyptian records were an advance-guard of the North-West-Greek-speaking barbarians who descended on the derelict Mycenaean Greek World eventually, after their advance-guard had wrecked the Mycenaean Greek society on which it had imposed its domination. The Greek of the 'Linear B' tablets will have been the native dialect of the Achaean Greek warlords' Greek subjects. If this is the truth,[94] the North-West-Greek-

---

[93] See Risch, E., '*Die Gliederung der griechischen Dialekte in neuer Zeit*', in Kirk, op. cit., pp. 90–105.

[94] The likelihood of this being the truth is suggested by facts that are well attested for a later period of Greek history, running from A.D. 1204 to the end of the Balkan Wars of A.D. 1913–14, during which Greeks—and between 1461 and 1821, all Greeks—were living under the rule of dominant minorities that had imposed themselves by conquest. The ruling minorities in this later age were not Greeks whose original mother tongue was merely a different dialect of their subjects' language. Their mother tongues were French, Italian, Catalan, and Turkish. Yet they came to speak, and even to write, their subjects' Greek language, though, for this series of rulers, Greek was an entirely foreign language. The French ruling minority in the Principality of the Morea (the Pelopónnêsos) during the thirteenth and fourteenth centuries, and the Turkish ruling minority in

speakers' eventual mass-migration into the Mycenaean Greek World—known retrospectively as the 'Dorian invasion' by the Greeks of the Hellenic Age—will have merely filled a vacuum that their forerunners' hands had created.[95] The 'Dorian invasion' of Greece in or after the twelfth century B.C. would then be comparable to the Slav invasion of Greece in the seventh century of the Christian Era, after the preceding depopulation of Greece by Slav and other barbarian raids.

The Mycenaean civilization had a meteoric career. The mainlanders' sudden encounter with the Minoan civilization of Crete at the transition from the Middle to the Late Helladic Age was evidently both immensely exhilarating and profoundly disturbing. Till then, the mainlanders' history had been relatively uneventful. Their reception of agriculture, metallurgy, Cycladic culture, and the Greek language had not been psychologically overwhelming experiences. On the other hand, the mainlanders' subsequent encounter with the Minoan civilization produced a seismic upheaval in the mainlanders' life, because of the extremeness of the difference between the cultural levels of the two civilizations at the time when they suddenly met. If the Achaean rulers of the mainland were recently arrived backwoodsmen, they must have been even less fit to cope with the problem of acculturation than their less barbaric Helladic Greek subjects were. The Achaean rulers of the Helladic World failed to adjust themselves and were consequently thrown off their balance.[96] The Minoan civilization's impact on the mainland suddenly transformed the backward Helladic culture into the Mycenaean civilization, but, within less than five centuries, this civilization came to grief as suddenly as it had originally come into existence. The most convincing explanation of the catastrophe is that the Mycenaean Greeks' Achaean rulers ran amok and destroyed each other.

In their brief heyday the Greeks of the Mycenaean Age had accumulated karma. How much of this karma was inherited by the Mycenaeans' Hellenic successors? And how did the Hellenic Greeks react to the surviving residue of their Mycenaean past?

Êpeiros and the Pelopónnêsos on the eve of the Ottoman Greek insurrection of 1821, are known to have been bilingual. This feature of the period A.D. 1206–1913—a period that is analogous to the Mycenaean Age in respect of the political structure of society in Greece—makes it credible that the dialect of Greek inscribed on the 'Linear B' tablets was the language of the subject majority of the population, not the original mother tongue of the ruling Achaean minority. The Achaeans' mother tongue may well have been ancestral to the North-West Greek, *alias* Doric, that, on the evidence of inscriptions, was the dialect spoken by the Peloponnesian and the Thessalian Akhaioi in the Hellenic Age. The use of the subject majority's Arcado-Cyprian dialect in the Mycenaean Age by North-West-Greek-speaking war-lords would have been all the more natural if it is true, as is now thought, that the dialects of the Greek language were less sharply differentiated from each other in the Mycenaean Age than they had come to be in the Hellenic Age.

[95] See Vermeule, op. cit., p. 279.
[96] See Starr, op. cit., pp. 57–8.

III

THE HELLENIC GREEKS' HERITAGE
FROM THE MYCENAEAN GREEKS

IF the Hellenic Greeks had inherited their Mycenaean predecessors' karma intact, they would have started their own career under a heavy handicap; but the Mycenaeans' failure had been so extreme that it annihilated some of the most burdensome elements of the karma that the Mycenaeans had accumulated. The significance of the Hellenes' inheritance from the Mycenaeans lies in its negative aspect.

The Hellenes did not inherit the Mycenaean princes' excessively sumptuous palaces. The ruins of these were not rebuilt and reinhabited; they were left derelict, buried under their own debris. The Hellenes did not inherit the Mycenaean principalities' excessively *dirigiste* administrative organization. The Mycenaean bureaucrats did not survive the catastrophe,[1] though the Mycenaean poets did. The Hellenes did not inherit the Mycenaean 'Linear B' script, which was the instrument with which the bureaucratic Mycenaean administration had been conducted. The art of writing and reading this script was lost, and, for at least 3,000 years, no one even knew that it had ever existed. The unearthing of some 'Linear B' tablets and their subsequent decipherment are achievements of the present century. 'The whole organization and the whole mentality at the top—that of the palace bureaucracy—went.'[2] 'The whole of Mycenaean society was overturned.'[3]

The Hellenic Greeks' good fortune in escaping these potential legacies from their Mycenaean Greek predecessors stands out in contrast to the untoward effects of the corresponding legacies from the Hellenes on the fortunes of the Byzantine and the Modern Greeks. The Byzantine Greeks did inherit from the Hellenes the Roman imperial palace at Constantinople, the Diocletianic-Constantinian system of administra-

---

[1] Desborough, *The Greek Dark Ages*, p. 23.

[2] Dow, in Kirk, op. cit., p. 164. Cp. Starr, op. cit., pp. 6 and 61. Desborough, *The Greek Dark Ages*, loc. cit., guesses that the dominant minority of the overthrown Mycenaean society may have emigrated to Cyprus.

[3] Finley, M. I., 'Homer and Mycenae: Property and Tenure', in Kirk, op. cit., pp. 191–217, on p. 201. The temporary loss of such practical amenities as razors and lamps (see Chapter II, Appendix, p. 291, shows how thorough the clearance was. This temporary squalor was a cheap price to pay.

tion, the Hellenic Greek alphabet, and—preserved in this alphabet, like flies in amber—the pre-Christian Hellenic classics, the Christian scriptures written in the Attic *koine*, and the works of the Greek Christian fathers written in the same form of Hellenic Greek. The cumulative weight of the Byzantine Greeks' Hellenic heritage was crushing. It was an initial handicap that goes far towards explaining the Byzantine Greek civilization's premature collapse. Conversely the Hellenic Greeks' escape from a comparable Mycenaean Greek legacy goes far to explain the Hellenic civilization's relative success.[4]

The Hellenic civilization lasted for about seventeen centuries (from the eleventh century B.C. to the seventh century of the Christian Era); the Byzantine lasted for less than twelve centuries (A.D. 284–1453).[5] The Mycenaean civilization had lasted for only about five centuries (*circa* 1600–1100 B.C.). Of course, longevity is a crude index of success, whether the careers that we are comparing are the individual careers of persons or the collective careers of societies. The significant indices are qualitative, not quantitative, and qualitative comparisons are odious because they are inevitably subjective.

The Mycenaean Greeks have perhaps been rated too high by their enthusiastic modern discoverers, and their Hellenic successors' vision of them was astigmatic. Through one eye, Hesiod saw the Mycenaeans as the grim 'Race of Bronze' that they truly were;[6] but the Hellenic poet's other eye transfigured these same repellent predecessors of his into a 'god-like Race of Heroes'.[7] The Byzantine Greeks have certainly been depreciated unduly by the modern Western representatives of a rival Christian civilization, and also by some Modern Greeks, who have wished to dissociate themselves from their own Byzantine past in order to identify themselves with their modern Western contemporaries. As for the Hellenic Greeks, they were regarded by their Byzantine successors with mixed feelings. As pagans they were frowned upon by the Byzantines, but as writers of Attic Greek they were admired and imitated by them. The Hellenes' paganism has been condoned by Modern Greeks and modern Westerners alike. These have agreed in idealizing Hellenism in all its aspects, and this idealization has to be discounted if Hellenism is to be appraised dispassionately. For a Modern

---

[4] 'Linear B literacy, had it lasted any length of time, would have been an incubus on the Greek mind.... The palace bureaucracies ... too, would have become an incubus' (Dow, in Kirk, op. cit., p. 165).

[5] There was a chronological overlap of about three centuries between the last phase of the Hellenic civilization and the first phase of the Byzantine. The period spanned by the reigns of the Roman Emperors Diocletian to Maurice is common to both these Greek civilizations. There was another chronological overlap of about the same length between the last phase of the Byzantine civilization and the first phase of Modern Greek history.

[6] Hesiod, *Works and Days*, lines 143–55.

[7] Ibid., lines 156–73.

Greek or a modern Westerner, this is not an easy exercise. In redressing his traditional obeisance to the Hellenes he may lean over backwards into an excessive castigation of the Hellenes' shortcomings. Yet he may still guess that an emotionally uninvolved enquirer—a Hindu, say, or a Chinese—would rate the Hellenic civilization the highest among the four Greek civilizations that have arisen so far in the course of mankind's history. It may also be guessed that, if Hellenism is awarded the palm, its superiority over the other historic Greek civilizations will be attributable in large measure to the negativeness of its heritage from its Mycenaean past.

The Mycenaean Greek civilization did have the benefit of one geo-political advantage that was subsequently enjoyed by the Hellenic Greek and by the Western Christian civilization, and also by the Russian offshoot (though not by the Asian and south-east European nucleus) of the Byzantine civilization. The Mycenaean Greek civilization, like these later specimens of the same species of society, lay on one of the outer fringes of the cluster of civilizations composing the Old-World *Oikoumenê*, and it thus had an opportunity for expanding at the expense of adjacent barbarians. However, this geographical location also exposed it to the risk of barbarian invasion, and, in contrast to both the Hellenic Greek and the Western civilization, the Mycenaean Greek civilization was unstable and fragile[8] because it was top-heavy and exotic.[9] If it is true that the Achaean rulers of the Mycenaean Greek principalities were barbaric Greeks from the backwoods, while their administrative system was—as it looks as if it were—a sophisticated import from the Levant, this incongruous combination of opposite extremes invited disaster; and it is not surprising that, when the disaster came, it annihilated the unsound social structure that had caused it. The literate bureaucrats who administered the principalities for their Achaean masters, and the Achaean princes themselves, together with their war-bands, were, all told, probably a mere handful compared with the numbers of the subject Greek peasantry; and the peasants, as well as the war-lords, were illiterate. The destructive inter-dynastic and intra-dynastic conflicts in the Mycenaean World that are commemorated in the Hellenic tradition[10] and that are attested by archaeological evidence

---

[8] See Dow, in Kirk, op. cit., pp. 163-4; Desborough, *The Last Mycenaeans*, pp. 242-3.

[9] See C. M. Bowra, 'The Meaning of a Heroic Age', in Kirk, op. cit., p. 25.

[10] This tradition is epitomized by Hesiod in his concordant accounts of the self-liquidation of the 'Race of Bronze' and of the 'Race of Heroes'. The bronze men 'were brought low by their own hands and went their way to the mouldering house of chilly Hades, nameless' (*Works and Days*, lines 151-5). The heroes 'were destroyed by evil war and dread battle—some below Seven-Gate Thebes in the land of Cadmus, as they fought for the flocks of Oedipus, while others were carried for destruction to Troy in ships over the great gulf of the sea, for the sake of Helen of the lovely hair. There verily they met their end and vanished in the embrace of death' (ibid., lines 161-6). The bronze men and the heroes both came to the same bad end, and both brought their destruction

would have been enough to bring the whole precarious superstructure of the Mycenaean civilization to the ground, leaving the peasantry's condition in the eleventh century B.C. much the same as it had been in the sixteenth century B.C., when the superstructure had been rather suddenly imposed on this old-established population of husbandmen and shepherds.

The peasantry of Greece had a culture of its own. It had had this since the dawn of the Neolithic Age, long before it had become Greek-speaking, and it has this historic culture still in so far as the peasantry still survives. The Greek peasants' culture is composed of the popular religion and folklore of the shepherd's and husbandman's recurrent annual round of seasonal events with the accompanying hopes and fears and joys and griefs. This peasant culture has outlived one civilization after another that has passed over the peasants' heads. It is only since the opening of the present century that this ancient rural way of life has been succumbing to the urban way of the modern industrial cities into which more and more of the population of the villages of Greece has been decanted. The Greeks who migrated to the United States before the First World War, and who have been migrating, since the Second World War, to Australia[11] and to West Germany and to Athens, have lost their peasant culture in the act of uprooting themselves from the environment in which this culture had been created and sustained. They now have to find a new culture that will make life endurable for them in a strange new world.

The one element in Greece's ephemeral Mycenaean cultural super-structure that survived the collapse of the Mycenaean civilization was the poetry in which the princes' exploits had been celebrated. This was Hellenism's principal Mycenaean heritage; and it was fortunate for the Hellenes that their poetic heirloom was both oral and secular.

If a corpus of Mycenaean poetry had been bequeathed to the Hellenes in writing, as the corpus of Hellenic poetry was subsequently bequeathed to the Byzantines, the Hellenes would have had to take this frozen hard in its original Mycenaean form. This might have happened, considering that it did happen in neighbouring societies, contemporary with the Mycenaean, in which literacy was more widely diffused, and in which the scripts were more efficient for conveying the languages. At Ugarit (Ras ash-Shamrah), at the northern end of the coast of Syria, tablets

upon themselves. The identity of their fates, as these are described by Hesiod, proves the identity of these two races whose characters Hesiod has depicted in strikingly different colours (see p. 25).

[11] The Greek-speaking components of the populations of the cities of Sydney and Melbourne now amount to more than 200,000 persons. There are reported to be five times as many Castellorizans in Sydney as there now are on the islet of Castellorizo itself, and the Castellorizans of Sydney are said to be a very close-knit community. (Information supplied by Professor Robert Browning.)

inscribed, like the Mycenaean 'Linear B' tablets, with administrative records and instructions.[12] No literary tablets have yet been discovered on any Mycenaean site, and it seems probable that none were ever made. The script was complicated and clumsy; we may guess that scribes were few; and there is not likely to have been a reading public for non-utilitarian writings.

It was also fortunate that the subject-matter of Mycenaean poetry was secular, not religious; for religious scriptures and liturgies readily set hard, even if they are transmitted orally and even if they are as long as the *Iliad* or the *Odyssey*. The purpose of religious literature is to propitiate or to spell-bind the Godhead; an incantation may be ineffective, or, worse still, may be 'counter-productive', if even one of the sacrosanct syllables is uttered incorrectly; and, if this is the accepted belief, acute anxiety will enforce meticulous accuracy. The Mycenaean civilization may have bequeathed some rigid ritual formulae to its Hellenic successor; for it certainly bequeathed to it a substantial heritage of religious practice and belief. Mycenaean poetry, however, was addressed, not to gods, but to human beings, and its purpose was, not spell-binding, but entertainment. Being thus un-sacrosanct, besides being oral, it was fluid.[13]

The poet-minstrels' original Mycenaean audience wanted, we may guess, to be entertained by the singing of flattering and exciting songs about notable contemporary events. After the Mycenaean civilization had collapsed, the school of poets that had outlived the Mycenaean dynasts and bureaucrats had to satisfy a two-fold demand. Their post-Mycenaean audience had a nostalgia for a vanished state of society which, in retrospect, appeared to have been much more glamorous than the squalid and dull life of these epigoni.[14] The epigoni therefore demanded that the Mycenaean heroes' deeds should still be celebrated. At the same time, they demanded that the past should be commemorated in terms that would be intelligible to a present-day audience. The collapse of the glamorous civilization had been so complete, and the consequent change in the epigoni's way of life had been so extreme, that

[12] See Webster, T. B. L., *From Mycenae to Homer* (London 1958), p. 9. The two sets of tablets were housed in different buildings and were written in different languages and scripts: the official documents in Akkadian, the literary works in the authors' native Canaanite language, conveyed in an alphabet constructed with Akkadian cuneiform characters.

[13] See ibid., pp. 134–5.

[14] See Bowra, in Kirk, op. cit., p. 34. An age is stamped retrospectively as having been heroic by the feelings of posterity. The belief in a heroic age 'is commonly formed after some defeat or disaster', and 'the memory of it may be strongest among people who suffer from a sense of deprivation or inferiority or servitude' (ibid., p. 48). Desborough, *The Greek Dark Ages*, p. 321, points out that the Hellenic Greek oral tradition concerning a pre-Hellenic age of Greek history concentrated on events in the latter part of the Mycenaean Age, and was not interested in the post-Mycenaean dark age, which was the period during which this tradition was gradually taking shape.

an archaeologically accurate reproduction of the authentic Mycenaean *mise en scène* would have been unintelligible and would therefore not have been entertaining.

If the post-Mycenaean poets had possessed this information, they might have withheld it in order to keep *en rapport* with their audience. If they had known and divulged the historical facts, they would have been derided, as Marco Polo was when he brought home authentic first-hand information about contemporary China. Polo was nicknamed *Messer Millione* as his penalty for telling what his audience believed to be tall stories. On the other hand, if the Mycenaean Greek poets had transposed their *mise en scène* entirely into matter-of-fact terms of contemporary life, their audience would not have found this performance entertaining either; they would have found it unsatisfyingly prosaic. The poets therefore had to keep on bringing their matter sufficiently up to date to make it intelligible for audiences in successive generations, while keeping it sufficiently archaic to preserve the illusion of its being authentically antique.[15]

Fortunately for the poets, the extemporized oral poetry which was their inherited medium enabled them to compromise successfully between the two demands that were being made on them. Poetry that has not been reduced to writing and that has no religious sacrosanctity is as plastic in the poet's mouth as clay is in a potter's hands. The age of illiteracy may have lasted for 450 years,[16] that is to say, for not less than eighteen generations in which the expectation of life was short. No 'Linear B' tablets of a later date than *circa* 1200 B.C. have been found.[17] The wide-spread devastation of the Mycenaean palaces at about the end of the thirteenth century B.C. seems to have put the 'Linear B' script permanently out of action. The dates of the earliest inscriptions in the Hellenic Greek alphabet that are known so far are later than 750 B.C.[18]

The epic poetry that had been inherited by the Hellenic Greeks from the Mycenaeans did not set hard till it had been drawn upon for the composition of two Hellenic masterpieces, the *Iliad* and the *Odyssey*, and until these two long poems had been recorded in writing in the Hellenic Greek alphabet. Did their makers compose them orally? Or were they already composing these poems in writing? This question is still being debated, and a conclusive answer to it may never be reached. It does,

---

[15] Post-Mycenaean Greek poetry 'had two faces', one turned towards the past, the other towards the contemporary audience (Webster, op. cit., p. 182). Cp. Hope Simpson, R., and Lazenby, J. F., *The Catalogue of Ships in Homer's Iliad* (Oxford 1970), p. 9.

[16] Desborough, *The Last Mycenaeans*, pp. 255–6, reckons the time-span of the Age of Illiteracy to have been 'almost five hundred years'. Cp. *eundem*, *The Greek Dark Ages*, p. 321.

[17] Taylour, op. cit., p. 177. The twelfth century B.C., however, is given as the terminal date for 'Linear B' in ibid., p. 42.

[18] Starr, op. cit., p. 169; Burn, A. R., *The Lyric Age of Greece* (London 1960), p. 54; Snodgrass, op. cit., pp. 351 and 421.

however, seem to be agreed that the eighth century B.C. saw both the composition of the two Homeric poems and the reception of the alphabet by the Greeks from the Phoenicians. It also seems to have been established conclusively that, whether the Homeric poems were composed orally or were composed in writing, the poetry that was their raw material had been transmitted orally, and that it had originated in the Mycenaean Age.

No specimens of this raw material have survived. (None could have, considering that this material was never reduced to writing in any of its pre-Homeric forms.) We have to argue back from the Homeric end-product, which was put into writing at least as early as the sixth century B.C. and possibly before the close of the eighth century B.C. The Homeric poetry, as we have it, is a cento of prefabricated metrical formulae. Extempore composition would have been impossible if the poet-minstrel's mind had not been stored with a sufficient number and variety of these metrical formulae to enable him to string together, impromptu, a poem in hexameter verse.[19]

The end-product of perhaps eighteen generations of improvised poetry constructed from metrical formulae is, for the most part, a presentation, in the eighth-century-B.C. Ionic Greek dialect, of eighth-century-B.C. Greek life in Ionia—for the most part, but not entirely. No work of verbal art is ever an exact replica of either the diction or the style of informal contemporary talk. This is true of written literature; and it is true, *a fortiori*, of poetry that has had a long history of oral transmission. Some of the Homeric formulae contain non-Ionic (presumably pre-Ionic) forms of Greek that were ineradicable because they could not have been turned into eighth-century-B.C. Ionic Greek without making them unmetrical and therefore unutilizable. Ancient oral poetry, composed of formulae, is like a glacier carrying boulders along with it.

[19] The theory that the Homeric poems are the end-product of a school of poetry was propounded by F. A. Wolf in 1795, but it remained unproved till the oral poet's method of composition was brought to light by Milman Parry (see his *L'Épithète traditionelle chez Homère* (Paris 1928) and his papers in *Harvard Studies in Classical Philology*, vols. 41 (1930) and 43 (1932)). By analysing the structure of the *Iliad* and the *Odyssey* and comparing this with the structure of still living Serbo-Croat oral poetry and also with the structure of a poem composed in writing by Apollonius Rhodius in the third to second century B.C. in what this Alexandrian scholar intended to be the Homeric diction and style, Parry showed that oral, unlike literate, poets compose by drawing on a stock of ready-made metrical formulae. The oral poet's art lies in having a maximum number and variety of formulae at his command, employing these felicitously impromptu, and coining new formulae to enlarge his store and thus to extend his range. Milman Parry's work has now been republished under the title *The Making of Homeric Verse: Collected Papers* (Oxford 1971). See also Dodds, E. R., in Kirk, op. cit., pp. 13–17; Lord, A. B., in ibid., pp. 68–78; Kirk, G. S., in ibid., pp. 79–89; Webster, op. cit., pp. 135 and 182. Webster here points out that the Mycenaean official documents committed to writing in the 'Linear B' script use formulae (e.g. set forms of style and title and of letters and orders). He suggests that this formulaic Mycenaean 'officialese' may have given the contemporary Mycenaean oral poets the idea of coining formulae to meet their own need for a mnemonic device.

The boulders of this simile are the metrical formulae, and we can date a number of them by their language and their subject. Some of them date from the latest stages of the poetry's transmission, others from the earliest stage, others again from stages between the starting and the ending dates. A formula would be likely to survive if it was metrically convenient. It would have a double chance of survival if its matter was either picturesquely archaic[20] or vividly modern.

Before noting the Mycenaean elements that the Homeric poems have preserved, we must take note of the far more important features of Mycenaean life that have fallen here into oblivion.

The poet of the *Odyssey* gives descriptions of the palaces, and the palace personnel, of Nestor at Pylos, of Menelaos in Lakedaimon, of Alkinoos on Skheria, and of Odysseus on Ithaca. No doubt these descriptions were convincing both to the poet himself and to his audience, but a present-day reader who is acquainted with the archaeologists' finds at Pylos and at Mycenae, not to speak of Knossos or of the 'Minoan Pompeii' that has been disinterred on the island of Santorini (Thera), will detect that the poet's descriptions convict him of being utterly ignorant of the historical facts. The poet has no conception of the Mycenaean princes' wealth,[21] or of the numbers of their palace personnel,[22] or of the administrative and social hierarchy in their principalities.[23] Alkinoos's palace, as described in the *Odyssey*, is a fancy picture set within a realistic picture of an Ionian city-state.[24]

Whether or not the poets of the *Iliad* and the *Odyssey* were literate in the Hellenic Greek alphabet, they were certainly not literate in 'Linear

---

[20] See Webster, op. cit., p. 287.

[21] See Bowra, in Kirk, op. cit., p. 25.

[22] 'Odysseus and Alcinous each keep fifty women to work in their houses, and there is no hint that this is not princely, but the Pylos tablets, which come from a single phase and a very short period, give the names of 645 slave-women, together with some 370 girls and 210 boys' (ibid., loc. cit.). Cp. Webster, op. cit., p. 110.

[23] 'In the tablets we have . . . a complex system of tenures, often interlocking, with a correspondingly articulated, hierarchical structure of the population and elaborate specialization of occupation and function, with allocations of manpower and supplies, payments to men and gods, all carefully recorded (in fractions, if required), catalogued and totalled' (Finley, in Kirk, op. cit., p. 135). The bureaucratic organization at Pylos and at Knossos that is revealed in the 'Linear B' tablets has parallels in contemporary Ugarit and Alalakh and Hattusaš (Page, op. cit., p. 180), but there is no inkling of any of this in the Homeric poems (ibid., pp. 186, 187, 202). The poets had no record of it (Finley, op. cit., p. 204), and how could they have had any? The Mycenaean governments' instructions could not have been given, and their records could not have been made, without the use of writing (ibid., p. 135); their archives had been lost; and, without the archives, a contemporary official, and, *a fortiori*, a later poet, would have been worsted by a mass of detail that no one could have memorized. Finley's confrontation of two sets of eight status words (ibid., p. 199)—one set Mycenaean and the other Homeric—is particularly revealing. Cp. Page, op. cit., pp. 187–93.

[24] Webster, op. cit., p. 157; Snodgrass., op. cit., p. 435. 'The Homeric political system, like other Homeric pictures, is an artificial amalgam of widely separated historical stages' (ibid., p. 389; cp. p. 435).

B'; they had never seen an inscribed clay tablet. The *folded* tablet that was given to Bellerophon by Proitos[25] cannot have been a clay tablet of the kind, derived ultimately from the Sumerians via the Minoans, that was used in the Mycenaean Age for writing 'Linear B'. It was presumably a wooden diptych with its two inner faces coated with wax in which letters or characters were scratched. This mention of a letter in a diptych does show that the poet was aware of the existence of the art of writing, but he may have known of it only as a contemporary foreign technique, the Cypriot syllabary, for instance, or the Phoenician alphabet. His description of a letter purporting to have been written in the Mycenaean Age may, in fact, have been one of his modernizing touches for making his audience feel at home in the strange vanished world that he was professing to be conjuring up. The poet may have believed that he was committing an anachronism which was warranted by poetic licence. If so, he will never have known that, by a freak of chance, he was recalling a genuine Mycenaean technique that had fallen into oblivion.

However, we cannot feel quite sure that the post-Mycenaean poets, besides being ignorant of the 'Linear B' script, were also unaware that some of the Mycenaean Greeks had been literate. Proitos's letter may have been, not a fanciful modernism, but an archaism founded on knowledge. An aura of archaism was part of this school of poets' stock-in-trade, and one of their devices for producing an old-world atmo-sphere was to retain, in their *mise en scène*, certain genuine features of the Heroic Age that were incompatible with some conspicuous features of contemporary life. One of their archaistic conventions was that the west coast of Asia Minor and its off-shore islands, except for the Dodecanese, were not yet in Greek hands, though the *Iliad* and the *Odyssey* were almost certainly composed in Ionia from poetic matter that had been sung in the Greek settlements there during the later stages of its transmission from the European Greece of the Mycenaean Age.[26] Another of their conventions was that the metal in general use was still bronze, and not yet iron.[27]

These well-known Homeric conventions make it conceivable that, in his account of Proitos's letter, the poet of the *Iliad* may have been deliberately recalling that the Mycenaean-Age princes were literate— or, at least that they employed literate amanuenses. This would have

---

[25] *Iliad*, VI, lines 168–9.

[26] See Page, op. cit., p. 259.

[27] 'The Homeric pattern of metal-using . . . is a comparatively clear-cut but totally artificial one . . . . There is nothing to suggest that the earlier dark age inspired any part of the picture' (Snod-grass, op. cit., p. 390). An immense variety of archaeologically attested burial methods can be claimed as being Homeric (ibid.). 'The problem is insoluble because the model never existed' (ibid., p. 391).

been an additional artifice for giving his poetry an antique flavour for the audience, if, by the date at which this passage was composed, the audience had not yet become literate again, but had also not forgotten that it had had literate predecessors. Considering this possibility, we cannot be so sure that the Homeric poets were unaware of the Mycenaean Greeks' literacy as we can be that these poets were ignorant of the 'Linear B' script and that they were unaware of the Mycenaean system of government and structure of society.

Compared to these two great lacunae in the post-Mycenaean oral poets' memory of the Mycenaean Greek World, the flotsam from the wreckage of this World that was carried down into the Hellenic Age in the oral poets' metrical formulae does not amount to much.

One piece of this flotsam is the non-Ionic element in Homeric Greek. It used to be thought that this non-Ionic element was Aeolic, and it was even conjectured that the poetry had been composed in Aeolic and had been transposed into Ionic subsequently. Recently, however, it has been suggested that the earliest versions of the poetic matter on which the Homeric poets eventually drew were composed in the Mycenaean Age in an undifferentiated South-Greek dialect of which we have specimens in the inscriptions in 'Linear B', and that it was not until after the collapse of the Mycenaean principalities, and the displacement of their South-Greek-speaking ex-subjects as a result of the North-West-Greek-speakers' *Völkerwanderung*, that the Arcado-Cyprian and Ionic dialects of the Hellenic Age took their distinctive shapes. If this is the truth,[28] the non-Ionic elements in the Homeric form of Ionic Greek would not be imports; they would be relics. They would have particularly strong survival-power in metrical formulae which would have become unmetrical if the Ionic modifications of the Ionic dialect's ancestral South Greek had been admitted here.[29]

This is linguistic evidence that oral poetry was being composed in the language of the documents written in the 'Linear B' script before the end of the Mycenaean Age, and we can also infer that the metre of this poetry, though not necessarily the number of feet in each line, was the same as in the Homeric hexameter, since the metrical formulae which are the poets' building-blocks are portions of hexameter lines. Circumstantial evidence that the Homeric poems stem from a body of Mycenaean-Age poetic matter is presented by the description, in the *Iliad*,[30] of a helmet coated with rows of boars' tusks. Mycenaean-Age

[28] For the suggestion that the Hellenic-Age dialects of Greek may not have become differentiated from each other till the time of the post-Mycenaean *Völkerwanderung*, see Risch, E., in Kirk, op. cit., pp. 90–105; Chadwick, J., 'The Greek Dialects and Greek Pre-history', ibid., pp. 106–18; Chadwick, J., 'Mycenaean Elements in the Homeric Dialect', ibid., pp. 119–25.

[29] See Taylour, op. cit., p. 42; Page, op. cit., p. 219.

[30] *Iliad*, Book X, lines 261–5.

representations of boars'-tusk helmets have been disinterred,[31] as well as
actual tusks that had once been fitted on to helmets; but the date of the
latest archaeological evidence so far found for this type of helmet is the
twelfth century B.C., i.e. the century in which the Mycenaean civilization
was in its death agonies.[32] Evidence that this poetry was being composed
before the fourteenth-century-B.C. revolution in Mycenaean military
equipment[33] is presented by the formula φέρων σάκος ἠΰτε πύργον[34]
('carrying a shield as if he were carrying a tower'); for this body-shield,
which is represented on one of the inlaid dagger-blades from shaft-
graves at Mycenae,[35] and which therefore must have been in use in the
early sixteenth century B.C., went out of use 200 years later, when it was
replaced by the small round shield, held in the left hand, not slung, like
the body-shield, by a strap over the left shoulder.

These are two out of nine 'certainly Mycenaean objects and practices
mentioned in Homer'.[36]

The siege of a city is a motif that appears right at the beginning of the
history of Mycenaean visual art. It is delineated, in repoussé relief, on
the fragments of the silver rhyton that has been recovered from shaft-
grave IV at Mycenae.[37] It may have been a theme of Mycenaean poetry
from as early a date, and it may have been applied to other sieges—for
instance, the two sieges of Thebes—before being applied to the siege of
Troy.[38]

The poets who, in retrospect, under-estimated the size and wealth
and man-power of the Mycenaean fortified palaces in Continental
Greece over-estimated the dimensions of Troy. The length of the *enceinte*
of Troy VI is little more than 550 yards,[39] yet is has been reckoned that
the Troy described in the Homeric poems would have housed a
population of more than 50,000.[40] All the same, the *Iliad* has inherited
authentic information about Troy that could no longer have been
obtained after the destruction of Troy VIIa *circa* 1260 B.C.[41] In the *Iliad*
and the *Odyssey*, Troy—the city itself—is known by two alternative
names, *Troiê* and *Ilios*. *Troiê* has ten standing epithets, *Ilios* has eleven.

---

[31] See Taylour, op. cit., plates 62 and 64; Vermeule, op. cit., plate XXXIX B.
[32] See Snodgrass, op. cit., p. 389, citing *Athenische Mitteilungen* 75 (1960), 44, Beilage 31, 4. See also Taylour, op. cit., pp. 42 and 143–4; Page, op. cit., pp. 218 and 259; Vermeule, op. cit., p. 135.
[33] For this, see Taylour, op. cit., p. 142, quoted already on p. 17.
[34] See Taylour, op. cit., pp. 42, 43, and 142; Page, op. cit., pp. 232–5 and 259; Webster, op. cit., p. 114.
[35] See Vermeule, op. cit., plate XII; Taylour, op. cit., plate 56.
[36] A list of these is given by Kirk in Kirk, op. cit., pp. 176–7.
[37] See Taylour, op. cit., pp. 127 and 139, with plate 59; Vermeule, op. cit., pp. 100–2, with plate XIV.
[38] See Vermeule, op. cit., p. 277; Webster, op. cit., pp. 59–60 and 61.
[39] Page, op. cit., p. 54.
[40] Blegen, op. cit., p. 13.
[41] Page, op. cit., p. 221.

Only one out of the twenty-one is attached to both names; this common epithet of theirs is *'euteikheos'* ('well-walled', in the genitive case);[42] and Troy has been found by its modern excavators to have been strongly fortified through all its successive phases from Troy I to Troy VIIa inclusive. Troy and the Trojans are also associated in the Homeric poetry with horses. Troy has a monopoly of the epithet *'eupôlos'* ('having fine foals'), and the Trojans are called *'hippodamoi'* ('breakers-in of horses') in nineteen passages.[43] The archaeologists have found that the horse was introduced into Troy simultaneously with 'Minyan' pottery, by the new occupiers (presumably the same people as the contemporary new occupiers of Continental Greece) who were the makers of Troy VI.[44] These new people came into the Aegean basin in the twentieth or the nineteenth century B.C.

The Homeric poems' heirlooms from the past are impressive, 'yet the society portrayed tends to be relatively (though not entirely) "modern"'.[45] The language has been brought up to date as far as metrical requirements have allowed. It has been transposed into the Ionic dialect that has differentiated itself from the original Mycenaean-Age South Greek, and this Ionification of the language suggests that there may have been a similarly far-reaching modification of the traditional story.[46] Homeric similes, above all, are taken from modern life;[47] there is no archaism here; and, in Page's opinion, even a majority of the metrical formulae are post-Mycenaean.[48]

It is unlikely that any historical traditions, beyond those that had originally been embodied in oral poetry, survived . . . the last northern invasions.[49]

If so, it is evident that the Hellenic Greeks were not overshadowed and dominated by their legacy from their Mycenaean predecessors, as the Byzantine Greeks were by their legacy from the Hellenes, and as the Modern Greeks have been by their legacies from both the Hellenes and the Byzantines. The oral poetry that was the Hellenes' principal heritage from the Mycenaeans was fluid; it could and did change to meet the demands of the poets' successive audiences, and there were perhaps as many as eighteen generations of audiences and poets between the date of the definitive collapse of the Mycenaean Greek civilization in Continental Greece and the date at which the oral poetry, in the latest

---

[42] Blegen, op. cit., p. 16.
[43] Ibid., p. 17. Cp. Page, op. cit., pp. 251–2.
[44] Page, op. cit., pp. 57–8.
[45] Finley, in Kirk, op. cit., p. 205 n. 1.
[46] Page, op. cit., p. 257.
[47] See Dodds, in Kirk, op. cit., p. 5; Webster, op. cit., p. 227.
[48] Page, op. cit., p. 267 n. 19.
[49] Forsdyke, op. cit., p. 123.

pre-Homeric stage of its evolution, was laid under contribution for the composition of the *Iliad* and the *Odyssey* in Ionia.

The Mycenaeans did not dominate the Hellenes posthumously. So far from that, the Hellenes dominated the Mycenaeans retrospectively. They re-shaped, to their own liking, the image of the Mycenaean World that had been transmitted in the Hellenes' heritage of Mycenaean oral poetry. The Hellenes modified this image, again and again, to make it conform with the constantly changing fashions of Hellenic life. They modified it till it had become unrecognizable except for a few deliberately retained archaic conventions and a few particular ana-chronisms, such as the pre-fourteenth-century-B.C. body-shield, that were preserved perforce by the intractability of a metrical formula. The Hellenic modernity of the eventual image of the Mycenaean World that has been immortalized in the *Iliad* and the *Odyssey* is hardly blurred by the presence of a few authentic Mycenaean traits.[50] The Hellenes virtually annexed the dead Mycenaean world to their own living world. For the next twenty-six centuries after the date of the composition of the Homeric poems, Mycenaean Greece was known merely as the setting of the themes, and the provider of the heroes and the villains, of the two earliest great works of Hellenic literary art.[51] At last, in the nineteenth century of the Christian Era, modern archaeologists discovered that the Mycenaean Greeks had created a civilization of their own which not only was pre-Hellenic but was un-Hellenic.

The Mycenaean Greeks had facilitated the Hellenes' literary *tour de*

[50] This point is made in extreme terms by Finley in Kirk, op. cit., p. 217: 'The Homeric World was altogether post-Mycenaean, and the so-called reminiscences and survivals are rare, isolated, and garbled.' The denial of the presence of any important Mycenaean features in the Homeric poetry has been challenged by Hope Simpson and Lazenby, op. cit. Their criticism is the more telling for being undogmatic and unpolemical, besides being carefully documented. It ought to be taken into account by enquirers whose position is, as the present writer's is, nearer to Finley's.

[51] The annexation of the material relics of the Mycenaean World to the Homeric epics began as soon as this Ionian poetry had been disseminated into regions of European Greece in which some vestiges of the Mycenaean civilization were still visible. The evidence for this consists partly of votive offerings and partly of paintings of scenes on Geometric vases and on seals, of dates that are all earlier than 700 B.C. The inscription, written *c*. 720 B.C., on a cup found at Pithekoussai (Ischia) is metrical, and it alludes to the description of Nestor's cup in *Iliad*, Book XI, lines 632-5, or *Odyssey*, Book III, line 63 (see the photograph of the cup and the transcript and translation of the inscription in Snodgrass, op. cit., p. 351). The earliest representations of mythological or heroic *motifs* on Geometric vases may even antedate the time at which the Ionian epic became a common possession of Hellas as a whole (ibid., pp. 431-2). In the dark age, the Hellenes' communion with the Mycenaean Age had been 'wistful'; in the eighth century B.C. it became 'deliberate' (ibid., p. 395; cp. Desborough, *The Last Mycenaeans*, p. 46; *eundem*, *The Greek Dark Ages*, p. 283). However, this deliberate search for contact with the Mycenaean past was in some cases misdirected. Cult offerings to Agamemnon at Mycenae and to Menelaos of Therapne began to be made before 700 B.C. (Snodgrass, op. cit., p. 192), but the late-eighth-century-B.C. shrines that were built at these two places were located on Mycenaean buildings that had been secular, not sacred (ibid., p. 397). At Athens, on the site that eventually became the Akademia, a private dwelling-house of Early Helladic date was evidently mistaken in the late Geometric period for an ancient holy place. A cult-building was erected alongside of it, and numerous sacrifices were made there (ibid., p. 398).

force by the thoroughness with which they had destroyed themselves. The Mycenaeans' collapse safeguarded the Hellenes, in the formative stage of the Hellenic Greek civilization, against being dominated either by superior Greek predecessors or by superior non-Greek contemporaries. One consequence of the Mycenaean civilization's fall and the subsequent *Völkerwanderung* in the Levant was that the Aegean was 'sundered from the Middle East for three centuries',[52] in contrast to the previous active intercourse between the two regions in the Mycenaean Age.[53] The opening up of relations between the Hellenic Greeks and the Phoenicians as early as the eighth century B.C. is attested by the Greeks' adoption and adaptation of the Phoenician alphabet, and in Hesiod's *Theogony* there are religious and mythological motifs, apparently derived from civilizations to the east of the Hellenic World, which must have been current in the Hellenic World itself already before Hesiod made use of them *circa* 700 B.C. Greek wares were being exported (not necessarily by Greek traders in Greek vessels) to Al-Mina, near the mouth of the River Orontes, by the beginning of the eighth century B.C. However, commercial relations between Greece and Egypt were in abeyance from *circa* 1200 B.C. until the seventh century B.C.[54]

This break was its [the Aegean's] decisive critical opportunity . . . .[55] The Greeks were to be free to work out their destinies essentially unaffected by external influences until they themselves were ready to look once more abroad.[56]

The Greeks of the Hellenic Age did indeed make magnificent use of this opportunity that had been given to them by the extremeness of their Mycenaean Greek predecessors' failure. The Hellenic Greeks and the Byzantine Greeks, in their turns, did their utmost to give similar opportunities to their successors. Hellas and Byzantium each ended almost as disastrously as Mycenae had ended, but on each of these two later occasions the heir of the wrecked Greek civilization failed to reap the benefit that had accrued to Hellas. The fallen predecessors' karma was not dissipated by their fall; it was handed on. Since the sixteenth century B.C., when the Helladic Greeks encountered the Minoans, the post-Mycenaean dark age has been the only spell, in the long subsequent course of Greek history, in which the Greeks have not been subject to pressure from importunate contemporaries and from perhaps even more importunate predecessors.[57]

---

[52] Starr, op. cit., p. 74. Cp. Webster, op. cit., p. 137.
[53] Starr, op. cit., pp. 115–19.
[54] Forsdyke, op. cit., p. 83.
[55] Starr, op. cit., p. 74.
[56] Ibid., p. 106.
[57] See Chapter II, Appendix, *The Post-Mycenaean Dark Age.*

IV

THE HELLENIC GREEKS' SUCCESSES
AND FAILURES

IN sheer potency the Hellenic Greeks stand in the topmost rank of the peoples who have made civilizations. Their only peers have been the Chinese and the Jews. The Hellenes hold their own against these two competitors, and excel all others, when we apply obvious tests.

The most obvious test is the extent of a people's geographical expansion. At the date of the Mycenaean Greeks' collapse, the area occupied by Greek-speakers was limited to Continental Greece, a beachhead round Knossos in Crete, the Dodecanese, Miletus, and possibly the Troad, if the new occupiers of the Troad at the beginning of Troy VI were the same people as those who occupied Continental Greece at the beginning of Middle Helladic I. Thereafter, 'during the Dark Ages, the Aegean turned into a Greek lake, focussed within itself'.[1]

In the Aegean, except along its north shore, only pockets of pre-Greek non-Greek-speaking population are known to have survived—at Praisos, for instance, at the east end of Crete—and, during the Hellenic Age, non-Greek-speaking intruders into the Aegean were rare. Tyrsenoi, speaking a language closely akin to that of the Tyrsenoi of Etruria, occupied the islands of Lemnos and Imbros at an unknown date before the engraving of the inscription in this language at Kaminia.[2] In the second century B.C. a few Italian business men, both Roman and non-Roman, settled at Delos and at other commercial centres in the

[1] Starr, op. cit., p. 108. Cp. ibid., p. 375. For instance, Embório on the south coast of Khios, where a Mycenaean Greek settlement had been founded and then destroyed during the Late Helladic III C period, was reoccupied by Hellenic Greek settlers in the Late Geometric period (ibid., p. 90), after having remained uninhabited during the intervening dark age (Desborough, *The Greek Dark Ages*, p. 221). The Hellenic settlements in insular and continental Asian Ionia may have begun to be founded in the eleventh century B.C., and Ionia became one of the most important regions of the Hellenic Greek World. On Lesbos and in continental Asian Aiolis, the earliest Greek pottery found so far is no earlier than the eighth century B.C. (Snodgrass, op. cit.; Desborough, *The Last Mycenaeans*, p. 255). Antissa on Lesbos seems to have had closer connections with Asia Minor in the dark age than with Greece (Desborough, *The Greek Dark Ages*, p. 221). However, in 1972, there had not yet been any archaeological investigation of the town-sites of either Mytilene or Khios (ibid.).

[2] This inscription must have been engraved before the eviction of these Tyrsenoi from Lemnos, and they had been evicted by Miltiades II, the Athenian despot of the Thracian Chersonese (the Gallipoli Peninsula) before 493 B.C., the date at which Miltiades fled to Athens.

Hellenic World. A few Roman colonies were planted in Southern Greece and in Macedonia and in the Troad by Julius Caesar and Augustus. But these intruders were all exterminated, evicted, or absorbed.

Beyond the Aegean, to the east, the Greek language also won beachheads in Pamphylia and Eastern Cilicia, and captured Cyprus, during the transition from the Mycenaean to the Hellenic Age. The Greek-speaking settlers in this region did not become Hellenes, in the cultural sense, until the post-Alexandrine Age of Hellenic history, but the massive settlements of Greek-speakers that occupied large tracts of territory in South-Eastern Italy and Sicily and Cyrenaica and along the shores of the Dardanelles and the Sea of Marmara and the Bosphorus, in and after the second half of the eighth century B.C., brought with them the Hellenic civilization that, by then, had taken shape in Greece and on the west coast of Asia Minor.

Beyond these massive Hellenic Greek settlements, there was a far-flung diaspora of Hellenic Greek beach-heads. The north-west shore of the western basin of the Mediterranean, from the western foot of the Maritime Alps to about half way down the Mediterranean coast of Spain, was sown with scattered Greek outposts, of which Massalia (Marseilles) was the chief, in the course of the first period of Hellenic Greek colonization, *circa* 750–550 B.C. In the same period, a similar diaspora of beachheads was planted along the north shore of the Aegean and round the southern, western, and nothern shores of the Black Sea. During the second period of Greek colonization, for which the way was opened by the overthrow of the Persian Empire by Alexander the Great, another diaspora of Hellenic Greek cities was broadcast over the Persian Empire's former dominions, from Egypt to the regions that are now Soviet Central Asia and Afghanistan. However, these diasporan colonial Greek cities did not succeed in Hellenizing their rural hinterlands.

The range of Hellenic settlement was exceeded by the range of Hellenic trade. Massalia's commercial hinterland expanded as far as Cornwall, the Black Sea settlements' as far as the Black Earth belt in the Ukraine, Alexandria's as far as the east coast of India and the upper Indus basin (Gandhara). The geographical expansion of Greek settlements and Greek trade in the Hellenic Age was never equalled before it was surpassed, in modern times, by the literally world-wide expansion of the West-European Christian peoples.

This comparison is a reminder of the truth that geographical expansion is, at best, only a crude criterion of success. Current Western experience suggests that gigantism may be a symptom, not of health, but of sickness. Present-day Westerners are becoming aware that inordinately large quantities and magnitudes are a menace to well-being, and perhaps even to life itself. The stage of Hellenic history at which the geographical extent of Greek settlement and Greek trade was at its maximum was the post-Alexandrine Age, and this stage was neither the most creative nor the happiest. A test of success that is more revealing than geographical expansion is attractiveness.

In the fifth century B.C. the Hellenic way of life captivated the king of the pastoral nomad Skyths in the steppe hinterland of the Greek colonial city-state Borysthenes (Olbia), at the mouths of the Dniepr and the southern Bug. When King Skyles' horde skirted Borysthenes in the course of its annual round, Skyles used to slip away into this Hellenic city for a month or so out of each year. As soon as the city gates had been safely locked behind him, he changed into Greek dress and enjoyed himself in the agora (ἠγόραζε). He led the Greek way of life, including participation in public worship. He committed himself to his adopted Hellenic city by buying house-property there and by marrying a Borysthenite wife. He did all this at the risk of his life, for he was committing an unpardonable act of cultural treason. The Hellenic and the nomad ways of life were at opposite poles. When his tribesmen eventually discovered his secret, they put him to death.[3]

An even more remarkable case of captivation by Hellenism was that of Skyles' approximate contemporary, Ducetius, who began his career as the leader of a Sikel (native Sicilian) resistance movement to the Greek settlers by whom the Sikels were being evicted and subjugated. When Ducetius was defeated by Syracuse, the most powerful of the Sikeliot Greek colonial city-states, he retired, not to his native mountains, but to Corinth, Syracuse's mother-city in Greece, and he afterwards returned to Sicily at the head of a fresh swarm of Greek settlers to found a new Greek city-state there. Thus, even when the Sikels were up in arms against their Hellenic Greek assailants, despoilers, and oppressors, they could not resist the attraction of the Hellenic way of life. In the end, all the native inhabitants of Sicily became Greek-speaking citizens of city-states organized on the model of the Greek colonial city-states that had been planted in Sicily at the natives' expense.

It was impossible for Hellenism to convert Skyles' fellow nomads, but it did convert the Sikels' neighbours, the peoples of Italy. These were not Hellenized as thoroughly as the Sikels; they did not take to speaking Greek instead of their mother-tongues, but they did adopt the Hellenic way of life. Hellenism's great prize in Italy was Rome,[4] a city-state that eventually conquered and united politically the whole perimeter of the Mediterranean Sea, including the whole of the Hellenic World to the

---

[3] Herodotus, Book IV, chapters 78–80.

[4] *Graecia capta ferum victorem cepit et artes | intulit agresti Latio*—Horace, Epist. II, 1, lines 156–7.

west of the River Euphrates. In Latin dress, the Hellenic way of life and culture were carried by the Romans into western Europe and into north-west Africa, far beyond the Massaliots' range.

Even the Babylonians accepted the Greeks as liberators from the Persian yoke. The Greeks did not attempt to force or to induce the Babylonians to give up their own age-old language and script and culture, and this tolerance opened the way for intellectual co-operation between Greek and Babylonian astronomers.

The most attractive feature of Hellenism was—deservedly—its visual art. Skyles' fellow Skyths, who rejected the rest of the Hellenic way of life, imported Hellenic works of art in exchange for the Skyths' agricultural subjects' cereals. The Greek manufacturers produced special goods, decorated in a semi-Scythian style, for supplying this lucrative market, but, along with these, unadulterated Hellenic Greek works of art have been found in Scythian chieftains' graves. In Britain, before the Roman conquest, local princes were minting coins bearing devices that were inspired, at many removes, by the fourth-century-B.C. coinage of King Philip II of Macedon.

In the field of visual art, Hellenism's greatest conquest was the Northern School of Buddhism (the Mahayana). In pre-Hellenic Buddhist art the Buddha had been represented by a blank, an appropriate symbol for a being who had achieved self-extinction by making his exit into Nirvana. The Hellenic style of art reached Gandhara (probably from Alexandria) in the early centuries of the Christian Era, when Northern Buddhism was in its formative stage, and when Gandhara was its geographical focus. Consequently the Buddha came to be represented at Gandhara anthropomorphically in the likeness of the Hellenic god Apollo, and it was in this Hellenic form that the Buddha's image was carried by the Mahayana on its long journey over the Hindu Kush and along the steppes to Eastern Asia. Thus, through the medium of its art, Hellenism captivated almost the whole of the Old World, from Japan to Britain inclusive, except for Africa to the south of the Sahara.

By contrast, Hellenic religion missed fire. The reactions of most non-Hellenes to it were either indifference or contempt or active hostility, and here again Hellenism received its deserts. The popular religion of the Greek peasants was—and is—both sincere and pertinent to the peasants' way of earning their livelihood; but, for these very reasons, rural Greek popular religion has been much like that of other agricultural peoples. Non-Greek peasants did not have much to learn from it. As for the official religion of the Hellenic city-states, this could not appeal to peoples who were living under other political dispensations. Each city-state had its own tutelary goddess (or, less usually, its tutelary god) who symbolized the state's collective power; and, since Hellenic city-states, like the city-states of other societies, were apt to be aggressive, their tutelary deities were not attractive to foreigners. Nor did they have much hold over the hearts of their own human fellow-citizens. Participation in public worship in an Hellenic city-state was a manifestation of political loyalty rather than an expression of spiritual devotion. Any warmth of religious feeling that the 'politicized' gods still aroused was preserved for them by their pre-political past. Most of them had originally been personifications of natural forces that could work weal or woe in their worshippers' private lives. They had, in fact, been conscripted from the peasants' pantheon to serve as patrons for city-states.

Meanwhile, however, these gods had been partially discredited by the poets whose poetry had culminated in the *Iliad* and the *Odyssey*. They had been brought down to Earth and had been placed morally on a par with the poets' human heroes and villains. When the gods had been degraded to this semi-barbaric human level, their chief residual super-human attribute was immortality. They were not even omnipotent, since they could, and did, thwart each other. Zeus's control over Apollo was as precarious as Agamemnon's over Achilles. A Hellene who had heard any pre-Homeric or Homeric poetry sung or recited must have had considerable mental reservations about the gods whom he had heard the poets satirizing. These disillusioning recollections must have haunted and disturbed him when he was called upon, as a citizen, to take seriously Sparta's Athana of the Brazen House or Athens' Athene Promakhos (Front-line Fighter).

Popular religion still could be, and still was, taken seriously by the citizens of Hellenic city-states; but, though popular religion was sincere, it was not altogether edifying; for its practical purpose was to promote fertility, and one of the means was sympathetic magic. The irresistible rustic god was Dionysos. His name is Indo-European, though it may not be Greek, and this convicts him of being of northern barbarian origin. He appears already in the Pylos 'Linear B' tablets as a member of the Mycenaean Greek pantheon. By the time when the post-Mycenaean darkness lifts, we find that Dionysos has won a footing in the Pan-Hellenic shrine at Delphi, side by side with Apollo and with the shrine's original owner, Mother Earth. Dionysos has also forced his way from the highland pastures and the lowland fields and vineyards into the rising Hellenic cities. He has not anywhere become a city-state's tutelary god, but, short of that, he has been accepted in the cities, and here his rustic fertility rites have been refined into sophisticated drama. In one Hellenic city, Athens, the Dionysiac drama has become the vehicle for one of the major achievements of Hellenic art. Yet, in submitting to this transfiguration of his rites, the god has not allowed these to be completely purged of their fruitful lewdness.

There was a persistent tradition that Dionysos had had to overcome resistance to his intrusion into the Hellenic 'Establishment'. Though he had won his way in, his presence was always felt to be something of a scandal; and, if his rites shocked the Hellenes themselves, they shocked non-Hellenes *a fortiori*.

> The Skyths are rude to the Hellenes about their practice of 'going Bacchic' (Βακχεύειν). They say that it is indecent to have invented this god who induces human beings to go mad.

The outrageous sight of their king Skyles 'going Bacchic' in a Dionysiac coven (θίασος) within the walls of Borysthenes shocked the Skyths so deeply that they became implacable. They could not rest till they had taken Skyles' life.[5]

About three centuries later, the same unruly Dionysiac outlet for pent-up Hellenic religious emotion caused the same shock and provoked the same savage reaction in the Roman Commonwealth and in Judaea. In 186 B.C. the Roman Government instituted a persecution of the devotees of Dionysos in Italy which anticipated the subsequent Roman persecutions of the Christians. In Judaea a Hellenizing movement had been started by one faction of the Jewish 'Establishment' *circa* 175 B.C.; the priests of Yahweh had taken kindly to Hellenic athletics; and this had not provoked the strait-laced Jewish conservatives to the point of revolting.[6] It was when the Jewish Hellenizers 'went Bacchic'[7] that they upset the apple-cart. This was one of the provocations that precipitated the revolt of the Hasmonaeans against the Seleucid Greek regime, and the anti-Hellenic reaction in Judaea in the second century B.C. has had momentous consequences for the whole of the western half of the Old World.

Hellenic religion, both in its uninspiring and in its provocative manifestations, was Hellenism's *côté faible*. The collision between Hellenism and Judaism in the second century B.C. was the most crucial confrontation between Hellenism and an alien attitude to life in the whole Hellenic chapter of Greek history. This encounter ended in two successive compromises: Christianity and Islam. In both compromises, Judaism gained the upper hand. The essence of both these Judaistic religions is Jewish monotheism, but Islam is still more Judaic, and still less Hellenic, than Christianity. In Christianity, the trinitarian interpretation of monotheism is a concession to Hellenic polytheism, while

---

[5] Herodotus, loc. cit.
[6] 1 Macc.: 1; 2 Macc.: 4.
[7] 2 Macc.: 5.

the visual presentation of the members of the divine trinity and of its attendant angels and saints is a concession to Hellenic visual art which, in Jewish eyes, is 'the abomination of desolation, standing in the place where it ought not.'

In the history of Christianity there have been several attempts to revert to the tabu against graven images which is part of Christianity's Jewish heritage; but in Eastern Orthodox Christendom the iconoclasts have been defeated, and in Western Christendom they have never more than partially prevailed. Islam has been faithful to the Jewish tabu, in spite of the sceptical Umayyad Caliphs' penchant for Hellenic visual art; but Islam has followed Christianity in acquiescing in a formulation of its beliefs in terms of Hellenic philosophy. This, however, has been only a minor victory for Hellenism. The dominance of Judaism in both the Hellenistic–Judaistic religions is demonstrated by their allegiance to Jewish monotheism.

Even at the price of submitting to Christianity, Hellenism proved unable to retain its hold over the major part of the regions that had been added to its political domain by Alexander. Fars, the nucleus of the former Persian Empire, reasserted its independence in the third century B.C., the rest of Iran in the third and second centuries B.C., Judaea in the second century B.C.; and in the second century B.C. the Egyptians, too, tried to throw off the yoke of their Greek rulers. Hellenism's Roman champions crushed the Jewish resistance movement and damped down the Egyptian resistance movement; but, in the fifth century of the Christian Era, anti-Hellenic mass-movements broke out within the bosom of the Christian Church. The Egyptians and Syrians and Armenians asserted their cultural independence by rejecting the Hellenic Christian 'Establishment's' creed, and they expressed their dissidence by organizing dissenting churches and translating the Christian liturgy from Greek into their own languages. In the seventh century they escaped from the rule of the Hellenized Roman Empire by acquiescing in a change of masters. The Muslim Arabs pushed back the Empire's frontier to the line of the Taurus Range.

At its maximum extent, Hellenism had expanded in Latin dress as far westward as Britain and Morocco, and, in Buddhist dress, as far eastward as Japan. In its last agonies, all that Hellenism retained of these enormous territorial acquisitions was Sicily and Asia Minor. Nevertheless, Hellenism's success in captivating so many non-Greek peoples, even temporarily, is manifest and incontrovertible evidence of the spiritual potency of this second of the civilizations that have been created by the Greeks.

Religion is the only field of human activity in which Hellenism failed signally. It was not conspicuously successful in technology. But in the visual arts,[8] architecture, literature, and philosophy it was pre-eminent. It is not possible to do justice briefly to Hellenism's achievements in these fields, and there is no need to make the attempt here; for these achievements are familiar and undisputed. Not the Hellenic achievements in themselves but their effect on posterity is the subject of the present book, and the pursuit of this subject confronts us with a truth that is ironical but pertinent. Hellenism's outright failures—for instance, its failure in the field of religion—have not bequeathed so awkward a legacy as its equivocal successes. Hellenism's history bears out Voltaire's epigram *le mieux est l'ennemi du bien*, if we may equate 'the good' with progress and 'the better' with an inhibiting ambition to perfect some particular stage of 'the good' that has already been attained. Hellenism's greatest achievements did, in truth, come so near to perfection that they became obstacles to further advance in their respective lines. The Old Masters' successors had to make a painful choice. Either they had to abandon a field in which their predecessors had left no room for further conquests, and this called for a deliberately revolutionary new departure, or else the epigoni had to lapse into an imitative archaism, adulating, Narcissus-like, inherited masterpieces that they could not emulate.

This dilemma is well known to modern Westerners from their own experience in at least two provinces of art. The naturalistic Western school of painting that had arisen in the thirteenth century, and the 'classical' school of music that had arisen in the seventeenth century, both found themselves in the nineteenth century destitute of new worlds to conquer. Since then, the Western practitioners of both these arts have been searching for a new *Lebensraum*. Their search has started inevitably with the negative gesture of repudiating their unsurpassable predecessors' too successfully achieved objectives. The Hellenes arrived at comparable impasses and reacted in the same revolutionary way. In their case, unlike our own, we know the end of the story. In fields in which the Hellenes' new departures proved to be blind alleys, they resigned themselves to lapsing into the opposite course. They took to imitating the predecessors whom they had proved unable either to surpass or to depose.

This disconcerting and depressing Hellenic experience is illustrated by the sequel to the Hellenes' supreme achievement in the art of oral poetry which has been considered in the preceding chapter of the present book. The *Iliad* and the *Odyssey* were the culmination of a style of oral poetry which, by the eighth century B.C., had been maturing for

---

[8] Not only in sculpture and in the shaping and decorating of pottery, but almost certainly in painting too, to judge by the post-Alexandrine-Hellenic-Age and Byzantine-Age imitations of lost Hellenic masterpieces.

perhaps as long as 800 years. It is no accident that the long-drawn-out development of this art not only culminated, but ended, in the composition of these two masterpieces.[9] Subsequent attempts to advance farther along this line did not succeed.

One of these unsuccessful enterprises was the coverage, in what was intended to be the Homeric manner, of the whole traditional story of the Trojan war, including its antecedents and its sequels. Apparently the whole of this poetic matter was familiar to pre-literate Hellenic audiences and to their literate successors. The pre-Homeric oral poetry, on which the poets of the *Iliad* and the *Odyssey* had drawn, must have ranged over the whole field, and, if this poetry was to be regarded primarily as being a record of past history, the selection of 'the wrath of Achilles' and 'the return of Odysseus' as themes for unprecedented works of genius in the traditional vein was arbitrary and unsatisfying. These themes that had now inspired poems of superlative merit were only minor incidents in the story. The fall of Troy was more important than a previous temporary crisis in the besiegers' fortunes owing to a quarrel between Achilles and Agamemnon. The return of Agamemnon to meet his death and to distract the most eminent of the Achaean principalities by adding to his house's burden of karma was more important than the happy ending of the return of Odysseus to an outlying Achaean principality. Of course the poets of the *Iliad* and the *Odyssey* had selected their themes with the eyes, not of chroniclers, but of artists. Out of the wealth of fluid traditional poetic matter, they had chosen not what was most informative, but what was serviceable for the great works of art that they were creating. They were followed by epigoni who set out to tell the rest of the story in supplementary poems on the Homeric pattern.

These addenda to the two Homeric epics have not survived. We have salvaged only epitomes of them and a few short textual quotations, and this, again, is no accident. Evidently the post-Homeric recordings of the residue of 'the Trojan cycle' were artistically inferior productions. They never won a place, side by side with the *Iliad* and the *Odyssey*, as components of an Hellenic counterpart of the Jewish Torah and the Christian Bible. But while second-rate seventh-century-B.C. poets were producing these uninspired and uninspiring addenda to the Homeric poems, some better-inspired contemporaries of theirs were making new starts.

A post-Homeric school of poets in Boeotia used, not the local dialect, which was a mixture of Aeolic and North-West Greek, but the Homeric metre, language, and diction to write on subjects that were not traditional themes of the Homeric poems and their antecedents. Hesiod

[9] See Kirk in Kirk, op. cit., p. 190; Starr in op. cit., p. 147.

and/or one or more anonymous Boeotian poets produced catalogues which must have been suggested, at many removes, by metrical versions of the lists of things and people that had once been inscribed on long-lost tablets in the forgotten 'Linear B' script by Mycenaean-Age bureaucrats.[10] A catalogue of the contingents of Agamemnon's armada has found its way into the Second Book of the *Iliad*.[11] It is not a field-state of the Achaean host in the Troad at the time—far on in the traditionally ten-years-long siege—of the quarrel between Agamemnon and Achilles. It is a muster-roll of the flotilla assembled in Aulis in Boeotia, before the Achaean expedition had set sail for Asia.[12] A fragment of a catalogue of Mycenaean-Age heroines has found its way into the Eleventh Book of the *Odyssey*.[13] Besides catalogues, the Boeotian school of poets produced a comprehensive account of the gods and of the genesis of these and of the Universe (the *Theogony*), and a farmers' year-book (*Works and Days*) which contains comment and advice on life, as well as on agriculture. The *Theogony* reproduces some myths that appear to have been derived from the Hittites, and perhaps ultimately from the Sumerians.[14]

This Boeotian poetry is original in the sense that it differs in matter from the Homeric poems; but it is pedestrian, and it had no future. Poetry that could hold its own against the Homeric masterpieces was produced by post-Homeric composers of lyrics. The themes of this new school of poetry were not traditional; they were unprecedented expressions of personal experience, and they broke with the tradition in their metres, as well as in their subject-matter and in their spirit. The elegiac couplet was a modification of the traditional epic metre, but there were poets of the post-Homeric personal school who broke right away from the age-old hexameter and wrote in a variety of other metres and in their own dialects, which were not Ionic and were not tinged with the archaism that was part of the legacy of the Homeric poetry's antecedents.

[10] See Webster, op. cit., pp. 71–3.

[11] Lines 484–779.

[12] The disinterred archives of Ugarit (Ras ash-Shamrah) include a catalogue of participants in a naval expedition in which, as in the catalogue in *Iliad*, Book II, the names of the commanders of the contingents, their districts, and the numbers of their men are recorded seriatim. This Phoenician catalogue resembles the Homeric Greek one in its form more closely than it resembles the mobilization-order inscribed in 'Linear B' on tablets (nos. 53–60) disinterred at Pylos. But the Ugarit document was inscribed *c.* 1400 B.C. (Page, op. cit., p. 158, n. 21) and the Pylos document *c.* 1200 B.C., whereas the catalogue in *Iliad*, Book II, may have been composed not earlier than the seventh century B.C. The word παvέλληvας (line 530) indicates that this catalogue's date is later than the date at which the Hellenic Greeks found a common appellation for themselves in the name of a small people, deposited in Central Greece by the post-Mycenaean *Völkerwanderung*, whose post-*Völkerwanderung* territory happened to contain the two meeting-places of the Delphic Amphictyony.

[13] Lines 225–332.

[14] See Starr, op. cit., p. 166; Walcot, P., *Hesiod and the Near East* (Cardiff 1966); West, M. L. (ed.), *Iambi et Elegi Graeci*, I Ante Alexandrum Cantati (Oxford 1972).

This sudden flowering of a wholly new kind of poetry demonstrated that the creativity of Hellenism's poetic genius was not yet exhausted, and this new act of creation was not the last in the field of Hellenic poetry. In the fifth century B.C. the personal poetry of the elegiac and lyric poets who had made their appearance all over an expanding Hellenic World, from the west coast of Asia Minor to Thasos and to Sicily, was followed by the dramatic poetry of Athens.

The fifth-century-B.C. Attic tragic poets drew their plots from the whole range of stories that had been transmitted from the Mycenaean Age in the oral poetry that had reached its peak and term in 'Homer'. The fifth-century-B.C. Attic comic poets preserved the original ribald spirit of the Dionysiac rites. Taking advantage of the Bacchic revellers' traditional licence, the comic poets lampooned eminent Pericleans and took controversial stands on burning questions. When this fifth-century-B.C. Attic exuberance had been damped down by the misery of the Atheno-Peloponnesian War of 431–404 B.C., the Attic muse was chastened without being silenced. In a lower key, she now produced a sophisticated comedy of manners. But even this subdued epilogue to the history of the Attic drama could not long survive the dwarfing of the Athenian city-state by the kingdoms that Alexander's successors carved out of the former Persian Empire's huge domain.

Athens was now replaced by Alexandria as the Hellenic World's literary centre, but this transplantation was fatal to the creative power of the Hellenic Greeks' poetic genius. The Museum fostered scholarship and science, but no new school of poetry germinated under its roof, and an academic *Ersatz* for genuine poetic inspiration was provided by an Alexandrian scholar, Apollonius (*circa* 235–165 B.C.). Apollonius reverted to the post-Homeric 'cyclic' poets' essay in writing epic poetry in the Homeric manner. Apollonius was gifted—perhaps more gifted than the 'cyclic' poets had been—and consequently his poem, the *Argonautica*, has survived. But scholarly virtuosity could not do duty for a centuries-long oral tradition. This had been the raw material out of which the poets of the *Iliad* and the *Odyssey* had created their master-pieces. The fiasco of the 'cyclic' poets had demonstrated, at least four centuries before Apollonius' day, that the Homeric poets' heritage and genius had made their achievement unrepeatable. Apollonius was as successful professionally as the Homeric poets had been. He, too, managed to give his public what it wanted, but this post-Alexandrine public was a very different one. It was not only literate; it was highly sophisticated.

Apollonius' poem 'smells of the lamp', and this artificial light attracted moths. The Hellenic Greek civilization remained in being for about 800 years after Apollonius' generation, and those eight centuries produced a series of imitators of Apollonius' imitation of 'Homer'—for instance, Rhianos (probably a younger contemporary of Apollonius), Nonnos, Quintus—who repeated, less ably, Apollonius' unfortunate performance. This had been unfortunate because it had set the fashion of aping not only the Homeric epic but also every later school of original Greek poetry. The only post-Alexandrine school of Hellenic Greek poetry that shows a touch of originality is Theocritus'. This school portrayed urban life realistically, and pastoral life with some affectation, in idylls written in hexameters in the Syracusan 'Doric' dialect. The technique is impressive; its artificiality is its defect.

There is a great gulf between the language and diction of Apollonius' *Argonautica* and the Attic *koine* that, in everyday life, was Apollonius' medium of communication with his family and his friends and with his fellow-scholars too. But, in this connection, the significant point is that, in a lesser degree, the language of the Homeric poets themselves had been out of touch with the language of their own time and place, and this beyond the normal extent of the inevitable difference between literary and colloquial speech. The Homeric poets' literary dialect had been inhibited from conforming to the contemporary Ionic vernacular of the poets and their audiences by two restraints. One of these had been the recalcitrance of metrical formulae that had been coined in Mycenaean-Age South Greek to transposition into the Ionic that was one of the sub-dialects into which this South Greek had gradually come to be differentiated. The second restraint on the modernization of the Homeric poets' literary dialect had been their audience's requirement that this poetry should combine intelligibility with an aura of archaism.

Thus the Homeric literary dialect was already divorced from the everyday language of the society in and for which the Homeric poems were composed; and this already perceptible gap widened immensely when the epic poetry which had flowered in Ionia captivated the rest of the Hellenic World, and when the Boeotian gnomic and didactic school employed the Homeric language and diction, as well as the hexameter metre, for addressing an audience that was originally a local one speaking the Dorico-Aeolic dialect of Boeotia itself, but which rapidly expanded to the Pan-Hellenic dimensions that the Homeric poems' public had already attained.

The Ionian poets of the personal school wrote in the elegiac variation of the traditional Homeric metre in a semi-Homeric language and style, and these poets, too, had the same Pan-Hellenic success as 'Homer' and Hesiod, with the same linguistic consequences. The Ionian elegiac dialect and metre were used in the seventh century B.C. by Tyrtaios, and in the sixth century B.C. by Theognis, for addressing audiences whose mother-tongue was the 'Doric' variety of North-West Greek and whose native lyric poetry, in its mother-tongue, was cast in quite a different metrical mode. Though distinguished and famous lyric poetry in non-dactylic metres was produced in the Aeolic (North-East Greek) dialect of Lesbos and in the Ionic dialect of the Cyclades, the 'Doric' dialect won for itself the prize of becoming the conventional dialect for the writing of lyric poetry in Hellenic Greek communities that had not given birth to any eminent school of lyric poetry in their own local dialect. The fifth-century-B.C. Attic dramas were dialogues interpolated between lyrics sung by choruses, and these lyrics were composed by the Attic-speaking playwrights in a conventional 'Doric', whereas their dialogues, being a new genre invented by the Athenians themselves, were written in an Attic that, even when elevated on to Aeschylean stilts, was a literary version of the colloquial Attic of the day.

Thus, since an ominously early stage of the Hellenic chapter of Greek history, the Hellenic Greeks had become accustomed to using different languages for literary and for utilitarian purposes. Apollonius, in his *Argonautica*, had merely carried an already established practice to a further length. Unhappily, this was not the limit. The epoch-making conceit in Hellenic Greek literary history—the conceit which was to bequeath a formidable legacy of karma to the Byzantines and, via these, to the Moderns—was the neo-classical Atticism that was imposed on the Greek-speaking World by nostalgic-minded men of letters in the Augustan Age. This archaizing school's perverse ambition achieved a resounding success because it chimed in with the Epimethean contemporary *Zeitgeist*. The Atticists of the Age of the Principate succeeded all too well in devaluing the prose literature that had been written in the post-Alexandrine Attic *koine*. They coerced themselves and a long series of successors into attempting to write the Attic of Isocrates and Demosthenes, or even, as a supreme *tour de force*, the highly individual Attic idioms of Plato and Thucydides.

The Atticists' achievement was doubly unfortunate. The Attic *koine* had evolved in response to the Hellenic World's need for a *lingua franca* when its geographical range had been vastly expanded, all of a sudden, by Alexander. The Attic *koine* had the second merit of being a living language that could and did change, as a healthy living language does, in the act of being transmitted from mouth to mouth and from generation to generation. This *koine* had been the natural product of historic events: the Athenians' fifth-century-B.C. political empire; their fifth-century and fourth-century commercial predominance; and King Philip II's momentous decision to make, not the native Macedonian variety of North-East Greek, but Attic, the official language of a kingdom of Macedon which, in the next generation, had generated the Greek successor-states of the Persian Empire. The Augustan Atticists sought to substitute for this Attic *koine*, which was alive and practical, a neo-classical Attic that was dead and academic.

The Atticists did succeed in establishing a dead language, that could be fully commanded only by professional *littérateurs*, as the sole entirely respectable form of Greek. Their success was prodigious, but it was incomplete. Before they had got to work, the Jewish Torah, which was to become the Christians' 'Old Testament', had already been translated into the *koine* with a spicing of Hebraisms. Before the Atticizing practitioners of 'the Second Sophistic' had delivered their lifeless set-pieces to appreciative audiences, the documents composing the Christians' 'New Testament' had been written, many of them in the Septuagint's Hebraizing style. When works written in this Hebraic Greek *koine* eventually became Holy Scripture, they automatically became sacrosanct. However, the Atticists anathematized Hebraisms and all other un-classical vulgarisms in any post-Demosthenic works of Hellenic Greek literature except the 'New Testament'. Even the Graecophone Christian Fathers were Atticists except for their biblical quotations and allusions.

The neo-Attic Greek that was demanded, though seldom completely achieved, during the last six centuries of the Hellenic Age was receding farther and farther not only from the constantly changing live form of the Greek language but also from the activities and concerns of practical life. The rhetors declaimed on themes, historical or fictitious, relating to the life of the pre-Alexandrine Hellenic World, and they were applauded by audiences that appreciated archaism for the reason that had once made the post-Mycenaean oral poets' audiences appreciate it. In the Hellenic World during the first six centuries of the Christian Era, as during the first three centuries of the last millennium B.C., a taste for archaism was fostered by a nostalgia for a vanished world that looked in retrospect more glamorous than the present age. Thus, in the opening as well as in the closing episode of Hellenic history, words, divorced from action, were valued for sentiment's sake. This tendency was characteristic of Hellenic life at all stages of Hellenic history except the four centuries that had started with the composition of the *Iliad* and had ended with the writing of the latest of the speeches of posthumously canonized fourth-century-B.C. Athenian orators.

The Atticists' canon of language and diction was limited to the literary products of those four centuries. This limitation was an arbitrary decision, even within the field of literary criticism, and it had unfortunate effects beyond this academic sphere. It generated the superstitious belief that the canonized standards of language and style were talismans for success in all the non-literary fields of human endeavour. The period of Hellenic history that had now been labelled

'classical' on the criterion of its literature was consequently deemed to
have been also pre-eminent in its military and political and architectural and artistic and intellectual and moral performance. Therefore,
conversely, so it was fancifully inferred, a period in which writers
allowed themselves to sink below the consecrated 'classical' standards of
writing was dooming itself to all-round decadence. It was implied that a
Greek who did not write like Aeschylus could not expect to emulate the
victors in the Battle of Marathon. This debilitating fantasy was proved
groundless, even before the close of the Age of 'the Second Sophistic', by
the heroism of the Elatean Mnesiboulos,[15] and in the next century by the
heroism of the Athenian Dexippos, who, like Xenophon, was both a
soldier and an historian, even if his neo-Attic was an imperfect imitation
of Xenophon's language and style. Yet the fantasy that was so promptly
confuted by facts continued to haunt Greek minds until within living
memory.

The Homeric poems are not the only link between the Hellenic and
the foregoing Mycenaean chapter of Greek history. Painted pottery is a
second link; and, though neither earthenware nor pigment can utter
'winged words', they do afford better historical evidence than 'Homer'
in one respect. In the field of Greek epic poetry, we possess only the end-
product, and the only way of guessing at its antecedents is the indirect
and uncertain procedure of making inferences from the internal
evidence of the surviving last phase of what is shown, by this evidence, to
have been a long-drawn-out process of development. On the other
hand, in the field of pottery, we have direct contemporary evidence, in
the shape of sherds, if not of intact vases, for each successive phase of
modelling and decoration.

Ware made in the eighth century B.C.—the time at which the
Homeric poems are believed to have been composed—is linked by a
continuous series of specimens with ware of the Mycenaean Age. From
mature 'Geometric' ware, back through 'Protogeometric' to sub-
Mycenaean, and to Mycenaean (Late Helladic) III C, the chain of
evidence furnished by pottery is continuous.[16] This visual and tangible
evidence tells us something that is not revealed by our inferences from
the verbal evidence of the Homeric poems. This poetry, in the final form

[15] Pausanias, *Descriptio Graeciae*, Book X, chapter 34.

[16] See the chart in Snodgrass, op. cit., on pp. 134-5. Desborough's second thoughts on the sub-
Mycenaean style of pottery are set out in *The Last Mycenaeans*, pp. 1-28 and 258-63. On this view,
with which Snodgrass concurs (in op. cit., pp. 31-3), sub-Mycenaean is not a ubiquitous style that
intervenes chronologically between Late Helladic III C and Protogeometric; it is a local style,
confined to Western Attica and Salamis, which is contemporary with Late Helladic III C in other
regions. In Western Attica and Salamis the duration of Late Helladic III C was exceptionally short.
Elsewhere, Late Helladic III C persisted until the beginning of Protogeometric. In *The Greek Dark
Ages*, pp. 64-79, Desborough gives a wider geographical extension to sub-Mycenaean Central-
Greek. See further the Appendix to Chapter II.

in which we have it, testifies that the Hellenic World of the eighth century B.C. had derived from the Mycenaean World a poetic tradition which, though changing all the time, and changing, cumulatively, almost out of all recognition, had not been broken at any point by a deliberate new departure of the kind taken afterwards by the seventh-century-B.C. Greek poets who expressed themselves in lyric instead of epic form. By contrast, the pottery series shows that a break of this kind—one so sharp that it can hardly have been unconscious and unintentional—did occur in the eleventh century B.C. in this other province of art.

Though the break was not absolute,[17] 'the change is a virtual revolution.'[18] 'The difference between sub-Mycenaean and Proto-geometric constitutes a major revolution in style.'[19] The innovations are both technical and aesthetic, and at Athens they were introduced before the replacement there of the sub-Mycenaean by the Protogeometric style.[20] The pot itself is made on a faster wheel.[21] The decoration is applied by the use, in combination, of a compass and a multiple brush.[22] 'The change is a technical one—a very simple one, admittedly, but one that no Mycenaean potter ever thought of.'[23] The aesthetic change is the deliberate co-ordination of the decoration with the shape.[24] This visual revolution is the expression of a spiritual one.[25] 'It is in the highest degree unlikely that this change was originally effected in more than one district.'[26] Protogeometric is most abundant in Attica;[27] and, though the new style appears more or less contemporaneously elsewhere—for instance, in the Argolid[28]—Attica, and, within Attica, Athens, is the place in which this style appears to have originated[29] and in which it certainly was developed most grandly. It is surely not just a fortuitous coincidence that Attica is the one region on the mainland of European Greece in which there appears to have been no political break. The acropolis of Athens was unique among the Mycenaean palace-fortresses

---

[17] See Desborough, *The Last Mycenaeans*, p. 262; *eundem, The Greek Dark Ages*, p. 41; Chadwick, in Kirk, op. cit., p. 116; Vermeule, op. cit., p. 270; Starr, op. cit., p. 89. The break between sub-Mycenaean and Protogeometric was, however, absolute on Kos and Rhodes according to Webster, op. cit., p. 147.

[18] Starr, op. cit., p. 90; cp. pp. 78, 92, and 102.

[19] Webster, op. cit., p. 76.

[20] Desborough, *The Greek Dark Ages*, p. 43.

[21] Desborough, *The Last Mycenaeans*, p. 262; id., *The Greek Dark Ages*, p. 145; Snodgrass, op. cit., p. 45.

[22] Desborough, *The Last Mycenaeans*, p. 262; id., *The Greek Dark Ages*, pp. 43 and 145; Snodgrass, op. cit., p. 47.

[23] Desborough, *The Last Mycenaeans*, p. 262.

[24] Desborough, *The Greek Dark Ages*, p. 147; Snodgrass, op. cit., pp. 45-7.

[25] Webster, op. cit., pp. 187, 189, 205, 292.

[26] See Desborough, *The Last Mycenaeans*, p. 262, and *eundem, The Greek Dark Ages*, pp. 106-11.

[27] Starr, op. cit., p. 96.

[28] Ibid., pp. 78 and 97.

[29] Ibid., p. 72.

in escaping devastation *circa* 1200 B.C., and the archaeological evidence indicates that Eastern Attica, at any rate, also escaped the post-Mycenaean *Völkerwanderung* of North-West-Greek-speakers which did swamp the Argolid at some date in the dark age.[30]

The 'Geometric' style of vase-decoration thus proves to have been indigenous[31]—in contrast to, for example, the 'Minyan' style that had been introduced into Continental Greece in the twentieth century B.C. by invaders who may also have introduced the Greek language there.[32] In this sense the 'Geometric' style was an original creation whose appearance marks the dawn of a new age—the Hellenic Age—of Greek history. In another sense this was the final break-through of a persistent previous tendency to revert to the pre-Minoan style of Helladic art which had been swamped by the sudden influx of Minoan culture into Continental Greece in the early sixteenth century B.C.[33]

The attested history of the 'Geometric' style of Greek vase-painting runs significantly parallel to the inferred history of oral Greek epic poetry. A long-drawn-out development works up to the creation of masterpieces that cannot be surpassed and that therefore necessitate a radical breakaway and a new departure. In poetry, the Hellenic Greeks achieved this new departure apparently without the aid of any stimulus from abroad. In the art of painting pottery, the Attic artists in the age of the 'Geometric' style's maturity and culmination had developed their form of it 'to a point beyond which it was difficult to go but which was equally difficult to abandon'.[34]

In the eighth century B.C., Continental Greece was exposed once again, as it had been in the sixteenth century B.C., to the impact of a foreign art which dealt, not in abstract patterns, but in representations of natural objects—the figures of plants and animals. In the earlier case the influence had come from Crete; in the eighth century B.C. it came from the Levant. On this occasion the Attic artists were recalcitrant; they admitted the figures of human beings and horses into their meticulously designed geometrical patterns only on condition that these awkward alien intruders should not disturb the harmony that the artists had achieved by an intense application of ability and effort. Consequently they 'geometrized' these grudgingly admitted natural objects to

[30] The relation of the sub-Mycenaean culture to Late Mycenaean III C on the one hand and to Protogeometric on the other is discussed further, in the light of Desborough's and Snodgrass's researches in particular, in the Appendix to Chapter II.

[31] Desborough, *The Greek Dark Ages*, pp. 43 and 340–1, holds that, though this Athenian cultural and spiritual revolution was indigenous, it was precipitated by a stimulus from abroad, and that the source of this stimulus was Cyprus.

[32] See p. 10.

[33] See p. 13.

[34] Starr, op. cit., p. 155.

a degree at which they were virtually caricaturing them.[35] The breakthrough of the new 'Orientalizing' style was achieved, not at Athens, but at Corinth and at Sparta, where the 'Geometric' style had not been carried to an Attic pitch of perfection.[36]

Thus, paradoxically, Athens started her artistic career as a 'die-hard' exponent of aniconic art, whereas Syria re-introduced into the Aegean the iconism that Crete had imposed on Continental Greece eight centuries earlier. Who, in the eighth century B.C., could have guessed that Syria would one day see first the Jews and then their Muslim disciples ban the representation of living forms, whereas Athens would make herself famous—or infamous, according to the spectator's ideology—as the workshop of iconic art in every medium? Yet, by the mid-point of the sixth century B.C., the Attic potters and painters had made a volte-face that enabled them to recapture the lead that they had lost in the seventh century B.C. They were now driving Corinthian and Spartan wares out of the international market by surpassing them in their own innovating iconic vein; and this was only the beginning of a long Attic story. Six centuries later, Saint Paul's 'spirit was stirred within him, when he saw the city wholly given to idolatry'.[37] More than seven centuries after Saint Paul's visit, an Athenian Byzantine Greek East Roman Empress, Eirênê (*imperabat* A.D. 797–802) re-established, for the first time, in A.D. 787 (as regent for her son), the cult of images that the Syrian Emperor Leo III had suppressed, except for some outlying beachheads in Italy that were not completely under the Imperial Government's control within the East Roman Empire's dominions.

In the Hellenic chapter of Greek history, painted pottery, like poetry, succeeded in taking two new departures which gave it three successive bouts of creativity. When the 'Geometric' style had exhausted its potentialities at long last, it was superseded by the 'Orientalizing' style; and this Corinthian and Spartan speciality was succeeded in its turn by a new Attic style that, like the Corinthian and Spartan styles, was a breakaway from geometric abstraction. This new Attic style began with black figures on a red ground and then changed over to red figures with a black surround. In this third style of the vase-painter's art, Athens was not merely the predominant producer; she held a monopoly.

The 'Orientalizing' style, as well as its successor the black-and-red style, found eager buyers in the expanding Hellenic World's still more widely expanding non-Greek markets. The affluent Etruscans readily exchanged their metalwork, and the affluent Skyths their Ukrainian peasant-subjects' cereals, for Greek painted vases that were exported as

---

[35] See ibid., p. 156, with plates 9, 10, and 11 between pp. 140–1 and 172–3.
[36] See ibid., pp. 241–2.
[37] Acts 17: 16.

alluring containers for Greek oil and wine. By the fourth century B.C. the non-Greek natives of the lowlands along the Adriatic coast of south-east Italy were showing their appreciation of the Attic red-figure ware's commercial value by producing uninspired imitations of it *en masse*. Hellenic painted pottery had proved to be a commercial success in virtue of its artistic merit. Yet, when the two successive Attic varieties of the black-and-red style had exhausted their potentialities in their turn, neither Athens nor any other Hellenic Greek community opened a new chapter in the history of Hellenic pottery and vase-painting by creating another new style. This Hellenic art, which hitherto had been so promi-nent, had no place in the repertory of post-Alexandrine Hellenic achievements. The Attic black-and-red ware's supreme excellence effectively deterred the Hellenes of the succeeding age from investing their ability in the creation of any further important new style in this province of visual art. A *chef d'œuvre* that cannot be surpassed or even be equalled cannot be superseded and replaced. Paradoxically, a *chef d'œuvre* condemns the art that has achieved it to languish.

In Hellenic painted pottery, the potter's three-dimensional art and the painter's two-dimensional art were mated, and the key to success was the achievement of harmony between the two partners. In the history of this Hellenic art, the harmony between form and decoration was worked out most exquisitely in the 'Geometric' style, which had a longer run than any of its successors. In Protogeometric already,[38] and subsequently in a supreme degree in mature Geometric, the shape of the vase and the pattern of the decoration were skilfully designed to enhance each other's aesthetic effect; and, in seeking and attaining this felicitous reciprocity, this earliest of the Hellenic styles of painted pottery was artistically sophisticated, not primitive.[39] In Hellenic sculpture, harmony became unity; for, though Hellenic statues and bas-reliefs, like Hellenic vases, were painted, the three-dimensional aspect here eclipsed the two-dimensional because a piece of sculpture imposes an awareness of its shape, more imperiously than a vase, in consequence of its reproducing, not the arbitrary play of the artist's imagination, but forms presented to the artist by the live world of Nature. Sculpture was, of course, one of the activities in which the Greeks of the Hellenic Age achieved outstanding success, and, in this field, the Hellenic Greeks' creative faculty lasted for as long as the Hellenic civilization itself.

In venturing to experiment in monumental sculpture, the Greeks of the Hellenic Age were taking a new departure. In the Mycenaean Age, and in the history of the Mycenaean Greeks' Minoan instructors,

---

[38] See p. 53, n. 20.
[39] Webster, op. cit., p. 205.

sculpture, though sometimes exquisite, had usually been in miniature.[40] Hellenic sculpture was inspired, not by buried and forgotten Mycenaean and Minoan statuettes, but by Egyptian statues that were extant in the sixth century B.C. The Greeks' first essays in emulating these Egyptian models were stiffer than the Egyptian originals; but, before the fifth century B.C. had yet run through the first half of its course, the Greek Pygmalions' lay figures had come to life, and, for the next 700 years, Hellenic sculpture retained, in a series of successive different manners, its mastery of the three-dimensional naturalistic representation of the human form.

Post-archaic pre-Alexandrine Hellenic sculpture sought to produce the effect of generality and of serenity but did not seek to be realistic. Realism and pathos were post-Alexandrine objectives, and, in this vein, Hellenic sculpture's final achievement was worthy of its long-since-surmounted 'classical' peak. The busts of the Roman Emperors who reigned during the terrible half-century A.D. 235–84 can look in the face the Egyptian busts of the pharaohs of the Twelfth Dynasty. The impact of excruciating experience on strong character has never been displayed more effectively in three-dimensional portraiture than in these two schools that are sundered from each other in time by twenty-two centuries.

A human being is a spiritual presence that is never more than partially revealed in the bodily form through which it is visible. The spirit, not the body, is Man's essence; and the spirit cannot be revealed visually even by the most cunning visual artist's hand; it can be explored only by itself; and, if Man is in truth mankind's proper study, Hellenic philosophy has made a greater contribution to this study than Hellenic visual art. Moreover, Hellenic philosophy did not confine its intellectual operations to human affairs. It took for its field as much of the Universe as was within an Hellenic observer's ken, and it began by questioning non-human nature. It then diverted more and more of its attention to ethics and to metaphysics as the Hellenes became more and more acutely aware, through bitter experience, that, for Man, human nature is the Universe's most unsatisfactory, most intractable, and most important constituent—a 'joker' in the demiurge's pack of cards that is no joke for Man himself.

Unlike Hellenic poetry and pottery and architecture, but like Hellenic sculpture, Hellenic philosophy retained its vitality till the end of the Hellenic chapter of Greek history. Hellenic philosophy and Hellenic sculpture were coeval. Both these magnificent Hellenic

---

[40] Usually, but not invariably. See Desborough, *The Last Mycenaeans*, p. 44; *eundem*, *The Greek Dark Ages*, pp. 280–1; Snodgrass, op. cit., pp. 395 and 399; and Taylour, op. cit., p. 69, for the fragments of life-sized Mycenaean-Age terracotta statues found on the island of Keos.

activities started in the sixth century B.C. and continued into the third
century of the Christian Era; and in philosophy, as in sculpture, the last
phase was worthy of its great past. In Plotinus, the third century of the
Christian Era produced a spirit who, in his own higher sphere, was the
counterpart in genius, though the antithesis in outlook, of the sculptors
of the busts of the Emperors Decius[41] and Trebonianus Gallus.[42]

In Hellenic architecture the dominant public buildings were temples.
These were not a legacy from the Minoans;[43] they may have had
Mycenaean forerunners;[44] but monumental temples, as salient architectural features of a city or a sanctuary, were an Hellenic new departure;[45] there was a 'prodigious growth in the number and size of
sanctuary-sites in the eighth century';[46] the architectural plan of an
Hellenic temple, which had originally been the same as that of a private
dwelling-house, eventually became something distinctive;[47] and the
Hellenic style of temple illustrates a characteristic of Hellenism which is
also revealed in the 'Geometric' style of pottery painting. In their
handling of both these media the Hellenic Greeks were content to work
with a small number of simple elements. Their ambition was to produce
superb artistic effects by attaining virtual perfection within these
voluntarily accepted limits. Even on vases of the mature phase of the
'Geometric' style, the patterns of the decoration are not intricate. The
art lies, as has been noted already, in making the decoration and the
shape of a vase enhance each other's intended effect. The Hellenic
temple is the geometrically decorated Hellenic vase's counterpart.

The Hellenic temple is a transfiguration of a log cabin with a
verandah resting on tree trunks set upright. Except for the gable roof, all
the components are set either vertically or horizontally, and, apart from
the roof, all the angles that the components make with each other are
right angles. This ostensibly artless plan is the one that the original
material had suggested. The Hellenic temple looks, in fact, much like
what a child would build from the contents of a box of toy wooden
blocks; and the Hellenic architects faithfully preserved this form when
they changed the material from wood to stone—a more durable

---

[41] In the Capitoline Museum at Rome.

[42] In the Metropolitan Museum at New York.

[43] Minoan places of worship were small chapels embedded in palaces whose labyrinths hid these
shrines from the eyes of the general public. In Continental Greece the Mycenaean-Age palace at
Asine is the only place where a Minoan-like shrine has been found so far (see Taylour, op. cit., p. 67;
Desborough, *The Last Mycenaeans*, p. 42; *eundem, The Greek Dark Ages*, p. 45).

[44] For instance, a Mycenaean-Age temple on the island of Keos, which contained the life-size
statue (see p. 57, n. 40), and three Mycenaean-Age buildings on Delos which may have been
temples (Taylour, op. cit., p. 69; Desborough, *The Last Mycenaeans*, p. 279).

[45] Snodgrass, op. cit., p. 408.

[46] Ibid., p. 399.

[47] Ibid., p. 412.

substance, and one which, in Greece, is also much more abundant. Gaze at a stone-built Hellenic temple—for instance, the Parthenon on the acropolis of Athens, which is the most famous example of all. It looks perfectly rectilinear. No curve meets the eye. But this is because the architect has actually introduced minute curves nicely calculated to produce the optical illusion of straightness.

The columns have been given a slight bulge because, if they had been exactly the same thickness from top to bottom, they would have looked, deceptively, as if, at mid-height, they had been constricted. For the same reason, the base of the building has been given a slight upward curve; if this had not been done, the base would make the deceptive impression that it was sagging. These precise and subtle curves show that, in spite of appearances, the architect did not lack the skill to do non-rectilinear work in stone; but they also show that he was not interested in using this skill to launch out into some wholly new style—an anticipation, say, of the future Byzantine Greek style or the future Western Rococo. The Hellenic architect reserved the use of his power of making curves for creating the effect of perfect straightness within the pattern of straight lines to which he had voluntarily confined himself. He was a perfectionist, not a pioneer.

The technique of arching and vaulting must have been within the Hellenic architect's knowledge. It was being practised in Etruscan and Roman Italy at least as early as the last quarter of the last millennium B.C., and, before the beginning of the Christian Era, Roman architects had further extended the range of possibilities for architecture by inventing concrete. This invention made it practicable to roof much larger spaces; for a roof made of concrete, being all of a piece, thrusts vertically downward, not outward, and a wall with a concrete core can carry a heavy load without cracking. The Romans themselves did use concrete in the Emperor Hadrian's reign (A.D. 117-38) to produce, at Rome itself, a revolutionary piece of architecture, the Pantheon.[48] Yet the Greeks continued to build temples and other public buildings in the toy wooden-blocks style till the end of the Hellenic chapter of Greek history.

What is more, this simple but exquisitely executed Hellenic style had captivated the Romans so thoroughly that they continued to build in it, side by side with buildings that were successful experiments in the new Roman techniques. The Romans' Etruscan instructors had modified the Hellenic temple's plan, but they had not departed from the rectilinearity that was its essence. The Romans built some of their

---

[48] For this Roman architectural revolution, see J. M. C. Toynbee in *The Crucible of Christianity* (London 1969), p. 193, with the plan and pictures of the Pantheon on pp. 178-9. See also Boethius, A., and Ward-Perkins, J. B., *Etruscan and Roman Architecture* (Penguin 1970).

temples in the Etrusco-Hellenic style and some (e.g. the *Maison Carrée* at Nîmes) in the original Hellenic style, but they had not the nerve to throw the Hellenic style itself to the winds and to devote themselves exclusively to exploring the new possibilities that their own Roman inventions had opened up. This exploration was postponed until after the Hellenic civilization had disintegrated. It was only after this that the Roman inventions were turned to account unreservedly by the Byzantine Greeks and by the creators of the Romanesque style of architecture in the Roman Empire's former western provinces.

Architecture, philosophy, sculpture, the shaping and decoration of pottery, and the art of poetry were particular fields in which the Greeks of the Hellenic Age achieved dazzling—and therefore daunting and inhibiting—successes. But the Hellenes' master institution was city-states; for these were the social setting of the Hellenes' particular achievements, and, without this setting, these achievements might never have been accomplished.

City-states were not a uniquely Hellenic social and political dispensation. There had been city-states in Sumer 2,000 years before any had arisen in the Hellenic World, and there have been city-states in the Western World in the medieval phase of Western history. One in Italy, two in West Germany, and several in Switzerland still survive. The Hellenes, however, set their characteristic stamp on an institution which they were not the first to adopt, though they may have reinvented it independently. The Hellenic city-states were marvellously fertile seed-beds for creative achievements in many fields of human activity; but, like Hellenic poetry and visual art and architecture, their excellence was bought at the price of some frustrating limitations. In their domestic life, Hellenic city-states were clubs whose amenities were accessible only for a privileged section of their inhabitants. In their relations with each other, they did not succeed either in coexisting peacefully or in coalescing. They were chronically at war with each other;[49] these fratricidal wars became more and more exhausting and devastating; they made sacrificial demands on each state's citizens, including those who had access to their state's domestic amenities; and, besides tormenting an increasing number of Hellenes, the interstate wars tore in pieces the Hellenic society itself.

The Hellenes never faced the failure of their city-state dispensation on the plane of interstate relations till this failure had become irretrievable. It is significant that the theorists who sought to salvage Hellenism by

---

[49] In the Hellenic World of the eighth century B.C., 'material progress by no means went hand in hand with security' (Snodgrass, op. cit., p. 420). The fortification of Hellenic settlements in this century is comparable in scale to the fortification of Mycenaean settlements in the thirteenth century.

working out blueprints for utopias in the fourth century B.C. thought and wrote in the unrealistic terms of a solitary single city-state, which they insulated on paper either by ignoring its foreign relations or by postulating that their imaginary city-state must be segregated by being kept un-industrial, un-commercial, and landlocked.[50] For a Hellene, the bounds of his local city-state were the bounds of human society itself. The Hellenic Greek word for 'social' was 'belonging to a polis' (πολιτικός); the converse word for being an outcast and an outlaw was 'having no polis' (ἄπολις).[51] The frontier of a Hellene's city-state was his social horizon.

Aristotle, in his treatise on the theory of the city-state, declares that *the* (sic) city-state comes into existence in order to make life possible, and remains in existence in order to make life worth living.[52] This dictum is historically correct as far as it goes. The two stages in the history of an Hellenic city-state that Aristotle has in mind are represented, in topographical terms, by the citadel and the *agora* respectively. 'Citadel' is the original meaning of the Greek word 'polis', and the citadel was all that there was of a *polis* at the start. It was a city of refuge, perched on a site that was a natural fortress and that needed only a minimum of supplementary artificial fortification to make it secure. It was not permanently inhabited, except perhaps by a few public officers, including priests if religious and secular functions were not combined in the same office. The rest of the population, with its flocks and herds, took shelter here only when it was threatened with attack by hostile raiders. The *agora* replaced the citadel as the heart of the *polis* if and when the state of insecurity abated sufficiently to make it safe to form an urban settlement at the citadel's foot, on terrain that could be made defensible only by the costly expedient of surrounding the settlement with a ring-wall.[53] It was the transference of the civic centre from the citadel to the *agora* that made life in an Hellenic sovereign city-state seem worth living in the days before inter-state warfare made this way of life intolerable.

'Agora' (ἀγορά) is the substantive corresponding to the verb 'ageirein' (ἀγείρειν). The verb means to assemble; the substantive means congregation or concourse, and, hence, the place in which people gather together. This word, in this usage, generated a secondary verb

---

[50] See Plato, *Laws*, Book IV, *ad init.*, 704A–707C.

[51] Aristotle, *Politics*, I, 1, 9–12 (1253 A). Cp. Sophocles, *Antigone*, line 370.

[52] γινομένη μὲν οὖν τοῦ ζῆν ἕνεκεν, οὖσα δὲ τοῦ εὖ ζῆν (Aristotle, op. cit. I, 1, 8 (1252 B)).

[53] The oldest ring-walls of an Hellenic city-state that have been discovered so far are those at Smyrna. The first was built in the mid-nineteenth century B.C., the second about a hundred years later. See Snodgrass, op. cit., pp. 298 and 413. Snodgrass points out (ibid., p. 415) that public works of this magnitude and of this high standard of technical accomplishment indicate that an efficient city-state government had already come into existence. The same political and social development is indicated at Sparta, Tegea, and Ephesus, not by the building of ring-walls, but by the rise of sanctuaries (ibid., p. 421).

'agorazein' (ἀγοράζειν), which means 'to pass time in the *agora*', with the imlication that this was the most enjoyable pastime that a Hellene could have. According to Herodotus, the Hellenized Skyth king Skyles ἠγόραζε as soon as he entered the Hellenic city Borysthenes on one of his clandestine annual visits.[54] The homesick Hellenic physician, Demokedes of Kroton, did just the same as soon as he had regained his native city-state after contriving to escape from his position at the summit of his profession as the Emperor Darius' personal physician in distant Susa— a city that was not a city-state, since it was the capital of the Persian Empire, with a palace, not an *agora*, as its centre-point.[55]

What made the *agora* so attractive to a Hellene and to a Hellenized Skyth? The *agora* attracted them because it was a focus of lively social intercourse, and Man is a social creature. The *agora* served a variety of social needs. The undifferentiated word 'agorazein'—to frequent the *agora*—acquired the specialized meaning 'to buy'; for the *agora* was the market-place for the city and for the countryside within the city-state's frontiers. But this economic service was not the *agora*'s most important function. The word generated another secondary verb, 'agoreuein' (ἀγορεύειν), which meant to talk in public, and this talk might be of diverse kinds. A politician might use the *agora* for talking to his fellow-citizens; a philosopher might use it for talking to his fellow inquirers into the nature of the Universe and of Man. The *agora* was, above all, a talking-place; and the talk there might take the various forms of a non-utilitarian discussion, a political speech or debate, and a haggle between a buyer and a seller.

The range of the economic business transacted in a city-state's *agora* depended on the character of each particular state's economy. The vast majority of the many hundred Hellenic city-states conformed closely to Plato's nostalgic ideal. The normal specimen was a tiny community consisting of an urban centre surrounded by half-a-dozen villages—each of them near enough to the single city within the territory for a peasant to be able, between dawn and nightfall, to walk into the city, sell and buy in the *agora* there, and walk home again by daylight. The only members of the community who did not make their living by agriculture or by animal husbandry were artisans, domiciled in the city, who made their living by supplying the rural population's modest demands. There were a few exceptional city-states that catered for more extensive and more variegated markets, and here the industrial and seafaring elements in the population predominated, and the city and its port overshadowed the local countryside. These exceptional Hellenic city-states are the

---

[54] Herodotus, Book IV, chapter 78, cited in p. 40.
[55] Herodotus, Book III, chapter 137.

most famous [56]—the names Athens, Corinth, Chalcis, Khios, Miletus, Massalia leap to the mind—but there were less than a score of these, all told.

Local sovereignty, or, short of that, local self-government, was the objective, in every Hellenic city-state, of those among its inhabitants who had an effective voice in public affairs. The 'politeuma' was the collective term for this politically privileged portion of the population. The normal *politeuma* was an oligarchy; and even in a state, such as Athens was for most of the time from 462 to 317 B.C., in which every male citizen, rural as well as urban, had a vote and served on juries and could stand for elective offices or win non-elective offices by lot, the *politeuma* amounted to no more than a minority of the adult population. The franchise was withheld from non-citizen freemen (resident aliens or freed slaves and their descendants), from un-freed slaves, and from women. The women, slave and free, must have accounted for about half of the total population, and in an industrial and commercial city-state, such as Athens was when she was officially a democracy, unenfranchised male slaves, male freedmen, and male resident aliens were numerous and were economically important. In Attica the peasants were freemen and were enfranchised; but in Lacedaemon and Thessaly and in the territories of Heraclea Pontica and of Syracuse they were serfs, and the opprobrious nicknames of the Epidaurian 'dusty-feet', the Argive '*sans-chemises*', and the Sicyonian 'fleece-wearers' suggest that these boors were not members of their states' *politeumata*, even if they were freemen and were also nominally members of these states' citizen-bodies.

By the date, probably in the eighth century B.C., at which the *Odyssey* was composed somewhere in Ionia, the Ionian city-states must have already come into being; yet, in the Hellenic society of this archaic age, as this is depicted in the *Odyssey*, the status of slaves and women was better than it had come to be by the fifth century B.C., when the Hellenic civilization was at its zenith.

Membership of the *politeuma* was the most highly valued prize in an Hellenic city-state. Exclusion from the *politeuma* aroused proportionately strong resentment; and this feeling sought relief in the sphere of religion, to compensate for political nullity. Resident aliens, and slaves and freedmen of alien origin, cherished their ancestral religions, and this all the more fervently because these were distinctive spiritual possessions of

[56] Sparta is the sole famous and temporarily powerful Hellenic city-state that eschewed industry and commerce, and Sparta, too, was exceptional in her own peculiar way. The privileged section of the population of her territory was an exceptionally minute fraction of the total population; in the seventh century B.C., this tiny Spartan dominant minority safeguarded its dominance by militarizing its life to an exceptionally extreme degree; and in the sixth century this militarism proved to be incompatible with the further development, and indeed with the survival, of the aesthetically admirable Spartan ceramics industry.

their own. The women retained the leading role in fertility rites that had come down from the early phase of agriculture in which this had still been women's work. When some of the major divinities had been 'politicized' by being conscripted to serve as the tutelary goddesses of particular city-states, the humbler and more intimate fertility rites survived their transference to the city from the fields and pastures. Even an industrial and commercial city-state did not dare to sever its religious links with agriculture or to dispense with female magic power to perpetuate the fertility of the human race and of its domesticated animals and crops.

The fertility cult at Eleusis had held its own after the incorporation of Eleusis in the Athenian body politic, and the Eleusinian rites were consoling to the 'under-privileged' because initiation into these 'mysteries' was open not only to Eleusinians but to all Athenian citizens, and not only to these but to women, slaves, and aliens as well. The worship of Dionysos was the ex-rural fertility-cult in which the women's predominance was the most conspicuous. When Dionysos drove his devotees murderously mad, the famous legendary murderers were women whose victims were males. Pentheus and Orpheus were torn in pieces by women's hands.

The Bacchae's sanctified atrocities were the women's revenge on the male *politeuma*. The *politeuma* never admitted into its ranks the politically penalized sections of the population of the Hellenic city-states, but, as the city-states lost their grip, the women's, slaves', and aliens' social position improved. Theocritus' idealized shepherds caught the fancy of his urban readers just because they were presented in a sylvan setting. Shepherds and swineherds had not been presentable previously in post-Homeric Hellenic literature, except perhaps, as butts for comedy.

The city-states fell because they failed to maintain the pan-Hellenic political unity, transcending local patriotism, which they had achieved momentarily at a crisis in Hellenic history. During the three years 480–478 B.C., a league of European Greek city-states was maintained under the joint leadership of Sparta and Athens, for the urgent purpose of preventing the Persian Empire, which had already annexed the Greek communities to the east and north of the Aegean, from conquering and incorporating the rest of the Hellenic World. This ad hoc anti-Persian league did not include more than a fraction even of the still independent city-states of European Greece, yet it was successful beyond all expectations. It not only repulsed the Persians' attack on European Greece; it also liberated the Greeks who had previously passed under Persian rule. Now or never was the moment for saving the Hellenic World's master institution by overcoming its principal malady before this had had time to produce fatal effects.

This malady was the disunity that bred chronic fratricidal warfare. If the league of city-states that had been formed voluntarily in 480 B.C. had been perpetuated in the form of a voluntary permanent federation, the subsequent course of the Hellenic chapter of Greek political history might have been very different from the actual tragic sequel. The accession of the Greek communities that had been liberated from the Persians might have been followed by the accession of the rest of the Hellenic World, and then the Hellenic World would have been united, while still physically and spiritually intact, by Greek hands, more than three centuries before the date at which it was united eventually by Roman hands[57] when Hellenism was already at its last gasp. This truth, which was so humiliating for Hellenes, was acknowledged retrospectively, in the latter days of the Augustan Peace, by one of the *virtuosi* of 'the Second Sophistic'.

At a moment when the states of the World were already laid out on the funeral pyre as the victims of their own fratricidal strife and turmoil, they were all at once presented with the [Roman] dominion and straightway came to life again.[58]

The Greeks who had defeated the Persians in 480–479 B.C. might have learnt the importance of political unity, not only from their own success in those two marvellous years, but from the previous success of their vanquished opponents. The Persians had become mighty because they had succeeded in uniting under their rule a territory that extended from the Panjab to the northern slopes of Mount Olympus and from the southern flank of the Caucasus Range to the foot of the First Cataract of the River Nile. The Persians had also given the Greeks a direct lesson in the art of transcending local particularism and thus ending the international anarchy that had been the nemesis of unmitigated city-state sovereignty. After the Persians had suppressed the revolt of their Asian Greek subjects which had broken out in 499 B.C., the Emperor Darius' brother and viceroy Artaphrenes had compelled the re-subjected Greek city-states in Ionia to make treaties with each other providing for the settlement of the claims of citizens of one state against citizens of another by taking legal proceedings in lieu of the barbarous practice of recouping themselves by piracy, which previously had been the only recourse open to them.[59] *Fas est et ab hoste doceri*;[60] yet, at this

---

[57] The year 168 B.C., in which the Romans overthrew and liquidated the Greek kingdom of Macedon, may be taken as being the date by which Rome had imposed her direct or indirect rule over the whole of the Hellenic World to the west of the River Euphrates. But Roman rule did not immediately bring with it the boons of peace and order. The *Pax Romana* was inaugurated only in 31 B.C. by the decisive battle at Actium, which ended a hundred-years-long bout of Roman revolution and civil war that had tormented all the peoples who had fallen under Rome's dominion.

[58] Publius Aelius Aristeides, *In Romam*, §69.

[59] Herodotus, Book VI, chapter 42.   [60] Ovid, *Metamorphoses*, Book IV, line 428.

turning-point in the Hellenic chapter of Greek history, the Hellenes ignored the Persian lesson that was so pertinent to their political needs; and the rest of the history of inter-state relations among the city-states of the Hellenic World is a melancholy tale of successive failures.

In 478 B.C. Athens and Sparta, whose co-operation with each other was the necessary condition for unifying the Hellenic World politically, turned their backs on each other. Athens then challenged Sparta by attempting to unite, under her own hegemony by force of arms, the whole of the Hellenic World to the east of the Straits of Ótranto. In 459 B.C. she committed herself to a war on two fronts. She attacked Sparta's Peloponnesian allies and simultaneously intervened in an Egyptian insurrection against the Persian Empire. The sequel proved that Athens' naval and military strength was not adequate for achieving her political ambitions. In 464 B.C. Sparta had been temporarily crippled by a lethal earthquake, and the Egyptian insurrection in 459 B.C. had been a heavier blow for the Persians than their reverses in 480–479 B.C. in the Aegean. Yet a series of Athenian naval and military disasters compelled Athens to make peace with the Persians in 448 B.C. and with the Peloponnesians in 445 B.C. on terms that were renunciations of Athens' twofold objective of dominating Continental European Greece and depriving the Persian Empire of the whole of its Levantine seaboard.

Athens compensated herself for these failures perversely by transforming into an Athenian maritime empire in the Aegean the voluntary alliance that had been made in 478 B.C. between Athens and the Persian Empire's former Greek subjects. The consequence of this oppressive Athenian policy was to alienate Athens' fellow Greeks, who found that, instead of having been liberated, they had merely exchanged one master for another.[61] The consequence of this, in turn, was a second Atheno-Peloponnesian War (431–404 B.C.), and this ended in Athens losing her empire because, once again, she involved herself in a war on two fronts. In intervening in Sicily in 413 B.C., Athens overestimated her strength as egregiously as she had overestimated it when, in 459 B.C., she had intervened in Egypt.

Athens' abortive attempt in the fifth century B.C. to unite the Hellenic World politically was the first in a series of similar failures that was brought to an end only by the eventual Roman conquest of the whole

---

[61] Since 461 B.C. political power at Athens had been in the hands of the indigent majority of the citizens who supplied the rowers for the Athenian navy—the arm which was the basis of the contemporary power of Athens herself. Between the years 461 and 404 B.C., the Athenian Government tried to win the allegiance of the indigent majority of the citizens of Athens' subject city-states by playing them off against the affluent minority of their fellow countrymen. This Athenian policy of 'divide and rule' did meet with some success, but this success was limited by Athens' failure to rise to the level of political generosity to which Rome rose in a later age. Athens lacked the Roman art of eventually transforming unwilling subjects into loyal enfranchised citizens.

perimeter of the Mediterranean. Athens' failure in the fifth century B.C. was matched by the successive failures of Sparta and Thebes in the fourth century B.C. to accomplish what Athens had unsuccessfully attempted. After that, no Greek city-states had any prospect of being able to give the Hellenic World the political unity that it needed more urgently after each of its more and more destructive fratricidal wars. Where the Hellenic city-states had failed, the culturally backward Greek kingdom of Macedon came within an ace of success; but Macedon, too, eventually missed the mark. In 338 B.C. King Philip II united in a confederation under his own hegemony all the Greek city-states, to the east of the Straits of Ótranto, except Sparta, that at this date were politically independent of the Persian Empire, but Philip's work was undone by his less prudent successor. Alexander repeated Athens' fatal mistake. He embarked on a twofold enterprise that was beyond Macedon's strength. He sought to hold the Hellenic World together and at the same time to enlarge its geographical extension enormously by conquering and incorporating the Persian Empire. After his sudden premature death in 323 B.C. the expanded Hellenic World relapsed into political disunity and consequently resumed its fratricidal warfare—now on a far larger scale.

Subsequent attempts to mitigate this fresh bout of international anarchy by forming voluntary confederations of Hellenic city-states were unsuccessful. The movement for confederation in Continental European Greece in the third century B.C. miscarried because, once again, as in the fifth century B.C., there were two rival nuclei which could not bring themselves to join forces with each other. The Aetolian and Achaean Confederations now repeated the failure of fifth-century-B.C. Athens and Sparta. A more promising attempt on a larger scale was made by the Persian Empire's Macedonian Greek successor state in Asia. The Seleucid monarchy was in process of evolving into a confederation of all Asiatic Greek city-states, including the post-Alexandrine foundations in former Persian territory, when the Seleucid power was shattered by an imprudent collision with the rising power of Rome.

The Romans eventually achieved what had not been achieved by the Athenians or the Spartans or the Thebans or the Macedonians or the Aetolians or the Achaeans or the Macedonian Seleucidae; but the Romans, in breaking the Seleucid power, lost for themselves and for the Hellenic World all the Seleucid Monarchy's dominions to the east of the Euphrates, and, though the Romans did unite the major part of the Hellenic World, they did not accomplish this until the Hellenic World had been exhausted by three centuries of warfare (459–168 B.C.) in which some of the worst of the damage had been done by the Romans themselves. This damage was aggravated by the Romans' flagrant abuse of their power for the next 137 years. The Hellenic World was not given a respite until the inauguration, in 31 B.C., of the Augustan Peace.[62]

This is a long and dismal story of unheeded lessons and of missed opportunities, and the failure of the Hellenic Greeks to federate their city-states on a pan-Hellenic scale in and after the year 478 B.C. is the more remarkable, considering that, in non-political fields, they had already shown their recognition that—notwithstanding their equation of 'polis' with 'human society'—city-states, in isolation, were not adequate containers for the Hellenic Civilization. The Hellenes had shown this by organizing a number of pan-Hellenic activities and establishing a number of pan-Hellenic institutions, as supplements and antidotes to the narrowness of life within the confines of a single insulated city-state. It has been noted already that, when great poetry was produced in some particular province of the Hellenic World, it was eagerly adopted as a common possession throughout the rest of the Hellenic World, including regions in which other dialects were the language of everyday life. Differences of dialect were no obstacles to diffusion if the poetry itself was admirable enough to be coveted. It has also been noted that the incorporation of Eleusis in the Athenian city-state's domain had not prevented the Eleusinian mysteries from becoming a common spiritual treasure for Hellenes of both sexes and of all statuses. The four periodical pan-Hellenic festivals—held at Olympia, Delphi, the Isthmus of Corinth, and Nemea—flourished because they gave to all Hellenes opportunities for social intercourse of a wider range than that of the *agora* of any single city.

Some of the pan-Hellenic sanctuaries and festival-places had the advantage of not being overshadowed by any city-state.[63] The island of Delos originally had no permanent inhabitants except for the personnel of the pan-Hellenic sanctuary there, and the island did not belong to any of the neighbouring insular city-states, though the sanctuary was controlled politically by each in turn of the powers that held, successively, the naval command over Aegean waters. Delphi lay in the territory of a very weak city-state, and, though the Delphians themselves did operate the oracle, the quadriennial festival was administered by an association of twelve neighbouring Greek peoples, and this regional 'amphictyony' was eventually extended to a pan-Hellenic range by politic interpretations of its constitution. Nemea lay within the frontiers of a small rustic city-state, Cleonae. Olympia lay on the extreme edge of the territory of

Elis—a rural canton which did not provide itself, with a civic centre before the fifth century B.C. At earlier dates, Elis' control over Olympia had not been uncontested.

On the other hand, Eleusis had been incorporated in the territory of the powerful city-state Athens, and the Isthmian festival was held on the home territory of another powerful city-state, Corinth. The Isthmian festival's attainment, and the Eleusinian Mysteries' preservation, of a pan-Hellenic status are impressive evidence that pan-Hellenic activities and institutions met a need that single Hellenic city-states, even states of Athens' and Corinth's calibre, were incapable of satisfying.

The social structure of an Hellenic city-state was not only oppressive for those elements in the population that were excluded from the *politeuma*; it was also exacting, as the price of being stimulating, for the members of the *politeuma* themselves, and this partly accounts for the popularity of the cult of Dionysos. Rampaging in a Dionysiac *thiasos* was not only an outlet for women; it was also a relief, even for politically privileged males, from the psychological strain of having to keep step in a phalanx, or to keep time on a rower's bench, in the dangerous game of inter-state warfare.

However, the history of Hellenic city-state social life ran the same ironical course as the history of Hellenic temple architecture. In each of these two fields of high endeavour, the Hellenes had so nearly attained perfection within narrow limits that they were unable to bring themselves to step out into a wider field. This necessary step was eventually taken for them, belatedly, by the high-handed intervention of aliens. In architecture, the Greeks left it to the Romans to carry them beyond the rectilinear style; in politics they left it to the same intruders to carry them beyond city-state particularism; and, since this political step forward was both belated and imposed, it was inevitably revolutionary. When city-state sovereignty had brought the Hellenic civilization almost to the point of committing suicide, this disastrous political disunity was ended by the imposition of the Roman imperial regime.

The Romans' policy was what the Persians' policy had been. The Roman Imperial Government sought to confine to a minimum its intervention in the Hellenic city-states' affairs. It banned inter-state wars and the resort to violence in a city-state's domestic politics, and it undertook to defend those Hellenic city-states that lay within the Roman Empire's frontiers against attack from abroad. But it intended to leave local government in the city-state *politeumata*'s hands. It wanted merely to subordinate and discipline its subject city-states, not to abolish them. The second-century-A.D. Greek man of letters, Publius Aelius Aristeides, in a eulogy of Rome that has been quoted already, draws an idyllic picture of the life that the Hellenes were leading in the latter days of the Augustan Peace.[64] He depicts this as being a continuous round of festivities in a world that had been laid out as a pleasure-park. He seems not to see that a perpetual holiday is intrinsically unsatisfying for the people who are treated to it (and, in Aristeides' world, these did not include the peasant majority of the population).

Moreover, Aristeides does not confess, though he must have been aware of this, that municipal civic life under the Roman Imperial regime was, in fact, politically unsatisfying even for the members of the *politeumata*—the *honestiores*, in Latin parlance, as distinguished from the *humiliores*, i.e. the poor, for whom the shows financed by the *honestiores* were accessible only if they were town-dwellers, not ploughmen or shepherds. The *honestiores* eventually grew tired of holding public offices that now involved expensive ceremonial duties but no longer conferred power. Now that they were no longer empowered to make war, the public officers of the city-states found no zest in being merely efficient administrators. By the beginning of the second century of the Christian Era, municipal finances were already falling into disorder, and the Imperial authorities were finding themselves compelled reluctantly to supervise them. When, in and after A.D. 284, the Empire was retrieved from a breakdown that had lasted for half a century, the Imperial civil service had to take over the major part of the work of local government too. Meanwhile, the ablest and most ambitious of the Empire's Greek citizens had become bored with municipal public life, and had been finding their way into the Imperial service. The ecumenical community had taken the place of the local community as the focus of political attachment. An Athenian's, and even an Alexandrian's, patriotism was now no longer just focused on his home town; it was extended to embrace the whole of 'Romania'.

In the ecumenical last phase of the Hellenic chapter of Greek history, the city states declined culturally as well as politically. In the course of the five centuries of creativity that had elapsed between the date of the composition of the Homeric epics and the generation of the playwrights who produced the Attic comedy of manners, Hellenism had accumulated a stock of works of art and intellect that has never yet been surpassed.

Some of the components of this Hellenic cultural capital could not be parted from their native soil. For instance, the temples at Athens and Ephesus and Akragas and Selinous could not be exported; they could only be imitated. Plays originally written for Athenian audiences assembled in the Dionysiac theatre at Athens could, of course, be re-performed in any theatre anywhere in the Hellenic World; but new plays were not written outside Athens, or even in Athens itself, in any of

[64] Aristeides, op. cit., §§ 94–9.

the Attic genres. Adherents and practitioners of all the Hellenic schools of philosophy were to be found all over the *Oikoumenê;* but the institutes of the four major schools—Plato's Academy, Aristotle's Peripatos, Zeno's Stoa, and Epicurus' Garden—did not change their original location; instead, they drew to Athens students from abroad, and Athens, which had once been the Hellenic World's political capital and had then been its commercial capital, ended by becoming its university city.

However, these untransferable components of Hellenism's cultural capital, though important, were exceptional; the bulk of it proved to be exportable. Greek athletics could be practised wherever there was a gymnasium or a palaestra; but the most portable of all Greek cultural exports were works of literature conveyed in writing. Together with athletics, the study of '*literae humaniores*' provided the materials for *paideia*—the Greek word corresponds to the German *Bildung* (the formation of a cultivated mind) rather than to the more technical *Erziehung* (the German counterpart of the English word 'education').

The attractiveness of this Hellenic *paideia* was immense, because its instruments were the mighty works of the Hellenic genius at its zenith. This exportable extract of Hellenism captivated the Hellenes' Roman conquerors. From before the close of the third century B.C. till after the opening of the third century of the Christian Era, every cultivated Roman was bilingual, and in the meanwhile the Romans had created for themselves a passable replica of Greek literature in the Latin language. However, when Hellenism's cultural capital was exported from the city-states in which it had been created, it lost its vitality, like these city-states themselves when they were saved from destroying each other by being converted into municipalities of the Roman Empire.

The fateful change from the spontaneous use of words to an artificial play with words had begun as early as the age of 'the First Sophistic', which had been contemporary with the Atheno-Peloponnesian War of 431–404 B.C. The speeches inserted by Thucydides in his history of this war are not verbatim records. The author himself frankly avows that they are compositions of his own. He has reproduced, as closely as possible, the general sense of the speeches that were actually delivered, but he has made up for his lack of authentic texts by putting into the speakers' mouths the words that have seemed to him to be the most appropriate for each particular historical occasion.[65] The speeches in Thucydides' history are works of art; and we may guess that the lost authentic speeches for which these are the historian's substitutes were less polished but were to that degree more spontaneous.

---

[65] Thucydides, Book I, chapter 22, § 1.

The post-Alexandrine scholars on the staff of the Museum at Alexandria did have the texts of speeches that had been delivered (and, no doubt, had then been polished for publication) by the fourth-century-B.C. Attic orators, and, thanks to the Alexandrians and their Byzantine successors, we can read these texts today. But a speech read by eye differs from the same speech heard by ear. It differs even if the hand that has edited it for publication after delivery is the speaker's own, and, when the written version of one of Demosthenes' speeches is imitated, five centuries later, in almost faultless, but insipid, neo-Attic, by Dio 'with the golden mouth' or by Aelius Aristeides, the product is not a live speech; it is an academic lecture.

Hellenisms' successes were numerous and immense. They have not been outdone by the achievements of any other civilization so far. But these Hellenic successes were perhaps peculiar—and, if so, were peculiarly tragic—in approaching so near to perfection that they inhibited the genius that achieved them from transcending them. An untranscended achievement turns into a failure; and, since the Hellenes' achievements were outstandingly great, the severity of their nemesis was proportionate. The karma that the Hellenes bequeathed was far more potent than the karma that they had inherited. What was the effect of this formidable Hellenic Greek legacy on the fortunes of the Hellenes' Byzantine Greek heirs?

V

THE BYZANTINE GREEKS' HERITAGE
FROM THE HELLENIC GREEKS

THE Hellenic Greeks' legacy to the Byzantine Greeks was potent and massive. In the course of the three centuries (A.D. 284–602) of cultural overlap, during which the Hellenic civilization was not yet extinct, while the Byzantine civilization was already in being, the Byzantines rejected a number of the key elements of Hellenism. City-states had already become incapable of serving even as non-sovereign municipal organs of local self-government. The Byzantine Greeks rejected the city-states' pre-Christian religion, the outward-facing rectilinear architecture of the Hellenic temples in which the rites of this religion had been performed, the naturalistic representation of the human form in monumental sculpture (bas-reliefs, as well as statues), and Hellenic philosophy. These rejected elements of Hellenism were of its very essence, and it might have been thought that so radical a cultural revolution would have enabled the Byzantine Greeks to jump clear of their Hellenic past. However, the Byzantines' repudiation of their Hellenic heritage, though sweeping, was not complete. The Byzantines failed to make a break with some of the naturalistic post-Alexandrine Hellenic minor arts, and they were haunted by two major bequests from Hellenism, the Hellenic *paideia* and the Roman Empire (a political dispensation which was the antithesis of city-states and was the nemesis of the Hellenic city-states' failure to give the Hellenic World peace, unity, and order). The *paideia* and the Imperial regime dominated Byzantine Greek life, and their dominance was one of the causes of the Byzantine Greek civilization's breakdown and disintegration.

In the Byzantine Greek World, there were still some city-states to be found, and some of these—for instance, Khersón (the Hellenic Khersónesos) in the Crimea and Neapolis (Naples) in southern Italy—were survivals from the Hellenic age of Greek history. Others, however—for instance, Amalfi on the Sorrento Peninsula, Ragusa, originally just off, and later just on, the coast of Dalmatia, and Venice in her lagoon—were settlements of refugees who had fled from their former homes during the age of anarchy and *Völkerwanderung* (*circa* A.D. 378–678). The constitutions of these Byzantine city-states differed, *de facto*, from those of the

former municipal city-states of the Roman Empire, and still more from
those of the previous sovereign Hellenic Greek city-states. The local
bishop now usually played an important part in the civil administration,
and in the Byzantine city-states in Italy and Dalmatia the principal lay
officers had originally been imperial officials and retained this status in
theory long after they had become, in practice, representatives of the
local population. Moreover, there were only fourteen Byzantine city-
states in all, including the nine on and off the Dalmatian coast, and all
of them were on the fringes of a Byzantine Greek World whose heart-
land was Asia Minor with a European ferry-terminal at Constantinople.
This heart-land was held by a resuscitated Roman Imperial Government, with Constantinople—'the New Rome'—as its capital. Compared
with the territories under the East Roman Imperial Government's direct
administration, the autonomous outlying city-states were insignificant
so long as the East Roman Empire flourished. The Empire's slow decline
and long-delayed fall opened the way for Venice—and for Ragusa, too,
on a smaller scale—to become sovereign city-states, and for Naples to
become eventually the capital of the Kingdom of the two Sicilies.

The Byzantine Greeks' repudiation of the Hellenic city-states'
religion was an even greater formal break with the Hellenic past than
the liquidation of the city-states themselves. This religious revolution
was symbolized in a change in the connotation of a famous name. For
Greeks of the Hellenic Age, the name 'Hellenes' signified 'civilized men'
in contrast to 'barbarians'; for Greeks of the Byzantine Age, the name
signified 'pagans' in contrast to 'Christians'. In other words the name
'Hellenes' meant, for the Byzantine Greeks, no longer 'insiders' but
'outsiders'; and these deplorable Greek-speaking recalcitrants, whose
survival had been a reproach to Christian Greek civilization, had
become extinct when their last representatives, the Maniots, had been
converted to Christianity in the reign of the Emperor Basil I (867–86).

This reversal of the connotation of the name 'Hellenes' was dramatic,
but the actual break in the continuity of the Greeks' religious life was not
so great as this terminological revolution suggests. The break was on the
surface; it did not extend to the subsoil. The popular religion remained
what it had been since the Neolithic Age. A *genius loci* who had been
honoured in the Hellenic Age as a hero or as a tutelary goddess was now
honoured as a saint or as 'the All Holy Mother of God' ('The Panayía',
'the Theotókos'). The religious revolution at the official level passed
over the peasants' heads, and most Greeks were still peasants till within
living memory.

The reversal of the fortunes of Hellenism and Christianity was abrupt,
because it could be, and was, brought about by acts of autocratic
Roman Emperors. Constantine I and Licinius lifted the ban on

Christianity in A.D. 313; Theodosius I imposed a ban on all non-Christian religions, except Judaism and the kindred religion of the Samaritans, in A.D. 380–92. The corresponding revolution in the architectural form of the Greek World's places of public worship was, by its nature, a change that could not be produced instantaneously by Imperial decrees; inevitably it was a gradual process.

This architectural revolution had two aspects: in being transformed into a Christian church, the Hellenic temple, like the word 'Hellenic' itself, was turned inside-out, and its rectilinear lines were dissolved into curves. Visually, the second of these two revolutionary changes is the more striking; psychologically, the first is the more significant.

The transfer of attention from the building's exterior to its interior was not only first in importance; it also came first chronologically. The Hellenic temple had been designed to please, not the god or goddess to whom it was dedicated, but the human public. The divinity's statue was housed—or immured—in lonely darkness within walls whose inner faces were not relieved either by windows or by decorations. The decorations were placed on the temple's outer faces, in the sunlight, for the delectation of the public. In the ensuing architectural revolution the contrast between the building's two faces was maintained, but their treatment was now reversed. This happened when the temple's lay-out was taken over for designing secular buildings in which the interior was to be used, not for housing the statue of a divinity, but by human beings.

Human users needed the comforts, namely sunlight and decorations, which had been unnecessary for a statue—however holy, and however great a work of art, this inanimate representation of the divinity might have been. Therefore, when the temple's layout was adapted for designing a basilica,[1] in which ceremonial, judicial, administrative, and other public business was to be transacted indoors, the basilica, unlike the temple, had to have windows. These might either be pierced in the walls or be provided by a clerestorey. The second alternative would require the replacement of the temple's traditional unitary gable roof by a roof in three sections, with the middle section elevated, in the clerestorey, to a higher level than the other two. For supporting the clerestorey and its roof, it was convenient to transfer to the interior the rows of columns that had previously been set along the long sides of the temple's outer face. Besides being useful for the architect, this transfer was agreeable for the human users of the basilica, since the columns were major elements in the decoration of the building.

[1] The word means 'a royal building', and this suggests that the first basilicas must have been built in one or other of the Persian Empire's monarchical Greek successor-states. However, the earliest surviving basilica is the Aemilia at Rome, and this was preceded there by the Porcia. Both these basilicas at Rome were built at the beginning of the second century B.C.

For the same reason, all the other decorations were now transferred from the exterior to the interior. They would be visible and enjoyable there, now that the interior was lighted by windows. The exterior could be stripped of its decorations, in order to embellish the interior with these, without any aesthetic loss for the human users. These, unlike statues, had sensibilities that required consideration. So long as the building had been a temple into which there was no admittance except, periodically, for a few priests, the public obtained its aesthetic satisfaction from the building by standing, or strolling round, outside it and enjoying its decorated exterior. Now that the interior of the building had become a place for the transaction of human business, no one would any longer wish to linger, gazing, outside; everyone would wish to enter promptly in order to get his business, inside the building, done. The exterior would not now receive more than a passing glance, so the architect could afford to leave it unadorned.

The rectilinearity of a basilica might be broken by apses, since an internal recess would be a convenient location for a public officer who was giving audience or was passing judgment in public. The public could then fill the main body of the hall. An apse would have to be roofed by a semi-dome, and this would break the rectilinearity of the roof as well. The way was now open for the development of the secular pre-Christian basilica into the Byzantine Christian church, in which the secular officer, transacting business with the public, would be replaced by a priest, officiating in partnership with a congregation.

In the architecture of the church, a square replaced the basilica's oblong ground-plan. This square was roofed by a circular dome, and the walls bulged out into apses roofed by semi-domes. These led the eye up, by stages, to the crown of the central dome. The Hellenic rectilinear gable-roofed oblong temple had thus been transformed into a non-rectilinear hollow pyramid. The roofing of a Byzantine church is pyramidal in its general effect; but, instead of mounting from its base to its apex in smooth surfaces meeting each other at sharp angles, the Byzantine church's roofing mounts in a crescendo of billowing curves. The optical effect is wave-like, and, to a modern observer, it feels like a piece of symphonic 'classical' Western music translated into visual form.

The Byzantine architects never carried their transformation of the Hellenic temple to its logical conclusion. This would have been a dome-roofed round building on the plan that, in the Pantheon at Rome, had been executed in concrete at an early date in the second century of the Christian Era.[2] The Byzantines did not take up the Roman invention of

---

[2] See p. 59. The Pantheon's Hellenic-style rectilinear portico is a perfunctory excrescence on the circular plan of the rest of the building.

concrete, and therefore, with a single famous exception, they did not build on the gigantic scale of the Baths of Caracalla and of Diocletian at Rome. The exception is, of course, the Church of the Ayía Sophía at Constantinople (532–7). The architects achieved their *tour de force* of building on this scale without using concrete by countering the outward thrust of the huge non-monolithic dome with massive buttresses, and by making the dome, at the first essay, of such light materials that it had to be replaced (558–62).[3]

The sixth-century Church of Saints Sergius and Bacchus at Constantinople ('the Little Ayía Sophía') is a variation on the plan of the Great Ayía Sophía, executed on a miniature scale, but the normal scale of later Byzantine churches is still smaller. The eleventh-century churches of the Kapnikaréa and the Saints Theodore at Athens are more characteristic, in both their scale and their style. The still tinier Old Metropolitan Church at Athens, whatever its date, conveys the quintessence of the Byzantine ecclesiastical architects' spirit.

The abandonment of monumental sculpture was, no doubt, partly a consequence of impoverishment. Statues of Emperors and even of popular racing charioteers continued to be made until the Empire's economic collapse in the East in and after A.D. 602.[4] But, though statues of human beings were still tolerated till then, statuary was too intimately associated with Hellenism, and Hellenism with paganism, to be looked upon with favour by the Christian ecclesiastical authorities. Moreover, when Hellenic temples were replaced by Christian churches, there was no longer a place for the statue of the divinity to whom a temple was dedicated. The statue had been the focal point of a temple's interior; the focal point of a church's interior was the place at which the rite of the Eucharist was performed. There was no room in a church for a rival centre of attraction in the form of a dominating statue. Nor could the Christian Trinity-in-Unity or the duality-in-unity of the person of Christ have been represented acceptably in the round. Christians fell out with each other in trying to convey these theological paradoxes even in the supple medium of the vocabulary of Hellenic Greek philosophy. In the use of art in the service of Christianity, the Byzantines eschewed sculpture in the round, and bas-relief too.[5] They compensated for this renunciation by decorating the inner walls of their churches two-dimensionally with mosaics and paintings.[6]

Even the flat representation of human forms is a breach of a Jewish

---

[3] See Grabar, A., in *The Cambridge Medieval History*, vol. iv, 2nd edn., part ii (Cambridge 1967), p. 317.

[4] Ibid., p. 322; Cameron, A.: *Porphyrius the Charioteer* (Oxford 1973), *passim*.

[5] Grabar, loc. cit.

[6] See Baynes, N. H.; 'The Icons before Iconoclasm', in his *Byzantine Studies and Other Essays* (London 1955), pp. 226–39.

tabu which the Christian Church has never avowedly repudiated; and
when it has failed, as it has at most times and places, to observe the
second of the Mosaic Ten Commandments, the Church has had
periodic misgivings about its laxity on this important point. These
misgivings have produced occasional outbursts of iconoclasm. There has
been the Protestant outburst in Western Christendom in and after the
sixteenth century; and this was anticipated by an outburst in the eighth
century which was let loose by an East Roman Emperor, Leo III
(717–41).

The conflict in the East Roman Empire over *eikóns* went on from 726
to 843. During these 117 years, except for the twenty-six years 787–813,
the iconoclasts were in power in the Empire, and they enforced their
veto on images in that part of Eastern Orthodox Christendom (and it
was the greater part) over which the East Roman Imperial Government's authority was effective in the eighth and ninth centuries. In 843
the conflict was ended by a compromise in which the champions of
images got the best of the bargain. Two-dimensional images were
reinstated, and it was agreed that the devotion paid to them was not to
be condemned as idolatrous. The images, so their champions[7] claimed,
were not being worshipped in themselves; they were being venerated as
visual symbols of the divine or saintly persons whom they depicted.

This decision, which has never been called in question, demonstrated
that the East Roman Imperial Government's autocratic power was not
so potent as public feeling. A majority of the Eastern Orthodox
Christian public was deeply attached to the cult of images, and its
devotion to them had not been weakened by two bouts of repression
which, between them, ran to ninety-one years. In the end the
iconoclastic-minded minority was compelled to recognize that, in spite
of having had the Imperial Government on its side, it must acquiesce in
a compromise that was a thinly disguised defeat. The settlement of A.D.
843 ensured that the two-dimensional representation of the human form
should be countenanced in Eastern Orthodox Christendom. The
veneration of *eikóns*, both publicly in church and privately in the home,
had been vindicated.

To judge by such evidence as we have for the style of the Hellenic art
of painting, the Byzantine and the Hellenic treatments of the human
figure were worlds apart. Their difference in style reflected a difference
of spirit and aim. Hellenic pictures, like Hellenic bas-reliefs and statues
and busts, were attempts to give a naturalistic portrayal of the human
body,[8] on the assumption that this was the best, and indeed the only

---

[7] e.g. Saint John of Damascus (d. A.D. 749). See Hussey, J. M., and Hart, T. A., in *The Cambridge Medieval History*, vol. iv, 2nd edn., part ii (Cambridge 1967), pp. 187–8.

[8] See p. 57.

possible, way of revealing human nature. On the other hand, Byzantine *eikóns* were attempts to adumbrate in visual form the invisible soul, on the assumption that the soul is Man's essence; and Byzantine painters and mosaicists did not hesitate to abandon naturalism if, by misrepresenting bodily appearances, they could succeed in conveying spiritual realities that a naturalistic treatment of the body would have failed to express.

At a previous point in this book,[9] it has been suggested that the Early Hellenic decorators of Protogeometric vases broke with the Minoan style of Mycenaean naturalism deliberately, and that their successors in the age of mature Geometric art were also acting deliberately when they 'geometricized' the figures of human beings and horses that they admitted into their subtly worked out abstract patterns. These are only guesses. But, in the apparently parallel case of the non-naturalistic style of the Byzantine *eikóns*, we have positive evidence that their departure from naturalism was not the involuntary consequence of a loss of mastery of the technique of painting or mosaic-making in the naturalistic Hellenic style. There are surviving specimens of the Byzantines' continuing use of this Hellenic style, side by side with their own non-naturalistic style. The Hellenic style was used by the Byzantines mainly for the trivial decoration of secular buildings; but they also used it, on occasion, for treating solemn religious themes. Moreover, their missionaries carried this Hellenic style, as well as the Byzantine style, to the regions beyond the East Roman Empire's frontiers that they converted. Examples of works in this Hellenic style survive in Russia and in Serbia.

Thus, in the field of painting and mosaic-making, the Byzantines' attitude towards their heritage from Hellenism was equivocal; and so was their attitude towards Hellenic philosophy. Christian theology had been elaborated in terms of Hellenic philosophy. The Greek texts—and these are the original texts—of the Christian Church's creeds are composed in the Hellenic philosophy's vocabulary, and the value of Hellenic philosophy's service to Christianity was always recognized even by the strictest guardians of Eastern Christian Orthodoxy. Moreover, Christian Greeks preserved, by the laborious copying of manuscripts, the writings of those Hellenic philosophers who happened to have written in a form of Attic Greek that had passed the censorship of the Atticizing purists of the Augustan Age. They also preserved even Aristotle's unpolished lecture-notes. Yet, in the Byzantine Age, to study Plato's works for their content, and not just for their style, was usually a dangerous adventure. The institutes of philosophy at Athens[10] were

[9] See p. 54.
[10] The separate institutes of the four major schools (Plato's Academy, Aristotle's Lyceum, Zeno's

closed by the Emperor Justinian I in A.D. 529. Seven philosophers who were unwilling to become apostates from Hellenism to Christianity had to find asylum in the Persian Empire; and they were able to return home, without having to choose between conversion and penalization, only because the Persian Emperor exacted from Justinian a special amnesty for them.[11] These were the last Greek students of Hellenic philosophy who were able to follow their bent with impunity. Phótios in the ninth century, Michael Psellós and John Italós in the eleventh century, and Yemistós Plêthon in the fifteenth century, each in turn got into trouble on this account. Italós and Plêthon asked for trouble; Phótios and Psellós did not; they tried to be discreet, but this did not save them. They were suspected of having secretly relapsed into the pre-Christian paganism that Plêthon afterwards professed openly and aggressively.

The two important elements in the legacy of Hellenism that the Byzantines failed to shake off were the Hellenic *paideia* and the Roman Imperial regime. In the latter part of the sixth century the monks succeeded in putting the *paideia* out of action temporarily,[12] but it was resuscitated in the ninth century. In the Eastern Orthodox Church's eyes the Hellenic *paideia* was innocuous, because all that it inculcated was an adulation of literary form. It had deliberately divorced form from content, and it did not take the content seriously; it did not regard this as having an intrinsic value of its own. As for the Roman Imperial regime, the Hellenes had begun by resenting and resisting its imposition but had ended by recognizing retrospectively that it had given the Hellenic civilization an unexpected and perhaps undeserved new lease of life. After that, the Hellenes had identified themselves with the Roman Empire and had appropriated it.[13] The Greeks' captivation of their Roman conquerors was completed when they took to calling themselves Romans (Rhomaíoi) instead of Hellenes. Now that the word 'Hellenes' had come to signify 'pre-Christian Greeks', the Christian Greeks needed a new appellation for themselves, and in 'Rhomaíoi' they found the word that they were seeking. In Byzantine Greek parlance, 'Rhomaíoi' came to mean, not Latin-speaking Romans, but 'Greeks who were Eastern Orthodox Christians', in contrast to outsiders, extinct and extant. The extinct outsiders were the Hellenes; the extant outsiders were the inextinguishable barbarians beyond the East Roman Empire's frontiers, and, in Byzantine Greek eyes, these

Stoa, Epicurus' Garden) had still been going concerns in the second century of the Christian Era. We do not know whether they retained their separate identities till 529. We know only that the teaching of Hellenic philosophy continued to be carried on at Athens until that date.

[11] In the Perso-Roman peace treaty of 532-3 (see Agathias: *Historiae*, Book II, chapters 30-1).
[12] See Haussig, H. W., *A History of Byzantine Civilization* (London 1971), pp. 80-3.
[13] See pp. 65 and 70.

now included Old Rome's barbarized and non-Greek-speaking inhabitants.

The evolution of the Hellenic *paideia* and of the Roman Imperial regime have been noticed in the preceding chapter of this book. The effect of these two legacies from the Hellenic chapter of Greek history on the Byzantine Greeks' fortunes is discussed in the next chapter.

VI

THE BYZANTINE GREEKS' SUCCESSES
AND FAILURES

(i) 'Economy'

I T was unfortunate for the Byzantine Greeks that they were not able to slough off their heritage from the Hellenic Greeks completely. The Byzantine spirit was so different from the Hellenic that the Byzantines' legacy from Hellenism was an incongruous element in Byzantine life. The *dirigiste* hierarchical Byzantine system of government and way of life had less affinity with Hellenism than with the Mycenaean system which has been revealed in the 'Linear B' tablets. Byzantine bureaucracy is also reminiscent of the Chinese bureaucracy that was developed first, in the fourth century B.C., in the Kingdom of Ch'in and then, from 221 B.C. onwards, in the politically unified China of the Imperial Age of Chinese history. However, the Byzantine Greeks also resembled the Chinese in contriving to combine rigidity with suppleness and arrogance with opportunism, and this not only in politics but in most other fields of human activity as well.

The Byzantines' own name for their opportunism was 'economy' (οἰκονομία), which means literally 'good housekeeping' and hence 'adroit management' of the business in hand, whatever this may be. Management involves making allowances and adjustments, and this is possible only if there is some room for manoeuvre and for negotiation. The Byzantines were masters of the art of arranging *combinazioni*. They therefore found diplomacy more congenial than litigation or argument, since precision is of the essence of both law and logic, and precision precludes the practice of 'economy' in the Byzantine Greek meaning of the word. 'Economy' requires elasticity. This must not be stretched so far as to make the departure from principle flagrantly apparent. Carried that far, 'economy' would be self-defeating, but elasticity within this limit is the necessary enabling condition without which 'economy' cannot be practised.

Two fields in which the Byzantine Greeks' practice of 'economy' is particularly striking are protocol and dogma, for these were fields in which the Byzantines were rigid and arrogant in principle.

According to Byzantine political theory, the (East) Roman Emperor —or college of co-emperors when the senior emperor had one or more junior colleagues—was the sole sovereign power in the World. Local rulers of outlying regions derived their authority from the Emperor by delegation from him, and exercised it under his suzerainty. The East Roman Imperial Chancery could not have demonstrated the validity of the Emperor's title to make this overweening claim. It could not have produced either documentary evidence or logical proof. The prerogative that was claimed for an East Roman Emperor was grounded simply on the assumption that it was his unquestionable prescriptive right, as was the identical claim of a Chinese Emperor to be sovereign of 'all that is under Heaven' in virtue of occupying the throne of the World's 'Middle Kingdom'.

An East Roman Emperor normally asserted his prerogative by arrogating the title 'Emperor' to himself exclusively, and refusing to concede it to any other ruler. But, on two historic occasions, the East Roman Government made this concession in consideration of counter-concessions that it considered to be valuable enough to justify a resort to 'economy' for the sake of securing them.

In an agreement concluded in 811 and ratified in 814, the East Roman Government implicitly recognized the legitimacy of Charlemagne's assumption of the title 'Emperor', which had been conferred on him by the Pope and by representatives of the people of Rome in the year 800. The quid pro quo was the cessation of Frankish pressure on Venice and Istria and Dalmatia—outlying East Roman possessions that were militarily at the Franks' mercy. This Frankish concession made it worth while for the East Roman Govenment to practise 'economy' by making an exception to its normally intransigent stand on the question of the Imperial title. If Charlemagne had not been in a position to take some East Roman pawns off the board, the East Roman Government would, no doubt, have welcomed the opportunity of humiliating him that he had presented to them. Charlemagne would have 'lost face' if the title that he had assumed by a unilateral act had not been recognized eventually by the party whose use of this title was unquestionably legitimate. The East Romans, however, reckoned that the extrication of Venice and Istria and Dalmatia from the Franks' grip was being purchased cheaply by their 'saving' of Charlemagne's 'face'. Moreover, the 'economy' with which Arsáphios, the East Roman envoy to Aachen, negotiated the deal 'saved' the East Roman Government's 'face' as well.

The recognition of Charlemagne as an 'Emperor' was a personal concession to him which did not hold good for his heirs. A permanent concession of the title 'Emperor' to the wearer of the crown of Bulgaria was made in 927, and at the same time it was conceded that the Bulgarian Emperor should have a Patriarch of his own, who would not be under the ecclesiastical jurisdiction of the Patriarch of Constantinople. The East Roman Government clinched these two remarkable concessions by giving the Bulgarian ambassador at Constantinople precedence *ex officio* over all other foreign ambassadors there; by giving in marriage to 'Tsar' Peter (as Khan Peter was now recognized to be) one of the granddaughters of the senior East Roman Emperor of the day, Rhomanós I Lekapênós; and by undertaking to pay to the Bulgarian Government an annual tribute. Face was saved by calling this tribute a personal allowance to the Lekapenid Tsárina from her family.

The princess and the tribute (camouflaged by a deft use of 'economy') were actually Bulgaria's only new gains; for Peter's father and predecessor, Khan Symeon, before his death in 927, had already styled himself 'Emperor' and given himself a Patriarch unilaterally. Thus the East Romans were merely conceding to Peter and to his Patriarch titles that they could not have stopped them from using. However, the East Roman Government's recognition of the Bulgars' right to use these titles saved the Bulgars' face. Consequently, the East Roman Government obtained, in exchange, relief from a state of war under which, since 913, all the East Roman Empire's continental European possessions, outside the walls of Constantinople, had been at the Bulgars' mercy. Manifestly the exercise of 'economy' over the East Roman claim to a monopoly of the title 'Emperor' was still more advantageous in 927 than it had been in 811–14.

In the East Romans' eyes, their church's orthodoxy was as sacrosanct as their Emperor's prerogative. When the competent authorities identified orthodoxy with a recognition of the legitimacy of the veneration of *eikóns*, a dead Emperor who had banned 'iconolatry' ought logically to have been condemned posthumously. However, the death of the iconoclast Emperor Theóphilos in 842 had opened the way for his widow Theodora, now regent for her son Michael III, who was still a minor, to reverse her deceased husband's policy, and Theodora had signified her intention of doing this on condition that Theóphilos should be spared a *damnatio memoriae*.[1] Theodora was devoted to the *eikóns*, but she was also devoted to her late husband. The party that shared her devotion to the *eikóns* harvested the victory that Theodora had placed

---

[1] There was a precedent for this in the acts of the Council of A.D. 787, which had rescinded the ban on the veneration of *eikóns* for the first time. On this occasion, too, the initiative had been taken by the widow of a deceased Emperor. Eirênê may not have been as devoted to Leo IV's memory as Theodora was to Theóphilos', yet care was taken to avoid any appearance of personal disrespect for Leo IV and his father and grandfather Constantine V and Leo III, whose iconoclastic policy was being reversed. To condemn them explicitly would have been an additional provocation to the Iconoclast party, and this provocation would have been gratuitous.

within their grasp by accepting it on Theodora's terms, and they gave a sop to the iconoclasts by refraining from reinstating sculpture in the round.[2] Thanks to these two 'economies' conceded by the victors in A.D. 843, the settlement arranged in that year has lasted till the present day without again being challenged.

The Eastern Orthodox Church frowns on a second marriage, penalizes a third marriage, and excommunicates any member of the Church who contracts a fourth marriage. The Emperor Leo VI (886–912) did, nevertheless, find a priest to marry him to his mistress Zoe 'Coal-eyes', who had borne him an heir (the future Emperor Constantine VII Porphyrogenitus) after Leo's three successive previous wives had died, each in turn, leaving him childless. Constantine was thus retrospectively legitimized, but the scandal split the church, from 906 till 920, into a party that condoned the uncanonical accomplished fact and a party that refused to countenance it. The breach was healed in 920 by a prohibition of fourth marriages which was not applied retrospectively to the deceased Emperor Leo VI's fourth marriage, and which therefore did not deprive Constantine VII of his status of being a legitimate child 'born in the Purple Chamber of the Imperial Palace'. This act of 'economy' was arranged between Rhomanós Lekapênós, who was in process of getting himself made Emperor as Constantine VII's senior colleague, and the Patriarch Nikólaos 'Mystikós' (ex-'confidential secretary'). Nikólaos' moderation was remarkable, considering that he had been deposed from the Ecumenical Patriarchate by Leo VI for having refused to recognize Leo's marriage with Zoe, and had been reinstated only after Leo's death.

These are not only fair samples of the practice of 'economy'; they also throw light on the outlook which justified the practice. In Byzantine eyes, 'economy' was not a venial concession to the weakness of human nature; it was positively virtuous, and in truth it was a saving grace, without which the Byzantine Greeks' proneness to rigidity and arrogance might have led them to go to intolerable and disastrous lengths in succumbing to these vices. Thanks to the practice of 'economy', 'Byzantium was never, in any period, totalitarian.'[3] The Eastern Orthodox Church 'has been shy of dogmatic definitions'.[4] The Byzantines were flexible on principle, not out of either moral frailty or intellectual incompetence. Their heritage of Hellenic *paideia* and Roman law—a *damnosa hereditas* if they had failed to temper it—would have enabled them, if they had chosen, to formulate precise definitions

[2] See p. 77, above.
[3] Grégoire, H., 'The Byzantine Church', in Baynes, N. H., and Moss, H. St. L. B. [eds.], *Byzantium* (Oxford 1948), p. 106.
[4] Runciman, S., *The Great Church in Captivity* (Cambridge 1968), p. 5.

where precision is manifestly unattainable and where, if it were attainable, if would nevertheless be inappropriate.

In the Creeds, the Christian Church's beliefs had been expressed in terms of Hellenic philosophy; yet, just because the Byzantine Greeks were theologically sophisticated, they recognized that the ultimate spiritual reality is incomprehensible for human intellects. They were masters of Aristotle's logic. The eighth-century Father, Saint John of Damascus, in his *Fount of Knowledge* (*Πηγὴ Γνώσεως*)—the nearest approach to an undisputedly authoritative *summa* that has been produced in the Eastern Orthodox Church[5]—starts by giving Aristotelian definitions of terms. Byzantine jurists had mastered Roman law, which had become the Greeks' law in A.D. 212, when the promulgation of the *Constitutio Antoniniana* had made the Greeks Roman citizens *en masse*. The late-ninth-century *Vasiliká* (*circa* 889-90) is virtually a reproduction of Justinian's corpus of Roman law in Greek. But the Byzantine Greeks did not make the medieval Westerners' mistake of applying Aristotelian logic and Justinianean law *à outrance*. For the Westerners, these relics of their lost Graeco-Roman past were exciting and intoxicating treasure-troves; for the Byzantines, they were familiar, and therefore unexciting, legacies; they were not open sesames to everything in Heaven and Earth.

Eastern Orthodox Christians have been reluctant to give a Western-like clear-cut 'yes or no' answer on the question whether, in the celebration of the Eucharist, there is a transubstantiation of the elements.[6] In Western Christendom, this question has been hotly debated since the Protestant Reformation, and in the seventeenth century the Orthodox were pressed, by both Protestant and Catholic Western theologians and diplomatists, to declare what the Orthodox Church's position was. The Westerners failed to extract from the Orthodox any conclusive or definitive answer. The Orthodox found the question itself distasteful and embarrassing. Evidently they felt that this was a question of a kind that had better have been left unasked.[7] Consequently the Orthodox have not sought to define the exact moment in the perfomance of the liturgy at which transubstantiation—if there is transubstantiation—takes place, whereas Roman Catholics pin-point the moment and announce it by the ringing of a bell.

Monasticism, too, is an Eastern as well as a Western Christian institution, and the fourth-century bishop Saint Basil of Kaisáreia and the ninth-century abbot Saint Theodore of Stoúdhios' House gave copious instructions for the conduct of monks, but neither of them promulgated

---

[5] See Runciman, Book II, chapter 9, pp. 338-59, 'The Definition of Doctrine', *passim*.

[6] See ibid., pp. 306-10, 319, 338, 352-4.

[7] See ibid., pp. 306-10, 319, 338, 352-4.

a 'rule' in the Western sense,[8] and the posthumous codifications of their instructions have remained unofficial. 'There was . . . both elasticity and a regulated norm.'[9] Since there are no Eastern Orthodox monastic 'rules', there are no monastic orders either, and this relative informality has left Eastern Orthodox monks freer than Western Catholic monks have been to choose between the alternative forms of monasticism—hermitage, convent, and *lávra* (the middle way)[10]—which had been created in Egypt and in Palestine in Christian monasticism's early days.[11]

Definition and regulation were also avoided by the Byzantines in their arrangement of the relations between Church and State. From A.D. 457 onwards, it was customary for an Emperor to be crowned by the Patriarch of Constantinople, but the constitutional and theological significance of this custom was never investigated, and consequently Eastern Orthodox Christendom escaped the ideological conflict over the question of the State's and the Church's respective powers by which medieval Western Christendom was plagued.[12]

(ii) *The Byzantine Greek Civilization's Attractiveness and its Limits*

When, in the light of this flexible Byzantine Greek mentality, we survey the Byzantine Greeks' successes and failures, we find that the Byzantines were strongest in the field of religion, in which their Hellenic predecessors had been weakest. The Byzantines' greatest achievement was the Eastern Orthodox version of Christianity. In the Orthodox liturgy they created a poetical and musical work of art which satisfies the spiritual need for congregational worship; but this collective expression of religious feeling has not inhibited the individual expression of it. Mysticism and asceticism blossomed contemporaneously with the liturgy and have coexisted with it. In the Orthodox Church the collective and the individual human approaches to God are not mutually exclusive. Orthodox Christianity also inspired creative new departures in architecture and in the visual arts, and in literature it inspired a new genre, hagiography, which combined edification with the kind of intellectual entertainment that, in the present-day West, is provided by novels and, for children, by fairy stories. The branch of

---

[8] Saint Benedict's 'rule' was inspired by Saint Basil's 'recommendations', according to Runciman; ibid., p. 38.

[9] Hussey, J. M., *The Byzantine World* (London 1957), p. 118.

[10] Justinian I, in his legislation, which was followed up by the 'Quinisext' (*In Trullo*) Council of A.D. 692, proved unable to eliminate *lávrai* (Runciman, op. cit., pp. 38 and 40).

[11] See Hussey, op. cit., pp. 125-6.

[12] See ibid., p. 92.

secular literature in which the Byzantines distinguished themselves was historiography. Their chronicles, as well as their more sophisticated and pretentious historical works, are impressive achievements.

In the economic and social field, the free peasantry which emerged out of the chaos in the seventh century was the Byzantine society's military and financial mainstay. The index of this society's economic soundness in its early days is the maintenance, for more than seven centuries, of the purity of the East Roman gold coin. This had been rehabilitated by Diocletian and by Constantine I after the previous currency had been debased to a degree that had put it out of circulation. The purity of the new gold coin was maintained until the reign of Constantine IX (1042–1054),[13] and in the meantime it was used as an international currency far beyond the geographical limits of the Byzantine Greeks' own economic activities.

These Byzantine Greek successes can bear comparison with those of the Byzantines' Hellenic predecessors, but, like the Hellenes, the Byzantines also experienced some signal, and eventually fatal, failures, In the field of literature, the Byzantines were weakest where the Hellenes had been strongest. Byzantine Greek secular poetry never fulfilled the promise of the fine ballads that it produced at the 'folk' level. In the social and economic field the Byzantine Age is the only time in the long course of Greek history in which the people of Greece have not been enterprising maritime traders.

About half a millennium before the introduction of the Greek language into Greece, the pre-Greek-speaking inhabitants of Continental Greece had colonized the Cyclades, and the islanders had then influenced the civilization of the mainland and had exported their artifacts to Crete, Troy, Bulgaria, Dalmatia, Sicily, and the Lipari Islands.[14] In the first century of the Christian Era, Alexandrian Greeks were trading as far afield as the east coast of India, and Massaliot Greeks as far afield as Cornwall. In the Modern Age, Greek shipping has been ubiquitous. In the Byzantine Age, too, the Greeks were adventurous travellers, but they travelled, not as traders, but as missionaries. In economics, the Byzantine Greeks were passive. They waited for non-Greek traders—Armenians, Muslims, Russians, Westerners—to visit them, and consequently even the domestic trade of the Byzantine Greek World passed into these more enterprising foreigners' hands. Worse still, the free peasantry, which was the Byzantine society's prime source of health and strength, was gradually ground away between an upper millstone—the Imperial tax-extracting service—and a nether one in the shape of rapacious large-scale land-owners. This was the main cause of

[13] See Hussey, op. cit., p. 51.
[14] See p. 12.

the Byzantine Greek civilization's untimely economic and military collapse.

The credit for the Byzantine Greeks' successes is all their own. On the other hand, their failures have to be debited in large measure to the untoward effects of their importunately tenacious heritage from their Hellenic Greek predecessors. The two principal components of this heritage were the Hellenic *paideia* and the Roman Imperial regime. Their effects on Byzantine Greek life are examined at the end of the present chapter.

It has been noted already that a civilization's geographical extension is, at best, only a crude test of its success or failure, and the application of this test to the Byzantine civilization is particularly inconclusive because in this case we have to take account of two criteria—the extension of the Greek language in this period and the extension of the Greek form of Christianity—and the application of these two criteria presents us with two widely different findings.

In the Byzantine Age the Greek language did not repeat the dramatic geographical expansion that it had achieved temporarily during the foregoing Hellenic Age. But religion, not language, was the main medium of the expansion that the Byzantine civilization did achieve; and, in this medium, its achievement was fully a match for its predecessor's. Moreover, the expansion of the Greek language in the Byzantine Age, though relatively narrow, was nevertheless remarkable, considering the adverseness of the situation from which this expansion had to start.

The Age of the Principate, which had seen the Greek language attain its maximum geographical expansion as a vehicle of trade and culture, had also seen the depopulation of Greece itself. On the mainland of South-Eastern Europe, by the end of the Age of the Principate, Greek had almost entirely replaced other languages[15] as far north as the southern foot of the Aímos (Balkan) Range and nearly as far north as the headwaters of the Rivers Strymón (Struma) and Axiós (Vardar). In the seventh century, this Greek-speaking population, which had already been decimated by previous raids of barbarians from the North, was largely replaced by a permanent settlement, *en masse*, of immigrant Slavs.

At the mouths of the Struma and the Vardar the Slav intruders reached the north shore of the Aegean Sea; and, though the rest of the Aegean coast of Greece, from Thessaloníkê to Monemvasía inclusive, continued to be held by its pre-Slav Greek-speaking inhabitants, the

---

[15] The Bessian dialect of the Thracian language survived round the headwaters of the River Marica till the seventh-century Slav *Völkerwanderung* to the south of the Lower Danube. The Illyrian language still survives in Albania.

west side of Greece, including the western side of the Pelopónnêsos, seems to have been occupied by the Slav invaders, to judge by the survival there of Slavonic place-names. Two Slav peoples, the Mêlingoí and the Ezerítai, undoubtedly established themselves in Laconia on Mount Taÿgetos and in the lower basin of the River Evrótas, and there is evidence that the Mêlingoí were still speaking Slavonic in the first half of the fifteenth century.[16]

On the other hand, the Greek language had, by then, regained, long since, most of the ground, as far north as the basin of the River Vistrica (Aliákmon) inclusive, that it had lost in the seventh century. This re-expansion of Greek had been achieved partly by systematic re-colonization in the reign of the Emperor Nikêphóros I (802–11), but to a larger extent by a process of simultaneous religious and linguistic conversion that was promoted by the Emperor Basil I (867–86).[17] These converted Slavs became, and remained, Greek-speaking Orthodox Christians.[18]

This geographical re-expansion of the Greek language in South-Eastern Europe in the Byzantine Age is remarkable, but it is dwarfed by the extent of the expansion of the Orthodox—that is, the Greek—form of Christianity. At the present day, Eastern Orthodoxy is the prevalent religion throughout an area extending southwards as far as Crete and Cyprus and the southern boundary of the Soviet Republic of Georgia, westwards as far as the eastern shores of the Adriatic and the head of the Gulf of Finland, northwards as far as the southern shore of the Arctic Ocean, and eastwards as far as the north-western shore of the Pacific Ocean.

This vast spread of Eastern Orthodox Christianity has been partly due to the Byzantine Greek ecclesiastical authorities' linguistic liberality. Highly though they prized the Greek language for its own sake, as well as in virtue of its being the language of their church's liturgy and of the

---

[16] See Vasmer, M., *Die Slaven in Griechenland* (Berlin 1941), p. 18.

[17] See Leo VI (Basil I's son and successor), *Taktiká*, Dhiátaxis 18, sections 99–101, cols. 968–9 in Migne, *Patrologia Graeca*, vol. cvii.

[18] The nascent Hellenic Greek World, like the nascent Byzantine Greek World, had had to cope with the effects of an influx of barbarians. The Slav *Völkerwanderung* into Greece in the seventh century of the Christian Era had had a counterpart in the *Völkerwanderung* of speakers of the North-West-Greek dialect in or after the twelfth century B.C. But the Byzantines' task of assimilating the barbarian intruders was more formidable than the Hellenes' task, and the Byzantines' accomplishment of the task was a greater feat of cultural assimilation. The North-West-Greek barbarians spoke a dialect of the same language as the Mycenaean Greeks, and they had been living in the immediate neighbourhood of the civilized Mycenaean World before they had squatted on its ruins. The Slavs spoke a non-Greek language, and they came, not from Êpeiros, but from somewhere in Eastern Europe to the north of the Danube. Yet the Byzantine Greeks succeeded in assimilating the Slav settlers in Greece. Their achievement was the greater of the two, but they were assisted by their possession of Orthodox Christianity. This was a cultural instrument of a kind that had had no counterpart in the Hellenic Greeks' cultural armoury.

earliest, and most of the greatest, of the Christian Fathers, the Byzantine Greeks did not seek to impose Greek on converts outside the frontiers of the East Roman Empire. So far from that, they provided their non-Greek-speaking converts with alphabets for conveying their own languages, and they helped them to endow these languages with literatures that included original works, as well as translations from Greek works, not only Christian but also pre-Christian. This linguistic liberality eliminated one possible obstacle to conversion. But Orthodox Christianity's success in winning converts was mainly due to its positive attractiveness—a quality that is a better criterion of success than mere geographical expansion, however extensive.

The attractiveness of the Byzantine Christian Greek civilization was the asset on which the Emperor Basil I relied in initiating the policy of assimilating the Slav settlers in regions under the East Roman Imperial Government's control. This policy was successful, and its success had been foreshadowed by previous instances of conversion that had been spontaneous. About two centuries before Basil I's day, a Greek city, Thessaloníkê, had fascinated Pervound, the king of a neighbouring Slav people, the Rhynkínoi, in the Struma Valley, as irresistibly as, more than a thousand years earlier, the Skyth king Skyles had been fascinated by Borysthenes (Olbia).[19] Like Skyles, Pervound fell in love with Greek urban life. He liked to spend his time in Thessaloníkê, living in the Thessalonians' Byzantine Greek way. Moreover, the Rhynkínoi, unlike the Skyths, shared their king's friendly feelings towards their Greek neighbours. Though they eventually took up arms against the East Roman Imperial Government after failing to obtain redress for the Imperial Government's arbitrary arrest and deportation of Pervound, they resorted to this retaliation only reluctantly, when a joint intercession by them and by the Thessalonians on Pervound's behalf had obtained no redress, and, though the Rhynkínoi then besieged Thessaloníkê, they made it clear that they had no quarrel with the Thessalonians themselves.[20]

A more remarkable, and more important, spontaneous convert to the Byzantine Christian Greek civilization was Khan Symeon of Bulgaria (Khan 893–925; self-designated Emperor of the Bulgars and the Romans, 925[21]–7). Symeon was the son and second successor of Khan Borís (852–89), in whose reign, in the year 864, Bulgaria had been converted to Christianity under pressure of an East Roman military

---

[19] See p. 40.

[20] See *Sancti Demetrii Martyris Miracula*, Book II, chapter 4, in Migne, *Patrologia Graeca*, vol. cxvi, cols. 1340–60.

[21] S. Runciman, in *A History of the First Bulgarian Empire* (London 1930), argues convincingly, on p. 163 n. 2, and on pp. 173–4, that 925 was the date. H. W. Haussig, in *A History of Byzantine Civilization* (London 1971), p. 254, dates Symeon's assumption of the title 917.

demonstration. Borís had sent Symeon to be educated at Constantinople, and here Symeon had been so thoroughly captivated by the Byzantine Greek civilization that he was nicknamed *emíarghos* ('semi-Greek'). After his accession to the Bulgarian throne, Symeon was twice at war with the East Roman Empire, from 894 to 896 and again from 913 till his death in 927. In the first of these wars he was reacting to a provocation. In the second war, however, he was the aggressor, and he appears to have been aiming at acquiring the East Roman crown and uniting it with his own. If this was in truth Symeon's ambition, he was foiled by the skill of East Roman diplomacy and by the impregnability of the walls of Constantinople, but the failure of Symeon's military trials of strength with the East Roman Imperial Government did not damp his enthusiasm for the Byzantine civilization.

Throughout his reign, Symeon actively pursued the policy, initiated by his father Borís, of introducing Byzantine literary culture into Bulgaria in the local Slavonic language conveyed in an alphabet of its own. Borís had welcomed the Slavophone clergy who had been expelled from Moravia after the death, in 885, of Methódhios, the survivor of the two Thessalonian missionary brothers who had been invited to Moravia *circa* 863. The other brother, Constantine-Cyril, had invented an alphabet to convey the dialect of the Slavs in the hinterland of Thessaloníkê. After the reception of Constantine-Cyril's and Methódhios' Slavophone clergy in Bulgaria by Borís, a new and simpler Slavonic alphabet—the script known as Cyrillic today—had been devised in Bulgaria, and the Macedonian Slavonic language, written in this alphabet, has become the liturgical language of all the Eastern Orthodox Slavonic-speaking countries. It was also the original liturgical language of the Romance-speaking Roumans. In this propagation of Eastern Orthodox Christianity and Byzantine culture in Slavonic dress, Symeon played an important part, and this gives the measure of the attraction that the Byzantine civilization never ceased to have for a Bulgar who was the East Roman Empire's obstinate adversary because he was a disappointed pretender to the East Roman Imperial crown.

Bulgaria, which was the East Roman Empire's immediate neighbour in South-Eastern Europe, was thus the country in which the Slavonic version of the Byzantine civilization was created; but Bulgaria's historic role in the cultural history of the Eastern Orthodox Christian World was to transmit this Slavized Byzantine culture to other Slavonic-speaking countries—for instance, to Serbia and, above all, to Russia. The captivation of Russia was the Byzantine Greeks' greatest cultural achievement. It was a counterpart of the Hellenic Greeks' captivation of Rome. The first Eastern Orthodox missionaries to Russia were Greeks;

possibly all but two of the metropolitans of Kiev were also Greeks from at least as early as *circa* 1039 until the Mongol invasion of Russia in 1237;[22] and the earliest churches built in Russia, and the mosaics and frescoes with which they were adorned, were probably the work of Greek and Georgian[23] architects and artists. Yet the amazing rapidity with which the Byzantine culture acclimatized itself in Russia after the conversion of Prince Vladímir of Kiev in 989 is probably due in part to the fact that, thanks to the Greek Church's linguistic liberality, a Slavonic version of the Byzantine culture had already been created in Bulgaria and was available for export from there to other Slavonic-speaking countries.[24]

The history of the Kievan Russians' relations with the East Roman Empire is not unlike the history of the Mycenaean Greeks' relations with Minoan Crete. In both cases, the encounter was sudden and the effect of the more advanced civilization on the more backward one was profound. In both cases, again, the younger civilization overtopped and outlasted the older one. The Mycenaeans actually occupied Knossos, the chief city of the Minoan World, in the fifteenth century B.C. The Russians have twice come within an ace of conquering Constantinople, first in 860 and then in 1878, but on each occasion they just failed to attain their alluring objective.

Western Christendom already had its own version of Christianity, and it competed with Eastern Orthodox Christendom for the conversion of Northern Europe. In Moravia and Bohemia and Hungary the Roman Church was victorious; yet the seeds of Eastern Orthodoxy that had been sown in these three countries died hard,[25] and, in winning the competition for the conversion of Bulgaria and Russia, the Eastern Orthodox Church outflanked the Roman Church and thus secured for itself the vast field for expansion into Northern Asia.

Moreover, till at least as late as the collapse of the East Roman Empire in A.D. 1182–1204, Western Christendom was still conscious of the superiority of the Byzantine culture. At Venice and in Sicily, which had once been parts of the East Roman Empire's dominions, this consciousness is commemorated in architecture and visual art. The Byzantine

[22] Baron Meyendorff and N. H. Baynes, in Baynes and Moss, *Byzantium* (Oxford 1948), p. 374, state this categorically, but the evidence is inconclusive. For more recent discussions of the question, see Dvornik, F., *The Slavs: Their Early History and Civilization* (Boston 1956), p. 212; *eundem, Byzantine Missions among the Slavs* (New Brunswick 1970), pp. 272–3; Vlasto, A. P., *The Entry of the Slavs into Christendom* (Cambridge 1970), pp. 268–70 and 277–86.

[23] See Haussig, op. cit., p. 254.

[24] For details of the reception in Russia of the Slavonic version of the Byzantine civilization, see Dvornik, *The Slavs*, pp. 223–37; *eundem, Byzantine Missions*, pp. 273–4; Vlasto, op. cit., pp. 270–1 and 293–4; Haussig, op. cit., pp. 253–9.

[25] See Dvornik, *The Slavs*, pp. 103–4; *Byzantine Missions*, pp. 194–229; Moravcsik Gy., in *The Cambridge Medieval History*, vol. iv., 2nd edn., part i, pp. 573–7 and 586–7.

churches at Venice[26] and on Torcello Island and at Palermo and at Monreale, and the mosaics with which these churches are decorated, are as impressive monuments of Byzantine culture as any in Bulgaria, Serbia, Russia, and other non-Greek yet Eastern Orthodox Christian countries. Still more impressive is the cathedral of Aachen, modelled on the church of San Vitale at Ravenna,[27] which is Charlemagne's audacious but clumsy attempt to equip his empire with a counterpart of the Ayía Sophía. Moreover, the sacristies of many Western cathedrals and monasteries, in places far beyond the farthest western bounds of the East Roman Empire at its widest westward extension, contain Byzantine Greek works of art—cloisonné enamel work, ivories, silks—which they have treasured ever since they acquired them, by gift or by purchase or by robbery, in the Middle Ages.

The one direction in which the Byzantine Greek civilization and the Eastern Orthodox form of Christianity met with rebuffs was towards the east. Here in the fifth and sixth centuries of the Christian Era, during the period of overlap between the Hellenic and the Byzantine chapter of Greek history, there was a linguistic and theological anti-Greek revolt. The Egyptian, Syrian, and Armenian Christians could not eradicate from their Christianity the expression of Christian belief in terms of Hellenic Greek philosophy, but they could, and did, translate the Bible and the liturgy into their own languages, and they rejected the terms in which Orthodoxy was formulated at the Council of Chalcedon in 451. To the east and south of the Antitaurus and Amanus Ranges there were mass-secessions from Chalcedonian Orthodoxy, and the local minorities that adhered to it were branded as Melchites ('running dogs of the alien and oppressive Roman Empire', in twentieth-century Chinese parlance).

In the seventh century the Syrian and Coptic and Armenian Monophysite Christians welcomed the Arab Muslims' conquest of their countries as a liberation from East Roman rule, in the spirit in which, in the fifteenth century, the East Roman Orthodox themselves felt that to submit politically to the Ottoman Turkish Muslim power was a lesser evil than to submit ecclesiastically to the Pope. Eastward, Eastern Orthodoxy prevailed only in Caucasian countries where Monophysite Armenia was felt to be a greater political and cultural menace than the more powerful but more distant Orthodox East Roman Empire.

The secession of the Monophysite churches undid partially—though only partially—what Alexander had done, eight centuries before, when,

---

[26] Saint Mark's at Venice was modelled on the Church of the Holy Apostles at Constantinople (Haussig, op. cit., pp. 391 and 401).
[27] See Haussig, op. cit., pp. 238 and 391.

in overthrowing the Persian Empire, he had opened up South-West Asia and Egypt as fields for penetration by the Hellenic Greek culture. But in every other quarter of the compass the Byzantine Greek culture proved to be attractive, and even on the east, where Greek culture had to contend with alien civilizations which had distinctive attractions of their own, Hellenism had succeeded in imposing itself, west of the Euphrates, for 800 years before it had evoked, at last, an effective reaction. Even then, Hellenic Greek science and philosophy were able to dig themselves into the intellectual foundations of non-Chalcedonian Christianity and of Islam. These pre-Christian secular products of the Hellenic Greek intellect were an indispensable constituent of all Christian theology— Nestorian and Monophysite, as well as Chalcedonian—and they were therefore also indispensable for Islamic theology, which was worked out on the existing Christian pattern.

(iii) *Eastern Orthodox Christianity*

Eastern Orthodox Christianity was the Byzantine Greeks' key institution, but it has not been confined within the Byzantine Greek World's geographical and chronological limits. The extent of its geographical expansion has been noted already. In this vast area, Eastern Orthodox Christianity is still a going concern today, more than five centuries after the date at which the Byzantine chapter of Greek history came to an end, and it has also outlived three potent imperial secular regimes—the East Roman, the Ottoman, and the Muscovite— with which it has had to coexist at different stages of its own history and in different regions within its huge domain. Eastern Orthodox Christianity is one of the major spiritual forces and ecclesiastical structures of the present-day world.

When Christianity was miscarrying as a new Jewish sect, it was making its fortune as a new ecumenical religion, and the Greek language and the Greek way of life were the media in which Gentile Christianity took shape after it had broken out of its Jewish matrix and before it had broken up into separate sects of its own. Consequently, in all of Christianity's subsequent differentiations, there is an indelible Greek, as well as Jewish, element. The Attic *koine*, which is the latest pre-Modern form of the evolution of the Greek language, was the original language of the Christian scriptures. The Christians took over, as their 'Old Testament', the third-century-B.C. translation into the *koine* of the Jewish Hebrew scriptures. The works that compose the Christian 'New Testament' were written in the *koine*, and so were the works of the

Apologists and the Fathers, the Acts of the Councils, the Creeds, and the whole of the Greek-speaking Church's liturgy.[28] This Greek liturgy has been adopted, in translation, by the non-Greek-speaking Eastern Orthodox churches. In the churches that are outside the Eastern Orthodox communion the liturgy has been elaborated along different lines. Among all the Christian churches that are in existence today, the Greek-speaking branches of the Eastern Orthodox Church are unique in possessing the whole original corpus of Christian religious literature, and the whole of the Eastern Orthodox liturgy too, in the Attic *koine* in which this literature was inherited by the Christians (as it was in the case of the Old Testament) or was written by them (as was all the rest of it).

A language is not an emotionally and intellectually neutral means of communication. Every language conveys a distinctive way of feeling and thinking, and the Attic *koine* made its own impress on the Jewish scriptures when these were translated into it and on the constituents of the Christian 'New Testament' when these were composed in the *koine* itself. The Epistles attributed to Saint Paul (most of them correctly, some perhaps erroneously) and the Gospel according to Saint John contain theological passages which could not have been written without some acquaintance with the Hellenic Greek philosophical vocabulary and without some grasp of the meaning of its terms. These passages indicate that, though the earliest converts to Gentile Christianity may have been mainly drawn from an only semi-educated Greek-speaking urban lower-middle class, some of the earliest propagators of Christianity in the Hellenic World were already addressing themselves also to people who had received the Hellenic *paideia*; and they must themselves have had the same Greek higher education, at least in some degree. The Apologists, the Fathers, and the ecclesiastical statesmen who argued out the decisions of the Councils and drafted the officially accepted creeds had certainly received the *paideia* in full measure.

This was a bond between Hellenically educated Christians and non-Christian Hellenes. The personal links were closest during the two generations between the lifting, in 313, of the Roman Imperial Government's ban on Christianity and the suppression of other religions by successive turns of the screw. Saint Basil of Kaisáreia (330–79) and his contemporary Saint Gregory of Nazianzós received an Hellenic education at Constantinople and Athens, and at Athens the future anti-Christian Emperor Julian (then still a nominal Christian) was their fellow student. Saint John Chrysostom (354–407) and Theodórĕtos of Mopsouhestía (d. 428) were pupils of the famous non-Christian man of

---

[28] The Greek-speaking Church has clung to the use of the Attic *koine* in the liturgy (Krumbacher, K.: *Geschichte der byzantinischen Litteratur* (*527–1453*) , 2nd edn. (Munich 1897), p. 790; Dölger, F., in *The Cambridge Medieval History*, vol. iv, 2nd edn., part ii, p. 208).

letters, Livánios of Antioch.[29] By the time of Julian's reign (361–3), Christians were not only studying the non-Christian Hellenic Greek literature; they were giving instruction in it; and the Christian professors of it were hard hit, as Julian foresaw and intended, when the Emperor disqualified them from teaching outside the field of their own Christian literature.

If it is true that the Greek language itself had an effect on the feelings and ideas of its users, this must have been true, *a fortiori*, of the literature written in Greek—above all, the magnificent non-Christian literature of the so-called 'classical' age. The Christian Fathers were committing themselves to the *paideia* when they wrote their own works in neo-Attic. These Hellenic Christian works could be appreciated and emulated only if the *paideia* continued to be transmitted; and, when the suppression of non-Christian religions in the Roman Empire had been completed, the whole of the responsibility for the transmission of the *paideia* devolved upon Christian instructors. Their task required the perpetuation of education in pre-Christian Greek literature, and this, in turn, required the adoption of an ambivalent attitude towards non-Christian Greek authors. As addicts to non-Christian religious beliefs and practices, these 'pagans' must be deemed to be suffering the torments of hell. At the same time, their works had to be sedulously studied and servilely imitated as models of correct language and style.

This was the official attitude towards Hellenism in the Greek-speaking nucleus of the Eastern Orthodox Church. It was deflected only temporarily by the monks' capture of education and attempt to suppress the *paideia* in the latter part of the sixth century.[30] The *paideia* re-emerged from an eclipse that lasted for about 300 years. It has been noted already[31] that the ground for the contorted Byzantine Greek Christian stance in regard to the *paideia* had been prepared unwittingly by the initiators of the neo-Atticist movement in the generation of Augustus. It was they who had made the Byzantine attitude toward the 'classical' Hellenic literature psychologically possible. The neo-Atticists had deliberately divorced the study of a 'classical' work's language and style from a concern for its contents, in order to concentrate attention on the words without regard to their purport.

Considering how highly the Greek Eastern Orthodox ecclesiastical authorities prized the Greek language, their linguistic liberality towards their non-Greek converts is remarkable.[32] The thirteenth-century canonist Valsamón pronounced that all languages were eligible for

---

[29] See ibid., pp. 213–14; Marshall, F. H., in Baynes and Moss, *Byzantium*, p. 222.
[30] See p. 80.
[31] Ibid.
[32] Grégoire, H., in Baynes and Moss, op. cit., p. 118.

liturgical use.[33] The historic case is Constantine-Cyril's invention, in the ninth century, of an alphabet for conveying the Macedonian dialect of Slavonic, but by that time it had already been established in principle that the acceptance of Eastern Orthodox Christianity did not commit converts to adopting the Greek language. During his mission to the Moravian Slavs, Constantine-Cyril rejected his Frankish opponents' thesis that Greek, Latin, and Hebrew were the only languages in which it was lawful to celebrate the Christian liturgy.[34] The first step taken by Constantine-Cyril himself in his previous abortive mission to the Khazars *circa* A.D. 861 had been to study the Khazar dialect of Turkish with a view to inventing an alphabet for the conveyance of this. A precedent had been set by the licence that had been given to the Georgian converts to Orthodoxy to practise their religion in their own language and in an alphabet specially created for conveying it. In Georgia the Byzantine Greek Orthodox Christian missionaries had been in competition with the Armenian Monophysites. These had arrogated to themselves the right to use their own Armenian language, and *circa* A.D. 400 they had invented an alphabet for conveying this. If the Greek Orthodox Church had not conceded the same rights to the Georgians, these might have been tempted to purchase these rights from the Armenians by adopting Monophysitism, even at the risk of falling under Armenian cultural domination.

In regions in which the local Christian community was not linguistically homogeneous, there are records of cases of mutual linguistic tolerance—as, for example, between Greek-speakers and Syriac-speakers in Syria in the fourth century.[35] Theodórêtos visited a monastery at Zévghma on the Euphrates, and another between Antioch and Vérrhoia (Aleppo), in which Greek-speaking and Syriac-speaking monks met in the same church to chant antiphonally, each in their own language, in separate choirs.[36] The bi-national monastery at Zévghma had been founded about half-way through the fourth century. In another passage, Theodórêtos notes that this amiable practice had started at Antioch and had spread from there,[37] and at Antioch in 387 Saint John Chrysostom exhorted his Greek-speaking congregation to welcome the Syriac-speaking peasants who flocked into the city for the celebrations on Easter Sunday.[38] There is also evidence for antiphonal

[33] Grégoire, H., in Baynes and Moss, op. cit., p. 126.

[34] See Dvornik, *Byzantine Missions*, p. 115; Vlasto, op. cit., pp. 44-7.

[35] See Wellesz, E.: 'Byzantine Music and Liturgy', in *The Cambridge Medieval History*, vol. iv., 2nd edn., part ii, p. 139; Jones, A. H. M., in *The Crucible of Christianity* (London 1969), p. 118; and the present work, Appendix I to the present chapter.

[36] Theodoret, *Religiosa Historia*, chapter 5, for Zévghma; Cp. *eundem*, *Historia Ecclesiastica*, Book IV, chapter 28, sections 1-2. See further Appendix I to the present chapter.

[37] Theodoret, *Historia Ecclesiastica*, Book II, chapter 24, section 9.

[38] This exhortation can, of course, be interpreted as evidence that the Greek-speaking

singing in Greek and Latin in South-Eastern Italy.[39] At the celebration of the Eucharist at Jerusalem, the early Christian pilgrim Aetheria listened to the lessons being read in Greek and then being translated into Syriac and into Latin for the benefit of non-Greek speakers.[40] It is unfortunate that the friendly relations between fourth-century Greek-speakers and Syriac-speakers in Syria did not survive the strain put upon them by the fifth-century conflict over Christology which triggered off the anti-Greek Syrian nationalist movement. Even within the surviving remnant of the Orthodox ('Melchite') community in the Patriarchate of Jerusalem, a Greek-speaking dominant minority has behaved oppressively towards the Arabic-speaking majority in the Modern Age.[41]

The language used by an Eastern Orthodox church could be left optional, because language was merely a vehicle for conveying Orthodox Christianity's content. In regard to the content itself, there was no corresponding latitude. The ecclesiastical languages of the Orthodox churches are various, but their theology, their liturgy, their mysticism, and their monasticism are uniform.

The distinctive feature of Eastern Orthodox theology has been noted already. In contrast to Western Christian theology—Calvinist as well as Roman Catholic—Eastern Orthodox theology deliberately refrains from attempting to define the ineffable, and, in the Orthodox Christian vision of the Godhead, the ineffable is the ultimate reality. For Eastern Orthodox Christians, the heart of religion is not theology; it is the liturgy.[42]

In the Eastern Orthodox liturgy the chanting of hymns plays an important part, and Christian Greek hymnology has made a break with Hellenic Greek choral singing, both in its music and in the metre of the poetry. Christian liturgical singing has followed the Jewish pattern.[43] Christian hymns in this Jewish style seem to have been composed first in Syriac. The words of these hymns were divided into stanzas, and each

---

population of Antioch was less well disposed than the bishop was towards the Syriac-speaking peasantry of the surrounding countryside. Many of these peasants will have been the Antiochene magnates' tenants or serfs.

[39] Wellesz, op. cit.

[40] Aetheria (or Silvia), *Peregrinatio* in *Itinera Hierosolymitana* Saeculi IIII–VIII, Geyer, P. (ed.) (Vienna 1898), pp. 35–101, on p. 99; Éthérie, *Journal de Voyage*, Geyer's text with introduction and French translation by Pétré, H. (Paris 1948), pp. 262–3.

[41] See Bertram, Sir A., and Luke, M. C., *Report of the Commission Appointed by the Government of Palestine to inquire into the Affairs of the Orthodox Patriarchate of Jerusalem* (London 1921); Bertram, Sir A., and Young, J. W. A., *The Orthodox Patriarchate of Jerusalem: Report of the Commission Appointed by the Government of Palestine* (London 1926).

[42] See Hussey and Hart in *The Cambridge Medieval History*, vol iv, 2nd edn., part ii, pp. 304–5; Haussig, op. cit., pp. 230–2.

[43] See Wellesz in op. cit., pp. 137–8.

stanza had to have an identical number of syllables, since each was sung to the same melody.[44] Hymns in the Syriac metre, sung to the Syriac music,[45] were composed in Greek from about half-way through the fifth century onwards.[46]

The Greek in which the hymns were written was the Attic *koine*, which was already established as the biblical and liturgical language of the Greek-speaking part of the Christian Church. By this time the living language of everyday speech had changed from the *koine* into an early form of Modern Greek, and the change in structure had been accompanied by a change in the nature of the accentuation. The pitch-accent of the Hellenic Age had been replaced already by the stress-accent of present-day Greek, and the *koine*, as well as the living language, was now pronounced with the stress-accent. Consequently, in the metrical structure of the stanzas of a Christian Greek hymn, the main stresses had to be made to fall in the same places in each stanza, and the accentual structure of the verse had to be harmonized with the melody to which it was sung.[47]

The man of genius who made hymnology one of the major Byzantine Greek arts was a Syrian,[48] Rhomanós the Melodhós. He took orders in the Orthodox Church, served as a deacon at Beirut, came to Constantinople in the reign of the Emperor Anastasius I (491–518), and did his life-work there, mainly during Justinian I's reign (527–65), as a composer in Greek;[49] but, though he sang in Greek, 'he thought in Syriac'.[50] Rhomanós launched Byzantine Greek hymnology on a career in which it ran through several phases. Rhomanós' own form of hymn, the *Kondákion*, was succeeded, and was eventually almost entirely replaced in the liturgy, by the *kanón*—a variation on the same fundamental form of poetry and music. Famous *kanónes* were composed by some of the leaders of the pro-*eikón* party—Saint John of Damascus, his adoptive brother Kosmás, and Theodore the abbot of Stoúdhios' House–during the conflict over the veneration of *eikóns*.[51] After the restoration of peace between iconoclasts and iconodules in A.D. 843,

---

[44] See Wellesz in op. cit., p. 140. Cp. Trypanis, C. A., *Medieval and Modern Greek Poetry* (Oxford 1951), p. xv.

[45] Wellesz, op. cit., p. 153.

[46] Ibid., p. 143. See also Mêtsákês, K., (Thessaloníkê 1971), Βυζαντινὴ ὑμνογραφία pp. 171–509, especially pp. 171–93.

[47] Wellesz, in op. cit., p. 154; Trypanis, op. cit., p. xv.

[48] In a hymn in honour of Rhomanós, he is said to have been a Jewish convert to Eastern Orthodox Christianity. This statement is rejected by Mêtsákês, op. cit., pp. 376–8.

[49] Wellesz, in op. cit., pp. 143–6; Trypanis, op. cit., p. xv. The Greek texts of notices of Rhomanós in the *Mênolóyion* of the Emperor Basil II (Cod. Vat. 1613) and in Cod. 40 of the Patriarchal Library at Jerusalem are printed in Krumbacher, op. cit., pp. 663–4. The style of the *koine* in which Rhomanós composed is described in Mêtsákês, op. cit., pp. 472–82.

[50] Emereau, C., *Saint Ephrem le Syrien* (Paris 1919), p. 104, cited by Wellesz in op. cit., pp. 143–4.

[51] Wellesz, in op. cit., pp. 146–9; Dölger, F., op. cit., p. 255.

there was a fresh outburst of hymn writing. The composers in this phase included the Emperors Leo VI (886–912) and Constantine VII Porphyrogenitus (913–59).[52]

In the field of mysticism, the counterpart of Rhomanós the Melodhós was another man of genius who was Rhomanós' approximate contemporary. His name is unknown, because he wrote under the pseudonym of Dionysius the Areopagite. The Pseudo-Dionysius was inspired by the pre-Christian Greek mysticism of Plotinus and his successors in the Neoplatonic school of Hellenic philosophy; and the goal of Neoplatonic mysticism was also the goal of Byzantine Christian mysticism from first to last. The mystic aimed at a union of his human soul with God, and this spiritual objective had been enunciated in the fourth century by Saint Athanasius of Alexandria in startlingly ambitious terms. 'Christ became man in order that we may become God.'[53]

Pseudo-Dionysius was followed up, within the next hundred years, by John Klímakos and by Máximos the Confessor. A fresh impetus to Byzantine Greek mysticism was given by Symeon the New Theologian (*circa* 949–1022), and Symeon's 'hesychasm' ('pursuit of spiritual tranquillity') was revived on Mount Athos by Gregory of Sinai (d. 1346) and found a fourteenth-century champion in the Athonite monk Grégory Palamás.[54]

Mysticism is complementary to liturgy and to theology. The mystic's approach to the Godhead is individual and autonomous, in contrast to the inevitably authoritarian regulation of corporate worship and doctrine. For this reason, the ecclesiastical authorities are apt to keep a jealous eye on the mystics' practices and beliefs. But, if and when the authorities fall out with the mystics and try to discipline them, it is the mystics, not the authorities, who are likely to win popular sympathy and support.

Eastern Orthodox Christian mysticism had in it a materialistic vein. From John Klímakos onwards, the mystics of this school recommended yoga-like breathing-exercises as a physical aid to attaining the beatific vision. They held that the divine light which the vision revealed was 'uncreated'. This tenet involved them in theological controversy, for, if the light that they saw was 'uncreated', they were seeing a direct manifestation of God's energies, and this implied that God's energies were knowable and were therefore distinguishable and separable from his unknowable essence. Symeon the New Theologian had had to leave

---

[52] Wellesz, in op. cit., p. 149.

[53] Αὐτὸς γὰρ ἐνηθρώπησεν ἵνα ἡμεῖς Θεοποιηθῶμεν (Athanasius, *Oratio de Humanâ Naturâ a Verbo Assumptâ et de eius per Corpus ad Nos Adventu*, Migne, *Patrologia Graeca*, vol. xxv, col. 192).

[54] See Hussey, J. M., and Hart, T. A., 'Byzantine Theological Speculation and Spirituality', in *The Cambridge Medieval History*, vol. iv, 2nd edn., part ii, pp. 199–204.

Stoúdhios' House, where he had been a monk. The controversy over Grégory Palamás, the fourteenth-century champion of hesychasm, was more violent.

It is hard to see how it was possible for the theological implications of hesychasm to be accepted as Orthodox; yet Palamás' defence of hesychasm was twice pronounced to be orthodox by a council—first in 1341 and then again in 1351. Palamás was appointed Archbishop of Thessaloníkê, and after his death in 1359 he was canonized. His paradoxical triumph was due to a combination of causes. His first opponent, the Westernized Calabrian monk Barlaam, incurred odium among the Eastern Orthodox hierarchy; at a later stage, a turn of the political wheel brought Palamás' supporters into power in the remnant of the East Roman Empire, and popular feeling was on Palamás' side; but perhaps the strongest force that worked in Palamás' favour was the Orthodox Church's rooted distaste for logical consistency. This was the spirit to which Palamás appealed. We may guess that, in a Western Christian Council, Barlaam's arguments would have carried conviction instead of giving offence.[55]

Mysticism is linked, through asceticism, with monasticism.[56] In Eastern Orthodox Christendom, monks, as well as mystics, have been popular. Hermits have won more admiration than coenobites ('common-life' monks); they have been admired in proportion to the degree of their asceticism; and therefore stylites have been elevated metaphorically, as well as literally, to the top of the tree. A fifth-century stylite could make the public authorities tremble if he chose to mobilize against them the popular enthusiasm that he had aroused by his feat of endurance.[57] A fifth-century gang of monks could sabotage an ecumenical council by organized physical violence.[58] During the conflict over the *eikóns*, the monks took a leading part in the resistance to the iconoclast Emperors and were therefore particularly penalized and were even systematically persecuted, especially in the reign of Constantine V (741-75). But, for the iconoclast Emperors' purposes,

[55] For the fourteenth-century controversy over hesychasm and this controversy's historical background, see Hussey and Hart in *The Cambridge Medieval History*, vol. iv, 2nd edn., part ii, pp. 197-204; Dölger in ibid, pp. 220 and 223; Grégoire in Baynes and Moss, *Byzantium*, pp. 114-16; and the detailed and acute exposition in Runciman, *The Great Church in Captivity*, chapter 6: 'The Theology of Mysticism', pp. 128-58.

[56] See Hussey, *The Byzantine World*, pp. 114-34; *eandem* in *The Cambridge Medieval History*, vol. iv, 2nd edn., part ii, pp. 161-84; Delehaye, H., in Baynes and Moss, *Byzantium*, pp. 136-65; Haussig, op. cit., pp. 212 and 328-31.

[57] e.g. Saint Daniel of Anáplous versus Basiliscus in 477. (See Delehaye, H., in Baynes and Moss, *Byzantium*, pp. 145, 159, and 161.) However, the stylite form of asceticism has not survived in Eastern Orthodox Christendom. The last known stylite in the East Roman Empire is one in the tenth century (Runciman, op. cit., pp. 45-6).

[58] e.g. at the 'robber council' of Ephesus in 449. The gangster monks on this occasion were Monophysites from Egypt.

their repression of their opponents among the monks was 'counter-productive'.

However, the monks' interventions in politics were rare, and interventions by stylites, which were the most effective, were the rarest of all. Hermits were even excused from participating in the liturgy.[59] It was recognized and accepted that they were concerned obsessively with their own individual salvation,[60] but this did not make the hermits unpopular or lead to their being condemned as being anti-social. They were popular,[61] and were consequently also influential,[62] because their performance was admired for its own sake; and their holiness was also regarded as being a social asset because it was deemed to win God's favour for the whole Christian community. Actually it was a social asset in a more direct way, as well. In the rapidly changing social conditions of the eastern part of the Roman Empire in the fifth and sixth centuries, the holy man had provided opportunely for new social needs by filling a social vacuum. He had served as an authoritative arbiter in the domestic quarrels of village communities, and as the spokesman for a community's collective interests *vis-à-vis* the Imperial authorities. The holy man had been able to play this key role because he had been recognized to be personally disinterested, in view of his having manifestly detached himself from mundane life by sensational asceticism.[63] He had performed, in fact, something like the service that the less austere, but likewise politically neutral, Prophet Muhammad performed at Yathrib during the years 622–32, in the more primitive social milieu of an agricultural oasis in the Roman Empire's Arabian hinterland.

The coenobitic monasteries, too, performed direct social services. They gave hospitality to travellers, alms to the poor, nursing to the sick, and care to the aged.[64] There were not, however, in Eastern Orthodox Christendom any counterparts of the Western Christian nursing, teaching, military, or missionary vocational orders[65]—though individual Eastern Orthodox missionaries were as adventurous, intrepid, and devoted as those of any other Christian church. The bishop whom the Ecumenical Patriarch Phótios planted at Kiev as a swift riposte to the

---

[59] Hussey in *The Cambridge Medieval History*, vol. iv, 2nd edn., part ii, p. 476.

[60] See Delehaye, H., in Baynes and Moss, op. cit., pp. 152 and 163.

[61] As is indicated by the colloquial Greek name for them, καλόγεροι, meaning 'good old men' (Delehaye in Baynes and Moss, op. cit., p. 163).

[62] Runciman, op. cit., p. 37; Hussey in *The Cambridge Medieval History*, vol. iv, 2nd edn., part ii, p. 167.

[63] See Peter Brown's illuminating paper, 'The Rise and Function of the Holy Man in Late Antiquity', in *J.R.S.*, vol. lxi (1971), pp. 80–101.

[64] See Runciman, op. cit., pp. 42–3; Hussey, *The Byzantine World*, pp. 128 and 139.

[65] Delehaye, H., in Baynes and Moss, op. cit., p. 164; Hussey in *The Cambridge Medieval History*, vol. iv, 2nd edn., part ii, p. 167.

Russian naval raid on Constantinople in 860 must have been both a daring and a capable man. The Thessalonian brothers', Constantine-Cyril's and Methódhios', mission to Moravia was diplomatically delicate (Moravia lay within the Roman See's patriarchal domain) and was also politically hazardous (it drew on itself the hostility of the German hierarchy). The second founder—in fact, the effective founder—of the local Christian Church in England was a Greek monk, Theodore of Tarsós, an *émigré* living at Rome. He was sent on his mission after he had turned sixty-six and he lived on to spend more than twenty-one years (669-90) on the strenuous work of putting Christianity in England in order.[66] Though they were Greeks, Theodore and the Thessalonian brothers were scrupulously loyal to the Roman Church, in whose domain they were operating.

The hermits performed some practical services for society without taking any toll from it. The coenobitic monasteries took, besides giving. The tenth-century East Roman Imperial legislation indicates that monasteries, as well as bishops and large-scale lay landowners, were encroaching on the peasant freeholds. One of the later novels (νεαραί) in this series, Nikêphóros II Phokás' No. 19 (964),[67] is directed against the inefficient management of monastic property. In this edict, Nikêphóros bans the foundation of new monasteries, and invites would-be lay donors to devote their charity to rehabilitating existing monastic estates. Nikêphóros is unlikely to have taken this drastic action without good cause. He was personally pious; in his private life he was ascetically austere; and he was a friend and admirer of Saint Athanásios, who, with Nikêphóros' approbation, had founded the Great Lávra[68] on Mount Athos in 963. Nikêphóros himself had intended to end his days eventually on Athos as an anchorite.

This edict of Nikêphóros II's, together with the rest of the tenth-century Imperial agrarian legislation, gives an unfavourable impression of the role played by the monks in the life of the East Roman Empire in that century. The same picture is painted in darker colours by the twelfth-century scholar-cleric Efstáthios, the Archbishop of Thessaloníkê.[69] In the fifteenth century, when the Byzantine civilization was in its last agonies in the Greek nucleus of the expanded Byzantine World, monastic life on Mount Athos sank to its nadir. The so-called

[66] See Stenton, F. M., *Anglo-Saxon England*, 2nd edn. (Oxford 1947), pp. 130–41.

[67] Printed in Zachariä von Lingenthal, C. E., *Jus Graeco-Romanum*, pars iii (Leipzig 1857), pp. 292–6.

[68] Notwithstanding its name, this was not a *lávra*; it was a coenobitic monastery. A *lávra* was a group of separate cells whose occupants were subject to an abbot and were convened, once or twice a week, for common worship (see Delehaye, in Baynes and Moss, op. cit., p. 139). Saint Athanásios' 'Great Lávra' on Mount Athos was a coenobitic monastery in which 5 out of the 120 monks were allowed to live as hermits (ibid., p. 158).

[69] See ibid., pp. 156–7.

'idhiorrhythmic' dispensation, which was introduced at this stage,[70] was a virtual repudiation of personal poverty and of corporate discipline, which are the twin pillars of coenobitic monasticism, both Christian and Buddhist.

This was a sad lapse from the standard of Gregory of Sinai, the ascetic reviver of hesychasm on Mount Athos during the first half of the fourteenth century.[71] Gregory had migrated from Mount Athos to Bulgaria before his death, and from Bulgaria Gregory's ascetic ideals were carried to Russia by his Bulgarian disciple Cyprian of Trnovo, who became Metropolitan of Kiev in 1390. The consequence for monasticism in Russia was a struggle between the 'non-possessors', who stood for monastic poverty and for independence—at the price of poverty—from the Muscovite state, and the 'possessors', who aimed at making the Russian monasteries, and indeed the whole of the Russian Orthodox Church, into instruments of the autocratic secular regime. This struggle in Russia ended in the sixteenth century in the defeat of the 'non-possessors'. In Western Christendom the struggle over the same issue in the Franciscan Order had ended in the defeat of the 'spirituals' in the fourteenth century.[72]

The defeat was not complete in either case. In Russia, the ascetic ideal survived, and the hermits in whom it was embodied won prestige and influence which the ecclesiastical authorities and their secular masters were unable to undermine. It is also true that in Russia the influence of the hermits on the masses was not an unmixed blessing. The blind were leading the blind, and, all too often, they fell, together, into a reactionary obscurantism.

In at least two points the Eastern Orthodox Church has been more liberal in its constitution than the Roman Catholic Western Church. In the Eastern Orthodox Church, the laity has retained some of the most important of its original rights, and the clergy has not been subjected to a single monarchical authority. In the Roman Catholic Church, it is only since the Pontificate of Pope John XXIII (1958–63), nearly four and a half centuries after the Protestant revolt, that the laity has begun to be readmitted to an active participation in the Church's life and that the episcopate has reasserted the principle of collegiality in its relations with the Papacy.

In the Greek, though not in the Russian, Eastern Orthodox Church[73] the laity has always succeeded in making its voice heard.[74] In the

---

[70] Ibid., p. 157; Runciman, op. cit., p. 49.

[71] See Hussey and Hart in *The Cambridge Medieval History*, vol. iv, 2nd edn., part ii, pp. 199–200.

[72] For the early stages in the history of this struggle, see Brooke, R. B., *Early Franciscan Government: From Elias to Bonaventure* (Cambridge 1959).

[73] For the difference on this point, see Runciman, op. cit., p. 325.

[74] Ibid., pp. 53–4.

Eastern Orthodox Church as a whole, the laity has continued to receive communion in both kinds.[75] It is true that, since the rail marking off the sanctuary has been heightened into an *eikonóstasis*[76]—the equivalent of a Western rood-screen—the clergy's action in the celebration of the Eucharist has been withdrawn from the sight, though not from the hearing, of the congregation, but the laity takes an active part in the performance of the liturgy. It is the clergy's partner in the antiphonal singing.[77] Moreover, the laity's presence and participation is indispensable. An Eastern Orthodox priest cannot celebrate the Eucharist without this.[78]

In Eastern Orthodox Christendom the clergy has been kept in check by the sanction of public ridicule to which it has been subjected with impunity. Devout critics have protested against clerical pomp by assuming the role of fools (*saloi*) who puncture the solemnity of even the most solemn rites by performing antics.[79] Ribald critics have produced the same effect by staging mock performances of the liturgy, not excluding the Eucharist itself. The Emperor Michael III's boon companions relieved, in this way, their own and their patron's feelings,[80] and though Imperial patronage made them conspicuous, they were not unique. The humourlessness and boringness of East Roman ceremonial, both ecclesiastical and secular, invited a vigorous retort, and it duly provoked one.[81]

The bond between the laity and the clergy has been maintained in Eastern Orthodox Christendom not only by the laity's continuing participation in the liturgy but also by the non-celibacy of the clergy below the rank of bishop. A bishop must be wifeless; but he may be a widower; he need not be a monk, though it has become customary, since the thirteenth century, for monks to be appointed to bishoprics of all degrees up to the summit, which is the Patriarchate. Below the rank of bishop, a cleric may be a married man if he has married before he has taken orders. A married priest may not contract a second marriage if he becomes a widower, but second marriages are frowned upon when they are contracted by laymen, though for laymen they are not prohibited.

[75] Runciman, op. cit., pp. 7 and 50. 'Men and women, and even newly baptised children, are given [both] bread and wine [at the Communion Service], and they [the Eastern Orthodox Christians] emphatically condemn the Papists [*de Paus-gezinden*] for withholding the wine from the laity.'—Cornelis de Bruyn, *Reizen door de Vermaadste Deelen van klein Asia . . . en Palestina* (Delft 1698), p. 111, col. 1.

[76] See Haussig, op. cit., p. 227.

[77] Hussey, *The Byzantine World*, p. 112; Dölger in *The Cambridge Medieval History*, vol. iv, 2nd edn., part ii, p. 254.

[78] Runciman, op. cit., p. 50.

[79] Haussig, op. cit., pp. 78 and 222.

[80] See *Theophanes Continuatus*, Book IV, chapter 38 (pp. 200-2 Bonn).

[81] An extreme case is the parody of the Eucharist called 'The Akolouthía of the man without a beard' (i.e. the eunuch). For details, see Krumbacher, op. cit., pp. 809-10.

Thanks to the Eastern Orthodox Church's closer adherence to the institutions of the early Church, its clergy has never lost touch with the people. In the Eastern Orthodox Church there has not been any counterpart of the Western Reformation,[82] and there has been no anti-clericalism among the laity[83]—at least, there was none until, in and after 1453, the Ecumenical Patriarch was invested by the Ottoman Imperial Government with civil authority over all Eastern Orthodox Christians within the Ottoman Empire's frontiers, in addition to his ecclesiastical authority over Eastern Orthodox Christians domiciled within the boundaries of his own Patriarchate.

This new role, which the Ecumenical Patriarch now had to play perforce, made it necessary to associate laymen—for instance, jurists and financiers—with clerics to serve the Patriarch in his performance of his civil duties as head of the Ottoman *Rum milleti* (the community of all the Eastern Orthodox Christian subjects of the Ottoman Empire).[84] This raised questions about the distribution of power between clerics and laymen on the Ecumenical Patriarch's staff, in his capacity as head of the *Rum milleti*. The clerics curbed the laymen's power in the eighteenth century.[85] In the nineteenth century, when the constitutions of the non-Muslim Ottoman millets were reformed under the Ottoman Imperial Government's auspices, the lay representation was strengthened in all of them, including the *Rum milleti*.[86] However, such tension as there was between clerics and laity in the *Rum milleti* arose, not out of the Ecumenical Patriarch's functions as an Eastern Orthodox prelate, but out of his functions as an Ottoman civil servant.

In spite of the Patriarch of Constantinople's assumption of the title 'ecumenical' (never recognized by the Papacy), neither the Patriarch of Constantinople nor the head of any other regional Eastern Orthodox Church has ever made the claim, made by the Pope, to be the head of the whole Christian Church. As a prelate (in distinction from his civil functions under the Ottoman regime), the Patriarch of Constantinople has never considered himself to be more than the head of one of a number of regional churches that hold an identical doctrine but are independent of each other administratively. The Patriarch of Constantinople and the heads of all the other independent Eastern Orthodox

---

[82] As is pointed out by Runciman, op. cit., p. 385.

[83] Ibid., p. 53.

[84] Ibid., pp. 171–6.

[85] Ibid., p. 176.

[86] See Davison, R. H., *Reform in the Ottoman Empire, 1856–1876* (Princeton 1963), chapter 4: 'The Reorganisation of the Non-Muslim Millets, 1860–1865', on pp. 114–35, especially pp. 126–9. Lay control and popular representation were not extended so far in the reform of the Orthodox Christian millet as they had been in the preceding reform of the Armenian (Gregorian Monophysite) millet, and the Orthodox laity did not press so strongly as the Armenian laity had pressed for having a greater say than before in the management of their millet's affairs.

Christian Churches have always conceded that the Pope is, not supreme over them, but *primus inter pares*, so long as he is not in schism. After the Roman and the Constantinopolitan Church had excommunicated each other in 1054, the Patriarch of Constantinople became *primus inter pares*, according to the Eastern Orthodox point of view, provisionally—that is to say, for so long as the Pope might continue to forfeit his traditional honorary precedence.[87]

When we trace the Eastern patriarchates' independence of each other back to its historical origins, we find these in the partition of the former dominions of the First Persian Empire among the successors of Alexander the Great. Antioch and Alexandria had been the respective capitals of the Seleucid and Ptolemaic Macedonian Greek monarchies, and, though both cities had been incorporated subsequently in the Roman Empire, it remained inconceivable that either of them would ever submit to being subordinated to the other. Nor, when they became the seats of Christian churches, was either of them willing to recognize the ecclesiastical supremacy of Rome; for, though Rome had become the political capital of the Mediterranean basin, the Christian community in Rome was at first an isolated outpost of Christendom, and the Christians in the West were, for long, outnumbered overwhelmingly by those in the Levant. Thus, from the outset, there were three major cities, two of them in the Levant, whose Christian churches were independent of each other *de facto*, in spite of the Roman Church's claim to supremacy over all others.

When Constantine became, in 324, the ruler of the entire Roman World, the churches of Byzantium and Jerusalem were still obscure. Byzantium was subordinate ecclesiastically to Heraclea (Hêrákleia) on the Thracian shore of the Sea of Marmara, and Jerusalem to Caesarea (Kaisáreia) on the coast of Palestine. Between the year 330, in which Byzantium, transformed into Constantine's city, was inaugurated as the New Rome, and the year 451, the date of the Council of Chalcedon, Constantinople, for political reasons, and Jerusalem, for sentimental reasons, were raised to the status of patriarchates,[88] and the whole

---

[87] See Runciman, op. cit., p. 23. The Patriarchates of Rome and Constantinople repealed in 1965 their respective excommunications of each other which had been in force since 1054, except for some brief intervals during which Constantinople recognized Rome's supremacy from the Western Christian powers for the East Roman Government. On 7 December 1965, the reciprocal anathemas of 1054 were cancelled simultaneously by the Ecumenical Patriarch Athênaghóras in the Patriarchal Church of Saint George in the Phanar quarter of Istanbul and by Pope Paul VI in St Peter's in the Vatican City. At each of these two simultaneous ceremonies, representatives of both churches participated. On the same day, a moving declaration was published in the names of Paul VI and of Athênaghóras I and his synod. The official English translation of this document was printed in The *New York Times* of 8 December 1965.

[88] See Runciman, op. cit., p. 21. The losers were Antioch and Ephesus, whose church had previously ranked not far below those of Antioch, Alexandria, and Rome. The Patriarch of Constantinople was given the second place in the order of honorary precedence in 381, thus taking

territory of the Roman Empire, save for Cyprus, was distributed among the five patriarchates that were now in existence.

The Church of Cyprus remained independent of all five patriarchates, and Cyprus' 'autocephalous' status, taken together with the increase in the number of the patriarchates to five from the original figure three, foreshadowed future increases in the number of the Eastern Orthodox churches. Countries converted to Eastern Orthodox Christianity that lay beyond the frontiers of the East Roman Empire—for instance, Georgia (*alias* Iberia) and other Caucasian states—were, in principle, added as a matter of course to the Patriarchate of Constantinople's ecclesiastical domain. This was, however, awkward politically for the governments of the converted states, since the Patriarch of Constantinople was the East Roman Emperor's, and subsequently the Ottoman Pādishāh's, political subject and was also one of his senior civil servants—virtually under the East Roman regime and juridically under the subsequent Ottoman regime. Consequently the government of a state converted to Eastern Orthodox Christianity has usually sought to safeguard its political independence by securing ecclesiastical independence for its church. The East Roman Imperial Government's recognition in 927 of a Bulgarian Patriarchate, independent of the Patriarchate of Constantinople, was therefore an epoch-making event; for it created a precedent that has been followed by the Eastern Orthodox successor-states, first of the East Roman Empire, and then of the Ottoman Empire.

Russia, being geographically remote from both the East Roman Empire and its heir the Ottoman Empire, was in no hurry to obtain ecclesiastical independence. It remained under the ecclesiastical jurisdiction of the Patriarchate of Constantinople till 1589, when a Patriarchate of Moscow was created, with the consent of all four eastern patriarchates, subject to its ranking below them all.[89] The Russian Orthodox Christian populations that had been incorporated, meanwhile, in the Roman Catholic Kingdom of Poland–Lithuania remained under the Constantinopolitan Patriarchate's jurisdiction till they became, first Uniate adherents of the Roman Church in 1594–6, and then once again Orthodox Christians—subject now to the Russian

rank above all the other four Patriarchs except the Pope. In 451 the Patriarch of Constantinople was assigned, for his ecclesiastical domain, the three secular dioceses Thrace, Asiana, and Pontica. This was a belated revival, on the ecclesiastical map, of the kingdom (capital, Ephesus) of Alexander's successor Lysimachus, which had been liquidated in 281 B.C. The praetorian prefecture of the Eastern Illyricum, and everything to the west of it in both Europe and Africa, was assigned to the Patriarchate of Rome. In terms of territory, Rome thus received the lion's share, but not in terms of population or of wealth. The Eastern Illyricum, Calabria, and Sicily were transferred from the Roman to the Constantinopolitan Patriarchate by the East Roman Imperial Government in 732, or at any rate by 751.

[89] See ibid., p. 331.

Orthodox Church—when they became subjects of the Russian state. This process was begun in 1667, was continued in the partitions of Poland–Lithuania in 1772, 1793, and 1795, and was completed after the Second World War, when Eastern Galicia and Carpathoruthenia were annexed to the Ukrainian constituent republic of the Soviet Union.

The most crippling of the progressive losses of ecclesiastical subjects that the Patriarchate of Constantinople has suffered have been due to the assertion of the ecclesiastical independence of the Ottoman Empire's Orthodox Christian successor-states. It they had not asserted this, their achievement of political independence would have been incomplete, for, though the Patriarch of Constantinople's political status in the East Roman Empire may be held to have been ambiguous, there is no doubt that he was an Ottoman civil servant until the *Rum milleti* was liquidated simultaneously with the Ottoman Empire itself. The most striking of the ecclesiastical secessions from the Patriarchate of Constantinople was that of the Kingdom of Greece in 1833. This was one of its earliest acts as an independent state. The Patriarchate of Constantinople recognized the *fait accompli* reluctantly in 1850. Every loss of territory by the Ottoman Empire in Europe brought with it a corresponding loss for the Patriarchate of Constantinople.

Thus the Eastern Orthodox Church is an association of administratively independent churches[90] that have an identical doctrine and an identical liturgy, though the liturgy and the scriptures and the corpus of patristic literature are conveyed in different churches in different ecclesiastical languages. The Eastern Orthodox Church has no central monarchical government,[91] and the ecclesiastical constitutions of the severally independent churches of the Eastern Orthodox communion

[90] This administrative independence of each of the local churches that adhere to the Eastern Orthodox creed and rite was asserted when the Churches of Constantinople and Rome excommunicated each other in 1054, and again when, in 1965, they each annulled their reciprocal anathemas. In 1054 the Patriarchates of Antioch and Jerusalem did not follow suit to the Patriarchate of Constantinople in breaking off relations with the Papacy. (See Runciman, S., *A History of the Crusades*, vol. i (Cambridge 1951), p. 97.) In 1965 the Eastern Orthodox churches of the Kingdom of Greece and of the Soviet Union did not follow suit to the Patriarchate of Constantinople in its reconciliation with the Roman Church. The act of reconciliation had been performed by the Constantinopolitan and Roman Churches on 7 December 1965. On 9 December the Holy Synod of the Church of Greece announced that it did not recognize the validity of this act. On 23 December the Church of the Soviet Union signified that, in its view, the Acts of 1054 had not been annulled juridically by the Act of 1965.

[91] The nearest thing in Eastern Orthodox Christendom to a common central institution is the federation of Basilian monasteries on the Athos peninsula. The earliest of these was the Greek Great Lávra, founded in 963 by Saint Athanásios the Athonite (see p. 104). Besides a number of further Greek foundations on Athos, a Georgian monastery was founded there *c.* 979, a Russian one in 1169, a Serbian one in 1197. In the eleventh century there was a short-lived Amalfitan monastery on Athos which observed the Latin rite (see Runciman, *The Great Church in Captivity*, p. 447). Next to Jerusalem, Athos has been Eastern Orthodox Christendom's most frequented pilgrimage resort. It is one of the curiosities of history that, until the eighth century, Athos lay within the ecclesiastical domain of the Pope.

are not monarchical either, except in so far as some of them are, or have been, controlled autocratically by the secular governments of the states with which these churches are respectively conterminous. In Russia, for example, the Patriarchate that had been created in 1589 was deliberately allowed by Peter the Great to fall into abeyance in 1700. After that, the Orthodox Church in the Russian Empire was administered virtually as a department of state from 1721 until 1917, when the Patriarchate was re-established by the Imperial Russian regime's Communist successors.

The Patriarchate of Constantinople has never been governed monarchically. Under the East Roman Imperial regime a Patriarch of Constantinople was chosen by the Emperor from among three candidates presented by a synod of metropolitans whose sees lay within the Constantinopolitan Patriarch's domain, and the synod was also empowered to depose the Patriarch.[92] There was also a resident synod (σύνοδος ἐνδημοῦσα) composed of bishops residing in Constantinople.[93] Under the Ottoman Imperial regime, the balance of power between the synod and the Patriarch changed in the synod's favour. The senior ecclesiastical permanent officials of the Patriarchate now became members of the synod *ex officio*, and Patriarchal decrees required the synod's endorsement to make them binding.[94] However, under both regimes alike, the Imperial Government could, and did, make its will prevail not only in the election and the deposition of Ecumenical Patriarchs, but also in their conduct of business while they were in office.

Wherever Eastern Orthodox Christianity was adopted beyond the frontiers of the East Roman Empire, it carried with it the melodies of its liturgy and the architecture and the art in which its tenets and its feelings were expressed. These aural and visual accompaniments enhanced Eastern Orthodoxy's attractiveness and were potent aids to the propagation of it. They established themselves in the converted countries simultaneously with the Church itself; and, though the first Byzantine clerics, monks, architects, and artists there were immigrant Greeks, the Byzantine culture that the Church thus introduced soon struck root locally and was maintained and developed by the converted peoples themselves. The rapidity of this process of acculturation was not surprising in Bulgaria; for Bulgaria's territory was former Roman ground; Bulgaria was the East Roman Empire's next-door neighbour; and Byzantine culture had already been seeping in before the conversion of Bulgaria to Christianity in 864. The rapidity of the conquest of Russia

[92] Ibid., p. 27.

[93] Herman, E., in *The Cambridge Medieval History*, vol. iv, 2nd edn., part ii, pp. 109–10.

[94] Runciman, ibid., p. 173; Βακαλόπουλος, Α. Ε., Ἱστορία τοῦ νεοῦ Ἑλληνισμοῦ, vol. ii, part i (Thessaloníkê 1964), p. 160.

by Byzantine culture, after the conversion of Russia in 989, is more remarkable, considering that Russia was insulated from the East Roman Empire geographically by the double barrier of the Black Sea and the Eurasian steppe, and that Russia was also a vast country by comparison, not only with Bulgaria, but with the East Roman Empire itself. Yet the penetration of Russia by Byzantine culture did not come to a halt at Kiev; it quickly spread still farther northwards to Novgorod.

The contrast between the Byzantine and the previous Hellenic style of Greek architecture has been noticed in the preceding chapter.[95] In the visual arts, too, the Byzantine civilization's greatest achievements were new departures. Though the Byzantines eschewed monumental three-dimensional sculpture and bas-reliefs, they cultivated the art of making miniature bas-reliefs on ivory[96] and metal plaques. In the two-dimensional art of painting, their virtuosity in reproducing the late Hellenic style is less interesting than their creation of an original style of their own for their *eikóns*. Haussig traces the origin of the Byzantine *eikón* back to the portraits on pre-Christian Egyptian mummy-cases. He believes that the earliest Christian Egyptian *eikóns*, too, were portraits of historical human beings; that their purpose was commemorative, not devotional; and that the representation on the *eikóns* of the Christian pantheon—saints, martyrs, the Theotókos, and Christ himself—was a subsequent new departure.[97]

Byzantine mosaic work was also virtually a new departure; for it, too, was used by the Byzantines for a new purpose and in a new style.[98] In the Hellenic Age, mosaic work, like the painting of vases, had been, in the Hellenes' own estimation, merely a minor decorative art. Hellenic mosaics are naturalistic, and their commonest use was for the decoration of the floors of courtyards and rooms in secular buildings. When the Byzantines transformed the dark *cella* of a temple into the interior of a church into which the sunlight was admitted through windows, they used mosaics to adorn the inner sides of a church's walls and the under sides of its apses and domes, and they made their mosaics into a medium for major works of religious art. They also discovered—whether accidentally or experimentally—how to make figures portrayed in mosaic appear to come alive. The Byzantine mosaicists set their tesserae

---

[95] In the present context, it may be noted that the development of the architectural form of Byzantine churches was partly governed by the development of the choreography of the Eastern Orthodox liturgy. See Grabar in *The Cambridge Medieval History*, vol. iv, 2nd edn., part ii, p. 329; Haussig, op. cit., pp. 230–2.

[96] See Grabar in *The Cambridge Medieval History*, vol. iv, 2nd edn., part ii, p. 323 and 344.

[97] See Haussig, op. cit., p. 226.

[98] See L'Orange, H. P., and Nordhagen, P. J.: *Mosaics* (London 1966), chapter i, 'From Floor Mosaics to Vault Mosaics,' and chapter vi, 'Technique and Intention in Monumental Mosaics'.

slightly unevenly,[99] so that, when the light catches them, they flicker and shimmer, and, when the spectator moves, the figures' eyes seem to follow him. The Byzantine mosaicists' creation of this optical illusion of movement was as subtle a feat of finesse as the Hellenic architect's creation of the optical illusion of straightness. In both cases the illusion was produced by a nicely calculated irregularity that was minute in terms of physical measurements but was magical in its optical effect.

(iv) *The Incubus of the East Roman Empire*

Runciman and Haussig have pointed out[100] that the Byzantine culture came into flower when the East Roman Empire went into decline. The Empire's decline was portended in its tenth-century agrarian legislation; and the tenth century was the age in which the Byzantine visual arts began to blossom. The tenth-century renaissance of the Hellenic style in miniature bas-reliefs was followed in the eleventh century by the animation of mosaic work which transformed this into a new art. As the Empire continued to decline, the arts continued to ascend. The East Roman Empire's last phase, which ran from 1261 to 1453, was politically and economically catastrophic but was artistically creative. On first thoughts, it seems paradoxical that, in the history of the East Roman Empire, the degree of artistic achievement should have varied inversely with the degree of Imperial power. On second thoughts, this can be seen to indicate that the East Roman Empire was an incubus on the life of its subjects, and that the alleviation of the political burden, thanks to the waning of the Empire's strength, released energy for non-political activities. The arts, at any rate, throve on the Empire's decline, in spite of the anarchy and impoverishment that this political and economic adversity brought with it.

Unfortunately for the Byzantine Greeks, two of their legacies from the Hellenic Greeks, the East Roman Empire and the Hellenic *paideia*, retained a hold over them which they failed to shake off, and they paid dearly for this servitude to the past. The East Roman Empire did not succeed in its attempts to subjugate the Eastern Orthodox Church. This Church survives today, more than five centuries after the liquidation of the Empire in 1453, and more than half a century after the liquidation, in 1922, of the Ottoman Empire, which was the last of the Roman Empire's five avatars in the Levant. But the Church had a hard struggle to escape from the Empire's toils, and it has not come out unscathed.

---

[99] See ibid., pp. 9–10. This could not be done in the setting of floor-mosaics; nor, on floors, could fragile materials be employed (ibid., pp. 47 and 57).

[100] See Runciman, *The Great Church in Captivity*, p. 16; *eundem*, *The Last Byzantine Renaissance* (Cambridge 1970), *passim*; Haussig, op. cit., pp. 302–3.

The Imperial regime's blighting effect on the economic life of its subjects was more thorough and more rapid, and the Empire's pretensions also bedevilled the Byzantine Greeks' political relations with their neighbours. As for the Hellenic *paideia*, its survival prevented the emergence, in the Byzantine Age, of a cultivated literature in Modern Greek, though Modern Greek had replaced Hellenic Greek as the Greek people's living language already during the transitional period A.D. 284-602, before the Byzantine Age of Greek history had begun.

The tenacity of both the Empire and the *paideia* is astonishing. In the seventh century the Empire seemed to be dissolving in anarchy. In the cities there was widespread civil war, and the open country was overrun by foreign enemies: the Persians, followed by the far more dynamic Muslim Arabs, in Asia and Africa, and in Europe the Slavs migrating southwards *en masse*. Yet, contrary to all reasonable expectations, the Empire survived its seventh-century ordeal. Moreover, it collapsed and revived twice more—in the eleventh century and in the thirteenth century—or three times more if the Ottoman Empire is reckoned, as it should be, to have been yet another revival of the East Roman Empire under Turkish, instead of Greek, management.

Meanwhile, the monks had failed as signally to kill the Hellenic *paideia*[101] as the Persians, Arabs, and barbarians had failed to kill the Empire. Half-way through the ninth century, the *paideia* was resuscitated after it had lain dormant—but not dead and buried—for more than 200 years. From Phótios' generation onwards, the *paideia* continued to hypnotize Greek men of letters until the liquidation, in the fifteenth century, of the last fragments of the Empire at Constantinople and in the Pelopónnêsos and at Trebizond. After that, it hypnotized Western men of letters when it was transmitted to the West in the fifteenth century by a handful of Byzantine Greek refugees. By that time there was a well-established literature in the Western peoples' living languages, and, in Dante, the West had produced a poet whose works in the vernacular were a match for anything that had ever been written in Latin or Greek. Yet the 'classical' Greek and Latin literature held the Western educated public spellbound in the early modern age of Western history, and the spell was not broken till the hard-fought 'Battle of the Ancients and the Moderns' was won by the Moderns towards the close of the seventeenth century. It was only then that the Westerners plucked up the courage to think and investigate for themselves, and to believe in the validity of

---

[101] According to Haussig, op. cit., pp. 80-3, the control of education—including higher education—had been captured, before the close of the sixth century, from the Hellenically educated lay men of letters by the monks, who were hostile to Hellenism. Other scholars dissent from Haussig on this point.

their own observations and discoveries, even when these conflicted with the lore of 'the Ancients'.

The master-institution of the Byzantine Greeks was the Eastern Orthodox Church, and therefore the East Roman Empire's impact on the Church was the most fateful of all the Empire's effects on Greek life in the Byzantine Age.

In theory, a Christian Roman Emperor's authority, like a Muslim Caliph's, was confined to the field of non-religious affairs. The taking of decisions on religious issues was the prerogative of the legitimate religious authorities. The Emperor's duty, like the Caliph's, in matters of religion was simply to support these authorities by putting the civil power at their service for giving effect to whatever they might have decided. But suppose that the Church was divided against itself: who, then, were the legitimate religious authorities, and where did the Emperor's duty lie?

Constantine the Great was confronted with this problem when he took the Christian Church under his patronage. By the fourth century the Church had become the most powerful non-political institution within the Empire. Its power had grown so great that any schism in the Church was bound to be a threat to the Empire's political cohesion, and this fact forced the Emperor's hand. His own undisputed political duty of trying to hold the Empire together compelled him to intervene in the Church's domestic disputes. The Emperor's interest was imperative, but it was negative. He was not concerned to take one side against the other in an ecclesiastical quarrel, but he was pressingly concerned to help the Church to recover its unanimity. Constantine and his successors on the Imperial throne tried but failed to save the Church from falling to pieces, and their unsuccessful endeavours involved them in taking sides, which was just what they had wished to avoid doing.

Constantine saw that the only organ of ecclesiastical authority that could possibly arrive at an authoritative consensus was an ecumenical council. He also saw that only the Emperor was in a position to convene a council, and that only he, again, had the power to give effect to a council's decisions—if it arrived at any decisions—by endorsing and promulgating and enforcing these. Unfortunately the decisions of ecumenical councils have never commanded universal assent, and consequently the Church has broken up. In the fifth century the Nestorians and the Monophysites hived off from the rest of the Church. In the eleventh century the Chalcedonian remnant split into an Eastern Orthodox and a Roman Catholic wing. In the seventeenth century the 'Old Believers' seceded from the reformed Russian Orthodox Church, as in the sixteenth century the Protestants had seceded from the unreformed Roman Catholic Church. The intervention of the Roman

Emperors and the subsequent local secular governments had proved ineffective on each of these successive occasions in the history of the Christian Church's progressive fragmentation.

When ecclesiastical factions have disagreed and have refused to be reconciled, all that any Roman Emperor or any subsequent local secular ruler has been able to do has been to align himself with the party that has seemed to him to represent the majority or at any rate to be the winner. But, even when he has guessed right, he has not been able to prevent the loser, even if this has been the weaker party, from seceding. When the secular ruler has guessed wrong, he or his heirs have been constrained to reverse his policy. Constantius II's and Valens' miscalculation in aligning themselves with the Arians was redressed by Theodosius I. The Syrian and Amorian Emperors' miscalculation in aligning themselves with the Iconoclasts was redressed abortively by the Empress Eirênê and definitively by the Empress Theodora. The Palaeologan dynasty's miscalculation in acknowledging the Papacy's supremacy over the Eastern Orthodox churches was exposed in the rejection of the Union that had been negotiated at Florence in 1439 by the Emperor John VIII. The union was rejected by the Russian Church in 1441, by the Constantinopolitan Church in 1454 virtually, and by all four Eastern Patriarchs in 1484 expressly.[102]

On religious issues, East Roman Emperors were always defeated in the long run if their policy fell foul of the preponderant public feeling.[103] But the eventual inclination of the balance was impossible to predict. When Leo III declared in favour of Iconoclasm in 726, he was correctly interpreting the will of his own army corps, the Anatolikoí, and he was also correct in reckoning that these Asian troops were more potent at this time than the troops of Greece and Italy. In 787, Eirênê had to transfer to Níkaia, beyond the range of the Iconoclast garrison of Constantinople, the council that reversed Leo III's policy for the first time. Even so, this first reinstatement of the *eikóns* lasted for only twenty-five years. Yet, by 843, the balance of public feeling had inclined so decisively against the Iconoclasts that Theodora was able to re-instate the *eikóns* effectively and lastingly.

In Constantine I's day, and again, for a short spell, in Justinian I's day, the seats of all five Patriarchates were under the Imperial Government's effective rule; but, of the five, the Constantinopolitan Patriarchate was always exposed to the heaviest pressure from the civil power, since its seat was the capital of the East Roman Empire, and the East Roman Imperial Government survived after the West Roman

---

[102] For the Council of 1484, see Runciman, *The Great Church in Captivity*, p. 228.

[103] This point is made by Grégoire in Baynes and Moss, *Byzantium*, p. 130, and by Runciman, *The Great Church in Captivity*, pp. 64, 70, 73–4.

Imperial Government's dissolution. In the trials of strength between East Roman Emperors and Eastern Orthodox ecclesiastical authorities, the Constantinopolitan Patriarchs had to bear, on behalf of all the Eastern Orthodox churches, the brunt of the civil power's invasions of the ecclesiastical authorities' rightful jurisdictional domain.

The Eastern Orthodox ecclesiastical authorities profited by the recession of the East Roman Empire's frontiers. By 726 the entire domains of the Orthodox Patriarchates of Alexandria and Jerusalem, and all but a fragment of the domain of the Orthodox Patriarchate of Antioch,[104] had fallen under Arab rule, and the protagonist in the opposition to Iconoclasm was Saint John of Damascus, who had been a civil servant of the Arab Caliphial Government at Damascus before he became a monk in the monastery of Saint Sávas in Palestine. The Umayyad Government had anticipated the East Roman Government in reasserting the veto against the representation of living creatures in visual art which had been inherited from Judaism by Islam as well as by Christianity, though it had been ignored by the Umayyads themselves in the decoration of their palaces.[105] Yet, since Saint John Damascene's championship of the *eikóns* was embarrassing for the Umayyads' adversary the East Roman Imperial Government at Constantinople, Saint John Damascene was able to write and publish his anti-Iconoclast polemical works under the Umayyad Government's protection.

The East Roman Imperial Government sought to strengthen its hold over the Eastern Orthodox Church by bringing under the ecclesiastical jurisdiction of the Patriarchate of Constantinople as much of Eastern Orthodox Christendom as still lay within the East Roman Empire's frontiers. The army corps district of Seléfkeia, for instance, was transferred to the Constantinopolitan from the Antiochene Patriarchate, and, in 732 or at some later date before 751, the Eastern Illyricum, together with Sicily and Calabria, was transferred to the Constantinopolitan Patriarchate from the Papacy's ecclesiastical domain.[106] In respect of these transfers, the interests of the Empire and of the Constantinopolitan Patriarchate were identical. The incumbents of the

[104] This fragment was the East Roman army corps district of Seléfkeia the former 'Rocky Cilicia'.
[105] The Umayyad Caliph Yazīd II (720–4) had issued a decree banning all representations of living creatures, not only in Christian churches but anywhere. However, Yazīd's successor Hishām (724–43) repealed Yazīd's decree as far as it applied to Christian churches (see Anastos, M. V., in *The Cambridge Medieval History*, vol. iv, 2nd edn., part i, p. 66; Haussig, op. cit., p. 213.) Hishām did not abstain from the representation of living creatures in the privacy of his palace at Khirbat al-Mafjar, a short distance to the north of Jericho. Besides mosaics portraying animals, you can still see there statues of dancing-girls and one of the Caliph himself.
[106] In Leo III's time the Exarchate of Ravenna was also still under East Roman rule, and the Ducatus Romanus and the four city-states Venice, Gaeta, Naples, and Amalfi were under East Roman suzerainty; but Leo III did not venture to detach from the Papacy's domain any of those disaffected Italian territories, nor the nine Dalmatian city-states either.

Constantinopolitan Patriarchate might be the Imperial Government's creatures or they might be its opponents, but they were invariably in favour of holding on to as much as possible of those portions of the domains of other Patriarchates that had been transferred to the Constantinopolitan Patriarchate by the Imperial Government for the Government's own purposes. In the eleventh century the Papacy recaptured Calabria and Sicily, thanks to the Norman Conquest, but it has never recaptured the Eastern Illyricum. This former Papal territory is occupied today by the three Eastern Orthodox Churches of Greece, Jugoslav Macedonia, and Serbia.[107]

The Imperial Government's attempt to make the Constantinopolitan Patriarchate conterminous with the Empire was eventually defeated by the contraction of the Empire's frontiers. By 1437 more than three-quarters of the sees of the metropolitans who were the Patriarch of Constantinople's ecclesiastical subjects lay in non-East Roman territory.[108] Considering that, at this date, the local head of the Russian Orthodox Church was still one of the Patriarch of Constantinople's metropolitans, and that Georgia, too, was part of this Patriarchate's ecclesiastical domain, the disparity in extent between the Constantinopolitan Patriarchate's and the East Roman Imperial Government's respective domains had become enormous. There was a corresponding disparity in power; and it is not surprising that the Imperial Government proved impotent to impose ecclesiastical union with Rome, under Roman supremacy, on Eastern Orthodox Christians. In the fifteenth century, Eastern Orthodox Christians, like Monophysite Christians in the seventh century, felt that submission to Muslim political rule was not too high a price to pay for the preservation of their ecclesiastical independence.

In the trials of strength between East Roman Emperors and Constantinopolitan patriarchs, Emperors won many battles but no wars. Emperors could depose, or could procure the deposition of, Constantinopolitan patriarchs. Till the conquest of Constantinople by the 'Osmanlis in 1453, the Emperors were autocrats and the patriarchs were their political subjects. But the ill-treatment of a patriarch who had been brave enough to oppose an Emperor on a matter of faith or of morals stimulated the resistance of the victim's supporters; and since, to an increasing extent, these were subjects of foreign governments and were thus beyond reach of an East Roman Emperor's arm, it became more and more difficult for the Imperial Government to defeat them. Even when a victimized patriarch obtained no personal redress,

---

[107] Western Thrace is the only portion of the present domain of the Church of Greece that is part of the original domain of the Patriarchate of Constantinople.

[108] Runciman, *The Great Church in Captivity*, p. 37. Cp. p. 65.

the cause for which he had sacrificed himself usually triumphed eventually.[109]

The Eastern Orthodox churches suffered from their long-protracted symbiosis with the East Roman Empire, but they have survived this ordeal. The Imperial regime worked greater havoc with the Greek people's economic life in the Byzantine period of Greek history. This is the only period in which the Greeks have lost to foreigners their maritime trade, even in their own home waters. In the Byzantine, as in the Hellenic, age, Greek industry was unsurpassed both in its technical skill and in the beauty of its products, but this potential advantage was offset by the cramping effect of the Imperial regulations and restrictions under which the Byzantine-Age industrialists were compelled to work. The most disastrous of all the untoward economic effects of the Imperial regime was the ruin of the East Roman peasantry.

The peasantry was the source of the East Roman Empire's power and wealth. It provided the major part of the Empire's military manpower and of its tax revenue. The provisions of The Farmer's Law (*Nómos Yeoryikós*), which was probably enacted at about the turn of the seventh and eighth centuries, show that, at that date, the peasantry was prospering and was increasing in numbers. New vineyards were being planted and new fields and pastures were being reclaimed from the wilderness. On the other hand, the tenth-century Imperial agrarian legislation shows that, by then, the Government was fighting a losing battle in trying to prevent the peasants' holdings—including those that supported soldiers and naval seamen—from being acquired by large-scale landowners.

The Government was aware that the peasantry was the Empire's mainstay; yet the Government itself was playing into the large-scale landowners' hands through fiscal sins of both commission and omission which the Government was powerless to abandon because its efforts at reform were obstructed by a virtual conspiracy between the large-scale landowners and the Government's own officials. Under regimes in which the official rate of taxation is inordinately high, the rich are usually more successful than the poor in evading the payment in full of the tax that is legally due from them. The East Roman tax officers extracted from the small-scale landowners the full tax, and sometimes more. They let the large-scale landowners off more lightly, partly because these were powerful enough politically to be able do defy the public authorities with impunity, but also because under-taxed large-scale rural property was an investment in which the civil servants themselves were eager to have a share when the improvement in public security made this form of investment attractive.

[109] For a list of courageous patriarchs, see Chapter VI, Appendix II.

The Government's restrictions on the operation of trade and industry made investment in the urban sector of the economy unremunerative, in spite of the security provided by city walls. Consequently there was a rush to invest in rural real estate as soon as security was established in the open country as well, and the open country became progressively more secure in the course of the tenth century—especially in regions on the fringes of the Empire, in which it was difficult for the Central Government, operating from Constantinople, to supervise effectively the transactions between the large-scale landowners and the Government's own itinerant tax-collectors and tax-inspectors.

It is no accidental coincidence that the series of Imperial agrarian enactments was contemporaneous with a series of Imperial military successes in the Romano-Arab border warfare. In this long-drawn-out military struggle the Empire went over from the defensive to the offensive in 926, and it reconquered in 934, 961, and 965 respectively the Arab bases at Malatiyah in eastern Asia Minor, at Candia in Crete, and at Tarsós in Cilicia, from which the Arabs had previously been raiding the Empire's territories. The agrarian legislation applied, at least retrospectively, to transactions carried out during and after the fiscal year 927/8, in which a severe famine had reduced the peasants to cruel straits and had given the rich a correspondingly favourable opportunity of making lucrative investments in rural land.

The climax was Basil II's agrarian law of 1003/4. In this law, Basil sought to redress the inequity of the incidence of taxation by saddling the large-scale landowners with the responsibility for producing the full aggregate sum that had been assessed collectively on the tax-payers in a taxation district. In a previous law,[110] however, Basil had confessed that he was being defeated by his own officials' collusion with the large-scale landowners whom the Emperor was attempting to bring to book. Within three years of Basil's death in 1025, this provision had been repealed, and the swift posthumous defeat of an Emperor who had been exceptionally energetic, ruthless, and determined, portended the definitive victory of the large-scale landowners over the Imperial Government.

From the middle decades of the eleventh century until the extinction of the East Roman Empire in 1453, the large-scale landowners, as well as the Church, had the upper hand over the Imperial Government. These two vested interests overlapped; for the monasteries and the episcopal sees were important constituents of the large-scale landowners' 'lobby'. The consequence was that the Imperial Government's former peasant taxpayers became the large-scale landowners' tenants or their landless labourers, and the Imperial treasury was impoverished by

[110] Novel 29, of 1 January 996.

being left eventually with few taxpayers who were not powerful enough to evade their fiscal obligations. Finance, which had been the East Roman Government's main source of strength from the fourth to the tenth century, became its most debilitating weakness during the last five centuries of the Empire's existence.

While the East Roman Government was thus sapping its own strength by its failure to preserve the health of its domestic economy, it was aggravating the difficulty of its relations with foreign powers whose relative strength was increasing. The East Roman Empire clung to the pretension that it was the sole sovereign power at the western end of the Old World, and that all other states within range of it were under its suzerainty. From the second century B.C. until after the opening of the third century of the Christian Era, the Roman claim to the possession of a monopoly of sovereignty and paramountcy had corresponded closely enough to the realities to be tenable. The international balance of power was changed irrevocably by the establishment of the dynamic Second Persian Empire in the third decade of the third century and by the Roman Empire's first breakdown in A.D. 235–84. Yet the traditional pretension was still being maintained when the Empire's territory had dwindled to Constantinople within the Theodosian Wall, together with the Pelopónnêsos.

The pretension to universal sovereignty made it impossible for the East Roman Empire and Bulgaria to coexist as separate powers on a par with each other in status. Only one relation between them was consistent with the doctrine that the title 'Emperor' implied world-wide dominion. One of these two geographically interlocked states must eventually assert the validity of this doctrine by subjugating and annexing its awkward next-door neighbour. Khan Symeon of Bulgaria tried to unite the two states in 913–24, but he failed. The East Roman Emperor Basil II tried in 986–1018, and he succeeded. But this East Roman military success was bought at so high an economic and social price that it accelerated the decline into which the Empire had already fallen. The significant point is the failure of the compromise of 927, in which the East Roman Government conceded to Khan Symeon's son and successor Peter the right to style himself 'Emperor' and to style the head of the Bulgarian Church 'Patriarch'. This compromise has been cited already as an example of the opportunism ('economy') which was the Greeks' saving grace in the Byzantine Age of Greek history. In this case, however, the East Roman Government's concession purchased, not a permanent peace settlement with Bulgaria, but merely a forty-two years' truce (927–69). The two powers share the responsibility for the resumption of the war between them—a fifty-years-long bout of hostilities that was disastrous for both the belligerents. The East Roman

Empire's responsibility for this common disaster was greater than Bulgaria's. Bulgaria's challenge in 969 was verbal; the East Roman Empire's response was military.

(v) *The Incubus of the Hellenic Paideia*

The second of the Byzantine Greeks' heritages from the Hellenes was the Hellenic *paideia*, and this has haunted the Greeks for more than half a millennium longer than the East Roman Empire. The Empire was liquidated in 1453; 'the language question' is still a vexed question in present-day Greece.

All living languages change unceasingly in the process of being transmitted from generation to generation. Each successive phase of a language is transient, and it is impossible to keep any one of these successive transient phases alive permanently. If a language has been reduced to writing, it is possible to 'freeze' some phase of it in which it has become the vehicle of a treasured literature, but the price of 'freezing' is death. Eventually there will be no one left who can speak the language in this obsolete 'frozen' form, while the size of the 'classically' educated minority that is literate in the 'frozen' form of the language will be constantly dwindling. The history of the Greek language illustrates this linguistic 'law' with unusual clarity, because the extant specimens of Greek, in its successive phases, range, in their dates, from the fifteenth century B.C. to the present day.

In the course of these thirty-four centuries, Greek has changed in the same general direction as the majority of the surviving languages of the Indo-European family. Our estimate of the technical merits or demerits of the Indo-European *Ursprache* as an instrument for communication from mouth to ear or from pen to eye has been affected by the immensity of the prestige of the literatures that have been written in three Indo-European languages: Hellenic Greek, Latin, and Sanskrit. These three languages are all close enough in structure to their common progenitor, the *Ursprache*, to have retained the *Ursprache*'s principal characteristic, and this can be seen to be also the *Ursprache*'s principal weakness, if we inspect the *Ursprache*, and the three famous archaic variations on it, critically.

Like the *Ursprache* itself, Hellenic Greek, Latin, and Sanskrit all use an unwieldy device for expressing the grammatical distinctions of person, case, number, gender, tense, and mood. They express these distinctions by differences in the terminations of words. This makes the quantity of word-forms large, and it therefore makes it difficult to master these and to use them correctly. This technical defect of the *Ursprache* and of the archaic variations on it has been partially remedied, in most surviving languages of the Indo-European stock, by a progressive simplification of their structure. This has been simplified by expressing the always necessary grammatical distinctions by means of a new device. As an alternative to continuing to ring changes on the terminations of words, the evolving Indo-European languages have expressed the grammatical distinctions to a greater and greater extent by shedding the various terminations and substituting for them prepositions and auxiliary verbs that are attached to other words as separate particles instead of being incorporated in them.

The unwieldy structure of the *Ursprache* has not been entirely eliminated even in present-day English, which, of all surviving Indo-European languages, has gone the furthest in replacing inflexions by compounds. This process has gone considerably less far, up to the present, in Modern Greek. Yet Modern Greek, like Modern English, has crossed the great divide between a structure that is fundamentally inflexional and a structure that is fundamentally analytic and compositional. The text of a surviving lampoon on the Emperor Maurice (A.D. 582–602)[111] tells us that the Greek language had already crossed the divide by the beginning of the seventh century of the Christian Era. From that time onwards, at the latest,[112] the living form of Greek has been radically different from the Mycenaean Greek of the 'Linear B' tablets and from the Hellenic Greek of the Homeric poems and of the Attic *koine*.

The merits or demerits of a language ought to be appraised in terms of its efficiency as a means of communication, and, on this criterion, we are bound to conclude that, in the history of the Indo-European languages, the progressive abandonment of the unwieldy device of inflexion has been a technical improvement. A present-day English-speaker readily recognizes that, on this criterion, Modern English is an improvement on Anglo-Saxon English. The present-day English-speaker's judgement is objective, because it is not affected by any pious feelings about Anglo-Saxon English literature. In order to read this literature, he has to learn Anglo-Saxon English, which, for present-day English-speakers, has become a foreign language. Few present-day English-speakers do take the trouble to learn it, for the literature written in this Anglo-Saxon

---

[111] The Greek text of this is printed in Krumbacher, op. cit., p. 792. See also Beck, H.-C., *Geschichte der byzantinischen Volksliteratur* (Munich 1971), p. 26, for this and other lampoons composed in the fifth, sixth, and early seventh centuries in the colloquial Greek of the day. But the language is not purely colloquial even in Byzantine lampoons and acclamations (ibid., pp. 3–4 and 25). The Spring Song, chanted antiphonally by the 'demes' (libretto in Constantine Porphyrogenitus, *De Caerimoniis*, vol. i, pp. 366 and 367 Bonn) is in the *koine*.

[112] Beck, in op. cit., p. 3, tentatively dates the decisive transformation of the living Greek language from its Hellenic to its modern form '*bereits zu Ende der Antike*'. He points out, ibid., p. 9, that there must have been not only local dialects of medieval Modern Greek, but also a common form of it that was current throughout the medieval Greek-speaking world.

English has little present prestige. Hellenic Greek is a greater linguistic incubus for present-day Greek speakers than Anglo-Saxon English is for present-day English-speakers. Modern Greek is not so extremely different from Hellenic Greek as Modern English is from Anglo-Saxon English. The relation between Modern Greek and Hellenic Greek is more like that between Modern English and Middle English— a language that is partially intelligible for a speaker of Modern English. Moreover, the prestige of Hellenic Greek is still enormous.

Hellenic Greek is the language of the pre-Christian Hellenic literature, of the Greek text of the Bible, of the works of the Greek Christian Fathers, and of the several Greek-speaking Eastern Orthodox Churches' liturgy. A present-day Greek's feelings about the works written in Hellenic Greek almost inevitably affect his judgement about the relative merits of the Hellenic and the Modern phase of his language. It is difficult for him to recognize that Modern Greek is a technical improvement on Hellenic Greek in so far as it is less inflexional. It is hard for someone whose living language is Modern Greek not to feel that it is a degenerate corruption of Hellenic Greek. The superiority of the literature in Hellenic Greek to any literature in Modern Greek that has been produced so far creates the illusion that the language in which the Hellenic Greek literature happens to have been written must be intrinsically superior to its present successor. Yet this illusion could hardly persist if, one day, someone were to compose in Modern Greek a poem that was unquestionably a match for the *Iliad* or for the surviving fragments of Sappho's lyrics or for Sophocles' play *Antigone*.

This diffidence about the merits of the Modern Greek language that a present-day Greek still feels was felt even more oppressively by the present-day Greek's Byzantine predecessors. Consequently, the living language, which had already developed the essential distinctive features of Modern Greek, did not, in the Byzantine Age, break through the crust of Hellenic Greek to become the vehicle for a literature that could compare with Byzantine Greek visual art and architecture. The beauty and sublimity of the Byzantine Greeks' achievements in these non-verbal arts indicate what they might also have achieved in a literature in their own living language if the prestige of their literary heritage in their Hellenic predecessors' dead language had not inhibited them.

The Byzantine Greeks' persistence in writing in Hellenic Greek was not either unnatural or culturally unhealthy in itself. Their Western contemporaries continued to write poetry in Latin till the fifteenth century, and it was not till towards the close of the seventeenth century that Latin was replaced in the West by French as the language of international intercourse. The point in which the courses of medieval Western and medieval Greek literature parted company was that, in the

West from the twelfth century onwards, a serious vernacular literature, created by and for cultivated men and women, arose side by side with the contemporary literature in Latin and quickly surpassed it. In the same century, some cultivated Byzantine Greeks, too, did produce some vernacular poetry written in an accentual metre—the so-called 'metropolitan verse'[113]—by cultivated authors, but, here, the only genre that showed any vitality in the twelfth century was satire,[114] while in the fourteenth century it was the romantic novel,[115] which was a flight from contemporary reality.[116] These romances are written in the contemporary colloquial language of an educated minority, but they are influenced by romances of the Hellenic Age written in the *koine*; these reminiscences of the Hellenic past appealed to a limited public only; and the authors revert from the colloquial language to the *koine* wherever their subject-matter invites this.[117] In contrast to Western vernacular literature, Greek vernacular literature was inhibited by the dominance of a literary heritage in a dead form of the language.[118]

Perhaps the decisive event in the history of Byzantine Greek literature was the choice of the Attic *koine*, in preference to the contemporary form of living Greek, as the language for hymnography.[119] A distinctive feature of the Eastern Orthodox Christian liturgy was the antiphonal singing in which the congregation was an active participant. This made the language of the *kondákia* and *kanónes* familiar to the public,[120] even if the uneducated majority did not fully understand the meaning of the hallowed words that they were constantly singing. Not all the meaning of the words of the seventeenth-century English translation of the Bible is comprehensible to twentieth-century English-speaking listeners and readers, though the difference between twentieth-century colloquial English and biblical English is slight by comparison with the difference between Modern Greek and the Attic *koine*. Yet biblical English, like *koine* Greek, has had an effect on the history of the language in its subsequent metamorphoses. The current use of the *koine* in the Liturgy encouraged the continuance of the use of it in secular works of literature, and even encouraged the writing of some works in an affected neo-Attic style that restricted their range to the narrow circle of their authors' fellow pedants.[121]

---

[113] Πολιτικοὶ στίχοι, meaning the verse of the Πόλις, i.e. of Constantinople. Accentual verse in this metre was also written in the Attic *koine*, which, like the living vernacular, had come to be pronounced with a stress-accent in place of the pitch-accent of Hellenic Greek.

[114] See Beck, op. cit., pp. 101–9.   [115] See ibid., pp. 115–43.

[116] Ibid., p. 128.   [117] Ibid., pp. 126–8 and 153.

[118] Ibid., p. 12.   [119] See p. 100.

[120] See Dawkins, R. M., in Baynes and Moss, op. cit., p. 256.

[121] Byzantine authors liked being esoteric (Beck, op. cit., p. 2). Their reluctance to make any concessions to a non-erudite public finds expression in a rueful annotation (quoted in Krumbacher, op. cit., p. 284) on the manuscript of an oration by Nikêtas Khoniátês, celebrating the Emperor

The scraps of folk literature in the vernacular that have survived from the Byzantine Age[122] show that, in that age, the Greeks did not lack the capacity to compose poetry in their own living language and to appreciate it. *Constantine and Areté* and *The Bridge of Arta* are a match for the finest poems of the same kind in Hellenic Greek or in any other language. The fifteenth-century elegies inspired by the final fall of Constantinople touch a present-day reader's heart through their sincerity and pathos. To find such masterpieces in so small a remnant of Byzantine folk literature in the vernacular is remarkable, but the smallness of this remnant of folk literature is, in itself, significant. When the folk literature was taken up and was worked over by educated men of letters, they spoiled it by translating the language from the vernacular into the *koine* and by adulterating the matter with inopportune importations from sophisticated works that had been composed in the *koine* and that lacked the vernacular literature's spontaneity and freshness.[123] Conversely, when educated people tried to produce popular works, they failed to reach the wider public with which they wanted to put themselves in contact. Even when they brought themselves to address this public in the vernacular, which was not only the public's mother tongue but was also the writers' own, they cut themselves off from the public by introducing sophisticated allusions to the works of their Hellenic-Age predecessors. They did this even when they were writing romances for diversion. In their serious works, the furthest that any would-be popular Byzantine Greek authors managed to go was to write the *koine* incorrectly.[124] Even the monks would not go beyond that, though they were hostile to Hellenism in principle. However, a slipshod *koine* was no more intelligible than a purist *koine* for a public whose only Greek was the contemporary vernacular.

The Byzantine Greek epic *Dhiyenês Akrítas*[125] seems to have been composed, like the *Iliad* and the *Odyssey*, by a poet who had derived his matter from an accumulated store of oral ballads, but unfortunately the outcome was different. 'Homer' had had no knowledge of anything that had been written by his Mycenaean Greek ancestors in the 'Linear B' script. He had had nothing to work with beyond his oral raw materials and his own uninhibited genius. The learned Byzantine who wrote an

---

Theodore I Láskaris' victory over the Saljūqs of Rum in A.D. 1210: ἐξεδόθη δὲ σαφηνείας πλῆρες τὸ παρὸν προσφώνημα διὰ τὴν τῶν ἀκροατῶν ἀσθένειαν.

[122] See Beck, op. cit., pp. 48–63. See, too, Constantine Porphyrogenitus' *Theophanes Continuatus*, p. 72 Bonn, for the existence, in the reign of the Emperor Michael II (820–9), of a rural minstrel who could improvise in colloquial Greek.

[123] See Krumbacher, op. cit., pp. 795–6.

[124] For instance, Michael Glykás (twelfth century). See Beck, op. cit., pp. 108–9.

[125] See Trypanis, op. cit., pp. 25–8; Krumbacher, op. cit., pp. 794 and 827–32; Beck, op. cit., pp. 63–97, with bibliography on pp. 65–8; and John Mavrogordato's edition of the Greek text, with an English translation, an introduction, and a commentary (Oxford 1956).

epic in the *koine*[126] was inspired by memories of life in the Arab marches of the East Roman Empire in the tenth and eleventh centuries, but he introduced into his work alien strands from the literature of the Hellenic Age that he had at his command.[127] Consequently his product is inferior to his sources of inspiration. It is even inferior to ballads that bear marks of having been subsequently derived from the literary epic when this had seeped down to the stratum of Byzantine society that was illiterate and was consequently free to use the vernacular as a medium for oral poetry.

In the lives of the saints the Byzantine Greeks had hit upon a new branch of literature which had a strong popular appeal. The saints were objects of curiosity as well as of veneration. Hagiography in the vernacular would have attracted many readers, and a still larger number of listeners. Some of the most celebrated saints were of humble social origin, and so, too, were some of their biographers. Like the chroniclers, the hagiographers wanted to reach a wide public; but, also like the chroniclers, they could not bring themselves to write in the vernacular.[128] Even those lives of the saints that have reached us in their original form are written in the *koine*. Yet the style was not sufficiently sophisticated to pass muster with the pedantic arbiters of Byzantine Greek literary taste.[129]

The major surviving collection has been processed by Symeon 'Metaphrástês', an epithet which indicates that Symeon's function was to transpose the works that he edited into a form of the *koine* that was more correct than the originals stylistically, and was consequently still more remote, intellectually and emotionally, from the spirit of the public for whom these works ought to have been made accessible. Symeon 'Metaphrástês' is believed to be identical with Symeon the chronicler, and the chronicler was a *loghothétês*—that is to say, a senior financial officer in the Imperial civil service. Symeon—or the two Symeons, if the chronicler and the hagiographer were different persons—was a tenth-century man of letters, and his date, as well as his diction, shows that his

---

[126] For the slightness of the ingredient of colloquial Greek in the language of the *Akrítas* epic, see Beck, op. cit., pp. vii and 97.

[127] This is especially apparent in Part II (see ibid., pp. 94, 96, and 96 n. 3). Part II is really a separate poem from Part I (ibid., p. 94). Beck holds (p. 92) that the author of Part II borrowed from the current popular ballads (τραγούδια), but that Part I is anterior to the ballads that have the same themes (p. 78).

[128] Professor Robert Browning has pointed out to me that, at this stage of Greek cultural history, a literate Greek was not literate in his own living mother-tongue. He had been taught to read and write Hellenic Greek only. He did not know how to write the contemporary form of Modern Greek; to teach himself how to do this would have been quite difficult for him; to write in the Hellenic *koine* was therefore the line of least resistance for a Byzantine-Age Greek who had been given an exclusively Hellenic-Greek education.

[129] For instance, the Patriarch Nikólaos IV Mouzalon (1147–51) inveighed against the biography of St. Paraskevê, on the ground that it had been written παρά τινος χωρίτου ἰδιωτικῶς (see Beck, op. cit., pp. 186–7).

education had been governed by the literary renaissance of Hellenism, which had been in progress since the generation of Phótios, about a hundred years before Symeon's time. The tenth-century *loghothétês* was on less familiar terms with the unsophisticated public than the two earliest Byzantine chroniclers, the monk Theophánês and the Patriarch Nikêphóros, whose lifetimes had bestridden the eighth and ninth centuries.

If the Akritic epic and the corpus of Byzantine hagiography had been written in the vernacular, the Byzantine Greeks might have created a cultivated vernacular literature that would have been worthy of their own folk poetry in the vernacular and would have been comparable to the cultivated vernacular literature of medieval Western Christendom. The incubus of the Byzantine Greeks' Hellenic literary heritage deterred them from harvesting the literary potentialities of their own Byzantine genius and experience. The bulk of the literature that the Byzantine Greeks did produce has suffered from having been written in a language that was not their own—namely, the Hellenic *koine*, re-minted into neo-Attic by those Byzantine purists who were capable of performing this academic *tour de force*.[130] The penalty for pedantry is insipidity, and this has blighted all genres of Byzantine literature in Hellenic Greek except for the single genre of historiography.

Byzantine historiographers are divided into two schools, which are distinguished from each other by the difference between their respective sources of inspiration.

The older of the two patterns of Byzantine historiography is the chronicle. This starts with the Creation of the World and comes down to the chronicler's own day if the chronicler has lived to carry his story that far. The prototype of all Byzantine chronicles is the work of the fourth-century chronicler and chronologist Efsévios (Eusebius) of Kaisáreia in Palestine. The inspiration of the Byzantine chronicle is the Jewish vision of God's action in time within the setting of eternity. Secular history is fitted into this theological framework. Byzantine Greek chronography, like Byzantine Greek hymnography and liturgical melody, was thus an import from the Syrian World. The historical horizon of the Byzantine chronographer was not only wider than that of the Hellenic writers of world-history (e.g. Herodotus or Ephorus or Polybius); its theological setting also gave it an additional spiritual dimension that had not been within the Hellenes' ken.

---

[130] The *koine* version of Attic Greek had been current for three centuries before the revival, in the last century B.C., of the pre-*koine* Attic of the fifth-century-B.C. and fourth-century-B.C. Athenian writers. This neo-Attic never succeeded in ousting the *koine*—not even after the *koine*, in its turn, had become a dead language (Beck, op. cit., p. 2). In Byzantine Greek parlance, Ἀττικῶς was synonymous with δοκίμως and with ἀρχαίως. It included not only neo-Attic but also the unpurified *koine* (ibid., p. 1).

This virtue of the chronographical way of writing history was recognized by Hellenically educated historians such as the eleventh-century chronicler John Skylídzês and his twelfth-century successor John Zonarás. Both these chroniclers were East Roman public servants; both of them held important and responsible offices. They were members of the East Roman 'establishment' of their day, and their education and career must have exposed them to the full force of the Byzantine literary renaissance of Hellenism. It is all the more significant that this did not deter them from choosing a non-Hellenic pattern for writing major historical works.

The second school of Byzantine Greek historiographers was less original. The influence of the literary renaissance did prompt the historiographers of this school to revert to the pattern of Hellenic Greek historiography that had been set by Thucydides and had been followed by a series of successors of his for the next thousand years. The Thucydidean, as opposed to the Herodotean, school of Hellenic historiography had switched attention away from the panorama of world-history to concentrate it on the study and recording of particular episodes. The last Hellenic historiographer of this school had been Theophýlaktos Simokáttês,[131] a contemporary of the Emperor Heraclius (610–41). There was an interval of about three centuries and a half between the lifetimes of Simokáttês and Leo Diaconus, the earliest of the Byzantine historiographers to adopt the episodic pattern of Hellenic historiography[132] in preference to the non-Hellenic pattern of the chronicle in which world-history is presented in a theological framework. The pattern revived by Leo Diaconus was followed by a series of successors of his for the next 500 years, running from the latter part of the tenth century to the latter part of the fifteenth century—the century that witnessed the extinction of the East Roman Empire in the two enclaves, Constantinople and the Pelopónnêsos, which were the Empire's last remnants, and also the extinction of the East Roman Empire's Greek successor-state, the Empire of Trebizond.

The Byzantine Greek historiographers' self-imposed handicap of writing in the Attic *koine*, or even in neo-Attic, and not in the vernacular inevitably restricted the number of their readers, but it did not prevent them from producing a corpus of historical works which, alone among all the products of Byzantine Greek men of letters, can bear comparison

---

[131] Latinized as 'Simocatta'.

[132] All the Byzantine historiographers of the episodic school were followers of Thucydides in adopting this pattern, but at least two of them—namely, Constantine VII Porphyrogenitus in his biography of his grandfather the Emperor Basil I (Book V of *Theophanes Continuatus*) and Michael Psellós—also followed Plutarch in recounting episodic history in the form of biography. In this they resembled the father of Chinese history, Ssu-ma Ch'ien, and the subsequent authors of the series of Chinese dynastic histories.

with the corpus of Hellenic Greek historical literature. When we overlook the Byzantine historians' cramping choice of language and focus our attention on the substance of their work, we find that this stands the test of the criteria by which historians of all times and places have to be judged. Like the most eminent of their Hellenic Greek counterparts, a majority of the Byzantine historiographers had taken a personal part in public affairs as civil servants,[133] diplomatists,[134] soldiers,[135] clerics,[136] or Emperors.[137] A majority of them, too, including those chroniclers who carried their story as far as their own times, were first-hand witnesses of some, at least, of the events that they have recorded. They were not disinterested witnesses in so far as they were implicated personally, but their partisanship can be detected and be discounted, and, when we have performed this discriminatory exercise, we can make use of their first-hand information without being misled by their propaganda.

Some of the first-hand witnesses were shrewd observers of character.[138] Some had the gift of describing vividly and movingly the events in which they had been personally involved.[139] Two of the latest three—Laónikos Khalkokondýlês and Kritóvoulos Imvriótês—had the vision that is an historian's supreme gift. Living and writing in the fifteenth century, they recognized that the state whose action was now the decisive factor in the political history of the Levant was the Ottoman Empire, not the East Roman Empire any longer. Portentous contemporary events made this truth difficult to ignore; yet it is greatly to the credit of these two Byzantine Greek historians that they faced the truth and wrote their histories in the light of it. In both these works, Ottoman history, not East Roman history, is made the main thread of the narrative. This is remarkable, considering that these two historians were *ci-devant* East Romans and that, by their time, the rulers and subjects of the Roman Empire had maintained, for 1,500 years, as the fundamental article of their political faith, the pretension that the Roman Emperor was the sovereign of the whole world, in spite of the evidence to the contrary that

---

[133] For example, Michael Psellós, Michael Attaleiátês, John Kínnamos, Nikêtas Khoniátês, George Pakhymérês, Nikêphóros Grêgorás, Dhoúkas, George Sphrandzês.

[134] For example, George Akropolítês, Laónikos Khalkokondýlês.

[135] For example, Nikêphóros Vryénnios, George Akropolítês (who was a bad soldier but a good diplomatist).

[136] For example, the priest John Kameniátês, the deacon Léon (Leo Diaconus).

[137] For example, Constantine VII Porphyroyénnêtos, John VI Kandakouzênós. Nikêphóros Vryénnios was a Caesar and was Aléxios I's son-in-law; Anna Komnênê was Aléxios I's daughter.

[138] For instance, Michael Psellós.

[139] Instances are the eyewitness accounts by John Kameniátês of the sack of Thessaloníkê by the Muslims in 904; by the Homeric scholar and Archbishop of Thessaloníkê, Efstáthios, of the sack of Thessaloníkê by the Normans in 1185; by Nikêphóros Khoniátês of the sack of Constantinople by the Venetians and the French in 1204; by Anna Komnênê of the behaviour of the Western crusaders at her father Aléxios I's court.

had been mounting up for the last twelve centuries. To shake off this delusion was a signal feat of historical insight and imagination.

Khalkokondýlês and Kritóvoulos did, however, harbour another delusion which was quickly dispelled by the unpropitious course of events. They assumed that, after the Ottoman conquest of the last remaining enclaves of politically independent Greek territory, there would continue to be a Greek public for works written in Hellenic Greek. They also assumed that, in the fifteenth century of the Christian Era, Greece would 'take her savage conqueror captive' once again, as she had done in the second century B.C. In that century, Polybius had reckoned on Greece's conquering the Romans culturally, and he had been justified by the event. Polybius had written in Greek a history of Rome's military conquest of the Mediterranean World, in the expectation that, under Roman rule, there would still be a cultivated Greek public to read his book and that Greek culture would also be attractive enough to the dominant Roman 'establishment' to induce the Greeks' new political masters to become their cultural converts and patrons. In entertaining similar expectations regarding the Byzantine Greek intellectuals' prospects under Ottoman rule, Khalkokondýlês and Kritóvoulos miscalculated, because they failed to reckon with two crucial differences between their own situation and Polybius'.

In the first place, Polybius was writing in an Attic *koine* which, in his day, was the Greek people's living language of everyday life, whereas the fifteenth-century Byzantine Greek historians—writing in Polybius' language, or in a neo-Attic caricature of it, sixteen centuries after Polybius' day—were operating with a long since dead form of Greek and were addressing only a narrow circle of readers whose esoteric culture did not appeal to the mass even of their fellow-Greeks in their generation. In the second place, there was no serious prospect that the 'Osmanlis would be captivated by Greek culture, as the Romans had been. The 'Osmanlis were the political heirs of the Roman Empire, but their religion was Islam, and the religious barrier between Muslims and Christians was a cultural barrier as well.[140] The Ottoman Pādishāh Mehmet II the Conqueror did appreciate contemporary Greek culture.[141] He was both a highly cultivated and a highly intelligent man. But he was also, for these very reasons, exceptional and unrepresentative. His appreciation of Byzantine Greek culture was a personal idiosyncrasy of his. It could not, and did not, inaugurate an Ottoman

[140] However, verses in the Greek language, written in the Arabic alphabet, occur in the mystical religious poetry of Mevlānā Jelāl-ed-Dīn Rūmī (1207–73), the founder of the Mevlevi Order of Dervishes, and of his son and successor Sultan Veled (1226–1312). See Beck op. cit., pp. 111–12, with bibliographical references.

[141] Mehmet II recognized that he needed the services of Greek and Italian employees (see Vakalópoulos, op. cit., vol. ii, part i, p. 10).

Hellenophil tradition. The seed sown by the last generation of Hellenically educated Byzantine Greeks fell on stony ground in their own homeland under Ottoman rule. It was on Western soil that this seed germinated and produced a harvest.

Two genres of Byzantine Greek literature that are closely akin to historiography are statesmen's handbooks and treatises on the art of war, and, in these genres too, the Byzantine Greeks achieved successes. The most interesting of all Byzantine Greek prose works is the Emperor Constantine VII Porphyrogenitus' tenth-century handbook on East Roman Imperial foreign policy. Modern scholars have labelled it, misleadingly, *De Administrando Imperio*. Actually it combines a description of foreign peoples and states with prescriptions for coping with them. The eleventh-century soldier and administrator Kekavménos wrote a handbook which, like Constantine's, combines precept with description in the form of illustrative anecdotes. This work, too, bears a misleading label. It has come down to us under the title *Stratêyikón*, but the author's precepts are concerned with personal conduct more than with the art of war. There are, however, three surviving tenth-century treatises that deal with the art of war exclusively: two written by officers who had served under Nikêphóros II Phokás[142] and one written by this Emperor himself.[143]

These three treatises have been written by soldiers in the light of their own professional experience. On the other hand, all but a fraction of the Emperor Leo VI's *Taktika*[144] is a cento of plagiarisms from earlier works, and so, surprisingly, is Nikêphóros Ouranós' *Taktiká*.[145] Ouranós was a successful general and ambassador in the reign of Basil II (976-1025), yet, in this work on one of his two professions, he does not cite any experiences or actions of his own.

The historical works and the handbooks dealing with public affairs that do draw on the authors' first-hand experience are the best products of Byzantine Greek literature. Its worst product is its sophisticated poetry in Hellenic Greek, and this is worst of all when it is written, as most of it is, not in the accentual verse that is used in the vernacular ballads, but in the Hellenic Greek metres, which are not accentual but quantitative. After the Greek accent had changed from a pitch-accent into a stress-accent, and after the consequent obliteration of the

[142] Περὶ Παραδρομῆς Πολέμου, published in C. B. Hase's edition of Leo Diaconus' history (pp. 179-255 in the Bonn edition); the 'Anonymus Vári's' Βιβλίον Τακτικόν (Leipzig 1901).

[143] Nikêphóros Phokás, Στρατηγικὴ Ἔκφεσις καὶ σύνταξις, ed. by Kulakovskii, J., in *Mémoires de l'Académie Impériale des Sciences de St. Petersbourg*, viiie série, Classe Historico-Philologique, vol. viii, no. 9 (1908).

[144] Leo VI, *Taktiká*, in Migne, *Patrologia Graeca*, vol. cvii, cols. 669-1094. R. Vári's critical edition is magnificent but unfinished (vol. i (Budapest 1917), Constitutiones I-XI; vol. ii, Fasc. Prior (Budapest 1922), Constitutiones XII, XIII, and XIV, §§ 1-36 only).

[145] *La Tactique de Nicêphore Ouranos*, ed. by Dain, A. (Paris 1937).

quantitative difference between long and short syllables, the Byzantine Greeks contrived to compose verses that scan quantitatively as iambics and accentually as scazons. But this ingenious harmonization of two different pronunciations could not be applied to quantitative hexameters and elegiac couplets. The Byzantines continued to write these too, but, if they pronounced them accentually, as presumably they did, the result, for the ear, must have been a metrical chaos.

The Hellenically educated Byzantine Greeks, who shrank from writing in the living vernacular of their time, could not help talking in the vernacular in their daily life, and their speech shows through their writing in the blunders that they made in using a virtually foreign form of Greek that they had not properly mastered.[146] These blunders are not confined to Byzantine works in the Attic *koine* whose authors were illeducated, as Malálas was, or were indifferent to points of style, as Theophánês was and as Constantine Porphyrogenitus was too when his attention was concentrated on his subject to the neglect of his style. The blunders are the most startling—and the most revealing too—in the works of writers like Psellós and Anna Komnênê who were not content with the simplified Attic of the *koine* but tried to write the neo-Attic of the Second Sophistic, garnished with duals, datives, and verbs in *-mi*. Their ambition outran their scholarship, and it inveigled them into errors that are more ludicrous, because they are more gratuitous, than those of simpler souls who were incapable of carrying their linguistic affectation to these absurd extremes.

A reader of the fourteenth-century emperor-historian John VI Kandakouzênós is pulled up short when the text changes abruptly from the Attic *koine* to Modern Greek in a passage in which the author is not writing words of his own but is quoting, verbatim,[147] a letter that he had received from the Mamluk Sultan of Egypt.[148] The historian's conscientious reproduction of a document in its original form betrays the stylist's preciosity. The Sultan did not share the Emperor's concern to maintain the *koine* and to suppress the vernacular. He let his Greek-speaking secretary write the letter for him in the living Greek of the day. He assumed that the Emperor would understand the meaning of a letter in this living Greek idiom, and he was not mistaken. The proof is Kandakouzênós reproduction of the letter as it stood, without transposition into the language in which the Emperor himself wrote but did not talk.[149]

---

[146] Khadzidhákis, G. N., followed by Dawkins, R. M., in Baynes and Moss, *Byzantium*, pp. 254–62.

[147] γράμματα οὕτως ἔχοντα τῇ λέξει.

[148] John Kandakouzênós, *Historiae*, on pp. 94–9 of vol. iii of the Bonn edition.

[149] The Ottoman Imperial Government and the Venetian Government conducted their diplomatic correspondence with each other in colloquial Greek till the close of the sixteenth century

Whenever and wherever the narrow circle of Byzantine Greek writers
and readers of Hellenic Greek was displaced or was deposed from power,
the thin crust of the dead language instantly crumbled away and left the
living vernacular form of Greek free to rise to the surface.[150] The
fifteenth-century Cypriot Greek chronicler Leóndios Makhairás testifies
that, until 1191, when Cyprus was conquered by Richard Coeur de Lion
for the Latins, the Cypriots had known how to write 'standard Greek'
('Ρωμαϊκὰ καθολικά), but that 'they then began to learn French and
took to using the barbarous Greek that they still use today. We now
write French and Greek, with the result that no one in the World knows
what our language is.'[151] The same thing had happened after the Latins'
conquest of the Pelopónnêsos in 1205. The fourteenth-century author—
or translator[152]—of *The Chronicle of the Morea* was a Greek-speaking
Frenchman or Franco-Greek half-caste; but the Greek in which he
writes is not the Attic *koine*; it is the fourteenth-century Peloponnesian
form of Modern Greek, though there is a perceptible tincture of the *koine*
in it.[153] After the reconquest of the Pelopónnêsos from the French by the
East Roman Empire, and after the subsequent extinction of both the
East Roman Empire and the Empire of Trebizond by the 'Osmanlis,
the Byzantine Greek literature in the Attic *koine* came to an end. It has
been noted already that two of its last practitioners were the historians
—Khalkokondýlês and Kritóvoulos—who lived to see the Ottoman
conquest of the last shreds of politically independent Greek territory.

The Eastern Orthodox Church survived the final fall of Constantinople and Mistrá and Trebizond because this Church's domain extended
far beyond the reach of the Ottoman Empire's arm. The domain of the
Greek language was much narrower; and this was a consequence of the
Eastern Orthodox Church's linguistic liberality. Neither the Attic *koine*
nor Modern Greek became the lingua franca of Eastern Orthodox

(see Vakalópoulos, op. cit., vol. ii, part i, pp. 10–11). The local Ottoman authorities in Greek-
speaking territories continued to use Greek for their decrees, letters, and local diplomatic
correspondence (ibid., p. 12).

[150] The remnant of this pedantic coterie came within an ace of being extinguished in 1422, when
the 'Osmanlis made an abortive assault on Constantinople. An account of this event by Ioánnês
Kananós is printed on pp. 455–79 of the Bonn edition of Phrantzês' (Sphrandzês') *Chronicle* (Bonn
1838; Bucharest 1966, ed. by Vasile Grecu); Krumbacher, in op. cit., pp. 300–1, notes that, as
Kananós approaches the climax of his dramatic story, he lapses from the *koine* into Modern Greek.
These lapses are, however, few and slight. Constantinople had not fallen; the Hellenically educated
minority of its Greek population still survived (see Skholários in Plêthon, *Nomoi*, ed. by C.
Alexandre (Paris 1858; reprint, Amsterdam 1966), p. 354); and accordingly the living vernacular
was barely able to break through the crust of the *koine* in Kananós' narrative.

[151] *The Chronicle of Makhairás*, ed. by Dawkins, R. M. (Oxford 1932), vol. i, p. 143.

[152] The Greek text is thought to be a version of a French original (Beck, op. cit., p. 158). This
original may be the *Livre de la Conqueste de la Princée de l' Amorée* written, probably, in the 1320s and ed.
by J. Longnon (Paris 1911). See Beck, op. cit., p. 159.

[153] See ibid.

Christendom, as Latin, and, later on, French, did become the lingua franca of Western Christendom. In Eastern Orthodox Christendom the Macedonian dialect of Slavonic, which had been equipped with an alphabet by the ninth-century Thessalonian missionary brothers, Constantine-Cyril and Methódhios, came to be used—when conveyed in the so-called 'Cyrillic' alphabet[154]—as the language of the liturgy and of literature, ecclesiastical and secular, by far more people, occupying a far larger territory, than the number of Eastern Orthodox Christians whose liturgical and colloquial languages were forms of Greek.

The Hellenically educated Byzantine Greeks' combination of this liberality towards other tongues with their hostility towards the living form of their own native language was paradoxical, and the consequences of this paradox were unhappy. There is no parallel in Greek cultural history to Western Christendom's successful effort, towards the end of the seventeenth century, to liberate itself from the constricting grip of the 'classical' languages and literatures. The shackles of the Hellenic Greek literature were struck off from the Greeks' wrists by Frankish and Turkish hands, not by the Greeks' own hands, and a cultural liberation that had not been of their own doing did not enable the Greeks to begin to think, in the post-seventeenth-century Western way, for themselves, instead of continuing to take information on trust from 'the Ancients'. The Greeks did not succeed in taking this momentous step until they had adopted the modern Western *Weltanschauung*, and the change in the Greeks' attitude towards the West from hostility to admiration was not completed before the turn of the eighteenth and nineteenth centuries.

[154] This 'Cyrillic' alphabet seems to have been invented in north-eastern Bulgaria at some date not long after the reception, in Bulgaria, of some of the survivors of the Slavophone clergy who had been expelled from Moravia after the death, in 885, of Constantine-Cyril's brother and fellow-missionary Methódhios, the Archbishop of Sirmium. The alphabet that had been invented by Constantine-Cyril himself seems to have been the Glagolitic (see above, p. 98). This Glagolitic alphabet survived in parts of Dalmatia till 1927 as the script of an old-Slavonic translation of the Roman Catholic liturgy (see Vlasto, op. cit., pp. 196–205).

VII

THE MODERN GREEKS' HERITAGE FROM THE BYZANTINE GREEKS

DURING the transitional stage (A.D. 284–602) between the Hellenic and the Byzantine Age of Greek history, the Greeks themselves decided which of the elements of the Hellenic way of life they should reject, and which they should retain. At this turning-point in Greek history the Greeks became, once again, their own masters, even in the political field; for, though they were still subjects of the Roman Empire, which had imposed itself on them in the second century B.C., the Empire itself was appropriated by the Greeks in the transitional period. In the fifth century of the Christian Era the Empire collapsed in the West and was overrun there by barbarians who set up independent, or virtually independent, successor-states. In the East Roman Empire, which survived, the only Latin-speaking districts were the northern parts of the Praetorian Prefecture of the Eastern Illyricum and the dioecesis of Thrace, and these economically backward and militarily hard-pressed districts were no match for the rest of the East Roman Empire, in which Greek had become the language of the whole of the population of Asia Minor and of a still dominant Greek-speaking minority in Syria and Mesopotamia and Palestine and Egypt. The Empire continued to be Roman in name, but it had become Greek in reality, and it remained Greek in spite of Justinian I's ephemeral re-conquests.

During the transitional stage (A.D. 1182–1461) between the Byzantine and the Modern Age of Greek history, the Greeks lost their political independence and, with it, their command over some of the non-political elements of their way of life as well. Which of the elements of the Byzantine way of life the Greeks were to keep, and which of them they were to lose, was decided for them by their Ottoman Turkish conquerors, not by the Greeks themselves.

The 'Osmanlis took over from the Greeks the burden of maintaining the Roman Empire. The Greek Roman Empire had been broken up in 1182–1204; the 'Osmanlis reassembled most of the pieces in the course of the fourteenth and fifteenth centuries, and the Ottoman Pādishāh was recognized by the heads of other Islamic states as being the Greek Roman Emperor's successor. They addressed him as Qaysar-i-Rūm

('Caesar of Rome'). The 'Osmanlis continued to carry the load till 1922, when the Ottoman Turks deliberately liquidated the Ottoman Empire and inaugurated the present Republic of Turkey. The Ottoman Turks' situation in 1922 was happier than the Byzantine Greeks' situation in 1461. After the conquest of the Greek Empire of Trebizond in 1461, there was no longer any territory inhabited by Greeks that was not under either Frankish or Ottoman rule. On the other hand, after the Ottoman Empire had lost almost all territories in which the Turks were in a minority or in which there were no Turks at all, the Ottoman Empire's youngest successor-state, the Republic of Turkey, started life in 1922 with a large territory in which the Turks were in an overwhelming majority.

Meanwhile, in the fifteenth century, the Greeks had been reunited politically under Ottoman sovereignty except for Greeks in a diminishing number of enclaves held by Western Christian powers; and, between the fifteenth and the nineteenth century, there was no independent Greek state before the establishment, in 1829–32, of the present national state of Greece within frontiers which, till 1913, included only a minority of the Greek people.[1]

Besides relieving the Greeks of the Roman Empire, the Ottoman conquest liberated them from the Attic *koine*[2] and from the previous impediments to Greek industry and trade.

The liberation of the Greeks from the *koine* was not complete, for, in the Greek-speaking Eastern Orthodox churches, the liturgy is still performed in the *koine*, and the Greek-speaking Eastern Orthodox hierarchy has always frowned on the translation of the liturgy and the Bible into Modern Greek. The seventeenth-century Patriarch of Constantinople, Cyril Loúkaris, incurred odium, among his Greek co-religionists, not only by inclining towards Calvinism, but also for having commissioned an edition of the New Testament in which the original text in the *koine* and a version in Modern Greek were printed in parallel columns.[3] A new translation into the demotic form of Modern Greek by A. A. Pallis, which was published in 1902, provoked a riot at Athens even in the present century.[4]

---

[1] See Runciman, *The Great Church in Captivity* (Cambridge 1968), p. 407.

[2] See Henderson, G. P., *The Revival of Greek Thought 1620–1830* (Edinburgh 1971), p. 3.

[3] This translation was made for Cyril Loúkaris by Máximos of Gallipoli and was printed for him at Geneva. It was published there in 1638, and copies did not reach Constantinople until after Loúkaris' death. According to Tsakonas, the translation was condemned by two synods; according to Bien, it was condemned and officially burned in 1704. See Runciman, op. cit., p. 275; Tsakonas, D., *Geist und Gesellschaft in Griechenland* (Bonn 1965), p. 46; Toynbee, A. J., *A Study of History*, vol. viii, p. 158 n. 5; Bien, P., *Kazantzakis and the Linguistic Revolution in Greek Literature* (Princeton 1972), p. 59 n. 53.

[4] Ἡ Νέα Διαθήκη κατά τό Βατικάνο Χειρόγραφο μεταφρασμένη (Liverpool 1902, 'Liverpool Bookseller', reprinted 1910).

However, since the fall of the last independent Byzantine Greek governments in 1453–61, and the deaths of the Greek men of letters who had survived these political events, there have seldom been attempts to write in the *koine* either literary works or secular official documents or private letters. While the ecclesiastical authorities in Eastern Orthodox churches in which the liturgical language was the Attic Greek *koine* continued, as a rule, to use this in their current official documents, there were exceptions even here. Theóphilos Korydhalléfs (1563–1646), who was head of the Patriarchal School at Istanbul and who rejuvenated the School during his incumbency, had an illustrious pupil, Evyénios Yiannoúlês 'the Aetolian', born somewhere in the neighbourhood of Náfpaktos *circa* 1595–1600, who conducted part of his voluminous correspondence in colloquial Greek. In 1575 the Ecumenical Patriarch promulgated three or four rescripts (κηρύγματα) in the colloquial language, ἡ δημοτική.[5] As for the new Greek social class of merchants engaged in business abroad—a class that grew in numbers, wealth, and influence after the liquidation of the East Roman Imperial regime— they inevitably conducted their business correspondence in the living language.[6]

Yet the Greeks in general continued to feel ashamed of their own mother tongue. The Philhellene Professor at the German University of Tübingen, Martin Kraus ('Crusius'), met with a rebuff when he sought[7] to learn Modern Greek in addition to Hellenic Greek. In 1577 John Zyghomalás, the Méghas Rhêtor of the Ecumenical Patriarchate, rejected a request, made on Crusius' behalf by the German traveller Stephan Gerlach, for a λόγος or a κήρυγμα in the 'κοινή' (i.e. in the Modern Greek δημοτική, not in the Attic κοινή).[8] This was two years after the actual promulgation of several Patriarchal κηρύγματα in the δημοτική. Crusius himself notes, in his book *Turcograecia*,[9] that the δημοτική was despised. That the Greeks themselves were actually speaking this despised form of their language is demonstrated by the words and phrases cited by the German traveller Arnold von Harff, who was in Greek lands in 1477.[10] Crusius reports[11] that the Greek written in his time by both clerical and educated lay Greek correspondents was not pure *koine* but a mixture of this with colloquial Modern Greek.

Since the completion of the Ottoman conquest in 1453–61, the Greeks have, in fact, used, for all these purposes, some form of Modern Greek,

[5] Vakalópoulos, op. cit., vol. ii, part i, pp. 258–9.
[6] Ibid., p. 405.
[7] See ibid., p. 247.
[8] Ibid., p. 258.
[9] Basel 1584, pp. 75 and 99.
[10] Vakalópoulos, op. cit., vol. ii, part i, p. 257.
[11] In op. cit., p. 273; cited by Vakatopoulos, op. cit., vol. ii, part i, p. 258.

with a gamut ranging from the 'purist' (καθαρεύουσα) form to an equally self-conscious and hardly less artificial 'slang' (μαλλιαρή). The Hellenic Greek language and literature have continued to be taught by Greeks to Greeks in Greek institutions for higher education; but, since the fifteenth century, when Hellenic Greek studies were introduced into Italy by a handful of Byzantine Greek *émigrés*, the Western World has been the place in which Hellenic Greek studies have been pursued the most intensively.

In the West, until my own generation, Greek and Latin were still the principal subjects of education in the humanities. In England, from 1899 to 1911, I was taught not only to read the works of Hellenic Greek authors but to write Hellenic Greek in imitation of these authors' various dialects, vocabularies, styles, and also metres when I was called upon to produce, not Greek prose, but Greek verse. The drilling in Hellenic Greek that I received from English classical scholars was, I should guess, as thorough and as correct as the instruction given in the second century by Dio Chrysostom or in the fourth century by Libanius (Livánios). I guess that, since 1461, the educational incubus of Hellenic Greek has weighed on the Modern Greeks less heavily than this. If so, the Modern Greeks ought to be grateful to the Franks for having appropriated the Hellenic *paideia*, as well as to the Turks for having temporarily extinguished Greek political independence. These robberies have also been reliefs.

The impediments to Greek industry and trade in the Byzantine Age had been twofold. First, the Byzantine Greeks' economic activities in these fields had been cramped by the East Roman Government's excessive superintendence and regulation of them; and then, while Greek manufacturers and merchants had continued to be handicapped by their own public authorities, the medieval Italian city-states had succeeded, from the eleventh century onwards, in extorting from the East Roman Government commercial privileges and immunities which gave these foreigners a decisive economic advantage over the Greeks in the Greeks' own home waters and territory.

The Ottoman Imperial Government was not positively benevolent to the commercial enterprise of its Greek subjects till towards the close of the eighteenth century, when it rewarded the shipping of Ýdhra, Pétses, and Psará for trading under the Ottoman flag, as a counterpoise to the right to use the Russian flag which had been conferred on Ottoman Christian shipping in the Russo-Turkish peace treaty of Küčük Kainarca (1774) as this treaty had been interpreted by the Russian Government.[12] By 1774, several Transalpine Western countries— France, the Netherlands, Britain—had already secured an economic

---

[12] See Dascalakis, A., *Rhigas Velestinlis* (Paris 1937), p. 11; Finlay, G., *A History of Greece, B.C. 146–A.D. 1864*, ed. by Tozer, H. F., vol. vi (Oxford 1877), p. 5 n. 1.

hold over the Ottoman Imperial Government that was as throttling as the medieval Italian city-states' hold over the East Roman Imperial Government had been. Moreover, in the Ottoman Empire's earlier days, the Ottoman Government had taken two steps that had been inimical to the business enterprise of its Greek subjects. It had imposed a tax on industry and commerce,[13] which, surprisingly, appear to have been tax-free, though not control-free, under the East Roman Imperial regime. In the second place, the Ottoman Government had given asylum to the Sephardi Jews who had been expelled from Spain in 1492, and it had planted them in some of the principal commercial centres of the Ottoman Empire—Istanbul, Izmir, Thessaloníkê[14]—where they were formidable competitors for the native Christian business community.[15]

However, on balance, the Ottoman Government had inadvertently promoted its Christian subjects' business interests, too, far more effectively than it had intentionally handicapped them. It had relieved its non-Muslim subjects from formidable foreign competition by ruining the Levantine business of the Italian city-states that had won a field of economic enterprise for themselves in the Levant before the Ottoman Empire had established itself there. The 'Osmanlis had conquered most of the Italian outposts in the Levant, one after another, and Italian trade had been interrupted by the constant wars.[16] In the second place, the 'Osmanlis had not cared to step into the commercial vacuum that they had created. This vacuum therefore offered golden opportunities for the Ottoman Government's non-Muslim subjects. The use that the Ottoman Greeks made of this opportunity is noticed in Chapter IX of this book. The present world-wide activity of Greek shipping, and of other forms of Greek business activity, is due to the free rein that the Ottoman Imperial regime gave to Greek commercial enterprise after this had been set free from the East Roman Imperial Government's constricting dirigism by the liquidation of the East Roman Empire itself.

Commerce is the field in which the Modern Greeks have been most conspicuously successful so far. Their greatest failure has been the miscarriage of their attempts to resuscitate the East Roman Empire, a

[13] See Woodhouse, C. M., *The Greek War of Independence: Its Historical Setting* (London 1952), p. 25.

[14] Jewish refugees had been planted at Thessaloníkê as early as 1478 (Vakalópoulos, op. cit., vol. ii, part i, p. 345). At Thessaloníkê in 1519, there were 1087 Christian households, 1374 Muslim, and 3143 Jewish (ibid., pp. 345–6).

[15] According to Vakalópoulos, op. cit., vol. ii, part i, p. 38, the economic activities of these Spanish Jewish immigrants upset the Empire's economy and led to the impoverishment both of the fief-holders and of the members of the Pādishāh's slave-household.

[16] The Venetian beach-head at Methónê, at the south-western corner of the Pelopónnêsos, had been a thriving commercial port till its fall in 1500 (Vakalópoulos, op. cit., pp. 334–40). In 1502/3, Bayezid II repeopled Methónê and the adjacent ex-Venetian beach-head at Korónê with deported dissident Kizilbash (Shī'ī) Muslim Turks from the former independent Turkish principalities of Tekke and Hamid in Asia Minor (ibid., p. 98 n. 2).

dream that they cherished as 'the Great Idea' (ἡ Μεγάλη 'Ιδέα). Both this Greek success and this Greek failure are consequences of the Ottoman Imperial Government's policy. The 'Osmanlis relieved their Greek subjects of the commercial handicap that had been imposed on them under the East Roman regime. On the other hand, in depriving them of political sovereignty, they did not exempt them from having to continue to bear political burdens.

The Ottoman Imperial Government, like the Roman Imperial Government in the Age of the Principate, sought to confine its own field of political activity to the minimum required for maintaining its sovereignty over its subjects. It reserved for itself a monopoly of the conduct of foreign relations, the control of armed forces, provincial government, the administration of criminal justice, and the levying of taxes to meet the Imperial Government's own financial needs. All public affairs of the Pādishāh's non-Muslim subjects that were outside the field of his Imperial prerogatives were disposed of by permitting—or, it might be nearer to the truth to say, imposing—a regime of far-reaching autonomy on the Empire's non-Muslim subjects of divers religions. The adherents of each religion were reorganized as a 'millet' (a civil community) and every millet's domain was conterminous with the Empire itself. Each millet had a head (*millet başı*), and the highest ranking ecclesiastical dignitary of the religious community in question whose seat lay in Ottoman territory was the head of the corresponding millet *ex officio*; but in this capacity his functions were not ecclesiastical; they were civil and political. He presided over the administration of the millet's communal affairs, in so far as these did not come within the scope of the Imperial Government's prerogatives, and he was personally responsible to his political sovereign, the Pādishāh, for the behaviour of all his, the *millet başı*'s, co-religionists who were Ottoman subjects.

It has been noted in the preceding chapter that, when, in and after the reign of Mehmet the Conqueror (1451-81), the Ottoman millet system was worked out systematically, the Patriarch of Constantinople was made *millet başı* of the *Rum milleti*, and that this millet comprised all Eastern Orthodox Christian Ottoman subjects, including those who were not the Patriarch of Constantinople's ecclesiastical subjects and those who were not Greeks.[17] The *Rum milleti* was the largest and most important of all the Ottoman millets,[18] and the Patriarch of

[17] See above, p. 107.

[18] Before the sixteenth-century Ottoman conquest of an Arab region extending to Algeria, the Yaman, and 'Iraq inclusive, the *Rum milleti* surpassed the Ottoman Muslim community in size, though not, of course, in political importance. The Ottoman Sunni Muslims were the Empire's first-class citizens. After the incorporation in the Empire of extensive Arab territories in which the Sunni Muslims greatly outnumbered the Shī'ī Muslims and the Christians, the Sunni Muslims were in an absolute majority in the Empire's population.

Constantinople's position, as head of this millet, was particularly delicate.

Like the heads of the Jewish and Armenian communities in the Ottoman Empire, the Patriarch of Constantinople had co-religionists living, outside the Empire's frontiers, under other sovereignties. The ecclesiastical head of the whole Gregorian Armenian Church was, and is, the Katholikos of Echmiazin, who was successively a Persian and a Russian subject and is now a citizen of the Soviet Union. However, neither the Armenian Patriarch of Constantinople, who was the head of the Ottoman Armenian millet, nor the Ottoman Chief Rabbi had any ecclesiastical subjects in non-Ottoman territory, whereas the Eastern Orthodox Patriarch of Constantinople was the ecclesiastical head of all the Eastern Orthodox Christian population of Muscovy and Poland–Lithuania till the elevation of the Metropolitan of Moscow to Patriarchal rank in 1589 and the consequent union of the Eastern Orthodox subjects of Poland–Lithuania with the Roman Church in 1594–6. Moreover, when, in 1516–17, the Ottoman Pādishāh conquered Syria, Palestine, and Egypt, the Patriarch of Constantinople, as head of the *Rum milleti*, became responsible to the Ottoman Government politically for the Eastern Orthodox Christians in the Mamluks' former dominions, though these were ecclesiastical subjects, not of the Patriarch of Constantinople, but of his ecclesiastical peers the Patriarchs of Antioch, Jerusalem, and Alexandria. The *Rum milleti* now included not only Greeks but Bulgars, Serbs, Roumans, Albanians, Georgians, Qāramānlis,[19] and Arabs. These were brigaded together in the *Rum milleti* in virtue of their all professing the same religion, but they did not feel any political solidarity with each other.

The pretext on which Sultan Murād IV was induced, by the Jesuits, to have the Calvinist-minded Patriarch of Constantinople, Cyril Loúkaris, put to death in 1638 was that the Don Cossacks, who were still ecclesiastical subjects of the Constantinopolitan see, had seized Azov, the Ottoman fortress commanding the River Don's mouth. This pretext had no juridical basis; for the Don Cossacks were not Ottoman subjects, and therefore the Patriarch had no responsibility for them in his political capacity as the civil head of the Ottoman Eastern Orthodox Christian community. Sultan Mahmūd II, on the other hand, was juridically within his rights in holding the Patriarch Gregory V responsible, as *millet başı*, for the insurrection of the Greeks in 1821; for, though Prince Alexander Ypsilándês himself was no longer an Ottoman subject, the Greeks whom he recruited in the Transdanubian Principalities and the insurgents in Greece itself were Ottoman subjects unquestionably,

---

[19] Turkish-speaking Eastern Orthodox Christians in Asia Minor.

and consequently their *millet başı* was answerable for their acts.[20] In his ecclesiastical capacity as Patriarch, Gregory V excommunicated Ypsilándês, but this did not exonerate him.

Thus, for the Patriarch of Constantinople, the task of serving as the head of the *Rum milleti* was always onerous and was sometimes dangerous.[21] For the Ottoman Imperial Government, on the other hand, the imposition of a far-reaching civil autonomy on the Ottoman millets was convenient and was not dangerous so long as the Government was able to preserve unadulterated the master-institution that had enabled the House of 'Osman to conquer and to maintain its Empire.

This institution was the Pādishāh's household, recruited from voluntary converts from Christianity—deserters, prisoners of war, and eventually the compulsorily conscripted (but never forcibly converted) children of the Pādishāh's own Christian subjects. In the household's heyday, its members were admirably disciplined—especially the native Ottoman Christian 'tribute children', who were the Pādishāh's slaves— and they were also carefully graded and selected. Each individual was given the education that accorded best with his ability. The ablest were educated to become the Empire's administrators, and the next ablest to serve in the household cavalry and in the Janissaries, a corps of

---

[20] But of course this does not justify the savagery of Mahmūd II's reprisals. He put to death not only the Patriarch Gregory V himself, but also two metropolitans, twelve bishops, the Dragoman of the Porte and his brother, and a number of other Phanariots (Runciman, op. cit., p. 406). Gregory V had not deserved this fate. He had behaved as a loyal servant of the Ottoman Government at the risk of being execrated by his Greek co-religionists. He has been debited—whether correctly or not—with having been the author of a book ascribed, on the title-page, to Anthimos, the Patriarch of Jerusalem, and published in 1798 under the title of *The Paternal Exhortation* ('H Διδασκαλία Πατρική), in which the Ottoman regime is commended to its Eastern Orthodox Christian subjects as having been the salvation of Orthodoxy. (The Greek text of this book is translated and discussed by Richard Clogg in 'The "Dhidhaskalia Patriki" (1798), an Orthodox Reaction to French Revolutionary Propaganda', in *Middle Eastern Studies*, vol. v (1969), pp. 87–115.) In 1805 the Patriarch (Gregory V's temporary successor) complied with a demand, from Sultan Selīm III, that he should issue a decree threatening with excommunication any priest or monk who failed to co-operate with the Ottoman authorities in suppressing the *klephts* in the Pelopónnêsos (see Theodore Kolokotrónês, Διήγησις συμβάντων τῆς 'Ελληνικῆς φυλῆς (1770–1836) (Athens 1901), p. 16; Runciman op. cit., p. 398). In 1807, Gregory V, on instructions from the Ottoman Government, had tried to persuade the insurgent Serb members of the *Rum milleti* to return to their allegiance (Bótzaris, N., *Visions balkaniques dans la préparation de la révolution Grecque (1789–1821)* (Paris 1962, Geneva 1962), pp. 69–70). After the foundation of the secret Society of Friends (Φιλική 'Εταιρία) in 1814, Gregory V, who was then living on Mount Athos, after having been deposed for the second time, refused to join, on the ground that he was bound by his oath to the Pādishāh (Runciman, op. cit., p. 400; Bótzaris, op. cit., p. 96). It was unfortunate for Gregory V that, after this, he was reinstated for the second time in 1818. If he had remained in disgrace and in retirement, he would have escaped the fate that he suffered in 1821.

[21] These drawbacks, for the Ecumenical Patriarch, of his being conscripted to serve as an Ottoman *millet başı* were not offset by the increase in the power—e.g. over the other three eastern Patriarchs and their flocks—which the office of *millet başı* brought to him. The three eastern Patriarchates did not recover their independence in civil affairs until 1856 (see Vakalópoulos, op. cit., vol. ii, part i, pp. 176–8).

uniformed regular infantry armed with muskets. The least able were
trained for humbler employments.

The total strength of the Pādishāh's household (excluding the household cavalrymen's own slaves who accompanied them on campaign)
was only about 56,000.[22] Compared with the size of the Empire's
population, this figure was minute, but the household was numerous
enough for its purpose; for the selection of ability and the cultivation of it
by discipline and education made for a high level of efficiency. In its
heyday, the Pādishāh's household was able to defend and expand the
Empire's frontiers, besides exercising an effective control over the
Empire's subjects. The slave-household kept in order not only the non-
Muslim millets but also the Muslim holders of the fiefs that maintained
the semi-professional provincial component of the army. The Pādishāh's slave-household was more successful than the East Roman
Imperial civil service had been in protecting the peasantry. The
Ottoman provincial fiefs were revocable, not hereditary, and the fief-
holders were restrained from maltreating the peasants by whose work
they lived. However, there were different categories of peasants on the
fiefs, ranging from tenants to serfs.[23] The fief-holders' peasants sometimes migrated from one fief to another, but a fief-holder was legally
entitled, if able, to compel a migrant peasant to return within a time-
limit of ten years.[24]

Vakalópoulos considers that it is an open question whether the
peasantry's lot was worsened or was ameliorated as a result of the
Ottoman conquest.[25] He holds that, for some categories of *ra'īyeh*,
the conquest did bring with it some alleviation.[26] Mehmet II did protect
the peasants, but the rates at which he had set their taxes were raised
later.[27] In any case, the Muslim peasants were as much oppressed as
their Christian fellow-victims.[28] Mehmet II's policy with regard to his
Eastern Orthodox Christian subjects was particularly enlightened. He
realized that they constituted the majority of his subjects. He wanted to
reassure them, and to encourage the anti-Uniates to persist in their
stance.[29] He imposed penalties for the ill-treatment of Christian
Ottoman subjects by Muslims.[30] In this deliberate practice of religious

[22] See the table in Toynbee, A. J., *A Study of History*, vol. iii, p. 45 n. 2.
[23] Vakalópoulos, op. cit., vol. ii, part i, pp. 16–19.
[24] Ibid., p. 30.
[25] See H. A. R. Gibb and Harold Bowen, *Islamic Society and the West*, vol. i, part i (London 1950),
pp. 235–8, for a detailed account of the Christian peasants' conditions, both *de jure* and *de facto*,
under the Ottoman regime in Rumelia and Anatolia.
[26] Vakalópoulos, op. cit., vol. ii, part i, pp. 23–4.
[27] Ibid., pp. 26–7.
[28] Ibid., pp. 28–9.
[29] Ibid., pp. 134–5.
[30] Ibid., p. 143.

tolerance, Mehmet II had been anticipated by Bayezid I in 1391 and by Murād II in 1430 on the occasion of the Ottoman annexation of Thessaloníkê.[31]

Mehmet II's measures for reassuring his anti-Uniate Eastern Orthodox Christian subjects were, of course, inspired by practical considerations of policy, which moved him to treat his Gregorian Monophysite Armenian subjects and his Jewish subjects, too, considerately.[32] But in his relations with George Skholários (*vivebat* 1405-75),[33] who was his principal Christian assistant in the implementation of this policy, there was also a human element of mutual esteem and perhaps even positive friendship. By the date of the Ottoman capture of Constantinople in 1453, Mehmet II must have informed himself thoroughly about Skholários' character and career, and have realized that, notwithstanding his studies of Latin Christian theology, his personal acquaintance with Western scholars, and his original acceptance of the ecclesiastical union of 1439,[34] Skholários had declared himself an anti-Uniate in 1443 and had quarrelled with the Uniate last East Roman Emperor, Constantine XI Dhrághasis.[35] After the Fall of Constantinople, Mehmet II made inquiries about Skholários' fate, and, finding that he had been enslaved, he ransomed him and caused him to be elected to the vacant post of Ecumenical Patriarch.[36]

On 6 January 1454, Skholários was consequently elected Patriarch, under the name Yennádhios, by a synod convened *ad hoc*. Though he was already a monk, he was still a layman, so he was ordained, through all the ranks of the ecclesiastical hierarchy, from deacon to patriarch, in the course of a single day.[37] The Pādishāh himself not only gave Yennádhios signal marks of honour on this occasion; he also re-conferred on the Ecumenical Patriarchate all the rights and privileges that it had enjoyed under the East Roman Imperial regime;[38] according to George Sphrandzês,[39] Mehmet II confirmed this in writing; but the passage is suspect, and no document to this effect has survived.[40] In any case, Mehmet II's personal regard for Yennádhios is not in doubt. He

[31] Ibid., p. 135.

[32] Ibid., p. 140.

[33] See the bibliographical note in ibid., p. 136 n. 1.

[34] Ibid., pp. 136-7.

[35] Ibid., pp. 138 and 157.

[36] Ibid., p. 139.

[37] Ibid.

[38] Kritóvoulos, *History of Mehmed the Conqueror*, English translation by Riggs, C. T. (Princeton 1954), p. 94 (part ii, § 7).

[39] Phrantzês, *Chronicon*, p. 308 Bonn; p. 446 Bucharest.

[40] See Vakalópoulos, op. cit., vol. ii, part i, pp. 141-2. F. Babinger, *Mehmed der Eroberer und Seine Zeit* (Munich 1953), p. 110, assumes that Mehmet II did put his charter to the Ecumenical Patriarchate in writing.

visited him three times at the Pammakáristos Convent,[41] and he did his utmost to dissuade him from retiring, as Yennádhios did retire in 1456, to Mount Athos[42] as a result of his having found, by experience, that, even with the Pādishāh's good will and support, the task of an Ecumenical Patriarch under the Ottoman regime was intolerable. In 1458, Yennádhios migrated from Mount Athos to the Monastery of Saint John the Precursor on Mount Meníkhion, near Serrhés, and remained there till his death.[43]

The Ottoman *arcanum imperii* was the slave-household's monopoly of the public service. The sons of members of the household were not ex-Christian slaves; unlike their fathers, they were Muslim freemen, and the superiority of their status debarred them from repeating their slave-fathers' careers. This rule was indispensable for the maintenance of the household's efficiency; for Muslim freemen—even those whose fathers were ex-Christian slaves—could not be made to submit to the slave-household's rigorous discipline and exacting education. However, the exclusion of a Muslim empire's free Muslim subjects from the public service was a paradox, and, before the close of the sixteenth century, the free Muslim 'Osmanlis had forced their way in.[44] The Pādishāh was compelled to admit into his household first the sons of household cavalrymen, then Janissaries' sons, and finally free Muslims who were free Muslims' sons. The size of the household increased; yet, even so, the pressure to gain entry, and to bequeath the right, was so great that, in the course of the seventeenth century, the recruitment of the household from conscript Christian children was reduced to a trickle.[45] In consequence, discipline broke down, efficiency was lost, and, after the failure of the second Ottoman Siege of Vienna (1682–3), the Empire was compelled in 1699, for the first time in its history, to make large cessions of territory as the price of peace. The Ottoman Empire's straits were its Greek subjects' opportunity.

Now that the Empire had been thrown on the defensive in its perennial warfare with the Christian powers, the Imperial Government was less able than ever to afford to do without efficient public servants. It could no longer supply itself with these in sufficient numbers by

[41] Vakalópoulos, op. cit., vol. ii, part i, p. 146.

[42] Ibid., p. 152.

[43] See Finlay, op. cit., vol. v, p. 139.

[44] Originally, the members of the Pādishāh's slave-household, like Roman soldiers in the Age of the Principate, had been debarred from contracting legal marriages. The *qullar* extorted from Suleyman I (*imperabat* 1520–66) the abrogation of this ban, and, for free Muslim aspirants, this concession removed a deterrent (Vakalópoulos, op. cit., vol. ii, part i, p. 58).

[45] See Toynbee, op. cit., vol. iii, p. 49 n. 4. The last *devrişme* (periodical conscription of non-Muslim children) for the recruitment of 'ajemoğlans was made at Náousa in 1705, and it provoked an *émeute* (Vakalópoulos, op. cit., vol. ii, part i, pp. 52 and 58–9). The last conscription for the recruitment of içoğlans was made about half-way through the eighteenth century (ibid., p. 59).

conscripting its Christian subjects' children as slaves. The free Muslim entrants had left too little room for slave Christian conscripts. The Government was therefore constrained to employ able Ottoman Christians unenslaved and unconverted; and, among the various Ottoman Christian peoples, the Greeks had become the best qualified for giving the Ottoman Government the kind of service that it now needed. Before the dilution of the slave-household, Serbs and Croats had figured prominently among the men who had risen to the top. Now that the Pādishāh had come to need diplomatists almost as much as soldiers, the Greeks monopolized the new posts that were created for unconverted non-Muslim Ottoman subjects.

The Ottoman Government itself had enabled its Greek subjects to qualify themselves for seizing this opportunity. The Government had allowed them to make fortunes in the international trade between the Ottoman Empire and the West and it had compelled their highest ranking ecclesiastical dignitary, the Patriarch of Constantinople, to become the head of the largest of the Ottoman millets. In the preceding chapter it has been noted that, in order to perform his new civil functions, the Patriarch had to take laymen on to his staff—for instance, lawyers and financiers.[46] This gave to financially successful Ottoman Greek businessmen, both aristocrats and plebeians, an opening—the first political opening for any Greeks since the Ottoman conquest of the last patches of politically independent Greek territory—for making their way into public life. They gravitated towards the Phanári ('Light-house') quarter of Istanbul, in the northern corner of the city, to which the Patriarchate had migrated after 1453.[47] The Patriarchate benefited from its association with these 'Phanariots'[48] though it also became financially dependent on them.[49]

Some of the Greek aristocrats who had lost their political power and their lands at, and indeed before, the liquidation of the East Roman Imperial Government had kept themselves temporarily afloat by farming the Ottoman Imperial Government's taxes and by engaging in commercial business.[50] These aristocrats also intermarried with the

---

[46] See Vakalópoulos, op. cit., vol. ii, part i, pp. 160–80; Runciman, *The Great Church in Captivity*, p. 175; Bótzaris, op. cit., pp. 11–12; and the present work, p. 107.

[47] Mehmet II had given to his Patriarch Yennádhios in lieu of the Ayía Sophía the Church of the Holy Apostles, which ranked second among all the churches in Constantinople. Yennádhios had voluntarily surrendered the Holy Apostles in 1454, and from 1454 to 1586 the Patriarchate was installed in the convent of the Pammakáristos. After 1586 it made two further moves before settling permanently at the Church of St. George in the Phanar in 1601 (Vakalópoulos, op. cit., vol. ii, part i, p. 144).

[48] See below, p. 217.

[49] See Runciman, op. cit., p. 202.

[50] Information from Theodósios Zyghomalás in a letter of 7 April 1581, to Crusius; see Crusius, *Turcograecia*, pp. 91–2, cited by Vakalópoulos, vol. ii, part i, p. 356 with n. 2.

nouveaux riches plebeian Greeks who had begun to make fortunes after the change of political regime. However, most of these noble families had become extinct by the close of the sixteenth century.[51] These temporarily surviving noble houses had included some of the Palaiológhoi, Kandakouzênoí, and Komnênoí.[52]

On the other hand, the Trapezoundian nobility, who had been deported from Trebizond to Adrianople and Constantinople by Mehmet II after his annexation of Trebizond in 1461, were more successful in the struggle for survival, and these, like the plebeian *parvenus*, took a leading part in the administration of the Patriarchate's affairs. For instance, in November 1462, the ex-*protovestiários* of the liquidated Empire of Trebizond, George Amiroúkês, engineered, through the influence of his kinsman the *vezīr* Mahmūd Paşa, the deposition of the Patriarch Joasaph I. The Trapezoundian deportees subsequently engineered the election to the Patriarchate of a Trapezoundian monk named Symeon. They achieved this through the influence of their sons, who had become *içoğlans* and had risen to high posts in the Ottoman administration. The transaction was clinched by a *douceur* to the Sultan.[53]

The Patriarch Yennádhios himself condoned laxity in general, and in particular he condoned, and even concealed, the practice of simony.[54] In 1577 the German traveller Stephen Gerlach observed[55] that ecclesiastical appointments and the decisions of the Patriarchal lawcourt were manipulated by a layman, Michael Kándakouzênós.[56] The increase of simony under the Ottoman regime put the Patriarchate at the mercy of wealthy Greek Ottoman subjects.[57]

The Phanariots' participation in the Patriarchate's administration of the *Rum milleti* brought the Phanariots into touch with the Ottoman Government, and in 1669 the rehabilitator of the Ottoman Empire, Grand Vezīr, Ahmet Köprülü, created the new post of 'Dragoman of the Porte' (Interpreter for the Imperial Government) for a Phanariot of Khiot origin, Panayiotákês Nikoússios Mamonás, who had been Ahmet Köprülü's private physician. Ahmet Köprülü also created another post—that of 'Dragoman of the Fleet'—to be held, likewise, by an unconverted free Greek Ottoman subject.

Ahmet Köprülü was the second in a series of six Grand Vezīrs of the same family who were in office during most years in the half-century

[51] Vakalópoulos, op. cit., vol. ii, part i, p. 357.
[52] Ibid., p. 355.
[53] Ibid., p. 164.
[54] Ibid., pp. 150–1.
[55] *Tagebuch* (Frankfurt am Main 1674), p. 267.
[56] Vakalópoulos, op. cit., vol. ii, part i, pp. 172–3.
[57] Ibid., pp. 164–6.

1656–1710[58] in which the tide visibly turned against the Ottoman Empire in its relations with the Western powers. The first five of the six Köprülü Grand Vezīrs were able men; they had not lost the 'Osmanlis' traditional concern for discovering ability, nor their traditional virtue of valuing and fostering ability wherever this might be found; they were free Muslims, not ex-Christian slaves; and they were willing to make use of the ability of their free Christian fellow Ottoman subjects, without requiring them to submit to the enslavement and the conversion that, under the original Ottoman dispensation, had been the price that ex-Christians had had to pay for being given a monopoly of political power.

At this crisis in Ottoman history the Phanariots promised to be useful to the Ottoman Imperial Government because they had acquired experience and knowledge that had now become pertinent to the Empire's needs. Through their business dealings with the West, the Phanariots had become familiar with the Western way of life, and the 'Osmanlis had now, for the first time, to take account of this, because they had now to negotiate with Western Governments whom they could no longer simply coerce by force of arms. The Phanariots perceived that education is one of the keys to power.[59] They had become accomplished linguists;[60] and they had deepened their knowledge and understanding of the West by completing their education there, particularly at the University of Padua, which was the University of the Venetian Empire and which admitted non-Roman Catholic Christian students without requiring them to become Roman Catholics. Panayiotákês Nikoússios had been a student at Padua. His more famous successor, Alexander Mavrokordháto, studied at Padua and then at Bologna. Both of them studied medicine, and Mavrokordháto succeeded Nikoússios as Ahmet Köprülü's private physician before succeeding him also as Dragoman of the Porte. Under the Ottoman regime, medicine, like commerce, was a free field for non-Muslim Ottoman subjects' enterprise.[61]

The creation of the two new posts of Dragoman of the Porte and Dragoman of the Fleet, to be held by free and unconverted Ottoman Greeks—in practice almost exclusively by Phanariots—was a revolutionary new departure in Ottoman policy. This innovation was followed up, after 1711, by giving the Phanariots the monopoly of holding two other high posts, the offices of prince (*hospodar*) of each of the two autonomous Eastern Orthodox Christian Principalities Wallachia and Moldavia.

[58] See Toynbee, op. cit., vol. vi, p. 208, with n. 3.

[59] See Runciman, op. cit., pp. 376–7; Bótzaris, op. cit., p. 10.

[60] See Tsakonas, D., *Geist und Gesellschaft in Griechenland* (Bonn 1965), p. 20; Dascalakis, A., *Rhigas Velestinlis* (Paris 1937), pp. 26–7.

[61] See Runciman, op. cit., pp. 213 and 363–9; Tsakonas, op. cit., p. 20; Vakalópoulos, op. cit., vol. ii, part i, pp. 271 and 354.

These two Principalities had been established in the fourteenth century by Rouman settlers from the eastern fringes of Hungary. Their settlement was the final victory of the ploughman over the pastoral nomad in a region that, before then, had been debatable territory between these two different economic dispensations. The soil was fertile, and, under cultivation, it yielded rich returns. The two Principalities had originally been under the suzerainty of Hungary, the country from which the Rouman settlers had come. But the Principalities had hardly been founded before the Ottoman Empire, expanding northwards, began to compete with Hungary for the Principalities' allegiance.

In this competition the Ottoman Empire was eventually the winner; but the Principalities put up a formidable resistance, and the power of their original suzerain, Hungary, was not broken by the 'Osmanlis till 1526. Consequently, the Principalities, when they submitted to the 'Osmanlis shortly before that date, were able to obtain terms that had not been granted by the Ottoman Government to any other conquered Christian countries. It was agreed that the Principalities should remain autonomous under Ottoman suzerainty, that they should always be governed by princes of their own religion, and that no Muslim places of worship and no Ottoman fiefs or Ottoman Turkish Muslim colonies should ever be planted on their territories.[62] Though the Rouman princes and population of the two Principalities had come from the Roman Catholic Christian Kingdom of Hungary, they themselves were Eastern Orthodox Christians. As such, they were ecclesiastical subjects of the Patriarch of Constantinople.

Between the years 1526 and 1683, the Ottoman Empire's suzerainty over the two Principalities was secure. But after 1683 it was threatened first by the Habsburg Monarchy's counter-offensive and then by the expansion of the Russian Empire. The Westernization of Russia by Peter the Great enhanced Russian power just at the time when Ottoman power had begun to decline. In 1711, Peter invaded Moldavia. This Russian venture ended in disaster. Peter was outmanœuvred by the 'Osmanlis, and he had to purchase his release from an encompassing Ottoman army's toils at a high price. The Ottoman Government, however, was not consoled by its military success for the treachery of the Prince of Moldavia, Demetrius Cantemir, who had no sooner been appointed than he had invited Peter to invade the Principality that the Ottoman Government had entrusted to him.

Cantemir was an Eastern Orthodox Christian, as he had to be under the terms on which Moldavia had submitted to Ottoman suzerainty. He was of mixed Graeco-Tatar origin (the native Rouman Bessaraba dynasty was extinct). The Ottoman Government took Cantemir's

[62] See Toynbee, op. cit., vol. ii, p. 225 n. 1.

treason to heart, and in Moldavia from 1711 onwards, and in Wallachia from 1716 onwards, the Pādishāh made a practice of conferring the hospodarships of the two Principalities on Phanariots. These were eligible, in virtue of their being Eastern Orthodox Christians, and the Ottoman Government reckoned that they would be amenable, considering that they were Ottoman subjects whose headquarters were in Istanbul and who were therefore, like the Patriarch, at the Pādishāh's mercy. The consequence, however, was not what the Ottoman Government had intended. Between 1711/16 and 1821, the Phanariot princes and their Greek entourage converted the Principalities into something like a sub-empire, under Greek control, within the Ottoman Empire's dominions.[63]

The ground had been prepared for this by the ecclesiastical jurisdiction of the Patriarchate of Constantinople over the Rouman Eastern Orthodox Christians, as well as by the Ottoman Empire's political suzerainty over the two Roumanian Principalities. Both these links had already enabled the Phanariots to gain a foothold in the Principalities before the Pādishāh put the political control over the Principalities into the Phanariots' hands. The native Rouman Bessaraba dynasty had been attracted to Greek culture by its attachment to Eastern Orthodoxy. It had endowed the Eastern Orthodox Patriarchates and the Metéora monasteries and the monasteries on Mount Athos with estates in the Principalities.[64] Phanariot families had intermarried with scions of the Bessaraba House and with other families that had been invested with the rule over the Principalities in the seventeenth century after the Bessaraba had become extinct. Like the Bessaraba themselves, the Rouman land-owning aristocracy in the Principalities, and the upper ranks of the Eastern Orthodox Christian hierarchy there, had found Greek culture attractive, and the Phanariots managed to insinuate themselves, side by side with the native notables, without arousing their hostility. The country was rich, the peasantry was exploited, and enough could be wrung out of them to satisfy their Greek as well as their native oppressors.

The Phanariots invested in land in the Principalities as much as possible of the wealth that they had gained in trade. Successful businessmen have always and everywhere aspired to become land-owners; the Phanariots had an additional incentive. Real estate in these autonomous Principalities was less perilously exposed to the danger of being

---

[63] See Runciman, op. cit., Book II, chapter 10, 'The Phanariots', pp. 360–84; Finlay, op. cit., vol. v, pp. 241–4.

[64] See Vakalópoulos, op. cit., vol. ii, part i, pp. 159–90 and 402. The native Rouman princes were more generous than their Phanariot successors, who had to recoup themselves, during brief tenures of office, for their heavy previous expenditure on purchasing the office by giving bribes to Ottoman officials (see ibid., pp. 189–90).

expropriated by the Phanariots' Ottoman masters than property in territory that was under direct Ottoman rule.[65] The Rouman peasants in the Principalities suffered in the seventeenth and eighteenth centuries what had been suffered in the tenth and eleventh centuries by the Greek peasants in Asia Minor.

In the seventeenth and eighteenth centuries, the Principalities had become important seats of Greek education and culture, thanks to their being exempt from direct Ottoman control. In 1680 a Greek printing press was established at Jassy in Moldavia by Dhosítheos, a Peloponnesian Greek who had risen to be Eastern Orthodox Patriarch of Jerusalem (1669–1707). The Patriarchate of Jerusalem had valuable estates in Moldavia which gave it local resources, and its press at Jassy became the most important one of any in Eastern Orthodox Christendom.[66] The Ottoman Greeks made themselves thoroughly at home in the Principalities in the course of the two centuries ending in 1821. Their local success there encouraged them to hope that, by the tactics of peaceful penetration which had proved so effective in the Principalities, they might eventually come to dominate the Ottoman Empire as a whole.[67]

This political hope was the incentive that induced the Phanariots to keep on bidding for the Principalities after the Ottoman Government had made these the Phanariots' political preserve. Financially, these appointments were ruinous. Candidates had to bribe the whole hierarchy of Ottoman court officials on an ascending scale; and, more often than not, a successful candidate would be deposed and replaced before he had had time to recoup himself at the Wallachian or Moldavian peasants' expense; for, the more frequently the princes were changed, the shorter, for the Ottoman officials, were the intervals between their opportunities for extorting bribes. Constantine Ypsilándês, who was successively Dragoman of the Porte, Hospodar of Moldavia (1799–1801), and Hospodar of Wallachia (1802–6 and again in 1806–8), looked forward to transforming the Ottoman Empire into an association of Principalities on the Wallachian and Moldavian model.[68]

This hope seemed reasonable at the time; for, after the signal defeat of the Ottoman Empire in the Russo-Turkish War of 1768–74, it looked as if the Ottoman dominions were breaking up into a mosaic of successor-states. Most of these were being carved out by Muslim adventurers; but at least one of these usurpers, 'Ali Paşa of Yánnina,[69] whose capital lay in

---

[65] See Runciman, op. cit., pp. 364–5.

[66] See ibid., pp. 347–52.

[67] See ibid., pp. 372 and 375–6; Woodhouse, C. M., op. cit., p. 20; Bótzaris, op. cit., p. 11.

[68] Bótzaris, op. cit., pp. 43, 64, 66.

[69] See Finlay, op. cit., vol. vi, pp. 53–95; Aravandinos, Sp. P., Ἱστορία τοῦ Ἀλῆ Πασᾶ τοῦ τεπελενλῆ (Athens 1895); Bótzaris, op. cit., pp. 48–9.

a region inhabited predominantly by Greeks, employed Greeks in his public administration and used the Greek language as his medium for correspondence and records.[70]

Thus, paradoxically, the incubus of the East Roman Empire, which the 'Osmanlis seemed to have taken over from the Greeks in 1453–61, had been partially reimposed upon the Greeks by Mehmet the Conqueror himself when he had constrained the Patriarch of Constantinople to become the head of the *Rum milleti*. This political burden had then become a political lure when the Ottoman Imperial Government had given its Phanariot Greek subjects the monopoly of occupying four key posts, the dragomanships of the Porte and the Fleet and the hospodarships of Wallachia and Moldavia. This lure led the Greeks into their greatest failure in the Modern Age of their history. In spite of the swift collapse of Prince Alexander Ypsilándês' invasion of Moldavia in 1821, the Greeks continued, for a century longer, to be haunted by 'the Great Idea'. The ghost was not laid till after the Greeks' catastrophe in the Graeco-Turkish war of 1919–22. In 1922 the Greeks and the Turks shook off the incubus of the East Roman Empire simultaneously.

The failure of the 'Great Idea' is dealt with in Chapter IX. The war of 1919–22 in Asia Minor demonstrated that the transformation of Asia Minor in the Byzantine Age from a Greek country into a Turkish country was irreversible, and this proved retrospectively that the Phanariots' dream of substituting a Greek for a Turkish hegemony over the entire Ottoman Empire had been moonshine. However, the Turks had not played the principal part in preventing the Phanariots from attaining their unrealistic objective. So far from that, the 'Osmanlis had actually reawakened the Greeks' political ambitions by improvidently thrusting political power into the Phanariots' hands. The adversaries who defeated the Phanariots were the non-Greek majority of the Pādishāh's Eastern Orthodox Christian subjects who had been made into the Greeks' unwilling yoke-fellows in the *Rum milleti*. Their unwillingness to see Ottoman Turkish Muslim domination replaced by Ottoman Greek Christian domination was the stumbling-block that the Phanariots could neither surmount nor circumvent.

The chief sufferers from the Phanariots' will to power were the Rouman peasants in the Principalities. From 1711 to 1821 these peasants were taxed, more mercilessly than ever before, by alien Greek princes who were always working against time to try to recoup as much as possible of their outlay in bribes to Ottoman officials. In 1821 the Rouman peasants' long-accumulated resentment came to light. By that date the Phanariots ought not to have been blind to the undercurrent, in the Principalities, of Roumanian national feeling. In 1679 the Greek

---

[70] See below, p. 218.

Patriarch of Jerusalem Dhosítheos himself had published at Jassy a translation of the Eastern Orthodox liturgy into Roumanian from Old Slavonic, and Roumanian continued to be the language of the liturgy in the Principalities thereafter,[71] though Greek became, temporarily, the language of higher secular education for the tiny minority that could afford to pay for this. The Greek prelate Dhosítheos' endowment of the Roumans with a version of the liturgy in their own national language did him credit. He was following the Byzantine Greek tradition of linguistic liberalism. At the same time, the Roumanian demand that he was satisfying ought to have opened his and his compatriots' eyes.

On the ecclesiastical plane, the Greeks appeared to have won victories in the eighteenth century over their Serb and Bulgar fellow members of the *Rum milleti*. In 1737 the Ottoman Imperial Government appointed a Greek to occupy the throne of the Serb Patriarchate of Peć, after this had been vacated by the reigning Serb Patriarch Arsenije IV's migration from Ottoman to Habsburg territory.[72] Thereafter, the Ottoman Government, at its Greek subjects' instance, abolished the Serb Patriarchate of Peć in 1766 and the West-Bulgarian Archbishopric of Okhrida in 1767, and placed these two hitherto autonomous Slavophone Eastern Orthodox churches under the Patriarch of Constantinople's direct ecclesiastical authority.[73] This looked, at the time, like a confirmation of the Greeks' hegemony over the non-Greek majority of the *Rum milleti*, and no doubt the Phanariots regarded it as an important step forward in their progressive 'take-over' of the Ottoman Empire. The actual effect, however, soon proved to be 'counter-productive'.

[71] See Jorga, N., *Geschichte der Rumänen und ihrer Kultur* (Hermannstadt [Sibiu] 1929), pp. 233-4 and 239-40.

[72] See Hadrovics, I., *L'Église serbe sous la domination turque* (Paris 1947), p. 153.

[73] See Gibb, H. A. R., and Bowen, H., *Islamic Society and the West*, vol. i, part ii (London 1957), p. 238 with n. 4.

VIII

THE MODERN GREEKS' HERITAGE
FROM THE HELLENIC GREEKS

THE Modern Greeks' heritage from the Hellenic Greeks is not on a par with their heritage from the Byzantines. Their Byzantine heritage is direct and has been inescapable. The Modern Greeks have inherited the Byzantine Greeks' religion and also the form of the Greek language that, in everyday life, the Greeks were speaking already in the Byzantine Age. On the other hand, the Modern Greeks are sundered from the Hellenic Greeks chronologically by the time-span of the Byzantine Age of Greek history, and culturally by the revolution in the Greek attitude to life, and way of life, at the transition to the Byzantine Age from the Hellenic. In casting back to their Hellenic past, the Modern Greeks have not been preserving a heritage; they have been raising a ghost, and they have been moved by desperation. They identified themselves with the Hellenes when, in 1182-1204, the Byzantine Greek World collapsed.

The culminating event in this collapse was the capture and sack of Constantinople in 1204 by the Venetians and the French and the installation of a French Emperor in the Imperial City. This was the first time that Constantinople had fallen since its inauguration in A.D. 330. In the course of the intervening 874 years, the City had experienced, and had survived, three great sieges: in 626, in 674-8, and in 717-18. It had survived against all likelihood, and these apparently miraculous escapes had created the illusion that Constantinople was impregnable. In 1204 this long-cherished illusion was shattered once for all. The shock in 1204 was therefore greater than it was in 1453, when the City fell for the second time. This time, the disaster had a precedent, and it did not come as a surprise. By 1453, Constantinople had been encircled and beleaguered for a century during which the noose had been drawn tighter and tighter.

From the date of the overthrow of the First Persian Empire by Alexander until A.D. 1204, the Greeks had felt that the Greek way of life was the only true form of civilization, and this Greek belief had not been shaken by the Roman conquest; for the Romans had quickly become converts to Greek culture, and the Greeks had eventually made the Roman Empire their own. As masters of the Roman Empire, they had come to feel that they were masters of the whole world politically as well as culturally. After the cataclysm in the seventh century this Greek pretension was quite out of relation with the facts, even at the western end of the Old World, not to speak of Eastern Asia. Yet the Greeks had continued to think of themselves as being the Imperial Roman people; and East Roman Emperors had taken offence when Popes and German self-styled emperors had called them emperors, not of the Romans, but of the Greeks (*Graecorum*). The name 'Greeks' had been applied to the Byzantine Greeks by these Westerners as an insult, and the Westerners had known that it would be taken as such.

Unsophisticated Greeks have clung to the name *Rhomaîoi* (pronounced '*Rhomyí*') till within living memory. Greek soldiers were still calling themselves 'Romans' during the Graeco-Turkish war of 1919–22.[1] On the other hand, a sophisticated minority realized, after the fall of Constantinople in 1204, that the Greeks' claim to be the Imperial people was no longer tenable. During the greater part of the eleventh and twelfth centuries the East Roman Empire had been multi-national; but, in the course of the last two decades of the twelfth century, both the Serbs and the Bulgars had recovered their independence, and, after 1204, the remnant of the Empire that had escaped being conquered by the Latins had broken up into three separate Greek successor-states.

These successor-states were sundered from each other geographically; their capitals were Arta in Êpeiros, Trebizond (Trapezoús) near the east end of the north coast of Asia Minor, and Níkaia in the Asian hinterland of the Sea of Marmara; but they had one feature in common: in each of them the Greeks were in an overwhelming majority. The largest, the best governed, and the most successful in expanding at both its Latin and its Greek competitors' expense, was the Empire of Níkaia. This was where most of the survivors of the Constantinopolitan Greek intellectuals had found asylum; and these refugees decided that, since it would be incongruous for exiles from the New Rome to continue to call themselves 'Romans', they were now going to claim, instead, to be Hellenes— using the name no longer in the depreciatory sense of extinct pagans, but in the laudatory sense of living heirs of the glorious Hellenic Greek civilization.

This revolutionary rehabilitation of the name 'Hellenes' to stand for something superior to the name 'Romans' seems to have been put into

---

[1] At that date the Turks were distinguishing between the Greek invaders of Turkey from the Ottoman Empire's successor-state, the Kingdom of Greece, and the Greek minority in Turkey itself, which, till 1922, was still *in situ*. The Turks noticed that the Greeks from the Kingdom were now spirited, whereas the Greeks who were still Ottoman subjects were still submissive. The Turks still called the Ottoman Greeks '*Rum*' ('Romans'), but they called the invading Greeks '*Yunan*' ('Ionians').

currency by the refugee scholar Nikólaos Vlemmýdhês (*vivebat circa* 1197–1272),[2] and it was adopted by his pupil the Nicene Emperor Theodore II Láskaris (*imperabat* 1254–8).[3] The neo-Hellenes' intention was to give the Greek people a new start. The Greeks had survived the fall of the East Roman Empire; they must extricate themselves from the Empire's ruins. But, in their effort to jump clear of the Empire, the neo-Hellenes were in danger of falling foul of the Church; for, in claiming to be the heirs of the Hellenes, they were identifying themselves with the whole of the Hellenic way of life, and Hellenism had been not only pre-Christian but anti-Christian—hence the depreciatory connotation that it had acquired for the ex-Hellenic Greeks after their conversion to Christianity.

The Byzantine Christian Greeks had continued to cultivate the Hellenic form of the Greek language, but exclusively for the sake of imitating its grammar, vocabulary, and style. The Byzantines had distinguished between the language itself and the *Weltanschauung* presented in the literature written in this language.[4] They had revered the letter of Hellenism but had repudiated its spirit. The neo-Hellenes were committing themselves implicitly to the spirit of Hellenism, as well as to the letter, in claiming affiliation to Hellenism, and professing allegiance to it, without making any reservations. It is remarkable that the first important exponent of neo-Hellenism, Nikólaos Vlemmýdhês, was a monk; but it is also significant that both the Nicene Emperor John III Vatátsês (1222–54) and his successor, Vlemmýdhês' own pupil Theodore II Láskaris (1254–8), shied away from appointing Vlemmýdhês to the post of Patriarch of Constantinople in exile.[5]

However, in the thirteenth century the potential conflict between neo-Hellenism and Eastern Orthodox Christianity did not come to a

---

[2] For Vlemmýdhês' literary works, see Krumbacher, op. cit., pp. 445–9.

[3] See Βακαλόπουλος, Α.; Ἱστορία τοῦ νεοῦ Ἑλληνισμοῦ, Α: Ἀρχές καί διαμόρφωδη του (Thessaloníkê 1961), pp. 67–70; Bótzaris, op. cit., pp. 14–15; Tsakonas, op. cit., p. 7. Professor Robert Browning has drawn my attention to one instance of the revival of the use of the word Hellene in an ethnic sense that antedates the sack of Constantinople and destruction of the East Roman Empire in A.D. 1204. George Torníkês employs the word to denote his own fellow-Greeks in contradistinction to Latins who had obtained high office in the East Roman Imperial Administration in the reign of the Emperor Manuel I (1143–80).

[4] The eleventh-century Neoplatonist, Michael Psellós, has recorded that, in 1055, the monks on the Mysian Mount Olympus crossed themselves at the mention of Plato's name and cursed him as an 'Hellenic' Satan. Platonic ideas were anathematized in the decisions of a synod that met in 1082 (note communicated by Professor Robert Browning). In the fourteenth century the Holy Synod of the Ecumenical Patriarchate of Constantinople formally anathematized all believers in 'Platonic ideas' Campbell, J. and Sherrard, P., *Modern Greece* (London 1968, p 22). The Council of 1082, which had condemned the Neoplatonist John Italós individually, had pronounced that Hellenic studies formed a valuable part of education but anathematized anyone who held Hellenic doctrines (Runciman, *The Great Church in Captivity*, p. 119).

[5] See ibid., p. 66. This can be read between the lines of Vlemmýdhês' own account of his career, for which see Krumbacher, op. cit., p. 446.

head. The ideological issue raised by the rehabilitation of the name 'Hellenes' was pushed into the background by the Nicene Imperial Government's success in attaining its political objective. The Nicene Greeks anticipated the achievements of the Ottoman Turks, whose fourteenth-century base of operations lay immediately to the south of Níkaia. In the thirteenth century the Nicene Greek Emperors expanded their dominions from Asia into Europe, encircled Constantinople, and took it eventually in 1261. For the next two centuries their energies were concentrated on fighting a losing battle for holding the reoccupied Imperial City, first against the Latins and then against the 'Osmanlis. In these circumstances the Greeks' Byzantine image of themselves as being Romans reasserted itself, and their modern image of themselves as being Hellenes temporarily receded.[6] But in the fifteenth century, immediately before and after the Ottoman Empire's annexation of the last politically independent enclaves of Greek territory at Constantinople and in the Pelopónnêsos and at Trebizond, the neo-Hellenic ideology found in George Yemistós Plêthon (*circa* 1360–1452)[7] an exponent who was more radical and more audaciously outspoken than Vlemmýdhês had ventured to be.

Plêthon was a Constantinopolitan who spent some time at Adrianople, which had been the capital of the Ottoman Empire since 1365. Thus he had a first-hand acquaintance with the 'Osmanlis, and he recognized that their vitality and their aggressiveness threatened to extinguish the last remnants of Greek political independence. He did not despair, however. He believed that the Greeks could still save themselves at the eleventh hour by an heroic act of national self-regeneration. Yemistós' recipe for this was a thoroughgoing revival of Hellenism. He was not content to confine this revival to the academic province of language and literature; he proposed to revive Hellenic Greek philosophy and even Hellenic Greek religion,[8] and he proposed this in earnest; though he was a pedant, he was not a poseur.

Yemistós hoisted his colours when he added the Hellenic Greek synonym 'Plêthon' to his ancestral Byzantine surname Yemistós ('Stuffed'). The name 'Plêthon' was intended to recall the name Pláton. George Yemistós was an avowed Platonist as a social and political

---

[6] Though it receded, it did not die out. Some fourteenth-century examples of the neo-Hellenic usage of the word 'Hellenes' are cited by Runciman, op. cit., pp. 119–20.

[7] For Plêthon see the surviving fragments of his own work, the *Nómoi: Πλήθωνος Νόμων Συγγραφῆς τὰ σωζόμενα*, ed. by C. Alexandre (Paris 1858; reprint Amsterdam 1966). See also Runciman, *The Great Church in Captivity*, pp. 119–25; Vakalópoulos, op. cit., vol. ii, part i, pp. 172–87 and 226–30; Campbell and Sherrard, op. cit., pp. 23–4; Masai, F., *Pléthon et le platonisme de Mistra* (Paris 1956). For the date of Plêthon's death see ibid., p. 54.

[8] See Vakalópoulos, op. cit., vol. ii, part i, p. 228; Runciman, *The Great Church in Captivity*, pp. 122–4; and the Appendix to the present chapter.

reformer, and a transparent Neoplatonist in his philosophy.[9] Moreover, for Plêthon, as for the historical *diadochi* and *epigoni* of Plotinus, Neoplatonism included an adherence to pre-Christian Greek religion, interpreted philosophically.

Plêthon's frank disclosure of his revolutionary outlook and pro-gramme made Constantinople, the seat of the Ecumenical Patriarchate, too hot to hold him, and, on a friendly hint from the Emperor Manuel II Palaiológhos (1391–1425), he withdrew, at some date soon after 1407, to Mistrá in Lakonía, which had been recovered by the Greeks from the French Principality of the Morea in 1261 and had been, since 1348, the capital of a Greek Despotate of the Pelopónnêsos, which was an autonomous dependency of the Constantinopolitan Greek Empire. Plêthon lived, taught, and wrote at Mistrá with impunity for nearly half a century ending at his death in 1452. For Plêthon, the fifteenth-century Pelopónnêsos was both stimulating and challenging.

It was stimulating because, here alone at the time, the Greeks were gaining ground militarily. In 1428–32 they reconquered the last remains of the French Principality of the Morea. It is true that, by the date of Plêthon's migration to Mistrá, the Ottoman Empire had already cast its shadow over the Pelopónnêsos. The 'Osmanlis had invaded it in 1397 and had compelled the despot to recognize the Pādishāh's suzerainty. They invaded the Despotate again in 1423 and 1446. But, to a neo-Hellene's mind, the Ottoman Empire's expansion, first in Asia and then into Europe, at the Greeks' expense, recalled the Persians' expansion in the sixth and fifth centuries B.C. In 480 B.C. and 479 B.C. the Persians had occupied Continental European Greece as far as Attica inclusive; yet in the same two years the Hellenic Greeks had inflicted on the Persians the celebrated decisive defeats at Salamis and Plataíai and Mykálê.[10]

At the same time, the Pelopónnêsos was challenging for Plêthon because of the flagrancy of the social injustice in the Despotate. This was brought home to Plêthon by his exercise of his profession. He was a judge.[11]

Plêthon proposed an Hellenic solution for both the domestic and the

[9] George Yemistós Plêthon's philosophy was inspired by Nikêphóros Grêgorás (*c.* 1295–1360). See Krumbacher, op. cit., pp. 293–8; Dölger in '*The Cambridge Medieval History*', vol. iv, 2nd edn., part ii, p. 246. According to Skholários, Ἅπαντα, vol. iv. 162, 8–12, Plêthon was inducted into Hebrew and Arabic commentaries on Aristotle and the Neoplatonists and Zoroastrianism at Adrianople by a Jew named Elisaeus (see Masai, op. cit., pp. 55, 57–8, and 60).

[10] In his memorial addressed to Theodore [II], the despot of the Pelopónnêsos, written not long after Theodore's accession in 1407, Plêthon cites a number of dramatic reversals of fortune. He draws attention particularly to recoveries that had followed social and legal reforms (see Masai, op. cit., pp. 70 1 and 387–8).

[11] Vakalópoulos, op. cit., vol. ii, part i, pp. 172–3.

foreign problem.[12] In memorials addressed to the Despot Theodore II
and to the Emperor Manuel II,[13] he called for social, political, and
military reforms on the lines of his exemplar Plato's utopian blueprints
in *The Republic* and *The Laws*. Plêthon would have been a more useful
counsellor if he had drawn on his own first-hand experience of Ottoman
institutions; for the military and administrative efficiency of the
Pādishāh's slave-household was the secret of the Ottoman Empire's
current success.[14] If the Persian Empire had created for itself corresponding institutions of equal effectiveness, the campaigns of 480 and
479 B.C. might have had a different ending. There is no evidence that the
Emperor Manuel or his sons the despots of the Pelopónnêsos paid any
more attention to Plêthon than the despot of Sicily, Dionysius II, had
paid to Plato.

It is true that the Palaiológhoi did not molest Plêthon, but he had
been discreet enough not to submit to them a work—his *Laws*—in which
he had divulged his philosophy and his religion. In this work Plêthon
called God 'Zeus' and referred to 'the gods' in the plural.[15] Before his
death, Plêthon had already engaged in controversy with his former
pupil and friend, George Skholários, who, like Plêthon, had been a
judge before he became first a monk and eventually Patriarch of
Constantinople.[16] After Plêthon's death and after the fall of Constantinople to the 'Osmanlis and after Skholários' appointment by Mehmet
the Conqueror to the Patriarchate, under the name Yennádhios, the
despot of the Pelopónnêsos Dhêmêtrios found a manuscript of Plêthon's
Laws and sent it to the Patriarch. Yennádhios read it and had it burned
during his second tenure of the Patriarchate (1463-5).[17] We know its
contents only from quotations and references. The Patriarch is said to
have stigmatized Plêthon as 'a new Julian'.[18] The Greek Eastern

---

[12] Vakalópoulos, op. cit., vol. ii, part i, p. 174.

[13] See Runciman, *The Great Church in Captivity*, p. 122; Vakalópoulos, op. cit., vol. ii, part i, p. 179.
The memorial addressed to Manuel II was written in 1418, according to Masai, op. cit., p. 387.

[14] Plêthon did praise Ottoman military institutions. In the same passage, he drew attention to
the 'Osmanlis' belief in Destiny, and he correctly divined that their success was partly due to this
Islamic tenet of theirs (Plêthon, Πρὸς τὸ ὑπὲρ τοῦ Λατινικοῦ δόγματος Βιβλίον in Migne, *Patrologia
Graeca*, vol. 160, col. 980, cited by Vakalópoulos, op. cit., vol. ii, part i, p. 228); the text of this tract of
Plêthon's is also printed in C. Alexandre's edition of Plêthon's *Nómoi*, pp. 300-11; the passage in
question is on p. 310.

[15] In the Máni, less than two days' walk from Mistrá, the Olympian gods had continued to be
worshipped until after the beginning of the reign of the Emperor Basil I (867-86) (see Constantine
Porphyrogenitus, *De Administrando Imperio*, chapter 50 (p. 224 in I. Bekker's edition (Bonn 1840));
p. 236 in G. Moravcsik's and R. J. H. Jenkins's edition (Budapest 1949)).

[16] The Greek texts of Skholários-Yennádhios' and Plêthon's tracts are printed as appendices to
Plêthon's *Nómoi*, ed. cit., and are discussed in the Appendix to the present chapter. See also
Krumbacher, op. cit., pp. 119-22.

[17] See Yennádhios' own defence of his action in his letter to Joseph the Exarch, printed in
Plêthon, *Nómoi*, ed. cit., Appendix XIX, pp. 412-41.

[18] See Vakalópoulos, op. cit., vol. i, p. 229, and vol. ii, part i, p. 152; Runciman, op. cit., pp. 124-5.

Orthodox Church was bound to oppose the identification of the Modern Greeks with the Hellenic Greeks when this was asserted explicitly and when it was pressed to its logical conclusion. But the 'Osmanlis' advance, which was pushing the Greek people geographically back towards the historical Hellas, played into the neo-Hellenists' hands.

Few of Plêthon's Greek contemporaries and pupils followed Plêthon in carrying their neo-Hellenism to the length of repudiating Christianity.[19] While the Constantinopolitan Skholários became Eastern Orthodox Patriarch of Constantinople, a pupil of Plêthon's, Vêssaríon of Trebizond,[20] became a cardinal of the Roman Church and was appointed to the Roman Catholic anti-Patriarchate of Constantinople in 1463. Thus Skholários and Vêssaríon turned their backs on each other. Skholários came to the conclusion that political subjection to the Pādishāh was a lesser evil than ecclesiastical subjection to the Pope. For Vêssaríon, the lesser evil was the acceptance of Papal supremacy and of expatriation. Yet neither of them turned his back on Christianity itself.[21]

However, Vêssaríon followed Plêthon in advocating social and political reform and military resistance to the 'Osmanlis,[22] in a letter addressed, *circa* 1444, to the despot of the Pelopónnêsos, who, as Constantine XI, was to become the last of the Greek East Roman Emperors (1449–53). Vêssaríon also shared with Plêthon the optimism with which Plêthon had been inspired by his identification of the fifteenth-century Greeks with the Hellenes.[23] In his letter to the Despot Constantine, Vêssaríon maintained that good institutions, diligently put into practice, could enable anyone to advance from small beginnings to greatness. He supported this thesis by citing the cases of Alexander, Cyrus, Rome, Spartacus, Timur Lenk, and, as the most pertinent case of all, the 'Osmanlis. He suggested that the little Pelopónnêsos could achieve comparable results by the same means, so Constantine need not be disheartened.[24]

Evidently for Vêssaríon, as for Plêthon, one of the attractions of neo-Hellenism was the implication that the fifteenth-century Greeks were

---

[19] At least one neo-Hellene, Michael Apostólês, was accused of polytheism, and was forced to confess and to recant, in Constantine XI's reign (1449–53) (see Vakalópoulos, op. cit., vol. i, pp. 245–6; Masai, op. cit., p. 312. Another, named Juvenal, was put to death in the Pelopónnêsos in 1450 (ibid., pp. 300–4)).

[20] See Krumbacher, op. cit., pp. 117–18.

[21] On the eve of the Ottoman conquest of Constantinople, Skholários declared that he did not call himself a Hellene, because he did not hold the Hellenes' religious beliefs, and that he preferred simply to call himself a Christian (Runciman, op. cit., p. 121). Yet in his Lament (Θρῆνος), dated 1460, Skholários calls the Greeks 'Hellenes' (Skholários, Ἅπαντα (*Collected Works*), vol. i, p. 285, cited by Vakalópoulos, op. cit., vol. ii, part i, p. 158; for Skholários' previous refusal to call himself a Hellene, see his *Collected Works*, vol. iii, p. 253, cited by Vakalópoulos, ibid., p. 179).

[22] See Vakalópoulos, op. cit., vol. i, pp. 230–4.

[23] Ibid., p. 237.

[24] Ibid., p. 235.

capable of repeating the apparently miraculous reversal of the Hellenic Greeks' fortunes in 480–479 B.C. In a desperate plight, people are tempted to await some miracle. On the last day of the siege of Constantinople in 1453, when the population learnt that the 'Osmanlis had broken their way in, they flocked to the Cathedral of the Ayía Sophía in the expectation that, when the enemy approached the threshold of Orthodox Christendom's chief shrine, an angel would appear and would annihilate the impious intruder. Mehmet II did arrive, but the expected angel failed to keep his appointment.

The social and political and military programme of neo-Hellenism was unrealistic. The Modern Greeks could not be regenerated instantaneously by an academic exercise. On the other hand, Greek neo-Hellenism did make an important contribution towards an eventual reconciliation between Greeks and Westerners; and, for the Modern Greeks, as for other non-Western peoples in the Modern Age, their relation to the ever more potent and ever more dominant West has been the most pressing of all their national problems.

Neo-Hellenism made a reconciliation with the West easier for fifteenth-century Greeks in so far as it weaned them away from the fanatical attachment to Eastern Orthodox Christianity which was the natural but unprofitable reaction of the majority of Greeks, at that time, to the West's arrogant insistence on the recognition of the Pope's ecclesiastical supremacy. Plêthon, Vêssaríon, and Skholários were all members of the Greek delegation at the Council of Florence in 1439. Plêthon seems to have regarded the proceedings as a sordid attempt, on his own countrymen's part, to buy material advantages by selling spiritual values. Skholários' eventual adoption of Plêthon's view on this point led Skholários, not away to Hellenic polytheism, but back to anti-Roman Orthodoxy. On the other hand, Plêthonian neo-Hellenism led Vêssaríon into the Roman Church. As for Plêthon himself, his overt indifference to the ecclesiastical issues that were being debated at Florence opened the way for him to fraternize, as a scholar, with his humanist Italian contemporaries, and they gave him an enthusiastic welcome.[25]

Neo-Hellenism was, in fact, common ground on which the Western humanists and the neo-Hellenic-minded minority of their Greek contemporaries could co-operate cordially. Hellenic Greek scholarship was a pursuit for which both these parties were enthusiastic. The Westerners had come to recognize that the classical Latin culture had been derived from the classical Greek culture, and that, without a revival in the West of a knowledge of the Hellenic Greek language and literature, the Western Renaissance would misfire. The handful of

[25] Runciman, *The Great Church in Captivity*, p. 124.

fifteenth-century Greek neo-Hellenists was able to transmit to the Western humanists the knowledge for which these were now thirsting, and the Greek neo-Hellenists were not inhibited by their fellow-Greeks' chauvinistic aversion from the West. The Greek neo-Hellenists had already taken their treasure out of Byzantine Greek culture and had placed it in Hellenic Greek culture. The neo-polytheist Plêthon and his pupil the ecclesiastical Unionist Vêssaríon had each reoriented himself culturally in this way. Their new treasure was something that they could share with eager Western recipients. Thus, in their relations with the West, they could play the gratifying role of generous cultural donors, instead of being cast for the humiliating role of political 'poor relations'.

Plêthon and Vêssaríon were therefore able to acknowledge, open-mindedly, the contemporary West's achievements. Plêthon took an interest in the political constitution of Florence,[26] as well as in the political constitutions—historical or Utopian—of Hellenic Greek city-states. Vêssaríon, too, had his eye on medieval Italian constitutional history, and he was also more alive than Plêthon had been to the technological superiority of the contemporary West.[27] In his letter to Constantine, Vêssaríon advised the despot to send able Peloponnesian students to Italy for technological training in a great variety of industries, but particularly in the iron industry, with a view to developing this industry in Lakonía, which is rich in iron-ores.[28]

Thus Modern Greek neo-Hellenism prepared the ground for an improvement in the relations between the Modern Greeks and the West. The Modern Greek neo-Hellenists' and the Modern Westerners' common admiration for the Hellenic Greek culture was an antidote to the traditional hostility between the Eastern Orthodox churches and the Roman church.

The Eastern Orthodox ecclesiastical hierarchy remained hostile to the Western *Weltanschauung* in all its successive manifestations: Roman Catholic Christianity, Protestant Christianity, and the post-Christian worship of collective human power that was associated incongruously with a cult of the human intellect.[29] The post-Christian Western *Weltanschauung* was more attractive to the Eastern Orthodox hierarchy's ecclesiastical subjects than either the two competing Western versions of Christianity or the native Greek neo-Hellenism had ever been. This nascent native Greek ideology had been extirpated in its homeland as a result of the Ottoman conquest. But the seed sown in the West by the handful of neo-Hellenic Greek refugees had borne a huge harvest on this

---

[26] See Vakalópoulos, op. cit., vol. i, p. 175 with n. 3.
[27] Ibid., p. 235 with n. 1.
[28] Ibid., pp. 237-8.
[29] See further Chapter IX (i), pp. 166-79.

foreign soil; and this Modern Western idealization of a long-since extinct Hellenic Greek civilization which, indirectly, was part of the West's cultural heritage too was closely connected with the progressive de-Christianization of Western life from the later decades of the seventeenth century onwards.

Few, if any, of neo-Hellenism's Western neophytes have ever followed Plêthon in reverting to the worship of the Hellenic Olympian pantheon, even in the Neoplatonic allegorical interpretation of it which Plêthon had adopted. But an increasing number of Westerners have 'dropped out' of Christianity, even if they have not consciously repudiated it, and by 1974 a great majority of Westerners—and of the Westernized intelligentsia of the non-Western civilizations as well—had unavowedly transferred their spiritual allegiance from their ancestral religions to the real religion of the Hellenic Greeks. These had really worshipped the collective human power symbolized by Athens' Athéne Polias, by Sparta's Athana Khalkioikos, and, in a later age, by the politically unified Graeco-Roman World's *Dea Roma* and *Divus Caesar*. This genuine Hellenic Greek religion has become the prevalent religion in the West and hence also in the rest of the World, including Modern Greece.

After having taken over the fifteenth-century Greek neo-Hellenism, the Modern West has developed it on lines of its own. For the first two centuries after 'the revival of letters' in the West, the Western attitude toward Hellenic Greek literature was Byzantine. This superb pagan literature was valued, cultivated, and imitated for the sake of its form as distinct from its content. This early modern neo-Hellenism was academic, not practical.

Towards the close of the seventeenth century the West came to the conclusion that, intellectually, it had now caught up with, and surpassed, the Hellenic Greeks and the Romans; but the West remained convinced that 'classical' Greek poetry and visual art were unsurpass-able, and it now began to be influenced in its political life by Hellenic Greek and Roman political institutions and ideas seen through Modern Western eyes. The vision was selective; it ignored the grim realities: the social injustice; the political violence in the domestic life of both the Hellenic city-states and the Roman Republic; the incessant wars that were ended only by the forcible imposition of the Roman Empire. Moreover, this selective Modern Western vision was interpreted, not in the light even of those historical facts of which it took cognizance, but in accordance with contemporary Modern Western political aspirations. In the Western imagination, Hellenism came to stand politically for constitutionalism, democracy, and freedom, as well as for the quin-tessence of art.

This Westernized vision of Hellenism was an integral part of that

Modern Western post-Christian *Weltanschauung* which began to fascinate the Modern Greeks from the later decades of the seventeenth century onwards. The vision appealed to the Greeks forcefully for two reasons. It had been derived from the Greeks by the Westerners, and it was an idealization of the Greeks' own pre-Byzantine past. *Omne ignotum pro magnifico.* For the Modern Greeks, their Byzantine past was familiar in the shape of its ecclesiastical residue, the Eastern Orthodox Church, and at the same time it was discredited politically by its historic defeats at the hands of the Westerners and the 'Osmanlis, and spiritually by the Modern Greeks' receptiveness towards Modern Western rationalism. On the other hand, the Hellenic phase of Greek history could be glorified just because there was no surviving relic of it to serve as an insistent reminder of the sober historical truth. Neo-Hellenism was, in fact, a 'myth';[30] and 'myths' are presentations of the past which are designed subconsciously to produce, not an accurate record, but a dynamic emotional effect. The potency of this effect is proportionate to the myth-makers' *naïveté*. On Western soil, the neo-Hellenic myth

grew with such vigour that when it was transplanted back into its native soil in the seventeenth and particularly in the eighteenth centuries it spread with an impetus that was astonishing.[31]

Westerners who gave more than the due credit to the Hellenic Greeks gave less than their due to the Western Hellenizers' Modern Greek contemporaries. Inevitably they saw in these the degenerate descendants of glorious ancestors.[32] For those Modern Greeks who accepted the Western estimate of the Hellenic Greeks, the antithetical Western estimate of the Modern Greeks was humiliating. But, though it was wounding, it was also stimulating. This imaginary vision of the Hellenic Greeks, which the Modern Greeks had come to share with the Westerners, made the Modern Greeks aspire to demonstrate that they were worthy scions of their illustrious ancestors.

When, in 1821, the Greeks eventually rose against the Turks, the decision as to whether the form of the society that was to issue from their struggles would be more in accordance with the Orthodox than with the 'Hellenising' myth had already been made in the national consciousness, and made in favour of the latter.[33]

---

[30] See Campbell and Sherrard, op. cit., p. 25.
[31] Ibid.
[32] Ibid., pp. 31–2.
[33] Ibid., p. 37.

IX

THE MODERN GREEKS' SUCCESSES
AND FAILURES

(i) *The Change in the Greeks' Attitude towards the West*

THE Modern Greeks have not been singular in having had to cope with the problem of their relations with the West. The 'Western Question' has confronted most other non-Western peoples too in the Modern Age. However, for the Greeks, this problem has been particularly acute. Eastern Orthodox Christendom is at closer quarters with the West geographically than any of the other non-Western civilizations, and it has a closer religious and cultural affinity with the West than any non-Christian civilization and also than any non-Chalcedonian Christian civilization (for instance, the Monophysite Christian civilizations of Armenia and Ethiopia). Geographical proximity has exposed Eastern Orthodox Christendom to Western pressure since a relatively early date; cultural affinity has made this pressure particularly irksome. When persons or peoples that are closely related fall out with each other, their quarrel is apt to be bitter. Its bitterness is likely to be aggravated when there has been a reversal of fortunes in the relations between the two parties, and when this reversal has taken the loser by surprise. All these exacerbating factors have entered into the relations between the Christendoms; and, among the Eastern Orthodox Christian peoples, the Greeks have been the most painfully affected, since the Greeks were the creators of the Eastern Orthodox Christian civilization and were also the most powerful and the most highly cultivated of the Eastern Orthodox Christian peoples in the formative first chapter of Eastern Orthodox Christendom's history.

The Greeks' relations with non-Greek peoples to the west of the Greek-speaking World have passed through a series of stages. The military and political subjugation of the Greeks by the Romans in the second century B.C. was compensated for psychologically by the Romans' reception of the Hellenic Greek culture and by their propagation of it, in a Latin dress, in Western Europe and North-West Africa. By Hellenic Greek standards, the Hellenization of the western provinces of the Roman Empire was superficial, except in Sicily and in the Italian

Magna Graecia, and therefore the Greeks were not greatly distressed when, in the fifth century of the Christian Era, these backward provinces of the Empire dropped off from the Empire's still sound core in the Hellenized Levant.

The Empire's Levantine subjects felt more distress and more resentment when, in the sixth century, they were heavily taxed for financing a re-conquest of the western provinces that was only partial and that proved to be ephemeral. After the death of the Latin-speaking Illyrian East Roman Emperor Justinian I in 565, his successors resigned themselves to the loss of one after another of the Empire's outposts to the west of the Straits of Otranto and the Syrtes in order to concentrate the Empire's dwindling resources on holding, in the first place, Asia Minor, and in the second place as much as possible of the Aímos (Balkan) Peninsula.

In this first chapter of the coeval histories of Eastern Orthodox Christendom and Western Christendom, the West had been a liability for the Greeks but not a menace to them. Even Charlemagne's empire had threatened only the north-western outskirts of the East Roman Empire in Dalmatia and Istria and at Venice, and this threat had been short-lived. In the eleventh century, however, there was a dramatic reversal (in Aristotelian language, a περιπέτεια) in the balance of power.

During the first half of the eleventh century the East Roman Empire seemed to be more powerful, militarily and politically, than it had been at any previous time since Justinian I's death. The Empire had annexed eastern Cilicia, Antioch, Bulgaria, and almost the whole of Armenia, and had imposed its suzerainty on Aleppo, the Caucasian states, Serbia, and Croatia. But these military and political successes were fragile, because they had been purchased at an excessive price in economic and social terms. In 1071 the Normans—(fifty years earlier a cloud no bigger than a man's hand) completed the eviction of the East Roman Empire from South-Eastern Italy by taking Bari, and in the same year the interior of Asia Minor—the Empire's heartland—was laid open to occupation by the Muslim Saljūq Turks after the defeat of the Emperor Rhomanós IV Dhioyénês at Melazgerd. The Saljūqs did not meet with the resistance that had once defeated the Arabs there. Since the tenth century the Greek peasantry in Asia Minor had become alienated from the East Roman Empire and from the Byzantine Christian civilization.[1] Their own government had taxed them mercilessly and had then failed

---

[1] See Michael Attaleiátês, *Historia*, ed. by I. Bekker (Bonn 1853), pp. 306 and 307; Nikêtas Khoniátês, *Kronikê Dhiêyêsis*, ed. by I. Bekker (Bonn 1835), p. 5; John Kínnamos, *Historiae*, ed. by A. Meineke (Bonn 1836), p. 22; all cited in Toynbee, A. J., *A Study of History*, vol. viii, p. 395 n. 4. See also Vryonis Jr., S., *The Decline of Medieval Hellenism in Asia Minor and the Process of Islamization from the Eleventh through the Fifteenth Century* (Berkeley, Los Angeles, and London 1971).

to check the encroachments of the big landowners at the ruined smallholder's expense.

The crumbling of the Empire's power could be measured in terms of the debasement of the East Roman gold coin, the *nómisma*, which had retained its purity, at least in issues intended for international circulation, for more than seven centuries running from the reign of Constantine the Great. In the reign of Constantine IX (1042–55) the *nómisma* was debased from 24 carats (κεράτια) to 18; in the reign of Michael VII (1071–8) it was debased further to something between 14 and 12 carats.[2] The reversal of fortunes could also be measured by the naval and economic rise of Venice, a Western city-state that had been under East Roman sovereignty originally. The East Roman Government had to purchase Venetian naval aid against the Normans by granting commercial privileges to Venetian traders that were ruinous for the Venetians' Greek competitors. In 1204 Venice inveigled French crusaders into joining with her to conquer Constantinople and to partition the East Roman Empire.

The Greeks had brought this reversal of fortunes on themselves. The East Roman Imperial Government had mismanaged its economy while over-straining it by expanding the Empire's dominions, and the Westerners had been given their opportunity by this Greek improvidence. But the Greeks did not face the facts. As they saw it, the West's triumphant aggression was inexplicable, besides being outrageous. The contemporary aggression of the Greeks' Eastern Muslim neighbours aroused less Greek resentment, because it did not give the Greeks so great a shock. The East Roman Imperial Government had dealt with the Sasanian Persian Empire and with its successor the Arab Caliphate as the Empire's equals *de facto*, and therefore the Greeks could reconcile themselves more easily to being dominated by the Arabs' Saljūq and Ottoman Turkish heirs than to being dominated by the upstart Westerners.

The Greek public—lay as well as clerical—was infuriated by the East Roman Crown's recognition, in 1274 and 1369 and 1439, of the Papacy's ecclesiastical supremacy. The Emperor Michael VIII's sister is said to have exclaimed in 1275: 'Better that my brother's Empire should perish than the purity of the Orthodox faith.'[3] An alleged proclivity towards the Western style of theology and scholastic philosophy had already been prejudicial to the Platonist scholar John Italós[4] in the eleventh century. He had been excommunicated.[5] In 1341 Barlaam,

---

[2] Hussey, J. M., *The Byzantine World* (London 1957), p. 51.
[3] Ibid., p. 77.
[4] See Krumbacher, op. cit., pp. 444–5.
[5] Dölger in *The Cambridge Medieval History*, vol. iv, 2nd edn., part ii, p. 245.

and in 1347 and 1351 Barlaam again, together, on these occasions, now with Akýndynos and Nikêphóros Grêgorás, was condemned by the ecclesiastical authorities for criticizing hesychasm on Western intellectual lines.[6] On the eve of the fall of Constantinople to the 'Osmanlis in 1453 the Grand Duke[7] Loukás Notarás is said to have declared that 'it is better to find the Turkish turban reigning within the City's walls than the Latin head-dress'.[8]

Byzantine Greek scholars, like Byzantine Greek traders, tended to stay at home and to wait for their Western confrères—or competitors— to visit them. Kydhônês, for instance, was moved to learn Latin by having to do business with Westerners in Constantinople as private secretary (*mystikós*) to the Emperor John VI Kandakouzênós. Kydhônês took lessons in Latin from a Dominican friar stationed in the Dominicans' house in Pera, and he was inspired to translate Saint Thomas's *Summa* by having been set, as an exercise, to translate a piece from another work of Saint Thomas's.[9] After the extinction of the East Roman Empire, however, Greek Ottoman subjects began to visit the West, first as traders and then as students. In the Greek territories that had fallen under Ottoman rule, Greek higher studies wilted, without dying out completely.[10] The University of Constantinople did not survive the Ottoman conquest, but the Patriarchal Academy was founded in 1454 by the Patriarch Yennádhios II to fill the gap,[11] and it continued to provide some secular higher education, though theological studies had to be its first concern.[12]

Greek learning was kept alive at Venice by the Greek refugee colony there in co-operation with Venetian Hellenists.[13] A Greek printing press was set up at Venice by two Greek *émigrés* in 1486,[14] and, in the same year, a Cretan *émigré*, Márkos Mousoúros, moved to Venice from Florence and became Aldus Manutius' editor for the Aldine series of editions of Hellenic Greek works.[15] The University of Padua, which was

---

[6] Hussey and Hart, in ibid., p. 197; Dölger, ibid., p. 220.

[7] Μέγας δούξ or Μεγαδούκας.

[8] κρειττότερόν ἐστιν εἰδέναι ἐν μέσῃ τῇ πόλει τὸ φακιόλιον βασιλεῦον Τούρκων ἢ κάλυπτραν Λατινικήν (Dhoúkas, *Historia Byzantina*, ed. by I. Bekker (Bonn 1834), p. 264.) The popular slogan at the same date was κρᾶττον ἐμπεσεῖν εἰς χεῖρας Τούρκων ἢ Φράνκων (ibid., p. 291). The same preference had been expressed by the Patriarch Michael III, who was in office in 1170–8, a century before there was any question of trying to buy Western military aid for the East Roman Empire at the price of submitting to the ecclesiastical supremacy of the Pope (see Every, G., *The Byzantine Patriarchate, 451–1204* (London 1947), pp. 182–3).

[9] Hussey and Hart in op. cit. loc. cit.

[10] Runciman, *The Great Church in Captivity*, pp. 208–10.

[11] Vakalópoulos, op. cit., vol. ii, part i, p. 221.

[12] Runciman, *The Great Church in Captivity*, p. 208.

[13] Ibid., pp. 210–12; Tsakonas, op. cit., p. 35.

[14] Vakalópoulos, op. cit., vol. ii, part i, p. 230.

[15] Ibid., pp. 233–4.

within Venice's dominions, did not impose a religious test, and Ottoman, as well as Venetian, Greek subjects studied there.[16] At Padua, at least two colleges for Greek Venetian subjects were founded by Greek Venetian subjects in the sixteenth century, and in 1657 the Collegio Cottuniano was founded there by John Kottoúnios, an *émigré* from Vérrhoia who had been appointed to the Chair of Philosophy at Padua.[17] The *Natio Ultramarina* at the University represented the University's Greek members.[18] In 1626 a rich Corfiot Greek named Thomás Phlangínês (1579–1648) founded an academy at Venice to prepare students for the University of Padua,[19] and this academy survived till 1797, the year in which Venice lost her political independence.[20] The Greek community at Venice founded a school there in 1593 for the children of overseas Greeks.[21]

Under the Ottoman regime, Greek traders were making money, and they began to found schools and colleges in Ottoman territory, particularly at Bucarest and Jassy, the capitals of the two autonomous Danubian Principalities, and on the island of Khios, which also had a certain amount of autonomy.[22] In 1593, the Ecumenical Patriarch Jeremias II convened a synod at which he exhorted his metropolitans to found schools,[23] and in the same year the Patriarch himself reformed the Patriarchal Academy. He broadened its field of study to include philosophy and science besides theology and literature, and the first heads of the new departments seem all to have been graduates of Padua.[24] The Church, as well as the Phanariots and other rich Greeks, endowed higher education, and, from about half-way through the eighteenth century onwards, these Greek educational efforts began to produce a Greek intellectual renaissance.[25]

Unfortunately, at this critical stage of Greek history, when, for the Greeks, so much depended on their handling of 'the Western Question', the clerics and the laity moved in different directions. From the eleventh century till the fifteenth, they had been unanimously anti-Western; but, from the sixteenth century onwards, the Ottoman Greek laymen who

---

[16] Márkos Mousoúros was appointed to a professorial chair in the University of Padua in 1503. Erasmus was one of his pupils there (ibid., p. 234).

[17] Ibid., pp. 238 and 240–1.

[18] Ibid., pp. 238–9.

[19] Ibid., pp. 238 and 270–1; Runciman, *The Great Church in Captivity*, p. 212 n. 2.

[20] Tsakonas, op. cit., p. 35.

[21] Vakalópoulos, op. cit., vol. ii, part i, p. 270.

[22] See Runciman, *The Great Church in Captivity*, pp. 217–18; Bótzaris, op. cit., p. 13; Toynbee, op. cit., vol. viii, p. 183 n. 3; Vakalópoulos, vol. ii, part i, pp. 269–70. Vakalópoulos notes that traders operating from Yánnina were active in founding schools, not only in Êpeiros, but elsewhere, and that Manolákês of Kastoriá founded schools at Khios, Árta, and Anatolikó.

[23] Ibid., p. 261.

[24] Runciman, *The Great Church in Captivity*, pp. 215–16.

[25] Bótzaris, op. cit., pp. 14 and 75.

were trading with the West and were making money by this came to be attracted towards the Western way of life and the Western outlook; and the last psychological barrier to their reconciliation with the West was removed when, before the close of the seventeenth century, the religious liberalism of the University of Padua was adopted throughout the Western World.[26]

On the other hand, the West continued, in each of its successive metamorphoses, to displease the Eastern Orthodox Churches, as has been noted already in the preceding chapter.[27] Roman Catholicism was literally anathema to them, and Protestantism did not please them any better. The Protestants had naïvely expected that the Eastern Orthodox Christians would fraternize with them over their common repudiation of the Papacy's claim to ecclesiastical supremacy. But the Protestants' overtures to the Eastern Orthodox Churches were quickly and curtly rebuffed. In Eastern Orthodox Christian eyes, Protestant and Catholic doctrines and rites were indistinguishably erroneous. When, from the later decades of the seventeenth century onwards, the West became progressively more secular-minded, this new Western *Weltanschauung* was as obnoxious to the Eastern Orthodox hierarchy as Roman Catholicism and Protestantism.[28] The Latin head-dress was not improved in Eastern Orthodox clerical eyes when it was transmuted from the Pope's triple crown into the sansculottes' Phrygian cap of liberty—a veritable red rag.

Protestantism in the Baptists' form of it has prospered in Russian Eastern Orthodox Christendom under the Communist regime. On the other hand, Protestantism has been repulsed more easily in Greek Eastern Orthodox Christendom than either of the other two Western ideologies with which Eastern Orthodoxy has contended. In Greek Eastern Orthodox Christendom, Protestantism in the Calvinists' form of it made a sensational but ephemeral lodgement in the time of the Calvinist-minded Patriarch of Constantinople, Cyril Loúkaris (*vivebat* 1572–1638; in office as Patriarch of Constantinople 1620–35 and 1637–8).[29] Loúkaris occupied a commanding strategic position, yet his enterprise was a forlorn hope. He had only a handful of supporters

---

[26] For the seventeenth-century revolution in the West's attitude towards Eastern Orthodox Christianity, see Toynbee, op. cit., vol. viii, pp. 165–8.

[27] See Chapter VIII, p. 163.

[28] See Bótzaris, op. cit., p. 14. The Eastern Orthodox ecclesiastical 'establishment's' abiding hostility to philosophy during the Ottoman regime is noted by Vakalópoulos, op. cit., vol. ii, part i, pp. 220–1.

[29] See Runciman, *The Great Church in Captivity*, pp. 259–88, with the bibliography on p. 259 n. 1; Toynbee, op. cit., vol. viii, pp. 152–60, with the bibliography on p. 152 n. 1; Vakalópoulos, op. cit., vol. ii, part ii, (Thessaloníkê 1968), pp. 447–66; Hofmann, G., 'Patriarch Kyrillos Loúkaris: Einfluss abendländischer Schriften auf seine Predikten', in *Orientalia Christiana Periodica*, vol. 7 (1921), pp. 250–65.

among his Eastern Orthodox co-religionists, and the support of the
Protestant foreign powers was counterbalanced by the opposition of the
Catholic foreign powers, while the balance was tipped against Loúkaris
by the conservatism of the majority of the contemporary Greek Eastern
Orthodox clergy. Loúkaris' Calvinism cost him his life. The Jesuits
persuaded Sultan Murād IV to put him to death. The Eastern
Orthodox Churches anathematized him posthumously.[30]

This repulse of Protestantism was remarkable, considering that, in
commending itself to the Orthodox, Protestantism had the negative
advantage of never having had an opportunity to persecute them.
Roman Catholicism had had the opportunity and had used it. At a
council held at Istanbul in 1484 and attended by all four eastern
Orthodox Patriarchs, the acts of the council of union held at Florence
in 1439 were declared invalid.[31] The Russian Eastern Orthodox
Church had repudiated the Council of Florence's acts immediately,
and had expelled the Greek Metropolitan of Kiev and all Russia,
Isidore, for having signed them. Isidore, like one of the other Greek
signatories, Vêssaríon, had taken refuge in Italy and had been made a
cardinal.

The massive and vehement rejection of the Union of Florence by the
Greeks, the Russians, and the other Eastern Orthodox Christian peoples
did not discourage the Roman Church from persevering in the pursuit of
a forlorn hope. In 1462 the Pope made Cardinal Vêssaríon the titular
Roman Catholic Patriarch of Constantinople, with jurisdiction over all
Uniates.[32] In 1472 the Vatican gave its support to the marriage of Zoê
Palaiolóyina, the Uniate niece of the last of the East Roman Emperors,
the Uniate Constantine IX, with the Grand Duke of Moscow, Ivan III.
However, Ivan rejected Uniatism, and Zoê renounced it.[33]

The Society of Jesus, founded in 1540, sought to win the Greek
Orthodox for Roman Catholicism by giving them facilities for modern
higher education. The College of Saint Athanasius, founded at Rome for
this purpose by Pope Gregory XIII in 1577,[34] admitted Orthodox, as
well as Catholic, Greek boys. In 1583 Gregory XIII sent six Jesuits to
Istanbul.[35] The Congregatio de Propaganda Fide was created in 1622.
The Jesuits founded schools for the Greek Orthodox in Ottoman

---

[30] See Runciman, *The Great Church in Captivity*, pp. 286–7; Toynbee, op. cit., vol. viii, pp. 158–9.

[31] Runciman, *The Great Church in Captivity*, p. 228.

[32] Vakalópoulos, op. cit., vol. ii, part ii, p. 171.

[33] Ibid., pp. 58–62; Runciman, *The Great Church in Captivity*, p. 323.

[34] Ibid., p. 231; Vakalópoulos, op. cit., ii, part i, p. 237; ibid., vol. ii, part ii, pp. 204–5. A Greek
college had already been founded at Rome, on the Quirinal, by Pope Leo X (*fungebatur* 1513–21)
(ibid., pp. 233 and 235), but this appears to have been a school of Hellenic Greek studies, not an
establishment for educating Greek boys.

[35] Ibid., p. 392.

territory, and their lead was followed by other Roman Catholic religious orders. Their first objective was the Island of Khíos, where the Roman Catholic minority of the population had been dominant, under Genoese suzerainty, from 1346 till the Ottoman Empire's annexation of Khíos in 1566. Here the Jesuits were followed by the Capuchins[36] —a French branch of the Franciscan Order whose members opened schools wherever they settled (they were pioneers in founding schools in the Levant for girls).[37] In 1635 a Greek Uniate, Nikólaos Rósês of Náfplion, started a school on Mount Athos.[38] In 1640 he was relegated to Thessaloníkê by the Ottoman authorities,[39] but in 1639–41 two Athonite monks studied at Rome in the College of Saint Athanasius.[40]

The Jesuits contributed to the defeat of Loukaris' attempt at a *rapprochement* between Eastern Orthodoxy and Calvinism, but they failed to coax the Ottoman Greeks into accepting the Union of Florence.[41] One of the most distinguished pupils that the College of Saint Athanasius ever had was Alexander Mavrokordháto, the future Dragoman of the Porte,[42] yet this Westernized Greek Orthodox Christian Ottoman high official helped the Orthodox to win para-mountcy over the Holy Places in Palestine at one point in the perennial struggle for this among the Christian Churches. The only Eastern Orthodox Christian populations that did temporarily accept the Union of Florence were some of those that were under the rule of Roman Catholic Christian governments, e.g. the Government of the United Kingdom of Poland–Lithuania, and their acceptance was not voluntary.

However, the Roman Catholic Christian power that had the greatest number of Greek Orthodox Christian subjects was Venice,[43] and Venice was reluctant to press her Orthodox subjects to become Uniates,[44] since she had to compete for their good will with her mighty neighbour and enemy, the Ottoman Empire.[45] There was an emigration from Venetian Tênos to Ottoman Mýkonos,[46] and from Venetian Crete to Ottoman

---

[36] For the Jesuits at Khíos see ibid., pp. 395 and 398; for the Capuchins, pp. 397 and 404–6.

[37] Ibid., p. 405.

[38] Ibid., p. 401.

[39] Ibid.

[40] Ibid., p. 403.

[41] For the Jesuits' activities in the Ottoman Empire, see Runciman, op. cit., pp. 230–7.

[42] See Camariano, N., *Alexandre Mavrocordato le Grand Drogman: activité diplomatique (1673–1704)* (Thessaloníkê 1970).

[43] Poland–Lithuania had more Orthodox Christian subjects than Venice had, but these were Ukrainians and White Russians, not Greeks.

[44] Vakalópoulos, op. cit., vol. ii, part ii, p. 175.

[45] *Siamo Veneziani e poi Christiani*—a Venetian saying quoted in ibid., vol. ii, part i, p. 177.

[46] Ibid., vol. ii, part ii, p. 217.

Istanbul.[47] In 1542 the Venetians were constained to allow the Inquisition to operate in their dominions,[48] but they were hostile, not only to the Inquisition, but to the Congregatio de Propaganda Fide.[49] In 1629 the Venetian Provedditore General in Crete, Morosini, prohibited the circulation there of pro-Union and anti-Orthodox literature, as well as the circulation of polemical Orthodox literature.[50]

Venice's Orthodox Christian political subjects were ecclesiastical subjects of the Patriarch of Constantinople, and the Patriarch was a political subject of the Ottoman Empire. Foscarini, who was Venetian Provedditore General in Crete during the years 1574–88, feared that, if Orthodox bishops were allowed to enter Crete, they might conspire with the Ottoman Imperial Government to try to turn Crete into an autonomous Orthodox Christian principality under Ottoman suzerainty, on the pattern of Wallachia and Moldavia.[51] The Venetian authorities therefore debarred Orthodox prelates from setting foot in Crete, and, in the War of Candia (1645–69), the 'Osmanlis had no sooner won a foothold in Crete than they imported an Orthodox Christian metropolitan in command of a team of seven bishops.[52] So long as the Venetians maintained their control over Crete, the Orthodox parish priests had had to fight the battle for Orthodoxy without the aid and guidance of an educated hierarchy. The parish priests were ignorant men,[53] and in Crete not all of them were of good character.[54] Yet, in the rural parishes especially, they had the confidence and support of their peasant flock, just because they themselves were peasants by birth and upbringing.

In Crete, the effectiveness of the parish priests' resistance worked together with the lukewarmness of the Venetian regime to defeat the Roman Catholic Church's campaign there in favour of Uniatism.[55] This failure of the Roman Catholic Christian Church to convert the Orthodox Christian Cretans to Uniatism while they were subjects of a Catholic Western Christian government contrasts strikingly with the rapidity and extensiveness of the Cretan conversions to Islam after the replacement of Venetian by Ottoman rule. There are said to have been 60,000 Cretan converts to Islam already by 1657,[56] and this year was only half-way through the long-drawn-out Turco-Venetian war of 1645–69. Unlike the Qaramanlis in Asia Minor, the Cretan Muslims did not become Turkish-speaking, but, though they retained their Greek mother-tongue, they became ardent Muslims; and they left their native

---

[47] Vakalópoulos, op. cit., vol. ii, part ii, p. 323.
[48] Ibid., p. 181.
[49] Ibid., p. 422.
[50] Ibid.
[51] Ibid., pp. 308–10.
[52] Ibid., pp. 491–2.
[53] Ibid., p. 451.
[54] Ibid., pp. 316–17.
[55] Ibid., pp. 173–4.
[56] Ibid., p. 512.

island and migrated to Turkey when Crete was progressively detached from the Ottoman Empire.[57]

Roman Catholicism failed to convert Eastern Orthodox Christendom, but it came nearer to success in influencing Eastern Orthodox theologians to formulate their doctrine on Roman lines. It has been noted already that the Greeks' animosity against the Westerners had not deterred some Greek scholars, even after the outrage in 1204, from studying Roman Christian theology and philosophy. Though, on the whole, the Eastern Orthodox Church deprecated the Western attempt to clarify the mysteries of Christianity by means of Aristotelian logic, this logic was, after all, a legacy from the Hellenic Greeks, and the Western Schoolmen's bold invasion of theological territory on which the Eastern Orthodox forbore to tread excited some Greek curiosity, though it did not win general Greek approval. In the Modern Age, this curiosity increased as the Eastern Orthodox Christians' animosity towards the Roman Church abated. It culminated in the seventeenth century in the Ukraine, where the presence of Roman Catholicism was closer, and its pressure stronger, than in any other Eastern Orthodox Christian country.

The Government of the Roman Catholic Kingdom of Poland–Lithuania had tried to impose union with the Roman Church, in the terms agreed at Florence in 1439, upon all its Eastern Orthodox Christian subjects. The Cossacks of the Dniepr and the Don—two autonomous Eastern Orthodox Christian communities—had compelled the Polish Government to tolerate Eastern Orthodoxy in the Ukraine; but the Jesuits were active in this debatable territory between Roman Catholic and Orthodox Christendom; and one of their intellectual weapons was logical precision. In 1633 a Moldavian who had been educated in Paris, Peter Moghila,[58] was elected Metropolitan of Kiev, and he saw that the Ukrainian Orthodox Church's best hope of holding its own was to compete with the Jesuits in the Jesuits' own style in the fields of education and theology.

Moghila founded a distinguished theological academy at Kiev, as well as schools in which Latin and modern Western science were included in the curriculum,[59] and, at some date before 1640, he wrote, in Latin, an Eastern Orthodox *Confessio Fidei* which was the first systematic exposition of Eastern Orthodox theology, apart from Loúkaris' controversial *Confessio*, since the publication of the eighth-century Father Saint John Damascene's *Fountain of Knowledge* (Πηγὴ Γνώσεως).

---

[57] In 1897 Crete became autonomous, with a Christian governor, under the supervision of the European Christian Powers; in 1913 the island was annexed to the Kingdom of Greece.
[58] See Runciman, *The Great Church in Captivity*, pp. 334–6 and 340–7.
[59] Ibid., pp. 334–5.

Moghila worked hard to persuade the Tsar of Muscovy, Alexis I Mikhailovitch (1645–76), to adopt his Westernizing system of education, and to persuade the Eastern Orthodox Churches to adopt his *Confessio*, but in both endeavours he fell just short of success.

In Muscovy Moghila's chances seemed bright after the acquisition of Kiev by Muscovy from Poland–Lithuania in 1667, but Tsar Alexis shied away and left it to Peter the Great to draw recruits from the Kievan Theological Academy to aid him in carrying out his Westernizing reforms.[60] As for Moghila's *Confessio*, its chances of being finally accepted were prejudiced by its Western flavour. 'It was clearly inspired by a Latin-trained mind.'[61] The Eastern Orthodox Churches found it less congenial than the Confession subsequently promoted and edited and published by Dhosítheos, the Peloponnesian Patriarch of Jerusalem (in office 1669–1707).[62] 'The "Confession of Dhosítheos" lacks the neat scholastic arrangement of Moghila's Confession,'[63] but it, too, runs counter to the Eastern Orthodox Church's traditional distaste for comprehensive formulations of theology. Neither of these modern statements of the Eastern Orthodox Christian faith has ever been ratified by an Ecumenical Council.

Dhosítheos, like Moghila, was on the defensive against the Jesuits,[64] and he, too, borrowed their intellectual weapons; but the Greeks did not go so far as the Ukrainians in Romanizing the exposition of Eastern Orthodox theology, and, for this reason, the Greek, not the Ukrainian, way of parrying Roman theological precision has prevailed.[65]

The third wave of Western influence that broke upon Eastern Orthodox Christendom was the secularizing rationalizing movement that, in the West itself, set in, before the close of the seventeenth century, as a recoil from the Catholic–Protestant Western wars of religion. This has been the most powerful wave of the three, and in Russian Orthodox Christendom it has had revolutionary effects. Here Peter the Great's revolution has been followed up by Lenin's. The effects were not so prompt, nor, till after the Second World War, so extreme, in any of those Eastern Orthodox Christian countries that were under Ottoman rule till after the opening of the nineteenth century; but the French Revolution shook all parts of Eastern Orthodox Christendom. The unfortunate Patriarch of Constantinople, Gregory V, took active measures for hindering the spread of the ideas of the French Revolution among his

[60] Runciman, *The Great Church in Captivity*, p. 335; Toynbee, vol. viii, pp. 128–9.
[61] Runciman, *The Great Church in Captivity*, p. 346.
[62] For Dhosítheos and his printing-press at Jassy, see Chapter VII, p. 152.
[63] Runciman, *The Great Church in Captivity*, p. 351.
[64] Ibid., p. 348.
[65] Ibid., pp. 352–4.

ecclesiastical subjects,[66] and in *The Paternal Exhortation* (Διδασκαλία πατρική), published at Istanbul in 1798 and possibly written by him,[67] though ascribed, on the title-page, to Anthimos, the Patriarch of Jerusalem, the Ottoman Empire is given credit for having served as a shield for Eastern Orthodox Christianity.

Since 1204, the Christian Westerners, not the Muslim Turks, had been the Greeks' arch-enemies.[68] In Greek lands under Western Christian rule, with the honourable exception of the Ionian Islands under the Venetian regime, the Eastern Orthodox clergy were harassed.[69] The Ottoman conquest of Western possessions in the Levant brought with it religious liberation for the Eastern Orthodox Christian inhabitants.[70] Skholários, who eventually made Notarás' choice, understood his countrymen's interests better than Vêssaríon. When Mehmet the Conqueror made Skholários Ecumenical Patriarch and head of the newly created *Rum milleti*, 'the integrity of the Church had been preserved, and with it the integrity of the Greek people'.[71]

Yet, even after 1204, some Greeks were attracted, in spite of themselves, by Western Christian intellectual culture.[72] The scholar-monk Máximos Planoúdhês (1260–1310)[73] translated into Greek a number of Latin works, including Boethius' *De Consolatione Philosophiae* —a belated Greek return for Boethius' translations from Greek into Latin. An impressive achievement was the translation of Saint Thomas Aquinas' *Summa*[74] by Dhêmêtrios Kydhônês (*vivebat circa* 1324–97/8).[75] Skholários himself, who eventually became the protagonist in the assertion of the ecclesiastical independence of the Eastern Orthodox Churches and consented to serve the Ottoman Pādishāh Mehmet II the Conqueror as the Ecumenical Patriarch Yennádhios II, was well versed in Western theology and scholastic philosophy, and he, too, translated some of Saint Thomas's works.[76]

When the last emperor of Constantinople began to subject the Oriental Church to Papal thraldom, the particular favour of Heaven raised up the Ottoman Empire to protect the Greeks against heresy, to be a barrier against

---

[66] See Daskalakis, op. cit., p. 19.

[67] See Chapter VII, p. 143 n. 20.

[68] Woodhouse, op. cit., p. 14.

[69] Runciman, *The Great Church in Captivity*, p. 227.

[70] Ibid., p. 228.

[71] Ibid. p. 182.

[72] See Hussey and Hart, in *Cambridge Medieval History*, vol. iv, 2nd edn., part ii, pp. 196–7.

[73] See Krumbacher, op. cit., pp. 543–6, especially p. 545; Dölger in *Cambridge Medieval History*, vol. iv, 2nd edn., part ii, p. 220.

[74] For this, see Hussey and Hart in op. cit., pp. 196–7.

[75] See Krumbacher op. cit., pp. 487–9.

[76] See ibid., p. 120.

the political power of the Western nations, and to be the champion of the Orthodox Church.[77]

The modern Western secularizing rationalizing movement has run, so far, through three phases: first the eighteenth-century 'Enlightenment', which was a recoil from the Wars of Religion; next, nineteenth-century liberalism, precipitated by the French Revolution; and then Communism, which captured Russia as a result of the First World War. The movement has risen crescendo in a steeply ascending curve; but even its comparatively moderate first phase frightened the Eastern Orthodox ecclesiastical 'establishment'. This church's retort, like the Roman church's, to 'enlightenment' was obscurantism; and, before the outbreak of the French Revolution, this obscurantism had frustrated the distinguished Corfiot Greek educationist Evyénios Voúlgharis (1716–1806).[78] Voúlgharis' offence was that he had had a German education in Modern Western secular philosophy. Unlike Plêthon, Voúlgharis was not provocative. He made a parade of being scrupulously Orthodox. For instance, he repudiated the neo-Hellenes' usage of the word 'Hellenes' to mean, not extinct pagans, but living Modern Greeks.[79] But Voúlgharis could not give satisfaction.

Voúlgharis was hounded out of a school that he had started at Yánnina. He was given a fresh opportunity when, in 1753, the Patriarch of Constantinople, Cyril V, founded a new academy on Mount Athos and appointed Voúlgharis to the chair of philosophy there. But, six years later, this Athonian academy was dissolved at the instance of Cyril V himself, who, by that time, had been deposed and had gone into retirement on Mount Athos. Voúlgharis was then given a post in the Patriarchal Academy at Constantinople, but he was forced out of this post too. In 1765 he withdrew from the domain of the Constantinopolitan Patriarchate to Germany, which was his spiritual home. In 1775 he found his opportunity at last, not in Greek, but in Russian, Eastern Orthodox Christendom. In that year the Russian Imperial Government, which believed in 'enlightenment' and had suppressed its own Patriarchate, appointed Voúlgharis to be bishop of the new see of Slavonia and Khersón, in territory recently acquired by Russia from the Ottoman Empire in the northern hinterland of the Black Sea.

The Russian Government's appreciation of Voúlgharis was a sign of the times. In the next generation after Voúlgharis', Western 'enlightenment' captured Ottoman Greek Orthodox Christendom too. Its

---

[77] Διδασκαλία πατρική, cited by Finlay in op. cit., vol. v, p. 285. There is now an English translation, by Richard Clogg, of the whole of this work: 'The "Dhidhaskalía Patrikí" (1798): an Orthodox Reaction to French Revolutionary Propaganda', in *Middle Eastern Studies*, v (1969), pp. 87–115.

[78] See Runciman, *The Great Church in Captivity*, p. 220; Toynbee, op. cit., vol. viii, pp. 160–1.

[79] See Toynbee, op. cit., vol. cit., p. 160 n. 3.

successful Greek apostle was Adhamándios Koraês,[80] the son of a Khiot business man who had migrated to Smyrna and had made money in the new commercial centre that had been opened up there by Western, seconded by Ottoman Greek, enterprise. Koraês followed the affluent Khiots' tradition[81] of completing their education in the West. In 1782 Koraês went to the University of Montpellier to study medicine there. In 1788 he went on to Paris and lived there serenely for the rest of his life. In Paris he witnessed, and survived, the French revolutions of 1789 and 1830; Paris had no terrors for an Ottoman Greek expatriate. The revolutionary cultural capital of the Western World gave Koraês a base of intellectual operations from which he could castigate Patriarchs and Pādishāhs with impunity.

By Koraês' time it was of no avail for the Greek Eastern Orthodox ecclesiastical 'establishment' to continue to set its face against all of the West's successive Protean metamorphoses. By this time, the Greek people as a whole had decided on its answer to a 'Western Question' that had been confronting it for seven centuries. The Greek people had at last decided for itself, as Peter the Great had decided for the Russian people more promptly, to seek admission to membership of the Western World. The impetus of the people's resolve overwhelmed the ecclesiastical 'establishment's' qualms and hesitations.

(ii) *The Greeks' Successful Engagement in the Economic Life of the Modern World*

Some of the performances of the Greeks at some of the stages of their long history have been ambiguous. For instance, the political performance of the Hellenic Greeks can be credited to them as having been a success, in virtue of their achievement of constitutional government, or alternatively it can be written off as having been a failure, considering that the Hellenic Greek city-states remained disunited, and continued to be chronically at war with each other, until unity and peace were imposed on them through the subjection of them all to the Roman Empire. By contrast, the greatness of the Hellenic Greeks' achievements in the fields of thought and art has never been questioned even by their bitterest enemies and least merciful critics. The political performance of the Modern Greeks has also been ambiguous so far. The Modern Greeks have succeeded in recovering and preserving their political independence against great odds, but they have been less successful in the management of their domestic political affairs.

There is, however, at least one field in which the Modern Greeks have

---

[80] See Toynbee, op. cit., vol. cit., pp. 178–80.
[81] For this, see ibid., p. 179 n. 1.

been successful—here, too, against great odds—to a degree at which their achievement can rank with the Hellenic Greeks' intellectual and artistic success. The Modern Greeks have not only entered into the commercial life of the Modern World; they have held their own in it with outstanding success. This commercial prowess of the Modern Greeks has been notable; for the Modern World's economy is a Western structure to which the Greeks have had to adapt themselves; and the Greeks have had to compete in this field with Western peoples who have far surpassed the Greeks in population, wealth, and power, as well as with non-Western commercial diasporas of the Greeks' own kind. Before the close of the fifteenth century, the Ottoman Greeks were having to compete in Ottoman territory with Jewish refugees from Spain whom Sultan Bayezid II (1481–1512) had planted at key points in the Empire.[82] Since the creation, by Western enterprise, of a global field of economic activity, the Greeks have also had to compete in this Western arena with Armenians, Lebanese, Syrian Christians, and Parsees.

To have succeeded so signally under these arduous conditions has been a notable Modern Greek feat. It is particularly remarkable, considering that, in the immediately antecedent Byzantine stage of Greek history, the Greeks' normal economic vitality had been depressed by the incubus of a rigid and ponderous political regime, and that the Byzantine Greeks' economic life had been at its lowest ebb during the quarter of a millennium (1204–1453) between the two catastrophic falls of Byzantine Greek Constantinople—the East Roman Empire's parasitic capital city.

During the last century before its second and final fall, Byzantine Constantinople had been a tiny enclave of East Roman territory, surrounded by the ever-expanding dominions of the Ottoman Empire. Bursa (Brusa), which had been the 'Osmanlis' capital before the transfer of this, *circa* 1365, to Adrianople, had replaced Constantinople as the terminus of the trade routes from Persia (via Trebizond) and from

---

[82] See above, p. 140. The immediate reason for the 'Osmanlis' hospitable reception of the Marranos was that these were victims of the 'Osmanlis' Western Christian enemies the Spaniards. However, the 'Osmanlis also saw in their Marrano guests an opportune counterpoise to their Greek subjects. The 'Osmanlis could count on the loyalty of the Marranos. These had become Ottoman subjects voluntarily, and they did not have any more desirable alternative asylum. The 'Osmanlis' Greek subjects were the conquered citizens of a Greek Empire that the 'Osmanlis had destroyed and had supplanted. The 'Osmanlis could count on their Greek subjects' loyalty too in so far as, for the Greeks, the Westerners, not the Turks, were their 'Enemy Number One'. But, from first to last, the 'Osmanlis were aware that the Greeks had not forgiven them for having reduced the Greeks from being a ruling people to being a subject people. For the Marranos in the Ottoman Empire, see Gibb and Bowen, op. cit., vol. i, part ii (London 1957), pp. 219–20 and 225–6. At the turn of the sixteenth and seventeenth centuries, there was a decline in the prosperity of the Ottoman Jews (ibid., pp. 240–1), whereas the Ottoman Greeks were becoming increasingly prosperous contemporaneously, by comparison with both the Ottoman Jews and the Ottoman Muslims.

Syria.[83] By the spring of 1453, when the Ottoman assault on Constantinople was launched, the city's population may have dwindled to about 50,000;[84] and, since the East Roman Imperial Government had rejected the prescribed three previous summonses to surrender, the city's fall brought with it the enslavement of the inhabitants and the pillaging of their property by the Ottoman troops.[85]

Sultan Mehmet II the Conqueror regretted the depopulation and devastation of Constantinople; for he was going to make it his capital. He had adopted the Byzantine doctrine that Constantinople conferred on its possessor the title to world-wide rule.[86] The ground, the buildings, and one-fifth of the booty (which included the enslaved inhabitants) belonged to the Government according to Islamic law. Mehmet II settled his quota of the slaves within their own city along the shore of the Golden Horn;[87] he allowed other captives who were able to ransom themselves also to remain in Constantinople;[88] and he deported to Constantinople other Greeks from Bursa,[89] the two Phocaeas, the Pelopónnêsos, Imvros, Lêmnos, Thásos, Ténedhos, Lésvos, Árghos, Caffa in the Crimea,[90] and Qaraman in the course of the years 1454–74.[91] The deportees were given house-property in Constantinople and a temporary remission of taxes.[92]

In the repeopled city there were about three times as many Muslims as Eastern Orthodox Christians according to the census of 1477,[93] and in 1490 the Muslims were in a great majority in the guilds.[94] However, 'economic life cut across sectarian lines'.[95] There were interdenominational guilds, as well as guilds that were exclusively either Muslim or Christian.[96] The Christians, including some of the surviving East Roman aristocrats,[97] quickly acquired customs-farming and mining

[83] Inalcik, H., 'The Policy of Mehmed II towards the Greek Population of Istanbul and the Byzantine Buildings of the City', in *Dumbarton Oaks Papers*, Numbers Twenty-three and Twenty-four (1969–70), pp. 229–50, on p. 231. See also Vakalópoulos, op. cit., vol. ii, part i, pp. 348–52.

[84] Inalcik, in op. cit., p. 231.

[85] See ibid., pp. 231–3.

[86] See ibid., p. 233.

[87] Ibid., p. 235.

[88] Ibid., pp. 237–8.

[89] The deportees from Bursa to Constantinople perhaps included some Turks.

[90] The deportees from Caffa were Genoese and Armenians.

[91] Inalcik, in op. cit., pp. 241–7. Cf. the repeopling of Constantinople by the Emperor Constantine V after the population had been reduced by the plague of 746–7.

[92] Ibid.

[93] See ibid., p. 247.

[94] Ibid., p. 248 n. 84.

[95] Vryonis Jr., Sp., 'The Byzantine Legacy and Ottoman Forms', in *Dumbarton Oaks Papers*, Numbers Twenty-three and Twenty-four (1969–70), pp. 251–308, on p. 279.

[96] Vryonis, op. cit., p. 284–5; and, for further details, Vakalópoulos, op. cit., vol. ii, part i, pp. 307–14, and Gibb and Bowen, op. cit., vol. i, part i, chapter 6, pp. 276–313.

[97] See Vakalópoulos, op. cit., vol. ii, part i, p. 356, cited on p. 147 of the present work.

concessions, and they began to gain wealth and influence, particularly in maritime trade.[98]

For nearly four centuries ending in 1453, the Greeks had suffered, not only politically, but also economically and demographically, from the progressive Turkish occupation of the East Roman Empire's former territories. This occupation had been carried out in three stages. The interior of Asia Minor had been occupied in the late eleventh and the early twelfth century; Western Asia Minor in the late thirteenth and the early fourteenth century; the Balkan Peninsula in the fourteenth and fifteenth centuries. The main mass of the Turkish invaders, at each stage, had been nomads whose conversion to Islam had hitherto been superficial. Their transformation into effectively Muslim sedentary peasants and town-dwellers was gradual. Meanwhile they inflicted grievous damage on the conquered communities on which they had imposed themselves.[99]

In Mehmet II's reign (1451–81) the Ottoman Empire was not only rounded off by the annexation of Trebizond, the Pelopónnêsos, several of the Aegean islands, and Qaraman; it was also stabilized; and the tardily established *Pax Ottomanica*[100] gave the Empire's Greek subjects an opening for economic recuperation. This can be gauged in the domestic market by the revival of the Byzantine Greek *panêgyreís* (religious festivals that were also fairs), with Muslim Turkish participation.[101] In maritime trade,

under Mehmed II the Greeks were enabled to engage in commerce under more favourable conditions than had existed before. Since they were *dhimmî*[102] subjects of the Sultan, the whole Empire was open to them as a field for their commercial activities, and they enjoyed protection, especially against the Italians, who were subjected to a higher customs tariff than the Greeks. Thus they gradually supplanted the Italians, particularly in the Black Sea trade and in trade with the countries of Northern Europe.[103]

One of the unforeseen consequences of the Ottoman conquest was the rebirth

---

[98] Inalcik, op. cit., p. 248 n. 84.

[99] See Vryonis in loc. cit., pp. 259–67.

[100] The Ottoman Empire was not peculiar among the would-be world empires in causing, during the process of conquest, devastation which was repaired only partially after the conquest had been achieved. The empire-building activities of Rome and Ch'in had followed a similar course.

[101] Vryonis, in loc. cit., p. 286.

[102] *Dhimmîs* are members of the *Ahl-al-Kitāb* (people with admittedly inspired scriptures, i.e. Jews and Christians). Muslim political authorities are under an obligation to protect *Dhimmîs*—as long as they have submitted politically and have agreed to pay a surtax.

[103] Inalcik, op. cit., p. 248 n. 85. Inalcik cites the customs registers for the ports of Kilia (in the Danube delta), Akkerman (at the mouth of the Dniestr, in 1490), and Caffa in the Crimea; see also Daskalakis, A., *Rhigas Velestinlis* (Paris 1937), p. 10; Runciman, *The Great Church in Captivity*, p. 196.

of Greek mercantile life. . . .[104] The Greek genius for commerce always flourishes in areas where the Greeks are debarred from political power.[105]

Indeed, any community or class that is penalized politically tends to make itself economically efficient and successful, partly because economic activity is an alternative outlet for repressed energies, and partly because wealth is some offset to the loss of political power. People who are politically impotent cannot afford to be indigent as well. The Jews developed their economic prowess after they had ceased to possess a national state of their own and had been prised off the land in what had once been Eretz Israel. The political blows that the Greeks suffered at the 'Osmanlis' hands during the century and a half culminating in the year 1453 had the same effect on them that the disasters of A.D. 70 and A.D. 135 had on the Jews. Like the Jews,[106] the Greeks reacted to military and political disaster by bringing into play an economic prowess that had been inhibited under the now defunct East Roman Imperial regime.

The Greeks in the fourteenth and fifteenth centuries had not been uprooted to the same extent as the Jews in the first and second centuries. During the Ottoman conquest of *Rum ili* (the Balkan Peninsula) there were mass conversions among the conquered Eastern Orthodox Christians.[107] East Roman Christian *pronoiárioi* saved their estates by becoming Ottoman Muslim timariots.[108] Apostasy even among monks and clerics was also common in this period.[109] Yet, in the greater part of the fertile lowlands, the Christian peasantry was ousted by Muslim Turkish settlers. The Ottoman Government secured its hold on its conquests by a planned policy of colonization;[110] and in any case the conquest would have been followed, as it actually was followed with official encouragement, by a spontaneous mass emigration into the Balkan Peninsula of the mobile nomadic Turkish *yürüks* who had been accumulating in Asia Minor since Alp Arslan's victory at Manzikert[111] in 1071 had opened the door for them, and since the subsequent explosion of the Mongols in the heart of the Eurasian steppe had driven further swarms of Turkish *yürüks* off the steppe into adjoining regions.

Under the pressure of the fourteenth-century and fifteenth-century *yürük Völkerwanderung* into the Balkan Peninsula, accompanied by the

[104] Ibid., p. 196. Cp. p. 360.
[105] Ibid.
[106] And, indeed, like the Japanese and the Germans after 1945.
[107] Gibb and Bowen, op. cit., vol. i, part ii, pp. 209–10 and 257; Vakalópoulos, op. cit., vol. ii, part i, pp. 44–50.
[108] Ibid., p. 48.
[109] Ibid., p. 49.
[110] Ibid., p. 75.
[111] *Alias* Melazgerd.

plantation of Ottoman fief-holders, the Rumelian lowlands mostly fell into Turkish hands,[112] and the Christian peasants who kept their footing here did so only at the price of submitting to conditions that were unenviable,[113] even if no worse than—or possibly not quite so bad as— their progressively deteriorating conditions during the last five centuries of the East Roman regime. The more enterprising and more high-spirited members of the conquered Christian rural population in *Rum ili* evaded this fate by withdrawing, and they had a choice of three alternative asylums.

They could retain liberty, at the price of embracing poverty, by ensconcing themselves in natural fastnesses in which the Ottoman Government could not make its authority effective, although these Christian asylums lay within the Ottoman Empire's frontiers.[114] Alternatively the Christians could emigrate either to regions under Western Christian rule or to urban areas under Ottoman rule. In both of these two alternative asylums, the Ottoman, or ex-Ottoman, Christians had economic opportunities. They duly seized these; for, under the Ottoman dispensation, the first concern of the 'Osmanlis' Christian subjects or emigrant ex-subjects was the acquisition of wealth. This now had, for them, the priority over such previous goals of their ambition as social status and literary culture.[115]

For Christians who did not evade Ottoman rule by either emigrating or withdrawing into the mountains, life was more tolerable, and economic prospects were more promising, in the cities than in the countryside; for although, as has been noticed already,[116] the Ottoman Government recognized that it was to its interest to protect its peasants, Christian as well as Muslim, against its fief-holders, and though, until the close of the sixteenth century, the Porte was more successful in this than the antecedent East Roman Imperial Government had been, the Ottoman central authorities could carry out their policy of protecting docile non-Muslims more effectively in Istanbul and in the other major Ottoman cities than in the countryside, where the degree of the Government's control varied proportionately to the proximity of the capital.

Accordingly, Istanbul and the other major cities of the Empire

---

[112] Vakalópoulos, op. cit., vol. ii, part i, p. 95. When the rural lowlands were occupied by Turkish settlers, the lowland cities became Turkish in still greater measure. Examples are the cities of Lárisa and Phérsala in the lowlands of Thessaly (ibid., p. 84).

[113] Ibid., pp. 13–35.

[114] Ibid., pp. 81–3. For the consequent differentiation between the Christian *vounísioi* and their Kambísioi co-religionists, whom the *vounísioi* despised, see ibid., p. 96.

[115] See ibid., pp. 252–3 and 268–9.

[116] On p. 144.

attracted Christians who had economic ambitions,[117] and many of these found their initial opportunity in the guilds of artisans and traders.[118] The Ottoman guilds were not direct successors of the East Roman guilds; they had originated in the twelfth century 'Abbasid Order of Chivalry or Virtue (*Futuwwa*),[119] in the form given to this by the Turkish *akhīs* ('brethren') in Anatolia.[120] The East Roman guilds seem to have been merged in the Ottoman guilds after the Ottoman conquest;[121] and the Christian guildsmen seem to have gained by this. In the guilds, at least down to about the close of the sixteenth century, the discrimination against non-Muslim Ottoman subjects seems to have been at a minimum, and the Ottoman Government's control over the guilds' activities seems to have been less stifling than the East Roman Government's control over the Ottoman guilds' predecessors.[122]

Moreover, the Prophet Muhammad had been a trader before he received his call; traders and artisans had always been highly esteemed in Islamic society; the 'Osmanlis had inherited this Islamic tradition;[123] they were eager addicts to technology in the days before their stagnation and decline.[124] In these circumstances, membership of guilds under the Ottoman dispensation gave non-Muslim Ottoman subjects an advantageous 'jumping-off ground' for making their fortunes. The guilds were the recruiting-ground for a new Greek bourgeoisie, and ultimately for the parvenu Phanariot Greek aristocracy.

The ex-East Roman aristocrats' attempt to make up for the loss of their official salaries and their rents by taking to tax-farming and trade had been a counsel of despair; for their ancestral tradition disqualified them for playing these novel roles. They quickly failed, whereas the rising Ottoman Greek guildsmen progressively made a success of these

---

[117] Indeed, Christians who had withdrawn into mountain fastnesses from the open country were subsequently attracted from the mountains into the cities by the prospect of economic opportunity combined with relative security. For instance, by 1605, half of the collective tax levied on the Thessalonian Christian community for the maintenance of the local garrison of Turkish *topcis* (artillerymen) was being paid by settlers in Thessaloníkê from the Ághrapha, the 'unregistered' (i.e. unassessed for tax) highland fastness at the southern end of the Pindus Range (Vakalópoulos, vol. ii, part i, pp. 359–64). Istanbul attracted Christians from Qaraman in south central Asia Minor (ibid., pp. 389–91). At Istanbul, the Qaramanli settlers prospered as traders, goldsmiths, and garment-workers (ibid., p. 390).

[118] See p. 181 n. 96.

[119] The founder was the Caliph Nāsir (*imperabat* A.D. 1180–1225). See Spuler, B., in *The Cambridge History of Islam*, vol. i (1970), pp. 156–7.

[120] Gibb and Bowen, op. cit., vol. i, part i, p. 283. The Akhīs had originally been unorthodox Muslims and disaffected political subjects (ibid., p. 290). See also Wittek, P., *The Rise of the Ottoman Empire* (London 1938), p. 42.

[121] See Gibb and Bowen, op. cit., p. 289.

[122] Vakalópoulos, op. cit., vol. ii, part i, p. 309.

[123] Ibid., p. 286.

[124] Ibid., p. 309.

new openings.[125] Thus the Ottoman conquest of the Greeks brought about a social revolution within the bosom of the Ottoman Greek community. The Ottoman regime in *Rum ili* and Anatolia, like the Tokugawa regime in Japan, hammered order out of anarchy at a heavy cost to its beneficiaries. The Ottoman Pādishāhs, like the Tokugawa Shoguns, sought to 'freeze' the order which they had established, but, like the Tokugawa, they were defeated by their inability to control the economic forces that had been generated by the rulers' own military and political feats.

The expansion of the Ottoman Empire into regions beyond the Danube which the East Roman Empire had never ruled, and into regions to the south and east of the Távros which it had not ruled since the seventh century, not only added to the number of Greek and other Eastern Orthodox Christians who were under the political superintendence of the Patriarch of Constantinople in his capacity as Ottoman *millet başi* of the *Rum Milleti;*[126] but it also enlarged the domestic field of commercial enterprise for the Ottoman Empire's Greek subjects. For instance, after the Ottoman conquest of Egypt, a Greek community made its appearance once again at Alexandria.[127]

The 'Osmanlis pushed the frontiers of their Empire far north-westwards into Central Europe, but the Ottoman Greek Christians anticipated their Turkish masters in making lodgements in Western Christendom, and, as traders, they penetrated it to distances that the Ottoman armies never even approached. The 'Osmanli invaders were preceded by Greek refugees. Some of these came as peasants who struck root in the Kingdom of the Two Sicilies without changing their way of life.[128] Others took service as mercenaries in the armies of the Kingdom of the Two Sicilies[129] and of Venice. The Ottoman conquest of the Peloponnêsos in 1460 produced a flow of Pelopennesian refugees into the Venetian possessions—for instance, to Pola and Parenzo[130] and to Venice itself.[131] The Greek settlers in Venice made their living by going into commercial business, and it is significant that the men who came to the front in the Greek community in Venice were, not the descendants of East Roman aristocrats, but parvenus of humble antecedents.[132] By

---

[125] Vakalópoulos, op. cit., vol. ii, part i, p. 312.

[126] See above, pp. 141–3 and 153.

[127] Runciman, *The Great Church in Captivity*, p. 177; Gibb and Bowen, op. cit., vol. i, part ii, pp. 259–60. The rise of this Greek community in Egypt was gradual. In the eighteenth century its numbers, and the scale of its economic operations, were still small.

[128] See Vakalópoulos, op. cit., vol. ii, part i, pp. 64–5 and 66–70.

[129] Ibid., p. 66. See Mozart's *Così fan Tutte*, first performed in 1790, for a Greek profession that, by that date, was at least 300 years old.

[130] Ibid., p. 64.

[131] Ibid., pp. 70–2.

[132] Ibid., p. 71.

1514 there was a colony of Greek traders at Ancona, mostly of North-West Greek origin.[133]

These settlements of Greek *émigrés* in Italy were substantial and durable, by contrast with the 'Osmanlis' brief military occupation, in 1480, of a solitary Italian beach-head at Ótranto. But the Greeks' lodgements in Italy were outmatched in range and scale and importance by their commercial penetration of Central Europe.

The Ottoman Greeks' base of operations for their commercial conquests in Central Europe was Thessaloníkê, an Aegean port which is linked with the interior of Europe by the two adjacent valleys of the Rivers Vardar (Axiós) and Strúma (Strymón).[134] Ottoman Greek traders established themselves in the German cities of Transylvania in the course of the sixteenth century.[135] By 1593 there were also Greeks as well as Armenians and Jews in Galicia at Lvov.[136] Indeed, by 1580, there were two Greeks as far afield as Posen.[137] Commercial relations between the Ottoman Greeks and Central Europe increased in volume during the seventeenth century.[138] In 1636 the Prince of Transylvania gave the Greeks of Hermannstadt (Sibiu) privileges that were renewed in 1701 and in 1777.[139] By 1639 there was a Greek Kompanía of Transylvania, governed by elected officers.[140]

The eventual recession of the Ottoman Empire's frontiers, which set in after the failure, in 1683, of the second of the two Turkish sieges of Vienna, gave further commercial openings to the Ottoman Greeks. In the eighteenth century the Greeks were the only European Ottoman Christian community in which there were traders and sailors, as well as peasants.[141] By this date, Ottoman Greek merchants, as has been noted, were travelling actively, both at home and abroad, long since.[142]

In the intermittent Hundred Years' War (1682–1791) between the Habsburg Monarchy and the Ottoman Empire, the military front changed repeatedly in both directions. In 1689, in the flood tide of the Habsburg counter-offensive after the Ottoman disaster in 1683, the

---

[133] Ibid., p. 394.

[134] The routes along the banks of both rivers are obstructed by a series of gorges; on the other hand, there is an easy passage over the watershed between the head-waters of each of these two rivers and the south-bank tributaries of the Danube. See the maps in Vakalópoulos, op. cit., vol. ii, part i, on pp. 396 and 399.

[135] Ibid., pp. 394–407.

[136] Ibid., p. 402.

[137] Ibid.

[138] Ibid., p. 394.

[139] Ibid., p. 398.

[140] Ibid., p. 400. This Kompanía was evidently more like a social fraternity than like a business corporation in the present-day sense.

[141] See Bótzaris, N., *Visions balkaniques dans la préparation de la révolution Grecque (1789–1821)*, (Paris 1962, Geneva 1962), p. 3.

[142] Ibid., p. 12.

Habsburg forces reached Skoplje, and they occupied Serbia in 1718–39 and again in 1788–92. The Habsburg Monarchy made no permanent territorial acquisitions to the south of the line of the Rivers Sava and Danube; but, even so, the Habsburg frontiers had been pushed forward, at the Ottoman Empire's expense, from a point only about half-way from Vienna to Pest to as far as the left banks of the Sava and the Danube opposite Belgrade; and this geographical advance of the south-eastern border of Western Christendom towards the parts of Ottoman *Rum ili* in which the population was Greek gave the Rumeliot Greeks an opportunity, which they seized, to open up a regular overland caravan trade between the Ottoman and the Habsburg dominions.

Greek family businesses were organized with their headquarters in *Rum ili* but with members of the family installed at Pest, Vienna, and even on the far side of the Habsburg Monarchy, at Leipzig. By 1797–8, when Rhêghas Velestinlés was arrested at Trieste by the Austrian police and was subsequently extradited to the Ottoman Government, this Habsburg–Ottoman trade, in Greek hands, had come to play such an important part in the Habsburg Monarchy's economic life that the Austrian authorities were chary of taking extreme measures against the eighteen business men of foreign origin, resident in Austria—ten of them Ottoman subjects, seven of them Habsburg subjects, and one a Russian subject—who were charged with conspiring on Austrian soil against the Ottoman Imperial Government. It was feared that judicial proceedings might have a seriously adverse effect, not only on the accused's own businesses, but on Austrian business in general.[143]

Moreover, this consideration was brought to the attention of the Habsburg Internuncio at Istanbul by the Dragoman of the Porte, Prince Constantine Ypsilándès,[144] who, in this affair, acted as a Greek patriot rather than as an Ottoman high official. The affair caused concern to the Greek business community as well as to the Austrian Government. When the Greeks in the Habsburg dominions became aware of Rhêghas' political activites, they began to realize their property there at a loss.[145] The news of Rhêgas' arrest created a panic among the Greek business houses of the Ottoman Empire.[146]

Meanwhile, German business men had been settling in *Rum ili*—for instance, in the Greek townlet Ambelákia, on the northernmost spur of Mount Ossa, overhanging the Témbê gorge. Here, local cotton was spun and was then dyed red with Valóna oak gall, and the product was exported overland to Pest, Vienna, Dresden, Leipzig, and even as far as

---

[143] See Daskalakis, op. cit., pp. 154 (with n. 2), 167, 175, 178.
[144] See Bótzaris, op. cit., pp. 23–4.
[145] Daskalakis, op. cit., pp. 73–4.
[146] Ibid., p. 121.

Hamburg.[147] The Greek caravan traffic between *Rum ili* and Central Europe was eventually put out of action by the building of a continuous line of railway from the Habsburg Monarchy to Istanbul in 1872–88, supplemented later by a branch line from Nish to Thessaloníkê and a further extension from Thessaloníkê to Monastir.[148] This was an Austrian business enterprise, but Ottoman Greek as well as Central European businesses benefited by this improvement in the means of communication.[149]

In the overland trade between *Rum ili* and Central Europe, the Ottoman Greeks had taken the initiative; in the maritime trade between other parts of the Ottoman Empire and Western Europe, the initiative had been taken by the French, Dutch, and English, who, since the sixteenth century, had inherited some of the maritime trade of the Levant which the Venetians and the Genoese had forfeited, partly as a result of Ottoman Greek competition and partly also, in Venice's case, as a result of recurrent hostilities with the Ottoman Empire in a long-drawn-out losing battle to hold Venice's Levantine possessions.

As a party to the Western anti-Ottoman coalition that had been called into existence by the Ottoman offensive in 1682, Venice had conquered in 1684–99 the whole of the Pelopónnêsos, where, in the Middle Ages, she had held only three beach-heads. But in 1715 the 'Osmanlis had reconquered from Venice the Pelopónnêsos and Tênos too, and, after that, the maritime trade between the Pelopóńnêsos and the West had passed into French hands.[150] The French, Dutch, and English had all taken part in the development of Smyrna[151] (Izmir) as an entrepôt for maritime trade between the West and the interior of Asia Minor and the more distant Asian hinterland, and this commercial opening, too, was seized by the Ottoman Greeks. Smyrna now became, once again, a Greek city, besides becoming a Frankish one. The Greek settlers in Smyrna mostly came from Khios and other Aegean islands.

---

[147] See Beaujour, F., *Tableau du commerce de la Grèce* (Paris 1800, 2 vols.), vol. i, pp. 272–5; Clarke, E. D., *Travels in Various Countries of Europe, Asia, and Africa*, part ii, section iii (London 1816), pp. 281 and 285–8. Clarke visited Ambelákia on 23–4 December 1801. These passages of these two books are reprinted in Toynbee, *A Study of History*, vol. viii, pp. 181–2.

[148] After the Orient Railway had been linked up with the Bulgarian and Serbian railway networks in 1888, Thessaloníkê was linked up with the railway network of Greece in 1916.

[149] Arriving at Thessaloníkê in July 1912 by ship from the Peiraeus, I was impressed by the sight of Hungarian, Austrian, and German railway-trucks at the quayside. At Shátishta in the Aliákmon basin, on 5–6 September 1921, I met an old man who, as a boy, had accompanied his father on one of the last of the caravan expeditions between Shátishta and Central Europe. I also visited a house in Shátishta in which there were eighteenth-century portraits of the owner's ancestors, in wigs and powder, that had been painted at Pest and Vienna when they had been resident there.

[150] See Sakellários, M. V., 'Η πελοπόννησος κατὰ τὴν δευτέραν Τουρκοκρατίαν (1715–1821) (Athens 1939), pp. 126–8.

[151] Smyrna captured Khios' export trade after the annexation of Khios to the Ottoman Empire in 1566. Smyrna also captured some of Aleppo's trade (Vakalópoulos, op. cit., vol. ii, part i, p. 412). By 1600, Smyrna was already flourishing (ibid., p. 378).

One of the ex-Khiot Smyrniots was the father of Adhamándios Koraês, who was to play such a prominent part in the history of the Modern Greek 'language question'.[152]

The Ottoman Greeks also benefited commercially from the naval and military successes of the Ottoman Empire's northern neighbour, Russia. Till the Russo–Turkish war of 1768–74, the Black Sea, including its backwater the Sea of Azov, had been a Turkish lake. Russia had conquered Azov, at the mouth of the River Don, in 1696, only to have to retrocede it in 1711. But in the peace-settlement of 1774 the suzerainty over the Khanate of the Crimea was transferred to Russia from the Ottoman Empire. Russia annexed Krim Tartary in 1783; in the Russo–Turkish war of 1787–92, Russia went on to annex the adjacent Turkish territory to the west, as far westward as the east bank of the River Dniestr along its lower course; in 1812 she annexed Bessarabia, the easternmost portion of the Principality of Moldavia, between the Rivers Dniestr and Pruth. The Russian Government promptly founded a row of port-towns along her newly acquired stretch of Black Sea coast: Khersón[153] in 1778, Nikolayev in 1788, Odessa in 1792–4. The hinterland of these new Russian ports was as vast and as fertile as the Mississippi basin, which the United States was beginning to open up at the same date. Odessa, in particular, rapidly grew into a flourishing centre for trade and shipping, and the Ottoman Greeks provided an important contingent of the cosmopolitan population which gathered there.

Russia sought to follow up her acquisition of a seaboard on the Black Sea by acquiring influence over the domestic affairs of the defeated Ottoman Empire, and her policy was to work through the Russian people's Eastern Orthodox Christian co-religionists who were Ottoman subjects—not, at this stage, through Russia's fellow Slavs so much as through the Ottoman Greeks, who were more mobile and more versatile. In the peace-treaty of 1774 it was stipulated that Russia was to have the same treatment, rights, and status in the Ottoman Empire as were enjoyed at that time by France and Britain under their capitulations, and that Russia might establish consulates, on the same footing as the French and British consulates, at any place in Ottoman territory. In the Russo–Turkish commercial treaty of 1783 it was expressly stipulated that Russian consuls should have the right, already enjoyed by the representatives of other capitulatory powers, of maintaining tax-free and otherwise privileged Ottoman servants. This right had already been flagrantly abused by the Western powers. The Russian Government

---

[152] See Chapter IX (iv).

[153] *Not* on the site of the original Hellenic Greek colonial city-state Khersón[êsos], which had lain in the Crimea, slightly to the south of the modern Russian naval base of Sevastopol.

now interpreted two clauses of the treaty of 1774, read together, as conferring on her a protectorate over all Eastern Orthodox Christian Ottoman subjects.[154] The Russian authorities licensed Eastern Orthodox Christian Ottoman subjects (i.e. in practice, Greeks) to trade at sea under the Russian flag. From 1818 onwards, Greeks were appointed as Russian consuls in the Ottoman Empire.[155]

The privilege of trading at sea under the Russian flag benefited the Ottoman Greeks indirectly as well as directly. The indirect effect was to move the Ottoman Government to show favour to Ottoman Greek ship-owners who were willing, in return, to continue to sail under the Ottoman flag.[156] At some date shortly before 1824,[157] the Ottoman Government granted 'most favoured foreign nation treatment' to Ottoman subjects, trading with foreign countries, who were not the official protégés of foreign embassies. We may guess that the date of this privilege—which included the limitation of the rate of customs duties payable by the beneficiaries to the 3 per cent *ad valorem* which was the maximum rate for the nationals and the Ottoman protégés of the capitulatory powers—was later than 1815. For, during the Napoleonic wars, ships flying the Ottoman flag had been enjoying the immense commercial advantage of being almost the only neutral ships in Europe, from Russia to Britain inclusive—and this at a time when the belligerency of the non-Ottoman European states was making it lucrative for ships flying the neutral Ottoman flag to export Ottoman grain to the French Empire and its compulsory allies, if the ships' masters were willing and able to run the gauntlet of the British blockade.

The ship-owners of four Greek islands—all so barren that there was no livelihood to be made by their inhabitants on shore—now rose to the occasion. The islands were Ýdhra and Pétses off the Aegean coast of the Pelopónnêsos and Psará and Kásos on the far side of the Aegean Archipelago.[158] The Kasiots and Psariots were Greeks; the Ydhriots and Petsiots were recently installed Eastern Orthodox Christian Albanians from the Pelopónnêsos. The enterprise was financed with Khiot capital; the seamanship and the gunnery, for trying conclusions with the British Navy if need be, were the islanders' own contribution, and but for this, the Khiots would have lost their money. The temporary opening for making high profits was so enticing that even the unmaritime-minded

---

[154] This interpretation of the terms of the treaty of 1774 will not bear examination, but the Russians were able to insist on it, thanks to Russia's decisive superiority over Turkey in military power at this stage.

[155] Khrysanthópoulos, Photákos, Ἀπομνημονεύματα (Athens 1899, 2 vols.), vol. i, p. 16.

[156] See Daskalakis, op. cit., p. 11.

[157] i.e. shortly before the publication, in 1824, of the seventh, and last, volume of I. M. d'Ohsson's *Tableau général de l'Empire Ottoman* (Paris 1788–1824, 7 vols.). See vol. vii, p. 509.

[158] See Woodhouse, C. M., *The Greek War of Independence: Its Historical Setting* (London 1952), pp. 31 and 59–60.

Muslim and Christian Peloponnesian landowners entered this hazardous overseas market for cereals.[159]

The four enterprising islands' brief economic boom had two historic consequences, one short-term and political, the other long-term and economic. The islanders' merchant marine, abruptly deprived of its lucrative earnings by the re-establishment of peace in Europe in 1815, became, at a terrible cost to the Psariots and the Kasiots and to their Khiot financial backers, the navy with which the insurgent Greeks won the war for independence from the Ottoman Empire which they started in 1821. On a longer view, the Ydhriot and Petsiot brigs which performed so brilliantly between 1792 and 1815 in the Mediterranean were the progenitors of the present Greek merchant marine, consisting of mechanically propelled ships of all sizes, which is plying today all round the globe.

The building-up of this Greek merchant marine in the course of the nineteenth and twentieth centuries has been an extraordinary achievement of Greek enterprise and ability. This was the age in which the British merchant marine was at its peak. The British ship-owners enjoyed the formidable advantage of being the oceanic carriers of the country that had been the first in the field in carrying out the Industrial Revolution. They made their fortunes in the age in which the United Kingdom was 'the workshop of the World', and was exporting its manufactures all round the globe in exchange for imports of raw materials and food from distant sources. In contemporary Greece, manufacturing industry was still rudimentary.[160] She was a poor country with a bare minimum of fertile soil and of accumulated capital. Yet she has held her own at sea 'under the strenuous conditions of the modern world'.[161] The only other people who have emulated the Greeks' modern maritime achievement are the Norwegians, and the Norwegians have been spurred by similar conditions at home. Norway and Greece have longer coastlines[162] and smaller rations of fertile soil than any other European countries. As for the Greeks, their global maritime achievement in the modern age is comparable to the Hellenic Greeks' achievements in the western basin of the Mediterranean in the pre-Alexandrine Age and in the Indian Ocean in the post-Alexandrine Age.

[159] The French traders in the Pelopónnêsos had been ruined by the abortive Peloponnesian Greek Christian insurrection of 1770 and by the local disorders that had followed it. After that, the French had been cut off from the Pelopónnêsos by the outbreak of the Revolutionary and Napoleonic Wars (Sakellários, op. cit., pp. 211, 218, 244).

[160] See Campbell and Sherrard, op. cit., pp. 299, 301, 309, 372–4. Manufactures accounted for only 3·4 per cent of the value of Greece's exports in 1963, and for not more than 11·6 per cent in 1965. Greeks preferred to invest their savings, not in industry, but in commerce.

[161] For this phrase, see the texts of the mandates of the 'A' class that were conferred on France and Britain for the temporary administration of some Arab countries after the First World War.

[162] See Woodhouse, op. cit., p. 60. Norway's coastline is even longer than Greece's.

Like the eighteenth-century and early nineteenth-century Greek overland trade between *Rum ili* and Central Europe, the present world-wide Greek maritime trade has been created and maintained by a diaspora. In the Middle Ages, except perhaps in the twelfth century,[163] the Greeks were not adventurous in settling far from home in order to expand the range of their overseas trade. They left long-range commercial enterprise to the Italians. In medieval and modern times, the area inhabited by Greeks in the Levant has been much reduced by the progressive expansion of the Turks there at the Greeks' expense. Yet, from this dwindling home base, the Modern Greeks have established footholds for themselves all round the globe on a par with their West European contemporaries and with the contemporary Armenians, Lebanese, Syrian Christians, Jews, and Scots. Moreover, like these other diasporas, the Greek diaspora has quickly come to play an important part in the life of the foreign countries in which it has established itself.

The Greek diaspora, like the others, has been recruited both from political refugees and from voluntary expatriates whose motive for migration has been economic. The most famous of the Greek refugees are the small band of fifteenth-century Greek scholars who inducted the Italians, and, through them, all other West European peoples, into the study of the Hellenic Greek language and literature. One of the most distinguished political refugees was Anna Notarás, the daughter of the Méghas Dhoux Loukás Notarás.[164] The refugee Greek instigators of Greek linguistic and literary studies in the West have played a more important part in Modern Western history than in Modern Greek history. The Modern Greek people's fortune has been made by the voluntary Greek expatriates who have migrated for economic reasons since the fifteenth century.

It has already been noted that Venice was the seat of one of the earliest important expatriate Greek communities in the West. The Greek colony at Venice included both refugees and voluntary migrants. The Greeks had not forgotten or forgiven Venice's action in diverting the Fourth Crusade to seize and sack Constantinople in 1204. However, in consequence of this outrage, Venice had acquired an empire in Greek lands which, though whittled away by successive Ottoman conquests

---

[163] See Hendy, M. F., 'Byzantium, 1081-1204: An Economic Reappraisal', in *Transactions of the Royal Historical Society*, 5th Series, vol. 20 (1970), pp. 31-52, on p. 40, for the presence, in the twelfth century, of Greek merchants at Alexandria, Barcelona, and Béziers. See further ibid., pp. 48 and 50, and also *eundem, Coinage and Money in the Byzantine Empire, 1081-1261*, Dumbarton Oaks Studies XII (Washington, D.C. 1969), p. 313.

[164] Anna's father and elder brother were eventually put to death by Sultan Mehmet II. The current version of their execution, and of the reason for it, is contested by Inalcik in loc. cit., citing Bakalopoulos, A. E., 'Die Frage der Glaubwürdigheit der Leichenrede auf L. Notaras von Johannes Moschos' in *Byzantinische Zeitschrift* (1959), pp. 13-21. Loukás Notarás' younger son was taken into the Pādishāh's household as a page (see Inalcik, in loc. cit., pp. 239-40).

from 1475 onwards, survived in the Ionian Islands till Venice herself lost her independence in 1797. Naturally, Venice's Greek subjects repaired to the capital of the Venetian Empire to do business and, when the Greeks' anti-Western animus abated, for the further purpose of getting a Modern Western higher education at Venice and at the Venetian Empire's university at Padua;[165] and the 'Osmanlis' Greek subjects soon began to follow this example in increasing numbers.

As Venice's economic and political power declined and the power of the West European countries and Russia increased, the Greek diaspora spread further afield. The Greek business communities that had established themselves, by the close of the eighteenth century, at Vienna and Trieste and Odessa have been noticed already.[166] In the Greeks' commercial penetration of Western Europe, Central Europe, and Russia, the Khiots played a leading part. Till *circa* 1791, the Khiots' main economic activities had been, not commercial, but agricultural and industrial.[167] Their staple had been the silk industry, a legacy from a Genoese chartered company, the Maona's, 220 years' rule over the island (1346–1566). The silk industry of Khios, like the cotton industry of Ambelákia by the time of Clarke's visit,[168] had succumbed, before the close of the eighteenth century, to Western industrial competition, and the Khiots had found alternative fields for investment and sources of profits, not only in financing the shipping of the four ship-owning islands,[169] but in engaging, on their own account, in the growing commerce between the Ottoman Empire and the regions to the west and to the north of it.

Like the Rumeliot Greeks, but on a grander scale, the Khiots conducted their commercial operations as family businesses, with members of each family posted at key points. Two members of the Ralli family can be traced at Leghorn (Livorno) as far back as 1780. Between 1780 and 1818, representatives of other Khiot businesses were operating at ports as far apart as Taganrog, Caffa, and Ismā'īl, along Russia's recently acquired and twice extended seaboard between the head of the Sea of Azov and the northern arm of the Danube delta. Khiots were also operating at Genoa, Marseilles, and Amsterdam.[170] After the catastrophe of 1822, there were further Khiot settlements in the places, mentioned above, where Khiots had already established themselves,

[165] See above, p. 149.

[166] See above, pp. 188–9, and Daskalakis, op. cit., pp. 19–20.

[167] See David, C. E., French Vice-Consul at Khios: dispatch dated 14 June 1824 (Ministère des Affaires Étrangères, Paris, Correspondance Consulaire de Scio, 1812–25 D, No. 39bis), enclosing 'Mémoire sur Scio', printed in Argenti, P. P., *The Massacres of Chios described in Contemporary Diplomatic Documents* (London 1932), on pp. 52–95.

[168] See above, p. 188.

[169] See above, p. 191.

[170] Argenti, *The Massacres of Chios*, p. xxiv n. 1.

and also at Trieste, Vienna, Paris, London, Liverpool, Manchester, and in the United States.[171]

After the annexation of the ex-Habsburg 'Illyrian provinces' to the French Empire in 1809, the Khiots took part, from the commercial bases that they had already established at Smyrna and Thessaloníkê, in the overland trade that the French proceeded to open up, via Bosnia, with the Ottoman Empire. From Istanbul, Khiot merchants, emulating the Rumeliots, exported cloth to Austria. Khios is said to have made a fortune in twenty years.[172] In 1798 the Habsburg Government had been nervous about the disturbing effect on Austrian business of the arrest of Rhêghas and his fellow detainees.[173] The massacre at Khios in 1822 was credibly reported, by the Habsburg Internuncio at Istanbul, to have been felt severely in many centres of commerce in Germany, France, Italy, and Britain.[174]

The most distinguished of all Khiot migrants to Western Europe was Adhamándios Koraês. His father had moved, as has been noted,[175] from his native Khios to the rapidly developing continental Asian port of Smyrna. The son moved on from Smyrna to Montpellier, not to transact commercial business, but to study medicine at the university there. From Montpellier he moved on to Paris, where he stayed for life.

Hellenic Greeks had planted colonies along the north shore of the Black Sea in the seventh century B.C.[176] On the French Riviera, Marseilles (Massalia) was an Hellenic Greek foundation, planted perhaps as early as 600 B.C. At Lyon (Lugdunum), far up the course of the Rhône, there was an Asian Greek community in the reign of the Roman Emperor Marcus Aurelius (A.D. 161–80). Alexander the Great and some of his second-century-B.C. Greek successors in Central Asia had conquered territories in India and had planted Greek cities there, and, under the Roman Empire, Alexandrian Greeks had traded with Ceylon and had planted an entrepôt on the east coast of the mainland at Arikamedu, just to the south of Pondichéry. But the range of Hellenic Greek conquest and colonization and trade in India was far exceeded by the range there of Modern Greek business enterprise. When, in the nineteenth century of the Christian Era, British conquerors united politically the whole of the Indian subcontinent, right down to its southern tip, the Khiot firm Ralli Brothers established a commercial empire of their own

---

[171] Ibid., pp. xxiii–xxiv; idem, *Chius Vincta* (*1566–1912*) (Cambridge 1941), p. cxxi.
[172] David, in Argenti, *The Massacres of Chios*, pp. 67–70.
[173] See above, p. 188.
[174] Argenti, *The Massacres of Chios*, pp. xv–xvi and 127.
[175] See above, p. 190.
[176] The names of some of these colonial city-states were applied, by the Russians, to the cities that they, in their turn, founded along this coast after the Russo-Turkish War of 1768–74; but the revived names were, in most cases, not affixed to the true original sites.

in India on a sub-continental scale. Indeed, Greek traders, great and small, followed the flags of the West European colonial powers into most of the then expanding West European overseas possessions in Asia and Africa.

As for the United States, the Khiots who established themselves there after 1822 were pioneers. The Hellenic Greeks had submitted to being barred out of North-West Africa and the greater part of Spain by the Carthaginians, and they had resigned themselves to renouncing the right of way through the Straits of Gibraltar. Even after the Romans had broken the Carthaginian cordon, the Roman Empire's Hellenic Greek subjects had not acted on the Spanish Roman philosopher and poet Seneca's prophecy that, one day, a new world would be discovered on the far side of the Atlantic. In America, as in the interior of India, the Modern Greeks were breaking new ground on which the Hellenic Greeks had never trodden; and the nineteenth century, which saw Khiot refugees set up business in the United States, also saw, before its close, the beginning of a massive migration of Greek ex-peasants[177] who entered American society at the bottom and who have since been working their way up towards the top as a reward for their stamina. These Greek migrants have survived the psychological strain of an abrupt removal from some secluded village in Greece to somewhere 'beyond the tracks' in American cities that were growing as fast as contemporary Smyrna or Odessa. Before the First World War checked the flow of European immigration into the United States, the wave of immigrants from Greece had surged westwards as far as the line of the River Missouri at Kansas City and Omaha. Since the end of the Second World War, a further massive migration, from the Greek islands, has been recruiting the labour force in the industrial cities of West Germany.[178]

Indeed, the Modern Greeks have spread over the face of the Earth at all levels of economic activity and social stratification. There has been a great initial gulf between the expatriate Khiot capitalist and the expatriate Rumeliot or Peloponnesian or Nesiot petty trader and shopkeeper and factory-hand. But, in the United States at any rate, this gulf is not 'fixed'; Greek-Americans who have started on the lowest rung of the economic and social ladder have been rising to, and above, the level at which their less indigent expatriate compatriots started. The Greek grocer in Brooklyn, as well as the Greek ship-owner whose vessels circumnavigate the globe, is a living witness to the Modern Greeks' success in engaging in the economic life of the Modern World.

---

[177] There were 250,000 emigrants from Greece to the United States between 1906 and 1914 (Campbell and Sherrard, op. cit., p. 97).

[178] In 1963, Germany was the destination of 64 per cent of all departures of Greek nationals from Greece (ibid., p. 328).

Thus, since 1453, the Greeks have snatched an economic triumph out of a military and political disaster. This Modern Greek economic triumph has been the reward of a characteristically Greek hardihood. Like Odysseus and the Hellenic Greek merchant adventurers for whom Odysseus was a prototype presented to them for them to emulate, the Modern Greeks have visited many foreign cities and have made fortunes by reading the alien minds of the foreigners with whom they have transacted business.[179] In the Byzantine Age of Greek history, only the missionaries of the Eastern Orthodox Christian Church equalled their Hellenic predecessors and their modern successors in playing the perennial Greek role of pioneering far afield. The pioneer, whether he is a missionary or is a commercial traveller, has to win his laurels at a high price in suffering.[180] Odysseus himself is grievously homesick, while his wife and son and aged father are no less grievously disconsolate. The *Odyssey* has transmuted into Hellenic Greek poetry the emotional experience of the eighth-century-B.C. Greek commercial pioneers and their bereaved families. The counterpart of the *Odyssey* in Modern Greek poetry is the genre of folk-songs whose theme is ξενιτιά—the emotional experience of the voluntary expatriate and of his family, for whose sake he has gone to win a fortune abroad, or perhaps to perish in this hazardous endeavour on their behalf.[181]

(iii) *The Modern Limitations of the Greeks' Freedom of Choice between Forms of Political Independence*

1. *The rise of autonomous local Greek communities during the decline of the Ottoman regime*

During the century beginning in 1354, the year in which the Ottoman Turks secured their first foothold in Europe, it had become increasingly clear that the Greeks who had maintained or recovered their independence were going to lose it. The restored East Roman Empire and the Empire of Trebizond were both doomed. Their Greek subjects were going to fall under Ottoman rule, and, for those Greeks who were already under Italian or French rule at that date, the only prospective change in their political fortunes was, not the recovery of their independence, but their transfer from their Western rulers to the 'Osmanlis.

For more than three centuries ending in 1683, the Ottoman Imperial Government was the dominant power in the Levant. In Europe, Asia,

---

[179] See *Odyssey*, Book I, line 3.

[180] *Odyssey*, Book I, lines 4–5.

[181] See Vakalópoulos, op. cit., vol. ii, part i, pp. 403–5, and Polítês, N. G., Ἐκλογαὶ ἀπὸ τὰ Τραγούδια τοῦ Ἑλληνικοῦ Λαοῦ (Athens 1914), pp. 195–202: Τραγούδια τῆς ξενιτείας.

and Africa it had continued to expand at the expense of other states, both Christian and Muslim. In 1676 it acquired Podolia from the Kingdom of Poland–Lithuania. After 1683, the date of the failure of the second Ottoman siege of Vienna, the Ottoman Empire began to lose its grip on its vast dominions. In Europe, it lost a fringe of territory permanently to the Habsburg Monarchy and to the Russian Empire. In Africa and Asia the Ottoman Empire's outlying territories became independent, in all but name, under local Muslim regimes, and wider local Druz and Maronite Christian regimes in the Lebanon. In the course of the eighteenth century the political future of the Empire's heartland in the Balkan Peninsula and Asia Minor also became problematical.

The non-Ottoman Turkish principalities in Asia Minor, as well as the Eastern Orthodox Christian states in both Asia Minor and the Balkan Peninsula, had been annexed by the 'Osmanlis by force of arms. Their populations had not ceased, during the intervening centuries of unchallengeable Ottoman rule, to remember their former independence and to repine at their loss of it. By the eighteenth century the Ottoman Government's hold had weakened, even here, to a degree at which Ottoman weakness reawakened the political ambitions of some of the elements in the *macédoine* of religions and nationalities that the Ottoman conquest and organization of this region had produced. Disloyal provincial governors, turbulent garrisons of Janissaries, and even private Muslim military adventurers now ventured to play for the *de facto* independence that other Muslim Ottoman subjects had already achieved in regions that were more remote from the centre of Ottoman power.

Muslims, even rebel Muslims, were privileged subjects of a Muslim empire; but in Ottoman Europe the Muslims were only a small, though powerful, minority of the population. Here the majority consisted of Eastern Orthodox Christians, and the intentions and prospects of these were enigmatic. The Balkan Christians were linked with each other by the ties of a common religion and a common political subjection to Ottoman sovereignty and to the administrative authority of the Patriarch of Constantinople in his capacity as an Ottoman official, the head of the Ottoman *Rum milleti*. At the same time, these Eastern Orthodox Christian subjects of the Ottoman Empire were alienated from each other by memories of pre-Ottoman chapters of their political history in which they had been mutually independent and had, at times, been at daggers drawn with each other.

The oldest-established of these now Christian peoples and Ottoman subjects were the Greeks; and, regarded in terms of past Greek history, the Modern Greeks' situation in the eighteenth century of the Christian Era, when the Ottoman Empire was visibly in decline, was not unlike the Hellenic Greeks' situation in the eighth century B.C., towards the close of the protracted 'dark age' that had followed the overthrow of the Mycenaean Greek political dispensation and the consequent eclipse of the Mycenaean phase of Greek civilization. At each of these two critical moments in the Greeks' long history, the Greeks were extricating themselves, at last, from a bout of anarchy, insecurity, and poverty, and, on each occasion, their recuperation was being achieved in the same way. New life was sprouting simultaneously, but independently, in a number of separate localities.[182] The forms taken at these different places by the new economic and social and political developments were highly individual and diverse. The common feature of these multiple growing-points was that they were becoming so many cultural and political oases in the previous social wilderness. Thucydides' account of the rise of the Hellenic Greek civilization[183] could be applied, with remarkably little modification, to the history of the Modern Greeks in the Ottoman prelude to the modern chapter of Greek history.

However, the respective sequels to these two similar overtures were not the same. When, in the eighth century B.C., the Hellenic Greek society flowered, it became a cultural unity to an ever-increasing extent, but, on the political plane, the local sprouts from which it had sprung evolved into mutually independent city-states which jealously maintained their independence, and recklessly asserted this by going to war with each other, till eventually political union was imposed on them from outside by their common incorporation in the Roman Empire.

It was possible for the political history of the Hellenic Greek society to take this course because, in the formative age of Hellenism, the Greek World was exceptionally free from external pressure. The same cataclysm that had swept away the Mycenaean political dispensation in Greece had simultaneously overthrown the Hittite Empire and had enfeebled Egypt. The Assyrian militarism that subsequently afflicted South-Western Asia and Egypt hit the semi-Hellenic Greek populations in Eastern Cilicia and in Cyprus but did not touch the heart of the Hellenic World. The Hellenic Greeks did not have an encounter with an aggressive alien great power till half-way through the sixth century B.C., when the First Persian Empire conquered the Hellenic Greek city-states along the eastern shore of the Aegean Sea; and though, in 480–479 B.C., some of the continental European Greek city-states co-operated in just sufficient numbers and for a just sufficient length of time to foil the Persians' attempt to incorporate in their empire the whole of the

---

[182] In the Ottoman Empire, in and after the eighteenth century, this was not an exclusively Greek phenomenon. It was likewise a Jugoslav phenomenon in Montenegro and (as has been noted already) an Arab phenomenon in the Lebanon.

[183] Thucydides, Book I, chapters 1–17.

Hellenic World, the political institution of sovereign city-states had set so hard by that date that the Hellenes failed to seize the golden opportunity of achieving a voluntary permanent union that the Persians had given to their Greek contemporaries by presenting them with both a threat and an example.

By contrast, the Modern Greeks did not have the Hellenic Greeks' initial freedom from pressure when, in the eighteenth century, the Modern Greeks, in their turn, burst into new life at a number of separate local points. They had still to liberate themselves from Ottoman rule—and the Ottoman Empire was relatively potent, even in its decline. Moreover, the Modern Greeks had also to cope with a number of adjacent great powers that were still in their heyday and that were eager to enter into the expiring Ottoman Empire's heritage. Simultaneously, the Modern Greeks had to come to terms with the post-Christian Modern Western Civilization, which had now become dominant all round the globe. The dominance of this civilization may prove to be temporary; but it already was, and still remains, more potent than either Christianity or Islam and more revolutionary than any traditional civilization or religion.

For these reasons, the two similar overtures to new manifestations of Greek life had dissimilar sequels. The natural sequel to both overtures was the sharp accentuation and obstinate maintenance of local political sovereignty that was the characteristic feature of Hellenic Greek history. The Modern Greeks were not in a position to take this Hellenic Greek course. If each local Modern Greek community had tried to turn itself into a miniature sovereign state on the Hellenic Greek pattern, the Modern Greeks would have had little chance of liberating themselves from Ottoman rule, and, even if they had achieved this, they would soon have fallen into subjection to some other power. For the Modern Greeks, the unavoidable price of political liberation was the sacrifice of local political autonomy, and eventually the loss of local cultural variety as well. The question confronting them was one, not of separatism versus unification, but merely of the form that the necessary unification was to take. In the event the political organization of the Modern Greek people has taken a form that has no native historical roots either in the realities of eighteenth-century Greek life or in any pre-Modern Greek traditions, Mycenaean or Hellenic or Byzantine. Political liberation has entailed, for the Modern Greeks, a violent break with all their cultural heritages. This has been a traumatic experience. The degree of the trauma can be measured by a survey of the local communities that were the seed-beds in which Greek life was sprouting, with a renewed vitality, in the last days of the Modern Greek people's subjection to Ottoman rule.

The characteristic and significant feature of eighteenth-century local

Greek life is its diversity.[184] In the part—then still a large part—of the Ottoman Empire in which a majority, or a substantial minority, of the variegated population was Greek, the local Greek communities that were burgeoning were widely dispersed, and they differed greatly from each other in their geographical setting,[185] in their economy, in their social structure, and in their political constitution, which largely depended on their relations with the Ottoman Imperial Government.

Geographically, these growing points of Modern Greek life were scattered from the interior of *Rum ili* to south-western Crete and from the north-western tip of Êpeiros to the west coast of Asia Minor and some of its offshore islands. The terrain might be a land-locked mountain fastness (e.g. Soúli,[186] and, in the Pindus Range, Zaghóri,[187] Malakási[188] [including the node of mule-paths at Métsovo], and Ághrapha[189]); a mountain-fastness with a seaboard (e.g. Khimárrha,[190] the Xerómero,[191] the Máni,[192] Sphakiá,[193] the Dhervenokhória,[194] Mount Athos[195]); a natural fastness (e.g. Kastoriá[196] [on the neck of a peninsula jutting into a lake], the forest of the Váltos district[197]); a highland district that was not impregnable but that lay off the beaten track of Ottoman armies, without being inaccessible for traders overland or by sea (e.g. Ambelákia

---

[184] Vakalópoulos puts his finger on this point in op. cit., vol. ii, part i, p. 95.

[185] Vakalópoulos, ibid., p. 85, points out that mountainous peninsulas lying off the main routes of traffic (i.e. routes frequented by Ottoman troops) were particularly favourable locations.

[186] Soúli is ensconced in a tangle of mountains between the upland basin of Yánnina and the coast of Êpeiros.

[187] Zaghóri is in Êpeiros, between Yánnina and Konítsa (*Admiralty Handbook of Macedonia and Surrounding Territories* (London 1921?), p. 194; Vakalópoulos, op. cit., vol. ii, part i, pp. 290–2).

[188] Malakási lies astride the upper waters of the River of Arta and the Aspropótamo (Akhelóios).

[189] The Ághrapha is a section of the Pindus Range round the headwaters of the eastern tributaries of the Aspropótamo (Akhelóios) river.

[190] Khimárrha is on the Akrokéravnos Peninsula, on the eastern shore of the Straits of Ótranto, facing the 'heel' of Italy.

[191] The Xerómero is the mountainous hinterland of the west coast of Akarnanía, whose inhabitants could find asylum, within easy reach, in the Venetian possession Santa Maura (Lefkádha). See Vakalópoulos, vol. ii, part i, pp. 89–91.

[192] The Máni is the central prong on the three-pronged southern coastline of the Pelopónnêsos. It is by far the most rugged prong of the three. See further ibid., p. 88.

[193] Sphakiá is on the south coast of Crete between the White Mountains—the westernmost of the three principal Cretan mountain massifs—and the sea. This coast is inhospitable, and Sphakiá is barely accessible overland from the north.

[194] The Dhervenokhória were five Albanian Christian villages commanding the overland route between the Pelopónnêsos and Central Greece where this route climbs over Mounts Yeráneia and Kithairón. See Finlay, op. cit., vol. vi, p. 30. See further Vakalópoulos, op. cit., vol. ii, part i, p. 316.

[195] Mount Athos is the north-easternmost, and by far the most rugged, of the three prongs of the Peninsula of Khalkidhikê.

[196] Kastoriá and its lake lie near the head of the Vistríca (Aliákmon) river basin, about midway between the Gulf of Thessaloníkê on the Aegean Sea and the Gulf of Avlóna on the Straits of Ótranto. Like its neighbour Shátista, Kastoriá is well-placed for serving as a centre for overland traffic in all directions.

[197] The Váltos is in Akarnanía, adjacent to the Xerómero.

and Ayía,[198] Náoussa [Nyáousta],[199] the Zaghorá,[200] the Madhemo-khória,[201] Sánta[202]); a navally and militarily indefensible island, or continental coastal district or port (e.g. Khios,[203] the Dhodhekánêsoi,[204] the four ship-owning islands,[205] Ayvalik [in Greek, Kydhoniés],[206] Kassándra,[207] Trikéri,[208] Ghalaxídhi[209]).

The economy of these budding communities was as diverse as their location. It has been noted already that the islanders made their living as sailors and traders, and that Ambelákia spun and wove cotton and dyed it with Valóna oak gall for export to Central Europe. The mines of the Madhemokhória and Sánta produced silver for the Ottoman Government. The mastic-pine gum—a unique product of a group of villages at the south end of Khios—was a perquisite of the Ottoman Imperial Seray. The Zaghorá and Ayvalik specialized in olive groves, and the Greek community at Ayvalik not only extracted the oil from the fruit, but manufactured from it excellent soap, which they exported in their own ships to Russia.[210] Kastoriá imported furs from far afield, worked them up, and re-exported them. Mount Athos (the Ayionóros) was a federation of monasteries in which almost all the Eastern Orthodox Christian peoples were represented. The monks imported alms given by pilgrims and rents extracted from their estates in the Ottoman Empire and in the two autonomous Roumanian Princi-palities, and they exported psychological satisfaction to their pious benefactors, though not to their sullen serfs.

The Khimarriots had nothing to export except themselves. They served as mercenary soldiers in the armies of Naples and Venice.[211] The Albanians in the Dhervenokhória were permitted by the Ottoman Government, in spite of their being Christians, to bear arms, and were

[198] Ambelákia stands on the northernmost spur of Mount Ossa (Kissavo), overhanging the Témbê gorge (see above, p. 188). Ayía stands on the same range, further to the south. See further Vakalópoulos, op. cit., vol. ii, part i, p. 87.

[199] Náoussa is in Macedonia, in the eastern foothills of Mount Vérmion, to the north of Vérrhoia.

[200] The Zaghorá is a cluster of villages on the westward slope of Mount Pêlion: twenty-four villages according to Finlay, op. cit., vol. vi, p. 200.

[201] The Madhemokhória ('Mining villages') lie on the north-east side of the Khalkidhikê peninsula, inland from the peninsula's Athonian prong. See further Vakalópoulos, op. cit., vol. ii, part i, 364–9.

[202] Sánta is a mining village in the hinterland of Trebizond.

[203] Khios lies off the Erythraí (Češme) peninsula, half-way down the west coast of Asia Minor.

[204] The chain of islands off the south-west coast of Asia Minor. The largest of them is Rhodes.

[205] Ýdhra, Pétses, Psará, Kásos, noticed already (see above, p. 191).

[206] Ayvalik lies on the west coast of Asia Minor, facing the island of Lésvos (Mytilênê).

[207] Kassándra (the Hellenic Pallênê) is the south-westernmost of the three prongs of Khalkidhikê.

[208] Trikéri is a portlet on the tip of the peninsula, jutting westwards from the southern end of Mount Pêlion, which commands the entrance into the Gulf of Vólos.

[209] Galaxídhi is a portlet on the west shore of the Gulf of Ámphissa (Sálona).

[210] See Toynbee, A. J., *A Study of History*, vol. ii, p. 40 n. 1, for an eyewitness account of Ayvalik in 1921, just before the exodus of the Greek minority from Turkey.

[211] See above, p. 184 with n. 115.

let off paying certain taxes, in return for their policing of an important overland route which would otherwise have attracted brigands.[212] The Ághrapha ('the Unwritten') were, as the name itself proclaims, a group of places that were not entered in the Imperial tax-registers—presumably because it was recognized that a tax-assessor would risk losing his life if he ventured to present himself there.[213] The Ottoman Imperial Government had had to come to terms with the Aghraphiots because it had been unable to disarm them.[214] It had regularized this embarrassing local situation by giving them the status of *armatoloí*[215]—that is to say, a licensed Christian 'home guard'.

[212] For the Dhervenokhorítai's privileges, see Finlay, op. cit., vol. vi, p. 30. These privileges had been granted to them by Mehmet II at the time (1460) of his conquest of the Pelopónnêsos (Vakalópoulos, op. cit., vol. ii, part i, p. 316).

[213] The Ághrapha had been a borderland between the East Roman Empire and the Bulgarian Empire after the 'rectification' of the Romano-Bulgarian frontier in Bulgaria's favour in 904. Perhaps this was the date at which the Ághrapha began to be omitted from the tax-registers. Armed highlanders astride an international frontier were well placed for refusing to pay.

[214] The earliest extant agreement between the Aghraphiots and the Porte is dated 10 May 1525 (Vakalópoulos, op. cit., vol. ii, part i, p. 290), but the Aghraphiots are said (Finlay, op. cit., vol. vi, p. 22; see also p. 18) to have received a previous written charter from Mehmet II, who had given a similar charter to the Dhervenokhorítai. The first Ottoman Pādishāh to give the status of *armatoloí* to the Aghraphiots may have been Mehmet II's predecessor, Murād II (*imperabat* 1421–51) (see Vakalópoulos, op. cit., vol. i, pp. 213–14, and vol. ii, part i, pp. 314–15). In the charter of 1525, the Porte recognized the autonomy of the Aghraphiot villages; it agreed that no Ottoman Muslims should live there, anywhere nearer than Phanári (a place on the fringe of the Thessalian plain, on the road between Kardhítsa and Tríkkala); it guaranteed access for the Aghraphiots to the plains as well as to the mountains; and it imposed an annual tax of 50,000 *ghróssia* (*gurush*) on each Aghraphiot community. Evidently the Aghraphiots' need for winter pasturage in the plains, which were under the 'Osmanlis' effective control, gave the Porte the leverage that enabled it in 1525 to exact a tax from these 'unregistered' Christian Greek highlanders.

[215] For the *armatoloí* and the *kléphtes* see Vakalópoulos, op. cit., vol. ii, part i, pp. 314–36. The word '*kléphtes*' means brigands, and the *kléphtes* did make their living by brigandage at the expense of their Christian co-religionists as well as of their Muslim Turkish enemies; but, besides being brigands, the *kléphtes* were also politically inspired guerrilla fighters who were in open-armed revolt against the Ottoman authorities. The word *armatolós* is a Greek rendering of the Italian word *armatore*, meaning 'outfitter' (sc. of pirate ships), according to G. Vlakhoyiánnês, Κλέφτες τοῦ Μοριᾶ (Athens 1935), pp. 14 and 17. It seems more probable that it is derived from the Turkish word *armatolik*, meaning a unit of gendarmes (ἀρμάτοι). In any case, the *armatoloí* were armed Christian subjects of the Porte who, in contrast to the *kléphtes*, had been licensed to bear arms and had been entrusted with the policing of districts that it was difficult for the 'Osmanlis to administer direct. The Porte's hope was that the *armatoloí* would put down the *kléphtes*. Actually they frequently gave asylum to the *kléphtes* and went into collusion with them (Vakalópoulos, op. cit., vol. ii, part i, pp. 326 and 329–30). The earliest of the *armatoliks* was the Ághrapha. The number of *armatoliks* in Greece was increased in 1537 by Suleyman I (Vakalópoulos, op. cit., vol. iii, p. 125). Each *armatolik* was under the command of a native *kapetános*, and the *armatoloí* were granted tax reliefs in return for the policing work that they were supposed to perform (Finlay, op. cit., vol. vi, p. 14; Vakalópoulos, op. cit., vol. ii, part i, p. 322). In reality, the *armatoloí* were less of a terror for the *kléphtes* than for the non-militant Christian Greek peasantry (Finlay, op. cit., vol. v, p. 192). In Êpeiros and Akarnanía, before the close of the sixteenth century, rival bands of *armatoloí* were fighting each other for the command of disputed territory (Vakalópoulos, op. cit., vol. iii, pp. 331–2). In 1637 and again in 1695 and 1704, the Porte tried, but failed, to abolish the *armatoloí* and to replace them by Turkish garrisons. (In 1704 the abortive measure was confined to Albanian *armatoloí*, and an exception was made for the *armatoloí* in the *sancak* of Tríkkala.) The institution itself was officially abolished in 1721

The Eastern Orthodox Christian Albanian Souliots' lair was as barren as Mount Athos, but, like the Athonian monks, the Souliot warriors lived as rentiers from the labours of subject peasant co-religionists,[216] supplemented, when necessary, by tribute levied from the Muslim land-owners in the neighbouring lowlands. Raiding less indigent neighbours was the main source of livelihood for the Maniots and the Sphakiots.

All these budding eighteenth-century local Greek communities had some kind of local self-government, and so, indeed, had every contemporary Greek village or townlet in both the Ottoman and the Venetian Empire. If the villagers were effectively under the Imperial Government's control, they were constrained to co-operate with each other by their collective liability for paying the tax that was assessed on the village as a whole[217]—a heritage of the East Roman fiscal regime. If the villagers were in some degree their own masters *de facto*, they co-operated voluntarily for defending the liberties that they had won for themselves against reassertions of the Imperial authorities' claims.

Village institutions—the village church, with its recurrent annual round of services and festivals, and, later on, the village coffee shop, which was both a general store and a club—gave the villagers opportunities for the lively talkative social intercourse that, in all ages and under all regimes, has been a characteristic feature of Greek life. The animated discussions, after divine service, in the village churchyard on the eve of the Greek insurrection of 1821 are described by Photákos Khrysanthópoulos, who was aide-de-camp to Kolokotrónis in the ensuing Greek War of Independence (1821-9).[218] In 1911-12, I had the same experience in tramping round Greece and listening to the conversation in innumerable village coffee shops, evening after evening.

The social amenities of Greek village life, simple though they were, inspired the sociable Greek people with a strong affection for their native villages. Photákos, a Peloponnesian Greek, migrated in 1813, at the age of fifteen, to Russia's newly acquired territories to the north of the Black Sea. He went into business there, first at Kishinyóv in Bessarabia, and then at Odessa. But his and his fellow emigrants' hearts were in their native villages.

(Vakalópoulos, op. cit., vol. ii, part i, p. 327). In 1787, 'Ali Tepelenli was appointed Dhervenci-Paşa, and he was more successful than any of his predecessors in bringing the *armatoliks*, including the Ághrapha, under control (Finlay, op. cit., vol. vi, pp. 21-2). Yet, on the eve of the Ottoman Greek insurrection in 1821, there were still seventeen *armatoliks* in *Rum ili* to the west and south of the River Vardar (ibid., p. 328).

[216] The Souliots' peasants were Greeks; the Athonian monks' peasants were Greeks and Roumans.

[217] Tsakonas, op. cit., p. 27; Campbell and Sherrard, op. cit., pp. 47 and 55.

[218] Khrysanthópoulos, op. cit., vol. i, p. 35.

Everyone sent his savings to his birthplace, to his parents or other relatives; and he sent his native commune and the village church a few books, a little lamp, or a little bell.[219]

The century ending in 1912 brought with it, for the Greeks, revolutionary social as well as political changes. Yet, on the eve of the Balkan Wars of 1912–13, the Greek emigrants' native village, not the Kingdom of Greece, was still, for him, his πατρίδα:[220] the fatherland for which he had been homesick and which he revisited as soon as he had saved enough money to pay for the return voyage. In 1911–12, Greek emigration to the United States was at its peak, and in many Greek villages there was at least one temporarily returned emigrant, enjoying, at last, the pleasure, to which he had been eagerly looking forward, of describing the seven wonders of America to a responsive audience of local compatriots. He too, like Photákos and his contemporaries, had brought some offering for his native village's adornment.

Greek local life was sociable, but it was not democratic, either politically or economically, and, in this point again, Modern Greek life in the eighteenth century of the Christian Era resembled Hellenic Greek life in the eighth century B.C. In most villages and townlets, local government was informal, and was conducted *ad hoc*, from hand to mouth. Others had constitutions which were recognized officially by the Ottoman Imperial Government. Among the growing-points listed at an earlier point in this chapter, only Soúli, the Máni, Sphakiá, and Khimárra seem to have maintained a merely *de facto* autonomy without any juridical basis.

One feature of the recognized local constitutions of Ottoman Greek Christian communities was the extreme lack of uniformity in their terms. This feature has not been peculiar to the Ottoman Empire. It is also to be found in other empires that have been established by conquest (as most empires have been hitherto). It had been Ottoman policy, as it had previously been Roman policy, and as it was subsequently British policy in India during the century ending in 1849 and was Prussian policy in Germany in 1866, to penalize resistance but to put a premium on submission, and a still greater premium on active co-operation, by granting to docile or co-operative communities favourable terms of capitulation and by honouring these terms thereafter.

The 'Osmanlis were also moved, by the same considerations of expediency, to grant unearned concessions in some cases. They considered that it was not worth their while to subdue poverty-stricken highland regions inhabited by warlike populations. The cost to the 'Osmanlis, in blood and treasure, of conquering regions of this kind and holding them

[219] Ibid., pp. 16–18.
[220] See Campbell and Sherrard, op. cit., pp. 47 and 52, borne out by my own experience.

down could never be recouped by the meagre tax revenue that could be extracted from them. This consideration accounts for the concessions made to the Ághrapha and to the other *armatoliks* in *Rum ili*.[221] The 'Osmanlis also perceived that it would be impolitic to impose onerous terms on regions that would be difficult for them to hold against attack by foreign powers who were strong enough, or remote enough, to challenge the Ottoman Empire's might. This consideration accounts for the leniency of the terms imposed on the two trans-Danubian Roumanian principalities, Wallachia and Moldavia,[222] and on Khios and other Aegean islands. The Roumanian principalities would have been difficult to hold against Western Christian military powers, and the islands against Western Christian naval powers, if the inhabitants had been given good reason by the 'Osmanlis to welcome a change of regime.

The most valuable, and most highly prized, of all alleviations was the exemption of a territory from the intrusion of Muslim 'Osmanli settlers. A corollary of this concession was the renunciation of the building of mosques and of the conversion into mosques of Christian churches. (In some cases this concession did not preclude the stationing, in the privileged territory, of a Muslim governor and *qādi*, or at any rate of a governor alone.) This crucial condition for the well-being of a subject but autonomous Christian community was secured to the two Roumanian principalities by treaty and to other communities by charter. Among the communities that enjoyed this exemption by charter were the Ághrapha,[223] the Zaghóri,[224] perhaps also Malakási,[225] the mining villages in the hinterland of Trebizond,[226] Nyáousta (Náoussa),[227] Týrnavos,[228] the federation of monasteries on the Athos Peninsula, and Ayvalik.[229]

This key privilege was not held sacrosanct by the Porte in all cases. Some of the villages in the Zaghóri were granted to 'Osmanli fief-holders about half-way through the seventeenth century and thus temporarily

---

[221] See above, p. 203 with n. 215.

[222] And on the Principality of Transylvania likewise, at times when this was under Ottoman, not Habsburg, suzerainty.

[223] See above, p. 203, nn. 214 and 215.

[224] See Vakalópoulos, op. cit., vol. ii, part i, p. 290.

[225] The charters given to the Zaghóri and to Malakási seem to have been identical (ibid., p. 292).

[226] See ibid., pp. 77–9. The privileges of this Greek Christian mining district were confirmed by Murād III (*imperabat* 1574–95). In this case the Porte was actuated by economic self-interest.

[227] See above, p. 202 n. 199.

[228] See below, p. 213.

[229] See Sakkárês, G., Ἱστορία τῶν Κυδωνιῶν (Athens 1920). Ayvalik was chartered in 1773 by an imperial firman. This document was lost when Ayvalik was evacuated in 1821. A summary of the provisions of the firman is given by Sakkárês in op. cit., pp. 20–1. Ayvalik was put out of bounds for all Turks except a governor elected by the local Greek community and a *qādi* appointed by the Porte. The salaries of both these Ottoman officials were paid for by the local Greek community.

lost their autonomy and their property rights. However, *circa* 1681-4, they were reunited with the rest of the Zaghóri in an autonomous federation of 47 villages which survived till 1868.[230] Malakási, too, was granted to 'Osmanli fief-holders in 1635, but in 1659 Métsovo, together with five adjacent villages, not only recovered the privileges previously enjoyed by the whole of Malakási but obtained additional rights.[231]

Other places were free from the presence of Muslims because these places were either economically unattractive or politically dangerous for them. For instance, no Muslims would have ventured to settle in Soúli or in the Máni or in Sphakiá, and none would have desired to settle on Mount Athos or at Ayvalik or on the four islands Ýdhra, Pétses, Psará, and Kásos. These islands are so barren that they were uninhabited when, in the eighteenth century, Ýdhra and Pétses were colonized by Peloponnesian Eastern Orthodox Christian Albanians,[232] and Psará and Kásos by Eastern Orthodox Christian Greeks.[233] Naturally the 'Osmanlis were pleased when these hitherto unproductive insular possessions of their Empire began to breed Ottoman Christian seamen who produced revenue for the Imperial customs and recruits for the Imperial navy. Similarly, it was more advantageous for the Ottoman Government to leave it to the Santiots and to the Madhemokhoriots to mine silver for it, and to the Khiots to grow mastic for it, than to attempt to conduct these skilled operations itself.

While exemption from the presence of Muslims was the most valuable of all privileges for an autonomous non-Muslim Ottoman community, the next most valuable privilege was inclusion in the estates of the Valide Sultana (i.e. the mother of the reigning Pādishāh). Ottoman crown lands in this category were more lightly taxed, and as a rule were more humanely administered, than other lands under Ottoman rule. This second privilege was enjoyed by the Zaghóri,[234] by Malakási,[235] and by the twenty-one villages on the island of Khios that tended the mastic-gum-producing pine-tree groves.[236] The inclusion of these villages in the Valide Sultana's estates brought disaster on Khios when, in 1822, the island became involved in the Greek insurrection. In the Imperial Seray at Istanbul the disloyalty of the mastic villages was taken as an aggravation of the Khiots' offence,[237] and this resentment was one of the causes of the savagery with which the revolt of Khios was put down.

[230] Vakalópoulos, vol. ii, part i, pp. 200-1.
[231] Ibid., pp. 292-4.
[232] See Finlay, op. cit., vol. v, p. 283, and vol. vi, pp. 30-3 and 168.
[233] See ibid., vol. v, p. 281, and vol. vi, pp. 166 and 167.
[234] Vakalópoulos, op. cit., vol. ii, part i, p. 290.
[235] Ibid., p. 292.
[236] See Finlay, op. cit., vol. v, p. 233.
[237] Ibid., vol. vi, p. 253.

Some of the autonomous non-Muslim Ottoman communities had federal constitutions. Examples are the federations of communities in the Zaghóri district of Êpeiros,[238] in the Ághrapha,[239] and in Malakási,[240] the Athonian federation of monasteries and the three federations of villages in Khalkhidhikê,[241] the federation of villages on Mount Pêlion (the Zaghorá),[242] and the federation of twenty-two villages with Ambelákia, which was negotiated in 1777.[243]

Khios had received a charter from the Ottoman Imperial Government in 1567, the year after it had been conquered from the Genoese Maona. In 1578, this charter was confirmed and amplified, and, though it was subsequently modified (mainly in favour of the Eastern Orthodox Khiots against the Roman Catholics), it was never forfeited till 1822.[244] After the death of the last Duke of Naxos, Joseph Nasi, in 1579, the constitutional privileges of Khios were extended to the islands that had constituted the Duchy,—namely, Naxos, Andros, Mêlos, Paros, Santorínê, Syros, Siphnos.[245] Mýkonos, which had passed out of Venetian into Ottoman hands in 1537, had a constitution from 1615 onwards.[246]

The Pelopónnêsos had a constitution that dated from the thirty years' interlude of Venetian occupation, and that had been maintained by the 'Osmanlis after their reconquest of the Pelopónnêsos in 1715. Though the Venetian regime had been liberal politically, it had been onerous and restrictive economically. The Peloponnesian Greek Christians found the Ottoman regime less distasteful on the whole, and the Ottoman Imperial Government, for its part, was concerned to avoid alienating a community that constituted the majority of the population in an outlying province that was difficult to hold. The constitution of the eighteenth-century Ottoman eyalet was an elaborate three-tier system of representative government, in which the provincial assembly held the power of the purse.[247] Moreover, the Greek Orthodox Christian

---

[238] Vakalópoulos, op. cit., vol. ii, part i, p. 290.

[239] Ibid., p. 291.   [240] Ibid., p. 292.

[241] See Finlay, op. cit., vol. vi, p. 202.

[242] See ibid., p. 200, and Campbell and Sherrard, op. cit., on p. 208 n. 2.

[243] Tsakonas, op. cit., p. 31.

[244] See Toynbee, *A Study of History*, vol. viii, p. 177 n. 3, citing Philip Argenti's works on the history of Khios. See also Vakalópoulos, op. cit., vol. ii, part i, pp. 285 and 299; ibid., vol. iii, pp. 226-33.

[245] Vakalópoulos, op. cit., vol. ii, part i, pp. 298-9; ibid., vol. iii, pp. 280-97. In these islands the native Greek population benefited by the substitution of Ottoman for Frankish rule (ibid., p. 211), but, even after the Frankish feudal lords had lost their political sovereignty, they fought an obstinate rearguard action for the maintenance of their privileges. Frankish feudalism was not completely liquidated in the Kykládhes until after the opening of the nineteenth century (ibid., pp. 280-4).

[246] Campbell and Sherrard, op. cit., p. 56; Vakalópoulos, op. cit., vol. ii, part i, pp. 155-6.

[247] See Toynbee, *A Study of History*, vol. viii, 'The Morea on the Eve of the Uprising of A.D. 1821', on pp. 681-3, following Sakellários, M. V., Ἡ Πελοπόννησος κατὰ τὴν δευτέραν Τουρκοκρατίαν *1715-1821, passim*, and Khrysanthópoulos, op. cit., vol. i, pp. 33-7.

community in the Pelopónnêsos, like the Athonian federation of monasteries, had political agents (*vekīls*) accredited to the Ottoman Imperial Government at Istanbul.[248]

At Khios, Mýkonos, and in the Pelopónnêsos, the local public officers were elected,[249] but a majority of them was drawn, *de facto* if not *de jure*, from a privileged minority. At Khios for instance, *circa* 1760, the all-Christian and all-Greek board of five *dhêmoyérondes* who governed the island consisted of two Eastern Orthodox patricians, one Eastern Orthodox plebeian, and two Roman Catholics.[250] In the eyalet of the Morea (Pelopónnêsos) the Ottoman governor's permanent council consisted of two Moreot Muslims, two Christian Greeks (elected annually, but at three removes from the primary elections in the villages), and one Christian Greek dragoman.[251]

Thus there was a striking increase in the degree of political autonomy that was accruing in the eighteenth century to a number of privileged or tolerated Ottoman Greek Eastern Orthodox communities, but this political amelioration benefited only an oligarchy.[252] There was a sharp division between patricians and plebeians even in the poverty-stricken Máni.[253] However, the position of these local Greek oligarchs was not secure. Even in the communities that had a regular constitution, recognized by the Ottoman Imperial Government, the Greek oligarchs were exposed to the risk of being arbitrarily, and perhaps savagely, punished by the Ottoman authorities if they failed to deliver the tax assessed on their communities, or if they failed to prevent their compatriots from breaking the peace. Consequently, the responsible Greek authorities were apt to treat their fellow Greeks with a high-handedness and a harshness which, according to Photákos, sometimes went to Turkish lengths.

Moreover, the Greeks were harsh to each other not only in the field of communal administration, in which the local oligarchs were under direct pressure from their Ottoman overlords, but also in the field of economic activity. For the 'Osmanlis' non-Muslim subjects, the winning of wealth was the only practicable means of offsetting, and

[248] Sakellários, op. cit., p. 94; Finlay, op. cit., vol. vi, p. 25.

[249] So, too, were the public officers of the Greek communities in the cities of Serrhés and Yánnina. At Serrhés, in the early seventeenth century, there was a council of twelve members, who were elected by the guilds. The Greek community at Yánnina seems to have had the same constitution (Vakalópoulos, op. cit., vol. ii, part i, pp. 285–6). In both these cities, the Greek Christian element in the population had continued to be large. But, in both, there was also a Turkish Muslim element, as there was in almost all Ottoman cities, and therefore the constitutions of the Greek communities in Serrhés and Yánnina must have provided only for the local Greeks' communal self-government, not for the municipal government of the city as a whole.

[250] Argenti, *Chius Vincta*, pp. clxxx–clxxxi.

[251] Sakellários, op. cit., pp. 90–2.

[252] See Tsakonas, op. cit., p. 33.

[253] Bótzaris, op. cit., p. 93 n. 1.

perhaps averting, the ill-treatment to which they were exposed by their political subjection. But this political subjection was also an initial economic handicap. For non-Muslim Ottoman subjects, the struggle to rise in the world economically was severe; only a small minority was successful, and the success was won in many cases at the expense of the minority's co-religionists and compatriots. Both the political and the economic cleavage between Greek and Greek was accentuated by the structure of Modern Greek society. A man's allegiance to his village was not his ultimate social loyalty. The basic social unit of Modern Greek life was not the village; it was the family.[254] It has already been noted that the widespread and large-scale Greek commercial houses that sprang up in the eighteenth century were family businesses. On behalf of his family, or at least in the name of his family's interest or of its honour, a Greek could reconcile it with his conscience to be merciless.

The mercilessness of life for Greeks under Ottoman rule, and the Greeks' consequent mercilessness to each other in each fighting for his own hand, is laid bare in the reminiscences of General Ioánnes Makriyiánnes (Μακρυγιάννης), who was one of the heroes of the Greek War of Independence and was perhaps the principal organizer of the successful revolt, in 1843, against the autocratic regime of Otto, the first king of the Kingdom of Greece.

Makriyiánnes was born into a poor family in the village of Avorítes in the Lidhoríki district, among the mountains of eastern Aitolía. When he was an infant, the village was attacked by some of 'Ali Paşa's men; three people, including Makriyiánnes' father, were killed in the family's house; and the surviving villagers fled for their lives to Livadhiá.[255] Makriyiánnes was put to work at the age of seven.[256] In 1811, when he was fourteen, he found work with a congenial employer at Arta. Here he won the confidence of the local Greek notables and traders, persuaded them to lend him money, re-lent this to peasants, bought grain in advance of the harvest, and sold it, during a famine, at four times the price that he had paid for it. By the date of the outbreak of the War of Independence in 1821, when Makriyiánnes was twenty-four, he had accumulated, by such means, a fortune of 40,000 *ghróssia* (*gurush*).[257] Makriyiánnes' sole comment on his business activities is that he had gained the amount that he had wanted, had made himself financially independent, and had won many friends.[258]

When, in 1821, Makriyiánnes switched his energies from money-

---

[254] See Campbell and Sherrard, op. cit., pp. 48–9.

[255] Makriyiánnes, I., Ἀπομνημονεύματα (Athens 1907, 2 vols.) vol. ii, pp. 11–13.

[256] Ibid., p. 13.

[257] Makriyiánnes himself, ibid., p. 15.

[258] Ἀπόχτησα ὅ, τι ἤθελα καὶ δὲν εἶχα τὴν ἀνάγκη ἀλλουνοῦ, Ἔκατζα εἰς Ἄρτα ὡς δέκα χρόνια, ἔκαμα πολλοὺς φίλους (ibid.).

making to war and politics, he was content to lose the fortune that he had accumulated; in the War of Independence he rose to be a general; after the achievement of independence he was a prime mover in the revolution of 1843;[259] and in 1864 he died famous and highly respected, but not rich. If he had been born a generation earlier, and had spent the whole of his working life on applying his great ability and energy to money-making, he would surely have become famous as the founder of a business house on the scale of the Khiot firm of Ralli Brothers.

The brief commercial chapter of Makriyiánnês' career is an example of how some Modern Greek peasants have succeeded in business with no initial assets except wits, vigour, and ruthlessness. However, only a tiny minority of the Modern Greek peasantry has made its fortune in this way, and the majority of the Modern Greek people have been peasants and shepherds till within living memory.

In the eighteenth century, when a few Greek peasants were making fortunes by going into business, the rest continued to be peasants, and, so far from growing richer, became poorer. In late eighteenth-century and early nineteenth-century Greek society, as in contemporary British society, a great gulf opened between the few who made money and the many who did not.

Since the rise of the earliest of the civilizations about 5,000 years ago, the growers of crops and breeders of livestock have not only had to provide for their own subsistence; they have also had to support the superstructure of civilization that has been imposed on them in one region after another. Usually they have been exploited. They have fared least badly under the rule of strong and intelligent governments which understood that the peasant's and the shepherd's productive labour was civilization's basis (as it continued to be till the Industrial Revolution). Governments of this kind have sought to monopolize the exploitation of the peasantry for themselves and have refrained from carrying this exploitation to ruinous extremes. Under the East Roman Imperial regime, the Greek peasantry had been comparatively well off from the late seventh century to the early tenth century of the Christian Era. Those of them who survived to become tenants of the Ottoman provincial fief-holders had been likewise comparatively well off from the late fourteenth century to the late seventeenth century. But in the eighteenth century the Ottoman Empire, in its turn, went into decline, and the weakening of the Imperial Government's hold on the provincial landlords was once again disastrous for the Greek peasantry, as it had been when the East Roman Government had been defeated by the provincial landlords in a competition for snatching the fruits of the peasants' labours.

[259] See Finlay, op. cit., vol. vii, p. 174.

When the Ottoman Imperial regime had been at its zenith, it had maintained an effective control over the fief-holders who had furnished the bulk of its cavalry. Fiefs had not been heritable as a matter of course, and their holders had been restrained from exacting too much from the peasantry on whose well-being the fief-holders' upkeep, and consequently their military efficiency, had depended. When the Ottoman Imperial Government lost grip, the peasants lost their security. The fiefs became, *de facto*, private property that could be bequeathed and could be sold and bought; and, as insecurity grew worse, there was an increasing competition to invest in land. Successful non-Muslim business men joined in the scramble with Muslim grandees. The peasants were the victims.[260] By 1821, the date of the outbreak of the Greek War of Independence, five-sixths of the Greek peasantry had sunk—so it has been reckoned[261]—to being hired labourers, owning no land of their own.

Thus, in the course of the eighteenth century, the economic condition of a majority of the Greek people deteriorated, and even the exceptional Greek communities that were becoming prosperous through engaging in commerce, industry, and the production of special crops, such as olives, were not secure. Their prosperity was contingent on their autonomy, and, under the Ottoman regime, the autonomy of those Ottoman Christian communities that possessed autonomy was always precarious. The 'Osmanlis granted autonomy where they felt this to be to their advantage, and they acquiesced in autonomy, where they had not granted this, only because it was not feasible, or was not worth while, to reassert their authority.

The Ottoman Government was indulgent to the Khiots and to the Peloponnesians for a reason that has been noted already. Experience had shown that Khios and the Pelopónnêsos were exposed to attack by hostile Christian naval powers. If and when the local Eastern Orthodox Christian population was more partial to the invader than to the Ottoman regime, the balance was tilted against the Ottoman garrison. The 'Osmanlis were able to reconquer Khios from the Florentines in 1599 and from the Venetians in 1695 because, at Khios, the local Roman Catholic Christians were in a minority, and the Eastern Orthodox Christians preferred Ottoman suzerainty to the rule of a Roman Catholic Christian power. The 'Osmanlis were able to reconquer the Pelopónnêsos from the Venetians in 1715 for the same reasons. On the other hand, the Peloponnesian Greeks did revolt, in spite of their favourable treatment by the 'Osmanlis, during the Russo-Turkish War of 1768–74, when a Russian squadron appeared

[260] See Campbell and Sherrard, op. cit., p. 55.
[261] Tsakonas, op. cit., p. 126.

in Levantine waters. The appeal of an Eastern Orthodox Christian power was irresistible; and, though the Peloponnesian Greeks were disillusioned at being abandoned by the Russians after having been incited and compromised by them, the 'Osmanlis had great trouble in suppressing the revolt. They achieved this only by first introducing into the Pelopónnêsos a horde of wild Muslim Albanian tribesmen and then mopping up these insubordinate auxiliaries. Moreover, the privileges granted to the Dhervenokhorítai[262] did not inhibit these Albanian Orthodox Christian guardians of the overland passage into the Pelopónnêsos from joining in the fresh revolt of the Peloponnesian Greeks in 1821.[263]

There were, however, as has been noted already,[264] some Ottoman Eastern Orthodox Christian communities that were privileged, not because they were hard to hold and not because it was particularly profitable for the 'Osmanlis to allow them autonomy either formally or tacitly, but because they had providently come to terms with the 'Osmanlis at the time of the original Ottoman conquest.

For instance, Evrenós Bey, the Ottoman conqueror and organizer of Macedonia, persuaded the people of Nyáousta (Náoussa) to submit and to move down from the town's original location on a spur of Mount Vérmion to a new site that was less defensible militarily but was more convenient for purposes of trade. In return, Evrenós obtained for Nyáousta from the Ottoman Crown a number of privileges: not only low taxation but the all-important exemption from having to receive any Muslim residents except the *qādi* and the governor. This favourable treatment enabled Nyáousta to develop a number of industries.[265]

Similarly Turakhan Bey, the Ottoman conqueror and organizer of Thessaly, founded a Greek Christian town at Týrnavos, a key-point on the line of communications between the basins of the Rivers Vistríca (Aliákmon) and Salamvriá (Pêneiós). Turakhan Bey obtained for Týrnavos the privilege that, notwithstanding its situation on a main route, Ottoman troops should be debarred from passing through it. He procured its exemption from the jurisdiction of the local Ottoman public authorities by obtaining for it the status of *vaqf* (i.e. a Muslim religious endowment). The only taxes to which its inhabitants were made liable were the *kharaj* (the surtax payable by *dhimmîs*) and the tithe, and they were exempted from corvées (ἀγγαρεῖαι).[266] Týrnavos is said to have been the first place in Europe to manufacture potash. Turakhan Bey is also credited with having introduced the art of dyeing into Thessaly,

[262] See above, p. 203 with n. 212.
[263] See Finlay, op. cit., vol. vi, p. 159.
[264] On pp. 205–6.
[265] Vakalópoulos, op. cit., vol. i, p. 224.
[266] Ibid., pp. 224–5.

and to have developed the silk, cotton, and wool industries there. If this is correct, Turakhan Bey's economic activities were the ultimate source of the prosperity of Ambelákia.[267] The history of the privileges conferred on Týrnavos and Nyáousta under the Ottoman regime may provide a clue to the origin of the privileges enjoyed by Shátishta[268] and by the Khasikokhória.[269]

However, in most cases, the political autonomy that had been acquired, in or before the eighteenth century, by a number of local growing-points of new Greek life was a consequence, not of an imaginative and bold pursuit of self-interest by the ʿOsmanlis in their prime, but of the subsequent decline of the Ottoman Empire; and this political dispensation was feasible only so long as the decline had not reached its terminus in a fall. These autonomous Greek communities were too small and too sparsely scattered for it to be possible for them to become so many separate independent successor-states of the Ottoman Empire after the Empire's demise. Unlike the germs of the Hellenic Greek city-states, the Modern Greek counterparts of these could not hold their own as sovereign polities in their post-Ottoman political environment. On the other hand, they were already holding their own successfully on the commercial plane by breeding dynamic merchants and mariners. On this plane these Greek communities had become part of the Modern World while they were still embedded politically in the decaying Ottoman Empire.

In the trade between the Ottoman Empire and the West the Greeks had replaced the Italians and had won a place side by side with the French and Dutch and British. They had also begun to play a leading role in the new trade between the Ottoman Empire and the Russian Empire that had now won a frontage on the Black Sea at the Ottoman Empire's expense. The traumatic break with their cultural heritages which, for the Modern Greeks, has been the price of political liberation has not extended to the commercial sector of Greek economic life. The industrial sector has not fared so well. Local Greek industries—for instance, the textile and the dyeing industry of Ambelákia,[270] the soap-manufacturing industry at Ayvalik, and the silk industry at Khios—had suffered from the competition of the recently mechanized industry of Western Europe before becoming victims of the hostilities in the Greek War of Independence. But in the commercial sector there has been an unbroken continuity and development from the date of the consummation of the Ottoman conquest down to the present day.

[267] See above, p. 188.
[268] See above, p. 189 n. 149.
[269] A federation of fifteen villages in the western part of Khalkidhikê (see Finlay, op. cit., vol. vi, p. 202).
[270] See Clarke, locc. citt., p. 189 n. 147.

2. *The impracticability of the 'Great Idea'*

The Modern Greeks could not recover their political independence by repeating the Hellenic Greeks' performance. It has been noted already that the autonomous local Greek communities that had arisen within the declining Ottoman Empire could not have held their own in the Modern World as so many separate sovereign states. For them, the price payable for independence was incorporation in some larger polity; and, since the Modern Greeks could not attain this scale of political organization through the spontaneous development of their own embryonic political institutions, they had to look elsewhere for possible models. They could look back to their heritage from their Byzantine Greek predecessors. Alternatively, they could look abroad to the contemporary Western World. The majority of the Ottoman Greeks, though not all the representatives of the Greek Orthodox ecclesiastical hierarchy, were no longer estranged from the West. Since the time when they had opted for falling under Ottoman, in preference to Western rule, their feelings towards the West had changed gradually from disdainful hostility to wistful admiration.

The memory of the Byzantine Greek past suggested that the recovery of political independence might take the form of a revival of the East Roman Empire; the spectacle of the contemporary Western World suggested, before the outbreak of the French Revolution, the construction of a counterpart of the Danubian Habsburg Monarchy, which was the nearest of the Western great powers and was familiar to the Ottoman Greeks through the commercial relations that they had established with it.

Naturally their own Byzantine past had a greater appeal for the Modern Greeks than anything in the contemporary West, in spite of the growing prestige of the West in Greek eyes, and in spite, too, of the misery, on the political plane, of the last chapter of Byzantine Greek history—a misery that had presented an invidious contrast to the contemporary flowering of Byzantine Greek art. The East Roman Empire's long-drawn-out decline—signalized by the sensational disasters of 1071 and 1204—had ended in the second and final fall of Constantinople in 1453; but that darkest hour of all had been lit up, surprisingly, by a glimmer of hope, and this gleam had not been extinguished. Though the expectation that the City would be saved at the eleventh hour by a miraculous intervention of God had been disappointed, this fallacious expectation had been replaced promptly by another. The City that had not been saved miraculously for the Greeks was going to be restored to them miraculously, and, with it, the Empire of which it was the divinely appointed capital. It was not for them to know the times or the seasons, but their faith in this new expectation gave them the strength to possess their souls in patience.

This faith went to earth in folk-songs and folk-tales. The angelic voice that interrupted the liturgy in the Ayía Sophía at the moment of the City's fall in 1453 bade the Theotókos cease to lament and to shed tears; for

$$\pi\acute{a}\lambda\iota\ \mu\grave{\epsilon}\ \chi\rho\acute{o}\nu o\upsilon s,\ \mu\grave{\epsilon}\ \kappa a\iota\rho o\acute{u}s,\ \pi\acute{a}\lambda\iota\ \delta\iota\kappa\acute{a}\ \sigma a s\ \epsilon\widehat{\imath}\nu a\iota.^{271}$$

At the same historic moment, seven half-fried fish came alive and jumped into a well, where they were to stay alive until Constantinople was retaken.[272]

This Greek optimism had been fortified by successive Ottoman acts of state. Mehmet the Conqueror himself had included a strong contingent of Greeks among the settlers with whom he had repeopled Constantinople.[273] He had preserved the Ecumenical Patriarchate by installing a new incumbent, and he had made the Patriarch *ex officio* the civil head of the *Rum milleti*—a civil community that embraced all Ottoman Eastern Orthodox Christian subjects, including those who were not Greeks and those Greeks and non-Greeks who were not under the Ecumenical Patriarch's ecclesiastical jurisdiction. In the seventeenth century the Ottoman government had abandoned the selective conscription of Ottoman Christian boys into the Sultan's slave-household, and had instituted two high offices of state for Ottoman Greek subjects who had received, not an Ottoman Muslim, but a Western Christian, education, and who had not renounced their ancestral Eastern Orthodox Christian religion. In the eighteenth century the Ottoman Greeks had been given the monopoly of two more high offices, the hospodarships of the autonomous Roumanian Principalities of Wallachia and Moldavia. In 1793, when the Ottoman Government at last recognized the necessity of establishing permanent Ottoman diplomatic missions at Vienna, Paris, London, and Berlin, it filled these new posts with Ottoman Greek Christian chargés d'affaires.[274]

This last-mentioned act brings out the point that, from first to last, the Ottoman acts of state that were advantageous for the 'Osmanlis' Greek subjects were prompted, as was to be expected, by regard for the 'Osmanlis' own convenience. Since Mehmet the Conqueror wanted to

---

[271] 'Again, with years, with time, again it is your own.'

[272] For the song about the interrupted liturgy, see Polítês, N. G., Ἐκλογαὶ ἀπὸ τὰ τραγούδια τοῦ Ἑλληνικοῦ λαοῦ (Athens 1914), pp. 4–5; Trypanis, *Medieval and Modern Greek Poetry*, no. 86, pp. 93–4. For the song about the fish-frying, see Passow, A., *Carmina Popularia Graeciae Recentioris* (Leipzig 1860), no. cxcvii, p. 147. Two versions of a folk-tale on the same theme have been published by Polítês in his Μελέται περὶ τοῦ βίου καὶ τῆς γλώσσης τοῦ Ἑλληνικοῦ λαοῦ (Athens 1904, 2 parts), part i, texts, p. 21; part ii, commentary, pp. 656–7.

[273] See above, p. 181.

[274] See d'Ohsson, I. M., *Tableau Général de l'Empire Ottoman*, vol. vii, p. 573.

re-equip Constantinople for serving, once more, as the capital city of a great empire, it was convenient for him to re-people it partially with urban Greeks. When, in and after the seventeenth century, the tide turned against the Ottoman Empire in its contests with the Western powers, Ottoman Greek Christians became more useful to the Porte as unconverted diplomats than as converted administrators and soldiers. The Porte had an increasing need for public servants who could negotiate on its behalf with Western powers which could no longer be coerced by Ottoman military strength; and the only Ottoman subjects who were fluent in Western languages and were well versed in Western manners and customs were the scions of Ottoman Greek families that had made money in trade with the West and had taken to investing some of their profits in Western education, first to serve their own business interests and then because they had come to admire the Western civilization and way of life more than either the Byzantine Christian or the Ottoman Islamic. Each of these successive promotions of the Ottoman Greeks had saved the 'Osmanlis trouble, but the policy had been improvident and its cumulative effect had been to imperil the 'Osmanlis' supremacy in the empire that they themselves had built by the device of converting the élite of their Christian subjects into the mainstay of the Ottoman Muslim ascendancy's own power.

By the close of the eighteenth century the Ottoman Greek *novi homines* whose rise had been not only tolerated but facilitated by the Ottoman Government itself had become the unacknowledged but apparently indispensable partners of the 'Osmanlis in the maintenance of the tottering Ottoman Empire. As high officials of the Porte, as patrons of the Patriarchate that administered for the Porte the *Rum milleti*, and as hospodars of the two autonomous Roumanian Principalities, the Phanariots[275] held three sets of strings. They were passed masters of the art of string-pulling, and, by the close of the eighteenth century, it might look, from their standpoint, as if they would be able to manœuvre themselves into the position of being, in effect, the senior partners in a Graeco-Turkish political firm, and perhaps eventually the firm's sole directors.

In that event, they would inherit an empire on the scale of Justinian I's (527–65), or at least on the scale of Manuel I Komnênós' (1143–80). Alternatively, if the Ottoman Empire were to break up into a mosaic of autonomous successor-states, the Phanariots might be able to gain control of some of these, as they already controlled the two Roumanian Principalities, and then they could manipulate the Ottoman Pādishāh's prestige, as the fount of legitimization, to build these fragments together

---

[275] So-called because their homes in Istanbul were in the Phanári (Lighthouse) quarter at the north-eastern corner of the city. See above, p. 147.

again into a replica of the kingdoms and lands that had been united under the Habsburg Crown, with the Greeks playing the part in this loosely reconstructed Ottoman Empire that, in the eighteenth century, the Habsburg Monarchy's German subjects were playing in the Habsburg dominions.

Muslim war-lords were carving out domains for themselves—some of them, for instance 'Alī Paşa at Yánnina, as disloyal Ottoman officials, others, for instance Pasvanoğlu at Viddīn,[276] as unauthorized adventurers. The position of both kinds of usurper was precarious. Might they not be induced to employ the Phanariots' services as mediators between them and the Porte, and thereby put themselves in the Phanariots' power? By 1818, 'Alī had gained control, not only of Êpeiros, but of Thessaly, Central Greece, the Pelopónnêsos, and western Macedonia[277]—that is to say, of almost all the continental European Ottoman territories in which a majority of the population was Greek.

Like the Ottoman Government, 'Alī found it convenient to employ Greeks in his administrative service; indeed, he used Greek as his principal language of administration,[278] and, under his regime, Yánnina became one of the leading Ottoman centres of the Westernizing movement in Greek education and culture.[279] Yánnina was well placed geographically for playing this role. Êpeiros was the nearest to the west of the Ottoman territories in which the Greeks were in a majority, and the Ionian Islands, with their Greek population and their Italianate Greek aristocracy and intelligentsia, were stepping-stones between Êpeiros and the West in the cultural as well as in the geographical sense. In 'Ali's domain, was not a 'take-over' by the Greeks already within sight?

In 1804 the Serbs rebelled, and the Ottoman Government proved unable to reduce them to subjection again. In Serbia, was there not, in the making, a new principality for a Phanariot Greek hospodar? Like the Roumanians in the two Transdanubian Principalities that were already under Phanariot Greek rule, the Serbs were members of the *Rum milleti*. Unlike the Transdanubian Roumanians, the Serbs had once been under Greek rule. From 1018 to 1180, some of them, previously subjects of Bulgaria, had been directly subject to the East Roman Empire, and the rest had been under its suzerainty. Why should not the status quo ante 1180 be re-established post 1804?

No doubt the sophisticated Phanariots did not believe consciously that the fifteenth-century prophecies of a restoration of the East Roman

---

[276] See Botzaris, *Visions balkaniques*, pp. 40–2.
[277] Campbell and Sherrard, op. cit., p. 61.
[278] See above, p. 153.
[279] For 'Ali Paşa's regime, down to his breach with Sultan Mahmūd II in 1819–20, see Finlay, op. cit., vol. vi, pp. 57–70.

Empire were fated to be fulfilled; but even a Westernized Greek mind must have been affected by the 'Great Idea' emotionally. However, by the date, at the turn of the eighteenth and nineteenth centuries, at which the 'Great Idea' had come to look, at first sight, like a rational and attainable objective for the Ottoman Greeks, a number of obstacles to its achievement had arisen.

The most formidable and insurmountable of these obstacles was the unwillingness of the non-Greek majority of the *Rum milleti* to acquiesce in a reimposition on it of a Greek ascendancy. The Bulgars' and Serbs' memory of Greek domination in the eleventh and twelfth centuries had been kept alive by their experience, under the Ottoman regime, of a partial resubjection to the Greeks for the 'Osmanlis' convenience. The non-Greek Ottoman Eastern Orthodox Christians did not want to be subject to either Turkish Muslim or Greek Christian masters; but, if they had had to make the choice between these two evils, they would probably have opted for remaining under Turkish rule, on the calculation that this was likely to be relatively easy-going.

The fate of the Roumanians was an object-lesson for their Slav fellow-members of the *Rum milleti*. Even while the two Roumanian Principalities were still being governed by Roumanian princes, the Eastern Orthodox Patriarchates and the Athonian monasteries had been endowed with estates in the Principalities by the native princes and nobles. In effect, these donors had been putting wealth into ecclesiastical Greek hands at the expense of the Roumanian peasantry; for the Patriarchates, and all but four of the Athonian monasteries, were held by Greeks. When, after 1711, the hospodarships had become Phanariot Greek perquisites, the Greek princes and their hangers-on had fleeced the Principalities in order to recoup themselves for the bribes with which they had bought their short and precarious tenure of office.

Another sign of the times was the failure of the Emperor Joseph II, when he was sole sovereign of the Habsburg dominions (1780–90), to standardize and unify these lands administratively and culturally by Germanizing them all. Joseph was defeated by the resistance of his non-German subjects. This precedent might have suggested that the Ottoman Greeks, who were still only junior partners in the Ottoman 'establishment', had little chance of Graecizing their non-Greek fellow-subjects.

In contrast to the Habsburg Monarchy, France was nationally almost homogeneous, and the makers of the French Revolution succeeded, in their more propitious circumstances, in achieving what Joseph had aimed at. They did transform the French monarchy into a French national republic 'one and indivisible'. Their achievement suddenly changed the ideal of what the structure of a Western state should be, and this change altered the outlook of all parties within the Ottoman Empire, as well as outside it. The creation of a homogeneous national state, embracing the whole of a nation, now became the objective, not only of every Western people, but also of all Westernized nationals of the non-Western peoples of the Ottoman Empire. Since the national heterogeneity of the populations of the Habsburg and Ottoman empires made it impracticable to reduce either empire to a nationally homo-geneous state of the revolutionary French kind, the French Revolution had condemned them both to eventual partition, and had therefore condemned their geographically intermingled populations to suffer the agony of being sorted out from each other by eviction or massacre. Between 1821 and 1922 the course of history demonstrated that the Ottoman Empire could not be Graecized; between 1908 and 1918 it was also demonstrated that the Empire could not be Turcized either. By 1918 both the Ottoman and the Habsburg Empire had broken up.

The only agency through which the Ottoman Empire could con-ceivably have been Graecized was the control over the *Rum milleti* that had been given to the Greek Ecumenical Patriarchate by the 'Osmanlis; but this control could not be used by the Patriarchate to dethrone the 'Osmanlis and to enthrone the Ottoman Greeks in their stead. The Patriarchate was at the Ottoman Government's mercy; its civil function was to keep the Empire's Eastern Orthodox subjects docile; and, if and when it failed to perform this service, it was held responsible, even though it might be powerless to carry out its mandate. One of Sultan Mahmūd II's retorts to the Ottoman Greek insurrection in 1821 was to put to death the Ecumenical Patriarch Gregory V. Probably Gregory was a loyal subject of the Sultan, and this not just out of prudence, but by conviction. The Eastern Orthodox Church had been opposed to Western ideas when these had taken the ecclesiastical form of an interpolation in the Creed and a claim by the Papacy to possess the prerogative of supremacy over the other Patriarchates. In the new secular form of 'the ideas of French Revolution' the ideology of the West was no less obnoxious to Eastern Orthodox clerical minds.

The French Revolution was advantageous for the Ottoman Imperial Government in its relations not only with the Eastern Orthodox Christian hierarchy but also with the Western powers. The Revolution reanimated the hierarchy's traditional view that Muslim rule was a protection for Orthodoxy against the contagion of Western error. At the same time it led the Western powers, including the semi-Westernized Russian Empire, to look at the Ottoman Pādishāh with new eyes. Before the French Revolution, they had regarded him as being an infidel ruler whom Christian sovereigns had the right and duty to despoil. After the Revolution, the representatives of the *ancien régime* who had survived or had been reinstated saw in the Pādishāh one of the Lord's anointed, or, in other words, one of themselves. Like his Western brothers, he, too, stood for the sacrosanct principle of dynastic legitimacy. Any rebellion against his authority was also a challenge to theirs.

Thus the Greek 'Great Idea' of re-establishing the East Roman Empire was foredoomed to failure before the fiasco, in 1821, of the first attempt to translate it into action. The 'Great Idea' was irreconcilable both with 'the ideas of the French Revolution' and with the counter-ideology of 'legitimacy'. Its incompatibility with these two ideologies is illustrated by the life, works, and death of Rhêghas Velestinlês (1757(?)–98).[280]

Rhêghas was a Rumeliot Vlach. His home town was Velestínos in Thessaly. He was educated at Ambelákia or in the Zaghorá (it is uncertain which of these two autonomous Thessalian Greek communities was the place).[281] After getting into political trouble at home, Rhêghas moved to Istanbul; became secretary there to Alexander Ypsilándês, who was at that time Dragoman of the Porte; followed his patron to Bucharest after Alexander Ypsilándês had become *hospodar* of Wallachia in 1774; and eventually became secretary to Ypsilándês' third successor at Bucharest, Nikólaos Mavroyénês, a non-Phanariot Greek interloper in the Phanariots' preserve who had been Dragoman of the Fleet in 1769–73. In 1787 the Porte appointed Mavroyénês commander-in-chief on the front in the Principalities against the Austrians and Russians; but in 1790 Mavroyénês had to evacuate the Principalities and was consequently put to death; Rhêghas, who in 1787 had been made ban of the Craiova district of Wallachia by Mavroyénês, was present at Mavroyénês' execution.[282]

In 1790 Rhêghas visited Vienna as secretary to a Phanariot Ottoman envoy, and he stayed there for several months. In 1791 he returned to Wallachia to look after properties that he had acquired there and to start a commercial business.[283] In 1794 he visited Trieste, and in 1796 he made a permanent move from Bucharest to Vienna, engaged in revolutionary literary activities there, was arrested in 1797 by the Austrian police, and was extradited, with seven other Ottoman subjects, in 1798. The eight prisoners were put to death at Belgrade by order of the Porte.

Rhêghas' literary works were all written in colloquial Greek (ἡ

[280] See Daskalakis, *Rhighas Velestinlis*; Bótzaris, *Visions balkaniques*; Vranoússês, L. I., *Rhêgas*; Manéssês, A. J., 'L'activité et les projets politiques d'un patriote grec dans les Balkans vers la fin du xviiie siècle', in *Balkan Studies*, vol. iii (1962), pp. 75–118; Pandazópoulos, N. I., *Rhêgas velestinlês*; Amandos, K., *Anékdhota éngrapha perì Rhêga Velestinlê*.

[281] Bótzaris, op. cit., p. 18.

[282] Daskalakis, op. cit., pp. 39–40.

[283] Bótzaris, op. cit., p. 19.

δημοτική), with inevitable lapses into 'purist' Greek (ἡ καθαρεύουσα). His political works were a map of 'Ellás' and a brochure that was printed secretly, in the course of two nights in November 1797, at Vienna in a Greek press operated by the two brothers Markídhês Poúlios, from Shátista,[284] who, since 1790, had been publishing, at Vienna, a journal called the *Ephêmerís* ('The Daily'), which was the earliest Greek journal to be published anywhere.[285]

Rhêghas' 'Ellás' embraced, according to the descriptive title of his map, the whole of the continental territory still under Ottoman sovereignty in Europe, including the two Transdanubian Principalities, together with the Ionian Islands, the Aegean Islands, and a strip of Asian Ottoman territory to the west of a line drawn from Lycia northwards to the Karamursal peninsula on the Asian side of the Sea of Marmara.[286] The labelling of this area as 'Ellás' is chimerical. The area does contain the original nucleus of the historical Hellenic Greek World, and this world had eventually expanded westward to the French Riviera and the Spanish Costa Brava, eastward to Uzbekistan and the Panjab, northward to the north coast of the Black Sea, and southward to Cyrenaïca and the Nile Delta; but the historical Ellás had never included the interior of South-Eastern Europe.

The brochure, which cost Rhêghas his life, consisted of a *Revolutionary Proclamation*, a *Declaration of the Rights of Man and of the Citizen*, a *Constitution*, and a 'war-song' or 'battle hymn', which the author called a *Thoúrios*.[287]

The *Thoúrios*[288] is the only one of these works of Rhêghas' that had any practical effect. It is said to have been sung by Rhêghas in October 1796.[289] Written, as it was, in colloquial Greek in rhyming couplets in the 'metropolitan' accentual metre (στίχοι πολιτικοί), it was easily memorized and it spread rapidly through the Greek World by oral transmission. Though the brochure, printed in Vienna, which included it, was successfully suppressed by the Austrian authorities, the *Thoúrios* was published separately at Corfú, perhaps as early as 1798.[290]

A manuscript copy of the Greek text of Rhêghas' brochure of 1797 has

[284] Daskalakis, op. cit., pp. 88–9.
[285] Ibid., p. 63. There is a facsimile of a specimen page, facing p. 64.
[286] See the French translation of the Greek descriptive title in ibid., pp. 52–3. The Greek original appears on sheet 4 of the 12 sheets, which is reproduced in facsimile in ibid., facing p. 96. There is also, facing p. 192, a facsimile of sheet 5.
[287] *Thoúrios* (θούριος) is an Hellenic Greek adjective meaning 'enthused with martial ardour'.
[288] Incomplete Greek texts in Fauriel, C., *Chants populaires de la Grèce moderne* (Paris 1824–5, 2 vols.), vol. ii, pp. 20–9; Thumb, A., *Handbuch der neugriechischen Volksprache*, 2nd edn. (Strasburg 1910), pp. 234–5; and in Trypanis, op. cit., pp. 137–8; complete French translation in Bótzaris, op. cit., pp. 205–9.
[289] Ibid., p. 20.
[290] Ibid., p. 29.

survived at Corfú, and a German translation of it in the Austrian public archives.[291] A complete French translation has been published.[292]

Rhêghas' works are significant because they are utterly unrealistic—and this is surprising, considering that, before he composed them, Rhêghas had had practical experience, in responsible official posts, of the political realities. After having labelled as 'Ellás' the area delimited in the descriptive title of his map, Rhêghas, in the *Revolutionary Proclamation* which is the preamble to his *Constitution*, calls the heterogeneous population of this area 'the people descended from the Hellenes'. The *Constitution* itself, together with the *Declaration of Rights*, is based on the French constitutions of 1793 and 1795. These two French constitutions had different political objectives—a difference of which Rhêghas seems to have been unaware—but they agreed with each other in one respect that had a vital bearing on Rhêghas' project: they were constitutions for a unitary state, and Rhêghas copies in detail the provisions in them that are designed to produce a state of this 'one and indivisible' kind.[293]

A single language, namely the colloquial form of Greek, is to be the medium of compulsory universal education[294] and to be the official language for laws and decrees.[295] Yet, even among the Greeks themselves, the 'language question' is still a contentious issue a century and three-quarters after the date at which Rhêghas made this proposal. *A fortiori*, it would have been an insuperable stumbling-block for the non-Greek majority of the motley population embraced within Rhêghas' imaginary frontiers. Moreover, though Rhêghas calls his state 'the Hellenic Republic' in his *Constitution*, Article 1, he calls it 'this empire' ($\beta\alpha\sigma\iota\lambda\epsilon\iota\omicron\nu$) in *The Rights of Man . . .*, Article 9, and in the *Thoúrios*, line 30, he demands that 'the fatherland' shall have 'a single leader'.[296]

Rhêghas counts on enlisting the Pādishāh's Muslim subjects in a general insurrection aiming at the overthrow of the Pādishāh's rule. This hope seems to have been based on a personal friendship with one Muslim usurper, Pasvanoğlu of Viddīn. Rhêghas, while he was ban of Craiova, seems to have done Pasvanoğlu some important service,[297] and Pasvanoğlu, like 'Alī Paşa of Yánnina in 1820, made promises to the Christians under his rule in the hope of winning their support for him

[291] Ibid., p. 25.

[292] By Daskalakis, A., *Les Oeuvres de Rhighas Velestinlis* (Paris 1937), pp. 75-125, reproduced in Bótzaris, op. cit., pp. 184-209.

[293] Article 1 of Rhêghas' *Constitution* declares that 'the Hellenic Republic' is one and indivisible, 'though it embraces in its bosom a number of different races and religions'.

[294] *The Rights of Man . . .*, Article 22.

[295] *Constitution*, Article 53.

[296] καὶ τῆς πατρίδος ἕνας νὰ γένῃ ἀρχηγός.

[297] Bótzaris, op. cit., p. 19. The Craiova district lies at the western extremity of Wallachia, just across the Danube from Viddīn.

against the Porte's attempts to suppress him. Pasvanoğlu, like Rhêghas in his *Revolutionary Proclamation*, adopted the French revolutionary slogans 'liberty' and 'equality', and he forbade the use of the derogatory term *ne 'īyeh* for designating his Christian subjects. Moreover, though almost all of his Christian subjects were Bulgars, not Greeks, he addressed his declarations to the Greeks.[298]

However, Rhêghas does not confine his appeal to Muslims to his professedly Graecophil Muslim friend Pasvanoğlu. In Rhêghas' *Thoúrios*, Pasvanoğlu does head the list of the Muslim Ottoman war-lords whom Rhêghas here names; but he cites them all. He exhorts the Mamlūks of Egypt to elect one of themselves as their king and to stop paying tribute to Constantinople. He demands 'a general conflagration from Bosnia to Arabia'—two Muslim lands that were at opposite extremities of the Ottoman Empire. But in the very next line he adjures these Muslims to crown their banners with a cross! In his *Revolutionary Proclamation* and in *The Rights of Man* . . ., Article 3, he proclaims the equality of Christians and Muslims.[299] Apparently he does not realize that he is not granting the Muslims a new right, but is asking them implicitly to renounce the old privilege of ascendancy which is the prerogative of Muslims according to Islamic doctrine. Moreover, subconsciously Rhêghas is not conceding even equality with the Greeks either to Muslims or to non-Greek Christians. All of them are to adopt the Greek language in its colloquial form, and the Muslims are to Graecize themselves under the sign of the Cross.

Even if Rhêghas had succeeded in making his way to the Máni instead of being arrested, extradited, and executed, he could never have induced any of his fellow Ottoman subjects who were not Greek Eastern Orthodox Christians to join him in risking their lives in order to set up an 'Hellenic Republic'—or to resurrect a Byzantine Greek 'Vasíleion'—on his terms. His abortive project for translating the 'Great Idea' into action was utopian. The action that was actually taken by Prince Alexander Ypsilándês[300] a quarter of a century later, in 1821, miscarried as swiftly and as disastrously as was to be expected.

It is astonishing that Alexander Ypsilándês should have supposed that, by crossing the Russo-Moldavian frontier, he would be able to subvert the Ottoman regime in Europe. It is even more astonishing that the reigning *hospodar* of Moldavia, Michael Soútsos II, should have made Ypsilándês' escapade possible by conniving at it. Soútsos and Ypsilándês had, like Rhêghas, a first-hand personal knowledge of the

[298] Bótzaris, op. cit., p. 42.

[299] He means Ottoman Muslims of all nationalities when he writes 'Turks'.

[300] See Finlay, op. cit., vol. vi, pp. 110-11. He was the son of Prince Constantine Ypsilándês, who had been twice Hospodar of Wallachia and once Hospodar of Moldavia. This Alexander is not to be confused with his homonym the Alexander Ypsilándês who had been Rhêghas' patron.

Roumanian Principalities; Ypsilándês had also had a military career in the Russian service and had risen to the rank of major-general. He ought to have known that Tsar Alexander I would frown on his enterprise, and that he would receive no support from the non-Greek Ottoman Christian peoples—Roumanians, Bulgars, Serbs—who constituted the majority of the population in the northern part of the Ottoman Pādishāh's European dominions—the region that Ypsilándês had chosen to invade. Yet, so far from recognizing facts with which he should have been familiar, Ypsilándês seems to have imagined that the Roumanian population of the Principalities would rise in his favour; that the native prince of Serbia, Miloš Obrenović,[301] would join forces with him;[302] that the Tsar would abet Ypsilándês' adventure; that at least he would not agree to the Porte's sending Ottoman troops into the Principalities;[303] and that anyway all the Ottoman troops in Europe would be fully occupied by the task of trying to liquidate 'Alī Paşa of Yánnina, in the quarter of *Rum ili* that was the most remote from the Principalities.

All these unwarrantable expectations were falsified by the event.[304] The Roumanians did rise, but not in support of Ypsilándês or against the Ottoman Government. The leader of the rising, Theodore Vladimirescu, petitioned the Pādishāh[305] to protect the Roumanian peasantry against their oppressors the *hospodars*, the native Roumanian nobles, and the Eastern Orthodox metropolitan of Hongrowallachia.

---

[301] When, in 1807-8, at the Ottoman Government's instance, the Ecumenical Patriarch, Gregory V, had tried, in his capacity as head of the *Rum milleti*, to mediate between the Porte and the Serb insurgents, these had insisted on being granted autonomy under a prince who was to be a Serb, not a Phanariot Greek (see Bótzaris, op. cit., pp. 69-70).

[302] In a proclamation dated Jassy, 24 February 1821, and addressed to the Greeks in the Principalities, Alexander Ypsilándês wrote, in Rhêghas-like language: 'The Morea, Êpeiros, Thessaly, Serbia, Bulgaria, the islands of the Archipelago, in a word all Greece [*sic*], has taken up arms' (text in ibid., p. 226). In a letter dated Tríkorpha, 25 July 1821, and addressed to the Ottoman governor of Crete and his troops, adjuring them to join in the insurrection, Alexander Ypsilándês' brother Dhêmêtrios, writing as Alexander's plenipotentiary, styles himself 'Generalissimo of the Nation of the Christians' (text in ibid., pp. 254-5). The Ypsilándês brothers had inherited Rhêghas' illusions.

[303] The Russian Government appears to have held that the Ottoman Government was bound by treaty not to send troops into the Principalities without having first obtained the Russian Government's consent. In the Russo-Turkish peace-treaties of 1774, 1792, and 1812, no article is to be found that can fairly be construed as giving the Russian Government this veto. However, from the Russo-Turkish war of 1768-74 onwards, Russia had the upper hand over the Ottoman Empire, and one of the uses that she made of her superior power was to put strained interpretations, to her own advantage, on the texts of her treaties with the Ottoman Empire. The Ottoman Government, for its part, appears simply to have notified to the Russian Government its intention of sending Ottoman troops into the Principalities after Alexander Ypsilándês' invasion of them. It may perhaps be inferred that the Ottoman Government did not consider that it was under any contractual obligation to apply to the Russian Government for permission.

[304] See Finlay, op. cit., vol. vi, pp. 116-38; Bótzaris, op. cit., pp. 133-66.

[305] French translation of this petition in ibid., pp. 217-21.

Miloš Obrenović did not stir.[306] Tsar Alexander I disowned Ypsilándês, dismissed him from his service, and agreed to the Porte's sending troops into the Principalities.[307] The Porte promptly assembled an army which annihilated the force that Ypsilándês had raised from among the local Greeks. Ypsilándês himself escaped ingloriously into Austrian territory and was interned there.

Ypsilándês fiasco in 1821 ought to have given the 'Great Idea' its quietus, yet it revived a century later, after the Ottoman Empire had doomed itself to destruction by intervening in the First World War on the side of the Central Powers. This time the chaser of the will-o'-the-wisp was Elefthérios Venizélos, a much greater man than Alexander Ypsilándês, and the consequences for the Greek people were far more serious. In 1915, the issue between intervention on the side of the Allies and non-belligerency in favour of the Central Powers split the Greek people into two factions whose hostility to each other became bitter. In the Graeco-Turkish war of 1919–22, Greek forces came within closer range of Constantinople than at any date since the Greeks' loss of the City in 1453, but the outcome in 1922 was the greatest military disaster that Modern Greece has suffered since the winning of her independence.

In 1915, John Metaxás, who was at that date acting chief of the Greek General Staff, had given warning that a Greek invasion of the mainland of Asiatic Turkey was bound to have a disastrous ending.[308] In 1922 his forecast was proved to have been correct. On the mainland of Asia Minor, in contrast to the offshore islands and to the southern extremity of the Balkan Peninsula, the Greeks were nowhere in a majority. They were only a diaspora, though a numerous one in the aggregate. Nor, in the hinterland of the west coast of Asia Minor, was there any 'natural frontier', in the shape of a river line or a mountain range, which the Greek army could reach and hold. In committing Greek troops to the Asian mainland in 1919, Venizélos made the fatal military error (against which Metaxás had given warning in 1915) of launching out into boundless space.

The Greek military disaster of 1922 was, for Greece, a blessing in

---

[306] Neither Miloš himself nor his Serb compatriots were willing to jeopardize the autonomy that Serbia had already won through an insurrection that the Serbs had started in 1804—that is to say, seventeen years before the date at which Alexander Ypsilándês crossed the Pruth and Petrobey Mavromikhálês made his sortie from the Máni. The recognition of Serbia's autonomy was obtained by stages, with Russia's aid. The boundaries of the autonomous Serbian principality were agreed by the Ottoman Government in 1833, the year after the date of the fixing of the original frontiers of the sovereign independent kingdom of Greece. The Ottoman garrisons were not withdrawn from the fortresses in Serbia till 1862–7. Serbia did not become a sovereign independent state till 1878.

[307] See Prokesch-Osten, A., Freiherr von, *Geschichte des Abfalls der Griechen*, vol. iii (Vienna 1853), pp. 59 and 76. Tsar Alexander I declared his consent on 7 March 1821. A protocol to this effect was drawn up on 12 March 1821.

[308] Campbell and Sherrard, op. cit., p. 118.

disguise, though it was a tragedy for the Greek diaspora in Asia Minor. If Greece had been able to dictate to Turkey peace-terms that would have left Greece in possession of a beach-head round Smyrna, Greece would have condemned herself thereby to having to hold down a hostile Turkish population which would have been divided from its free compatriots only by an artificial frontier that would have been difficult for the Greek Army to defend. For Greece, this position would not have been permanently tenable. The disaster that overtook the Greek Army in Asia Minor in 1922 would have been bound to overtake it sooner or later; and, the longer that the inevitable *dénouement* was staved off, the more damagingly Greece would have exhausted herself by persisting in an endeavour that was beyond her strength.

The 'Great Idea' was exorcized definitively by the Greek military disaster of 1922, by the mass exodus of the Greek diaspora from Asia Minor, by the retrospective regulation and ratification of this accomplished fact,[309] and, perhaps not least, by the metamorphosis of the remnant of the Ottoman Empire into the Republic of Turkey—a substantially homogeneous national state of the same post-revolutionary French type as the Greek national state that had been created in 1821–9.

For the Greeks, it was painful to have at last to face the truth that the City of Constantinople was never going to pass back into Greek hands, in spite of the confident prophecies that had been current in folk-songs and folk-tales since the Greeks' loss of the City in 1453. Yet a dispassionate examination of Constantinople's role in the Greek people's history suggests that the Greeks' failure to regain the City was not the loss of a treasure, but was a relief from an incubus.

Constantinople had been one of the legacies of the compulsory political unification of the Hellenic Greeks by the Romans after the Hellenes' persistent failure to achieve this unification voluntarily for themselves. The City had been founded by a non-Greek Roman Emperor for Roman Imperial purposes, and, when subsequently the East Roman Empire had been taken over by the Byzantine Greeks, the Imperial capital had been a burden to them. Its maintenance had become too heavy a tax on the Empire's resources after these had been drastically reduced by the loss, in the seventh century, of the productive provinces to the south of the Távros Range. It is significant that, after the temporary loss of Constantinople by the Greeks to the Western 'Crusaders' in 1204, the Empire's refugee Greek successor-state whose provisional capital was Níkaia prospered, but that this Greek state fell into adversity again after its recapture of Constantinople in 1261.[310] Part

---

[309] See Boulter, V. M., in *Survey of International Affairs, 1925*, vol. ii (London 1928), pp. 257–99.

[310] Professor Robert Browning has drawn my attention to a passage in George Pakhymérês' *History* (Bonn 1835, 2 vols., vol. ii, p. 149), in which Pakhymérês has recorded that Michael

of the price that it paid for this apparent triumph was the loss of its territory in the north-western quarter of Asia Minor; a portion of this ex-Greek territory became the nucleus of the Ottoman Turkish Empire. The two centuries between 1261 and 1453 were the most melancholy period of the Byzantine Greeks' political history.

During this period the one relatively prosperous part of the re-established Greek East Roman Empire's constantly dwindling dominions was the Pelopónnêsos. This was geographically the most remote from Constantinople of all the surviving fragments of Imperial territory, and, from 1348 onwards, it was administered as an autonomous appanage of the Empire, governed by despots who were junior members of the Imperial House. This autonomous Pelopónnêsos was the only quarter in which the declining Empire gained territory instead of losing it. The progressive Greek reconquest of the Pelopónnêsos from the French had been completed in 1432, and the inevitable Ottoman conquest was delayed here till 1460, seven years after the Ottoman capture of Constantinople.

These historical facts were more veracious auguries of the future than the prophecies that had been the Greeks' emotional response to the unacceptable loss of the Imperial City. The history of the Pelopónnêsos from 1348 to 1460 portended the eventual defeat of the 'Great Idea' by the incompatible 'Ideas of the French Revolution'.

3. *The inevitability of the National State*[311]

The last three surviving shreds of politically independent Greek territory—Constantinople, the Pelopónnêsos, and Trebizond—were conquered respectively in 1453, 1460, and 1461 by the 'Osmanlis. Some Greeks in the generation that lived to see this completion of the extinction of Byzantine Greek independence were moved to console themselves for their tragic experience by prophesying that one day the Ayía Sophía would once again be a Christian church and that the Greeks would once again rule, from Constantinople, a resuscitated East Roman Empire. In the preceding section of this chapter, an account has been given of the eventual miscarriage of this Greek 'Great Idea' which had been kept alive under Ottoman rule in folk-poetry and folk-tales and had captivated the imaginations of Westernized Greek intellectuals: Rhêghas, Alexander Ypsilándès, Elealthérios Venizélos. In the generation that had lived through the events of 1453–61, one of the last of the Byzantine Greek men of letters, the Athenian Laónikos Khalkokondýlês, prophesied a different and more modest future for the Greek people.

Senakherim, an ex-professor of rhetoric and poetry who had become the Emperor Michael VIII Palaiológhos' chief minister, prophesied that the reoccupation of Constantinople in 1261 by the Nicene Greek Government would turn out to be an unmitigated disaster.

[311] See Dakin, D., *The Unification of Greece 1770–1923* (London 1972).

καὶ κλέος μέν αὐτῇ [τῇ τῶν Ἑλλήνων φωνῇ] μέγα τὸ παραυτίκα, μεῖζον δὲ καὶ εἰσαῦθις, ὁπότε δὴ ἀνὰ βασίλειον οὐ φαύλην Ἕλλην γε αὐτὸς βασιλεὺς καὶ ἐξ αὐτοῦ ἐσόμενοι βασιλεῖς, οἳ δὴ καὶ οἱ τῶν Ἑλλήνων παῖδες ξυλλεγόμενοι κατὰ σφῶν αὐτῶν ἔθιμα ὡς ἥδιστα μὲν σφίσιν αὐτοῖς, τοῖς δὲ ἄλλοις ὡς κράτιστα πολιτεύοιντο.[312]

In contrast to the fallacious 'Great Idea', Khalkokondýlês' prophecy was substantially fulfilled in the course of the century and a quarter 1821–1945. By the year 1974, all Greeks except two dwindling Greek communities in Istanbul and Alexandria and a local Greek majority in the population of Cyprus had become citizens of a Greek national state, and they had all come to be domiciled within this state's frontiers, save for Greek citizens who were temporarily resident abroad on private or public business or who had become naturalized citizens of foreign countries to which they had emigrated. The only point in Khalkokon- dýlês' prophecy that was disputable in 1974—that is to say, about 500 years after the date at which his prophecy was made—was his optimism about the Greek way of life under the future dispensation. All the rest of his prophecy had come true. He had, in fact, foreseen the kind of state that has been engendered, in Greece and elsewhere, by 'the Ideas of the French Revolution'.

Khalkokondýlês' foresight is remarkable, considering that he had lived to see the extinction of Byzantine Greek independence, and that his own Greek home town, Athens, had been under alien rule since 1204. The same gift of discernment that Khalkokondýlês displayed as a futurologist was displayed by him as an historian. Though he was a Byzantine Greek, writing in an affected imitation of the Attic *koine*, he made the rise of the Ottoman Turkish Empire his theme,[313] and this was in truth the major historical development in the Levant during the period which he had set himself to record in detail. His objective view and lucid understanding of the history of his own time gave him insight into the future. In describing the downfall of the East Roman Empire and the creation of its Ottoman successor on its ruins, he was illustrating the mutability of affairs. A clear-sighted historian of this reversal of fortunes could foresee that the Ottoman Empire would fall in its turn, but Khalkokondýlês did not fall into his more simple-minded Greek contemporaries' mistake of imagining that the sequel would be a

---

[312] Laónikos Khalkokondýlês, Ἀπόδειξις Ἱστοριῶν, ed. I. Bekker (Bonn 1843), Book I, chapter 1, pp. 4–5. 'The Greek language is famous today and will be more famous in the future. This future time will see an empire [or a kingdom] of no mean stature being ruled by an emperor [or king] and by his imperial [or his royal] descendants who will be Hellenes. These [Hellenic sovereigns] and the children of the Hellenes will be gathered together by themselves. They will have a state of their own in which their way of life will be congenial to them and admirable in the eyes of others.'

[313] Ibid., p. 9. See above, pp. 130–1.

restoration of the Byzantine Greek past. He foresaw for the Greeks the post-Ottoman future that was actually in store for them.

The 'ingathering'[314] of the Greek people within the frontiers of a Greek national state has been accomplished in seven stages, spread over a century and a quarter. The price of four stages out of the seven had been war: the Greek War of Independence (1821–9); the Balkan Wars (1912–13); the Graeco-Turkish War in Asia Minor (1919–22); the Second World War (1939–45). The first and the third of these wars inflicted cruel losses on the population of the war-zone, in which Greeks and Turks had been living intermingled with each other geographically until they were sorted out by the massacres and evictions for which the hostilities gave occasion. The only territories that Greece has gained without bloodshed are the Ionian Islands in 1864; Thessaly, together with a slice of Êpeiros, in 1881; and the Dodecanese in 1945.

In 1821 the Greeks—and, with them, their Albanian and Vlakh co-religionists—revolted in almost all those parts of the Ottoman Empire in which they were in a majority at that date: that is to say, in the Empire's continental European dominions as far to the north-east as the Khalkidhikê peninsula inclusive, and in many of the Aegean islands. The exception was Êpeiros, where the Greeks and the Orthodox Christian Albanians, though they were in a majority, were unable to rise because a powerful Ottoman army was already concentrated there against 'Alī Paşa of Yánnina. In 1821–2 the 'Osmanlis succeeded in resubjugating the Greek insurgents in all continental European Ottoman territories to the north of the Pelopónnêsos except for Trikéri and Mesolónghi. Trikéri fell in 1823 and Mesolónghi in 1826, but in 1822 the 'Osmanlis failed to reconquer the Pelopónnêsos. The cause of this failure was the Greeks' ascendancy at sea over the Ottoman Navy. This forced the 'Osmanlis to confine their attack on the Pelopónnêsos to an overland expedition from the north, and the 'Osmanlis' base of operations in resubjugated territory was too distant to allow of their resubduing the whole of the Pelopónnêsos too within a single campaigning season.[315]

The 'Osmanlis' military failure in 1822 was politically important. It preserved the *de facto* independence that had been won in 1821 by the Ottoman Greeks within the limits of the Pelopónnêsos and the Kykládhes Islands, and this military success of the Greek insurgents confirmed a radical change in the Western attitude towards the Modern Greeks. Western devotees of an idealized Hellenic past who hitherto had

---

[314] Khalkokondýlês' word ξυλλεγόμενοι aptly forecasts the process by which the Greek people has come, since 1821, to be concentrated as a compact homogeneous population in a national territory of its own.

[315] For this strategic point, see Campbell and Sherrard, op. cit., p. 66.

pitied, despised, and patronized the Modern Greeks as degenerate descendants of glorious ancestors now saw in the insurrection an heroic act which had demonstrated that the Modern Greeks were worthy of their Hellenic forebears after all. Liberal Westerners also saw the insurrection as a political event of ecumenical importance. For them it was the first revolt against the post-Napoleonic restoration of the *ancien régime*, and the sponsors of this restoration shared the Liberals' view. The Western Liberals' philhellenism and the Western Governments' fellow-feeling for the Ottoman Pādishāh were complementary, though antithetical, aspects of the Western reaction, and the pro-Greek sentiment that had now been kindled in the Western World and in Russia was strong enough to move the Christian powers, notwithstanding their governments' current concern for the principle of 'legitimacy', to save the Greeks' precarious *de facto* independence from being extinguished.

When Sultan Mahmūd II purchased the aid of his vassal Mehmet 'Alī, the viceroy of Egypt, Greek independence would not have survived if Russia, France, and Britain had not intervened. Kásos and Psará was overwhelmed in 1824, and in 1825 Mehmet 'Alī's son Ibrahim, landing at Módhon at the south-west corner of the Pelopónnêsos, reconquered almost the whole of the Pelopónnêsos with his Western-trained regular troops. It was the three foreign powers, not the Greeks, who compelled Ibrahim to evacuate the Pelopónnêsos; these powers decreed that Greece was to become a juridically sovereign independent state; and it was they that drew, in 1832, this state's original frontiers. The original land-frontier on the European mainland ran, west and east, from the Gulf of Preveza to the Gulf of Vólos. The Kykládhes, but not Crete and not the Greek islands off the West coast of Asia Minor, were also included in the new Greek state.

In the Greek War of Independence, both the Muslim and the Christian population suffered severely. No Muslims, either Turkish or Albanian, survived within the frontiers eventually assigned to an independent Greece. Here the Muslim minority was massacred, evicted, or rescued by the armed forces of Western Christian powers. Outside these limits, Nyáousta (Náoussa) in western Macedonia and Khíos, as well as Kásos and Psará, were punished savagely for having revolted, and, on the Asian mainland, the Greek communities at Smyrna and Ayvalik, which had not revolted, were harshly treated nevertheless. In 1821 Sultan Mahmūd II put to death the Ecumenical Patriarch Gregory V, the Dragoman of the Porte, and other Ottoman Greek notables in reprisal for the massacres of Muslims in the Pelopónnêsos. But Mahmūd soon called a halt to unauthorized attacks by his Muslim subjects on his Christian subjects, and the great majority of these survived the Greek

War of Independence under Ottoman rule without losing their lives, property, and means of livelihood.

It has been estimated that in 1832 there were still about 2,500,000 Greeks in Turkey, as against only about 800,000 in the newly established Kingdom of Greece.[316] The Greeks who had been evacuated from Ayvalik were allowed to return to their home, and Ayvalik remained a Greek community until the wholesale exodus of the Asian Greeks in 1922. On the other hand, few Ottoman Greeks whose homes lay outside the frontiers of the new kingdom migrated to Greece.[317] Istanbul, Smyrna (Izmir), and Thessaloníkê continued to be the chief centres of Greek commercial activity—Istanbul till as late as the close of the nineteenth century.[318] A majority of the Greek people did not come to be included in the Kingdom till 1913, after the successive acquisitions of the Ionian Islands, Thessaly, and, in the Balkan Wars, Crete, Mytilênê, Khíos, Êpeiros, and southern Macedonia.

From 1832 to 1912, Greece was a nationally homogeneous state, if its Eastern Orthodox Christian Albanian and Vlakh citizens are reckoned, as they should be reckoned, as being Greeks in virtue of their feeling themselves to be Greeks, in spite of their non-Greek mother tongues.[319] The Turkish minority in the territory that had been acquired by Greece, without war, in 1881, was neither massacred nor evicted and dispossessed, but it numbered only about 6,000 persons. On the other hand, the further continental European territories that Greece acquired by conquest in 1912–13 contained 370,000 Turks and 104,000 Bulgars, and from 1913 to 1922 the non-Greek minority in Greece amounted to 13 per cent of the total population. In 1913, the Greeks amounted to only 42 per cent of the population in the part of Macedonia that had been annexed to Greece in that year.[320] If, in the Graeco-Turkish war of 1919–22, Greece had succeeded in acquiring a beach-head round Smyrna and also Eastern Thrace, in addition to Western Thrace, which was ceded to her by Bulgaria in the Peace Treaty of Neuilly (27 November 1919), Greece would have become a replica of the multi-national Ottoman Empire whose liquidation had been completed by the course of the First World War and in the subsequent peace-settlement.

---

[316] See Campbell and Sherrard, op. cit., p. 93. Cp. ibid., p. 79.

[317] One notable migrant was John Koléttês, a Vlakh (his surname is Romance) from the Métsovo district in the Pindus Range. Koléttês had been physician to ʿAlī Paşa of Yánnina. He became Prime Minister of Greece after the inauguration of a constitutional regime in 1843.

[318] Campbell and Sherrard, op. cit., p. 93.

[319] Their readiness to throw in their lot with the Greeks contrasts with the aloofness and hostility of other non-Greek members of the *Rum milleti*: for instance, the Vlakhs' Roumanian kinsmen in the Transdanubian Principalities and the Slavonic-speaking Serbs and Bulgars. The Roman Catholic Christian and the Muslim Albanians naturally did not share the Eastern Orthodox Christian Albanians' feeling of national solidarity with the Greeks.

[320] For these figures, see Campbell and Sherrard, op. cit., p. 143.

Actually, the exoduses of the Asian and East-Thracian Greek diaspora in 1922 and of the Bulgarian Greek diaspora in and after 1920, and the corresponding exoduses of Turks and Bulgars from Greece, together with the exchange of populations between Turkey and Bulgaria, reconverted Greece into a nationally homogeneous state, and turned Turkey and Bulgaria into states of the same kind.[321] The Greek element had risen, in the population of Greek Macedonia, from 42 per cent to 88.8 per cent by 1926, and, in the population of Western Thrace, from 17 per cent to 62.1 per cent by 1924. The Bulgarian minority in Greece had been reduced to 80,000.[322] The size of the non-Greek minority in Greece was not increased appreciably in absolute numbers, and was diminished in relative numbers, by the acquisition of the Dodecanese in 1945, since the small Turkish community in Rhodes was greatly outnumbered by the Greek majority in the population of this group of islands.

Thus, between 1821 and 1945, the Modern Greeks had built for themselves a Greek state that had gathered together within its frontiers almost all the Greeks in the world and had left scarcely any non-Greeks within these frontiers. This unitary homogeneous Greek national state was constructed on the Modern Western pattern. 'Enlightened Europe' (ἡ φωτισμένη Εὐρώπη)[323] was, for Adhamándios Koraês (1748–1833), the model that the emancipated Modern Greeks ought to copy in all things, including their political institutions.

In a letter[324] to the Greek delegation that was negotiating for the loan raised by the Greek insurgents in London in 1824, Koraês holds up Washington, Franklin, and Jefferson, side by side with Aristeides and Phokiôn, as examples of political integrity; cites a saying of Franklin's, 'one of the celebrated founders of the liberty of the Americans, which is the only true liberty'; and exhorts the Greek delegates, while in England, to seek advice from Bentham. In a letter of 4 July 1823, to Prince Alexander Mavrokordháto,[325] apropos of the Greek constitution of 13 January 1822 and the desirability of improving it, he adjures Mavrokordháto to act as if he were in the invisible presence of 'our ancestors the pioneers of liberty and civilization', or, alternatively, as if he were under the eyes of 'the healthy part of Europe and of the whole of the felicitous American nation', and he counsels Mavrokordháto to

---

[321] For these exchanges of populations see further V. M. Boulter in *Survey of International Affairs 1925*, vol. ii, pp. 257–66 and 288–99.

[322] Figures in Campbell and Sherrard, loc. cit. Cp. V. M. Boulter in loc. cit., p. 279.

[323] See Koraês' letter of 8 November 1810 to the Khiot community in Smyrna in Ἀπάνθισμα ἐπιστολῶν Ἀδαμαντίου Κοραῆ (Athens 1839), p. 30, and his letter to Odhysséfs of 17 June 1824, in ibid., p. 15. Koraês' 'Enlightened Europe' did not include the Ottoman Empire's geographically European dominions and successor-states.

[324] In ibid., pp. 20–5.

[325] In ibid., pp. 254–9.

persuade the Greeks to adopt the American Constitution as their first choice.

Manifestly, for Koraês, 'Modern Western Enlightenment' and 'Classical Greek Hellenism' were interchangeable terms. By 're-Hellenization' he meant 'Westernization'. The 'enlightenment' of Europe was admirable in his eyes because he saw it as a derivative light emanating from an original Hellenic Greek source. Koraês had no use for the East Roman Empire[326] or for the Eastern Orthodox Church or for the Phanariots,[327] and his blueprint, not Rhêghas', for the structure of the post-Ottoman Greek state has proved to have been 'the wave of the future'. Yet Rhêghas' project, impracticable though it was in the Modern Age, bore some resemblance to the historic structure of the East Roman Empire during the century ending in 1180, whereas Koraês' programme, which has eventually been translated into an accomplished fact, had no precedent in either the Byzantine or the Hellenic Age of Greek history.

The Hellenic Greek World had been, on the political plane, a galaxy of sovereign independent city-states. These had never succeeded in uniting with each other voluntarily into a single Greek state. A majority of them had at last been united forcibly by a non-Greek power, Rome. But the Roman Empire had never included all the Greeks. The colonial Greek city-states to the east of the Euphrates had remained outside the Empire's bounds, while on the other hand the Greeks within those bounds had been brigaded with many non-Greek peoples under Roman rule. It is true that when, in the sixth century, the Greek language had completed its gradual replacement of the pre-Greek languages of Asia Minor, and when, in the seventh century, the Arabs had detached from the Empire all its former dominions to the south of the Távros Range, the domains of the East Roman Empire and of the Greek language had come to coincide approximately. But this coincidence was accidental. The Byzantine Greeks thought of themselves as being Romans, not Hellenes, and, from 1018 till 1180, the East Roman Empire once again included numerous non-Greek-speaking subjects and vassals.

Thus the unitary homogeneous Greek national state that was built up between 1831 and 1945 had no true precedents in previous stages of Greek history. Nor had it any roots in Modern Greek life. The Modern Greek people's indigenous institutions were the Eastern Orthodox Church, the village community, and the family. None of these could provide an infrastructure for a state of the Modern Western pattern in any of this pattern's nineteenth-century variations to which Koraês had given his blessing.

---

[326] Letters of 10 January 1822, in ibid., p. 4, and of 12 October 1822, ibid., pp. 46-7.

[327] Letter of 4 July 1823, to the Phanariot Prince Alexander Mavrokordháto, ibid., p. 254: 'Can any good thing come out of Nazareth?'

One of the first acts of the new Greek national state was to assert the independence of the Orthodox Church within the new state's frontiers. The insurrection of 1821 had automatically severed, *de facto*, the relations between the Ecumenical Patriarchate and the hierarchy and clergy within the area that the insurgents controlled. Kapodistrias rejected overtures for the re-establishment of these historical relations which were made to him by the Patriarch when, in 1828, he became President of the new Greek state. In 1833 the Bavarian Regency that, by then, was governing Greece on King Otto's behalf declared the independence of the Orthodox Church within the Kingdom's frontiers; set up a separate ecclesiastical synod for the Kingdom; and remapped the episcopal sees to correspond with the new map of secular administrative districts. The Ecumenical Patriarchate recognized in 1850 the independence of the Church in the Kingdom of Greece.[328]

The creation of a national church of Greece was perhaps a necessary corollary of the Kingdom's achievement of political independence. The Ecumenical Patriarch was an officer of the Ottoman Imperial Government in his role as head of the *Rum milleti*, and therefore the re-establishment of his ecclesiastical jurisdiction over Greece would have carried with it the re-establishment of Ottoman political sovereignty in an indirect form. Even under the pre-Ottoman East Roman Imperial regime, under which the Ecumenical Patriarch had not been an Imperial official juridically, he had been virtually an official in fact, and this fact had been a stumbling-block in the relations between the Empire and Bulgaria after the conversion of Bulgaria to Christianity in 864.

Moreover, there were precedents for the carving of separate autocephalous churches out of the Ecumenical Patriarchate's domain. The creation of a national synod for Greece entailed only a small reduction of the Ecumenical Patriarchate's domain by comparison with the effect of the creation, in 1589, of an autocephalous Patriarchate of Moscow. The Eastern Orthodox Churches had always stood for the principle of autocephaly. They had never more than momentarily accepted the Papacy's claim to supremacy, and no counter-claim to supremacy had ever been made by the Ecumenical Patriarchate or by any of the Churches, outside its ecclesiastical jurisdiction, with which this Patriarchate was in communion. The new feature in the secession of the Eastern Orthodox Church in Greece from the Ecumenical Patriarchate was that, this time, it was not a Slavonic-speaking or a Roumanian-speaking but a Greek-speaking portion of the Ecumenical Patriarch's flock that was parting company with him.

[328] See Finlay, op. cit., vol. vii, pp. 126–30; Campbell and Sherrard, op. cit., pp. 86, 193, 196; and the present work, p. 110.

For the Eastern Orthodox Church in Greece, autocephaly has meant, not emancipation, but a change of masters. Here the political control of the Church has been transferred from an Islamic Ottoman government to a Greek government of the post-Christian Western type.[329] The intellectual climate in a Westernizing Greece has also been inimical to monasticism,[330] which is one of the key institutions of Eastern Orthodox Christianity. Yet today Greece is the solitary surviving officially Eastern Orthodox Christian country,[331] and the military junta that seized power on 21 April 1967 made much of this official fact.

The second indigenous Modern Greek institution with which the national state has contended is local autonomy and its concomitant, local oligarchy.[332] If allegiance to the Ecumenical Patriarchate was incompatible with the new Greek national state's sovereignty, it is equally true that this state's unity and indivisibility could not be reconciled with a local autonomy which put political power in the hands of local notables. The supremacy of the Central Government is one of the fundamental principles of the Modern Western national state. It is the rule even in Britain and in countries that have derived their constitutions from her, where centralization has not been carried to extremes. *A fortiori*, the Central Government's supremacy is a common feature of the French Revolutionary regime and of all the manifold variations on it, in France and abroad, that have been tried since the outbreak of the French Revolution. Kapodistrias, who was President of Greece for nearly three years before his assassination in October 1831, was a Corfiot Greek who had been born under the authoritarian Venetian regime and had been in the Russian Imperial Government's service. Both he and his Bavarian successors were imbued with the ultra-authoritarian spirit of the temporarily rehabilitated Western *ancien régime*; but the campaign for the assertion of the Central Government's power has also been carried on in Greece by all subsequent regimes of all complexions. They have all sought to wrest local government out of the local notables' hands and to transfer it to nominees and agents of the Central Government itself.

Consequently, sovereign independence in the Modern Western style has not given the Greeks a government that is of, by, and for the people. The Greeks still see in the government of their country, whatever its complexion, not an instrument for the execution of their collective national will, but an imposed authority: τὸ κράτος ('the power'). This relation between the people and the government is nothing new for the

[329] See Campbell and Sherrard, op. cit., pp. 9 and 356.
[330] Ibid., pp. 208 and 357.
[331] Ibid., p. 189.
[332] See Finlay, op. cit., vol. vii, pp. 40–1 and 119–21; Campbell and Sherrard, op. cit., pp. 83–5.

Greeks. They have felt aloof from their government ever since the turn of the third and fourth centuries, when the Roman Empire was converted into a bureaucratically administered centralized state. But this long familiarity has schooled the Greeks in the art of resistance. A Greek Central Government's attempts to impose its authority are countered by the solidarity of the Greek family; for the family is not only the basic Greek social unit; it is also the basic unit of Greek economic activity, and this not only in agriculture and animal husbandry but also in commerce and industry. Moreover, these family units are knit together by a network of individual relations between patrons and their clients.

Regimes in Greece that have ignored these fundamental realities of Greek life, or that have set out to override them, have ended in having to recognize them and to conform to them.[333] Under a top-dressing of various regimes in the Modern Western style, the pre-Western Greek way of life has lived on with a vitality and a tenacity that have defeated the most determined attempts to reshape it to the exotic Western pattern. This has been the experience of all Western-style regimes in Greece since the inauguration of President Kapodistrias in 1828, and the political history of the Greek state has to be viewed in this light. The ethnic unity and homogeneity that Greece has achieved has not been matched by a corresponding unification and homogenization on the social and political planes.

In the Modern Western World, where the centralized national state, which the Greeks have sought to copy, is indigenous, the system of government has passed through three phases: absolute monarchy has been followed by parliamentarism, and parliamentarism by the dictatorial rule of a junta of professional military officers. This was the series of regimes in seventeenth-century England, and the cycle recurred in eighteenth-century France.

England was exceptional in managing, after the brief taste of military rule (1655–60), to revert to parliamentary government and to make this system work well enough thenceforward—down to the present day at any rate—to preclude relapses into any form of arbitrary rule. This is, no doubt, what Koraês had in mind when he called the English 'the first founders and fathers of modern liberty', and when he put them on a par with 'the first fathers of ancient liberty',[334] that is to say, the Hellenic Greeks. The parliamentary element in the constitution of the United States was likewise, no doubt, the feature of it that led Koraês to commend it, above all others, to Prince Alexander Mavrokordháto in 1823.[335] However, the recovery of political stability, on a parliamentary

---

[333] See, for example, ibid., pp. 102, 113, 116, 117, 349–51.
[334] Ἀπάνθισμα, ed. cit., p. 24.
[335] Ibid., p. 255.

basis, after a state has passed through the typical series of Modern Western political regimes, has been exceptional in the West itself, and it is not surprising that it should have been rare in non-Western countries in which the attempt has been made to graft Western political institutions on to native political realities that are allergic to innovations of alien origin.

Parliamentary government is a peculiar political product of British history; and, outside Britain herself and the overseas Western countries of British origin, a successful acclimatization of parliamentarism has been rare. In most cases, experiments in this form of government have been followed, as in seventeenth-century Britain, by military regimes, and, if these have provoked a return to parliamentarism, this return has usually been short-lived. Since 1917, countries in which parliamentarism has failed to work have had a choice between three arbitrary authoritarian regimes, namely military government and Fascism and Communism. The feature that professional armies and Fascist or Communist parties have in common is a rigorous discipline which looks like a promising antidote to a parliamentary government that has proved to be incompetent or corrupt.

The history of Greece since the inauguration of President Kapodistrias in 1828 has followed the course that has been common in countries in which parliamentarism has not been indigenous. Since 1828 there have been two spells of more or less successful parliamentary government in Greece: the first in 1882–95 under the auspices of Kharílaos Trikoúpês, and the second—a shorter but more brilliant spell—in 1910–15 under the auspices of Elefthérios Venizélos. The second spell of successful parliamentary government in Greece might perhaps have lasted longer if the Western Powers had not stumbled into the First World War and if the Ottoman Empire had not then wantonly intervened in it. In 1915 the Greeks in Greece split into two factions over a question of foreign policy; the issue between intervention in the war on the side of the Allies and non-belligerency in favour of the Central Powers.

The schism over this momentous issue disrupted Greek political life, and Greece has not yet recovered from this traumatic experience. The first of the military pronunciamentos by professional officers of the Greek armed forces had been made in 1909. In this instance, the military junta called in Venizélos to re-establish a viable civilian government on a parliamentary basis; but, since 1915, Greece has oscillated between parliamentary government and military government. The Italian and German military occupation in the Second World War would have been succeeded in Greece, as it has actually been succeeded in Jugoslavia, by a Communist regime, if Britain had not intervened militarily on the anti-Communist side in the ensuing civil war in Greece, and if this

British military intervention had not been followed up by American economic aid.

Politics has not been one of the fields in which the Greeks have been successful since their recovery of their political independence. Yet τὸ κράτος—the exotic Western-style national government that the Modern Greeks have imposed on themselves in a variety of typically Western forms—has at least three major achievements to its credit. One achievement is the Greek people's heroic resistance to its 'Osmanli rulers in the War of Independence (1821-9) and to the Italian and German invaders in the Second World War (1940-4). The second great achievement of the Modern Greek state has been the division of the land among the peasantry. The third great achievement, which has a close connection with the second, has been the settlement of the Greek refugees from Asia Minor and Eastern Thrace after the Greek Army's disaster in 1922.

Each of the two heroic resistance movements was a *tour de force*. On each occasion, rival factions of Greek freedom-fighters fought each other with one hand while they were fighting their foreign oppressors with the other hand. The results of the division of the land have also been paradoxical. The division has been a response to the demands of the peasantry, who are still a majority of the population; and the social effect has been beneficial; but the price of social justice has been the creation of economic problems. The settlement of the refugees is the finest of all the achievements of the Greek people since 1821. The credit is shared by the League of Nations commissions for the exchange of populations and for the settlement of the Greek refugees in Greece, by the non-Greek subscribers of the loans by which the resettlement was financed, and by the Greek government. But the Greek people itself is the true hero. The refugees' endurance and resilience were magnificent. The accommodatingness of the previously established population was admirable.

It has been noted already that in 1821, at the outbreak of the War of Independence, five-sixths of the Greek peasants owned no land.[336] By 1860, a majority of the peasants in the Kingdom within its original frontiers had become owners of holdings averaging something between 10 and 15 acres in size.[337] The redistribution of the ownership of land continued during the next two decades, and the acquisition of Thessaly by the Kingdom of Greece in 1881 made the agrarian question acute; for Thessaly, which contains the largest single continuous area of lowlands in the whole of Greece, was in 1881 a country of large estates (*chiftliks*) owned by Turkish landlords who found it profitable to keep their land

---

[336] See above, p. 212.
[337] Campbell and Sherrard, op. cit., p. 92.

under grass, and to rent it to Vlakh transhumant shepherds as winter pasture for their flocks, instead of developing its potentialities for agriculture, particularly for the cultivation of wheat.[338] The expropriation of large estates was approved in principle by the National Assembly in 1911,[339] during the first period of Venizélos' administration. In 1917, after Venizélos had set up his 'provisional government' at Thessaloníkê in opposition to King Constantine's government at Athens, Venizélos' regime enacted drastic legislation for the expropriation of large estates, not only in Thessaly, but throughout the Kingdom.[340]

The agrarian history of the Kingdom of Greece during the century ending in 1922 shows that, at least on the issue of land-ownership (and this was the most important of all issues in the Kingdom's domestic politics), τὸ κράτος was not irresponsive to the needs and the demands of the rural majority of the population. However, even if the Greek government had been indifferent to Greece's agrarian problem, its hand would have been forced by the arrival in Greece, within its limits after the acquisition of Western Thrace, of at least 1,200,000 permanent refugees who had to be settled inside the Kingdom's frontiers.[341]

The main resource available for providing the refugees with a livelihood was cultivable land, since in Greece urban industry was, and still is, on a relatively small scale. About half of the land required was provided from the former property of evacuated Muslims who, under the arrangements for the exchange of populations, had ceded their property in Greece and had been compensated out of the property in Turkey that had been ceded by the Greek refugees.[342] The rest of the land required for the rural settlement of refugees was provided from state lands and by the expropriation of large private estates.[343] By 30 June 1926, 552,000 individual refugees had been settled in rural colonies— over 430,000 of them in 1,378 settlements in Macedonia.[344] By 1930, 145,758 refugee families had been settled on the land. The consequences were revolutionary. On the one hand, the area under cultivation in Greece increased by 55 per cent during the decade 1922–32. On the

---

[338] Campbell and Sherrard, op. cit., p. 97.

[339] Boulter, V. M., in *Survey of International Affairs 1925* vol. ii, p. 277 n. 2.

[340] See Campbell and Sherrard, op. cit., p. 145.

[341] For the settlement of the refugees in Greece, see ibid., pp. 138–44; Boulter in loc. cit., pp. 272–9; and the League of Nations document *Greek Refugee Settlement* (II Economic and Financial, 1926, ii, 32), of 1 September 1926, which carries the record down to 30 June 1926.

[342] The Muslim ex-inhabitants of Greece were the descendants of Turkish Muslim colonists or of ex-Christians who had become converts to Islam in order to retain the ownership of their land. Hence the average size of their land-holdings per head was much larger than that of the Christian ex-inhabitants of Turkey, though the number of the Muslim migrants from Greece to Turkey was much smaller: about 400,000 as against at least 1,200,000 permanent migrants to Greece (see Boulter in loc. cit., p. 259).

[343] Campbell and Sherrard, op. cit., p. 139.

[344] Boulter in loc. cit., p. 277.

other hand, by 1928 the cultivated area had been divided up into 953,000 farms, 90 per cent of which were only 12.5 acres or less in size.[345]

The increase in the cultivated area was made possible partly by the reclamation of potentially fertile marshes. The draining of Lake Kopaís, in Central Greece, had been put in hand as early as 1883.[346] During the settlement of the refugees after 1922, 300,000 acres were reclaimed from marshes in Macedonia.[347] By 1968 about 13 per cent of the cultivated area was irrigated,[348] and agricultural machinery was being used on a considerable scale in a zone extending from Attica north-eastwards to Macedonia, especially in the Thessalian and Macedonian plains.[349] The greater part of the land-surface of Greece is rocky and arid; it provides only marginally utilizable agricultural land or meagre grazing-grounds. The pockets of good soil are relatively few and small, but their fertility is high.[350] For Modern Greece, as for Hellenic Greece, it is profitable to use the rare good soil—especially the irrigated ex-marshlands[351]—for growing valuable cash-crops for export, and to buy from abroad part of the wheat-supply that the population requires.[352]

The main agricultural products exported from Hellenic Greece were oil and wine, and olive groves and vineyards still figure prominently in the country's rural landscape. But, since the Hellenic Age of Greek history, the olive has been propagated all round the shores of the western basin of the Mediterranean, and the vine as far to the west as the Atlantic and as far to the north as the Rhine. The most profitable export-crops of Modern Greece are currants, tobacco, and cotton, and the area under these crops is inevitably reduced by any increase in the area under wheat, because of the scarcity of soils capable of producing good yields of any crop.

Tobacco accounted for about 35 per cent of the total value of Greece's exports in the 1960s, cotton for 12 per cent in 1963, currants for 11 per cent in 1964.[353] Thus these three crops, between them, made a major

[345] Campbell and Sherrard, op. cit., p. 139.

[346] See Baedeker, K., *Greece*, 4th edn. (Leipzig 1909) English translation, pp. 183-4; Admiralty *Handbook of Greece* (First World War), pp. 19-20. At the time of my first visit to Greece, 1911-12, the Scottish engineers were still at work, and, though the lake bed was now dry, it had not yet been transformed into the irrigated garden that it is today.

[347] Boulter in loc. cit., p. 277 n. 1.

[348] Campbell and Sherrard, op. cit., p. 331.

[349] Ibid., p. 323. This mechanization of agriculture in these parts of Greece catches the eye even of a passing traveller.

[350] Ibid.

[351] e.g. in the lower basin of the Rivers Akhéron and Kokytós, as well as in Boeotia, Thessaly, and Macedonia.

[352] In 1957, Greece was self-sufficient in home-grown wheat; but 31 per cent of the cultivated area was under wheat in that year, and about 60 per cent in 1965, and this was costing twice as much as the world price for wheat (Campbell and Sherrard, op. cit., pp. 298, 323, 332).

[353] Ibid., pp. 325-6.

contribution to Greece's earnings of foreign exchange. At the same time, the profits from them, for the country's economy as a whole and for the individual farmer, were subject to the fluctuations of world prices,[354] and the farmers—still a majority of the population—could be tempted to support a government that subsidized them to grow, instead, wheat for home-consumption at a guaranteed price, above the world-price, at the expense of the urban Greek consumer.[355] The allocation of Greece's scanty supply of good soil between wheat and export-crops has thus become a political as well as an economic issue.

A maximum number of the refugees who arrived in Greece in 1922 was settled on the land by the joint efforts of the Greek government, the League of Nations Settlement Commission, and the refugees themselves. The number established as farmers in the refugees' new homes was greater than the number that had been farmers before the exodus. A majority of the refugees had been village shopkeepers and urban artisans and professional workers, and a majority had to be resettled, not on the land, but in towns[356]—above all, in and around Athens and the Peiraeus.

Before the War of Independence (1821-9), Athens had been the seat of the Ottoman governor of a minor province. It was made the capital of Greece in 1835, partly out of historical sentiment and partly because of its location towards the north of the Kingdom within the Kingdom's original frontiers.[357] Thessaloníkê, which is today the second largest city in Greece, is destined by Nature to be the Mediterranean port for a large part of the interior of the European continent. Its natural lines of communication with the interior are as good as those of Marseilles. By contrast, Modern Athens's only major industry has been to serve as the capital of a Greek national state. Greece's territorial expansion reached its limits in 1945 with the acquisition of the Dodecanese,[358] but her population has continued to expand, and Athens has become the receptacle for as much of this ever-growing population as is unable or unwilling to continue to live by agriculture or by animal husbandry and is also unwilling to seek a livelihood abroad.

The growth in the size of the population of Athens is an index of the progressive urbanization of Greece.[359] The pace has accelerated. In 1855 Athens still had only 20,000 inhabitants and 2,000 houses.[360] Its

[354] Campbell and Sherrard, op. cit., pp. 97 and 108-9.

[355] Ibid., p. 272.

[356] See Boulter in loc. cit., p. 276 n. 5.

[357] As a result of the successive extensions of Greece northwards and north-eastwards, Athens now lies to the south of the country's centre of gravity.

[358] In later years this dictum would have been contested by many Cypriot Greeks.

[359] See the four maps of Athens, showing its sizes at different dates, on p. 197, figs. 179-81, of Doxiadis, C. A., *Ekistics* (London 1968).

[360] Campbell and Sherrard, op. cit., p. 92.

population was 44,510 in 1870, 107,846 in 1889, 111,486 in 1896, 175,000 (including its outlying suburbs) in 1907,[361] 293,000 in 1920.[362] In 1920 the population of the Peiraeus was 133,000.[363] The steepness of the rise of the curve delineating the growth of Athens up to the date of the arrival of the refugees is striking, but, from that epoch-making date onwards, it is staggering. By 1961, the population of Greater Athens was 1,852,709,[364] and the combined population of Athens and Thessaloníkê was 2,226,000.[365] Between 1961 and 1971, the population of Greater Athens rose from 1,852,709 to 2,530,200.[366]

The most significant and most disconcerting feature of this acceleration of the rate of Athens's growth is that the pace did not slacken after the settlement of the urban refugees had been completed. The growth has been fed by subsequent immigration from the rural parts of Greece, and these migrants to Athens from the villages include people whose ancestors had lived in their ancestral village from generation to generation, since time immemorial. In the five years 1956–60, 250,000 people migrated from the Greek countryside to the towns, and Athens was the destination of 80 per cent of these.[367] During the ten years 1951–61, the net increase in the population of Athens through immigration was 330,861.

For an observer who has known Athens since 1911, the growth which that city has undergone is disconcerting. Greece is a country in which, till within living memory, Nature has been dominant over Man. Athens lies in a natural theatre, bounded by the sea and encircled by mountains: Ymêttós, Pendelikón, Párnês, Aigháleos. In 1911–12 there were still wide expanses of open country between the encircling mountains and the outermost fringes of the city. There was also still open country even between Athens and the Peiraeus, though the electric railway connecting the two cities had already been built. At the Peiraeus, only about half of the club-headed peninsula was yet covered with buildings. By 1974, Athens had engulfed the Peiraeus to the south-west and Maroúsi and Kêphisía to the north-east. The whole sea-front between the southern extremities of Mounts Ymêttós and Aigháleos had been built up, and the rising tide of streets and houses had not only reached the foot of all the surrounding mountains; it had surged up their slopes as far as the steepening gradient had allowed, and it had found its way through the gaps between them. Lió pesi to the east of Mount

---

[361] Baedeker's *Greece*, ed. cit., p. 17.
[362] Campbell and Sherrard, op. cit., p. 364.
[363] Ibid.
[364] Ibid., p. 365. This figure is given there as being for the year 1968.
[365] Ibid., p. 351.
[366] *ATO, ACE Newsletter*, vol. 8, no. 70 (April 1971), published by the Athens Center of Ekistics.
[367] Campbell and Sherrard, op. cit., p. 228.

Ymêttós, and Elefsís to the west of Mount Aigháleos, have now been trapped within Athens's built-up area.

Not content with bursting out of her mountain girdle, Athens—Greece's urban octopus—is reaching out to the frontiers of the state. In 1974 an autobahn already carried a tentacle of Athens as far as Lamía (Zeitoúni). This was destined to reach Thessaloníkê. It could be foreseen that a second autobahn would soon link Athens with Pátras, Aghrínion, Yánnina, and Êghoumenítsa. It was no longer fanciful to imagine the ferry between Rhíon and Andírrhion being replaced by a bridge spanning the mouth of the Gulf of Corinth. Comparable feats of bridge-building were already accomplished facts at San Francisco and at Sydney and astride the Bosphorus. The tentacles of Athens were threatening to clutch the whole of Greece in a throttling embrace.

This spectacle was disconcerting for two reasons: it exhibited the obliteration of Nature by Man, and at the same time it was an example of the social defeat that can be the nemesis of a technological victory. The growth of Athens's manufacturing industry had lagged behind the growth of her population. It is true that the refugees who, in 1922, had swollen Athens's population had brought with them some new industries: carpet-making, pottery manufacture, and the art of glazing tiles in the Kutahya style.[368] But these new sources of remunerative urban employment were utterly incommensurate with the number of additional Athenian mouths that now had to be fed.

Yet, in spite of the poorness of the prospects of employment in Athens, farmers from the countryside have been flocking into the city, in preference to retaining the rural properties that they had won in a political struggle that had lasted for a century. One motive for the massive internal migration has been economic. A plot of 12.5 acres no longer provides an acceptable standard of living, even for a farmer who has the good fortune to own fertile land, and who has had the good sense to plant it with a valuable cash-crop. However, the most potent motive has not been economic discontent; it has been psychological malaise.[369] Greek villagers who have migrated to Athens or to Germany or to the United States have put out of countenance their rural neighbours who have stayed behind. Rusticity has become a reproach, and the peasant has been lured into the city by a glamour which has concealed the gloominess of the outlook there for the migrant and his family.

The Modern Greeks are not peculiar in succumbing to the lure of urban life. All over the world, the expanding cities are being encircled today by an outer ring of shanty-towns, or by slums inserted in their hearts, next door to the luxury apartment-houses and hotels. The failure

[368] See Boulter in loc. cit., p. 279 with n. 2; Campbell and Sherrard, op. cit., p. 140.
[369] See ibid., p. 160.

of the 'Great Idea' has saved Greece from saddling herself again with the urban incubus of Constantinople. The success of the national state has imposed on her the urban incubus of Athens. And Athens threatens to be an even heavier burden for the Modern Greeks than Constantinople was for their Byzantine predecessors.

(iv) *The Greek Language's Vicissitudes in the Modern Age*

At each of the successive stages of the Greek people's history, the number of their heritages from the past has increased. Moreover, with the passage of time, these heritages have naturally become more and more alien. Yet their increasing irrelevance has not automatically diminished their prestige or caused them to lose their grip. In Greek history, the power exercised by heritages from the past has manifested itself strikingly in the field of language and literature. For two centuries, by now, Greek life has been plagued by a 'language question'. At times this has aroused acrimonious controversies; it has not yet been settled; and it has been a serious handicap for both education and literature. The modern 'language question' is the supreme example of the bewildering and inhibiting effect of the Greeks' heritages from the past on Greek life since as long ago as the latter part of the Hellenic Age.

The potency of the prestige of the 'classical' form of the Hellenic Greek language and literature revealed itself as early as the inauguration of the Augustan Peace, just before the beginning of the Christian Era. That age saw the initiation of a movement to revive the 'classical' Attic Greek of the fifth and fourth centuries B.C., as represented by the literary works of the great Attic Greek writers of that date. In the process of becoming the *lingua franca* (*koinê dhiálektos*) of an expanding Hellenic World, the Attic dialect of Hellenic Greek had changed. This had been natural and inevitable. All languages always tend to change, even when determined efforts are made to 'freeze' them. The Augustan neo-Atticists' objective was to remould the current *koine* into 'classical' Attic and to keep it 'frozen' in this form—the form in which, in their judgement, the language and literature had been at their acme. The neo-Atticists have never fully achieved their extravagant ambition,[370] but, as a result of their persistence, the Attic *koine*, in a form that has at least a recognizable affinity with 'classical' Attic, is today still the liturgical language of the Greek-speaking members of the Eastern Orthodox fraternity of Christian churches.

---

[370] According to Sextus Empiricus, *Contra Mathematicos*, section 1, paragraph 234, Atticists in the second century of the Christian Era spoke neo-Attic to each other and to the audiences at their lectures, but used the contemporary form of the *koine* in giving orders to their servants (see Bien, P., *Kazantzakis and the Linguistic Revolution in Greek Literature* (Princeton 1972), p. 16).

Neo-Atticism was an indication that the Greeks of the Augustan Age felt themselves inferior to their ancestors of the 'classical' Age of Hellenic Greek history. Under Roman rule they could not recapture the lost sovereign independence of their city-states, so they concentrated their efforts on trying to recapture their linguistic and cultural past, in the naïve hope that, if they succeeded in this, they would also recapture their ancestors' greatness and glory. Ever since the Augustan Age, successive generations of Greeks have clung to the illusion that a mastery of the 'classical' Hellenic language is a talisman that has the magical power of raising them to their ancestors' cultural and political stature.

This nostalgic cult of their linguistic heritage survived the turn for the better that the Greek people's fortunes took at the transition from the Hellenic to the Byzantine Age. The Greeks then repudiated the rest of their Hellenic past. They became proud of having become Christian Romans instead of having remained pagan Hellenes, but they continued to be devotees of the Hellenic Greek idiom and style; and their response to their subsequent six centuries of humiliation, from 1204 to 1821, was to reassume the name of 'Hellenes' and to treasure the Hellenic form of the Greek language. The modern form of Greek had become the Greek people's living language since at least as early as the sixth or seventh century. Yet, when, in the seventeenth and eighteenth centuries, the Ottoman Greeks renovated the Patriarchal Academy at Constantinople and supplemented it by founding new schools and academies, with contemporary Western philosophy and science now included in the curriculum, they still confined their teaching of Greek language and literature to Hellenic Greek, to the exclusion of the living form of the language.

In the early Modern Age, as in the Byzantine Age, Modern Greek was the language of everyday life. It was the language of folk-poetry and folk-tales throughout the Greek-speaking world. Greeks who had had an Hellenic education spoke their mother tongue, Modern Greek, not the *koine* that they read and wrote, and—in the diminishing number of Greek communities that were under Western, not Ottoman, rule—there were even educated Greeks who did not disdain to write sophisticated literature in their own living language. One reason for this was that, in the Western World's colonial dominions in the Levant, the native Greek upper class had been supplanted to a large extent by a Western French-speaking or Italian-speaking 'ascendancy', and the tradition of cultivating the *koine* had thus been broken locally. Another reason—which perhaps counted for more—was that the Western conquerors of these Greek lands had brought with them a literature in their own living languages; and their example inspired their Greek subjects to overcome their age-old inhibition against writing in the language that they spoke.

A sophisticated literature in Modern Greek sprang up under French rule, followed by Venetian rule, in Cyprus, under the rule of the Knights of Saint John in the Dodecanese, and under Venetian rule in Crete and in the Ionian Islands.[371]

Unlike the Byzantine and post-Byzantine Greek literature in the Attic *koine*, the literature in the living Modern Greek language was not the esoteric possession of an erudite élite. The sophisticated poetry, as well as the folk-poetry, in Modern Greek became a treasured possession of Greeks of all classes in those Greek lands in which it was produced. In Greece, as in Iran, there have been peasants who have been technically illiterate, but who have known by heart so much sophisticated poetry that they have actually been more highly cultivated than some contemporary Westerners who have been taught to read and write. There have been, for instance, Cretan peasants who have known by heart all the 10,052 verses of the seventeenth-century Cretan Greek epic *Erotókritos*.[372] The author, Vidzendzos Kornáros, bore a Venetian name; his poem is inspired by French and Italian models; and, though his metre is the native Greek 'metropolitan verse' (στίχοι πολιτικοί), he uses rhyme, which is a Western importation into the Greek *ars poetica*. Yet, in spite of its being so strongly impregnated with Westernism, the *Erotókritos* has become a national possession of the Greek people in virtue of its being a poem in their living mother-tongue.[373]

The captivation of the Greek people by Western-style poetry in the living Modern Greek language shows that they are capable of breaking the spell cast over them by the potent literature in Hellenic Greek. The Cretan school of Greek literature in Modern Greek rose to a climax in the seventeenth century; but its career was then cut short by the Ottoman conquest of Crete in 1645–69. The Rhodian literature in Modern Greek had already been cut short by the Ottoman conquest of the Dodecanese in 1522, and the Cypriot literature by the Ottoman conquest of Cyprus in 1571. After 1669, the Ionian Islands were the last surviving asylum for literature in Modern Greek. The local Greek aristocracy had become Italianate; but a folk-literature in Modern Greek was kept alive here by the local peasantry, reinforced, after 1669, by Cretan refugees.[374] This survival in the Ionian Islands of a tradition

[371] See Browning, Robert, *Medieval and Modern Greek* (London 1969), pp. 93–6; Campbell and Sherrard, op. cit., p. 221; Trypanis, op. cit., pp. xlii–xlv; Bien, op. cit., pp. 39–40; Politis, N., *A History of Modern Greek Literature* (Oxford 1973), pp. 54–67 and 69–73.

[372] Campbell and Sherrard, op. cit., p. 215; Trypanis, op. cit., p. xliii; Politis, op. cit., pp. 62–7.

[373] Popular Greek feeling for the *Erotókritos* is ignored in Koraês' slighting reference to this poem in a letter of 2 February 1805 (cited by Thereianós, D., Ἀδαμάντιος Κοραῆς (Trieste 1889–90, 3 vols.), in vol. ii, p. 224). See also Koraês' own *Vios Adhamandíou Koraê synghrapheis parà tou idhíou* (Paris 1833; reprinted in Dhêmaras, K. Th., Ὁ Κοραῆς καὶ ἡ ἐποχή του (Athens 1953), pp. 240–50).

[374] Browning, op. cit., p. 96; Campbell and Sherrard, op. cit., p. 221; Bien, op. cit., p. 40; Politis, op. cit., pp. 70–1.

of poetry in Modern Greek was to have an important effect on the history of the 'language question', after this question had arisen towards the end of the eighteenth century. Meanwhile the use of the living language, both viva voce and in print, as a vehicle for a sophisticated culture, had been promoted by an incidental effect, on the Ottoman Greek community, of the Protestant Reformation in Western Christendom.

In an earlier chapter[375] it has been noted that, after the abortive union of the Eastern Orthodox Church with the Roman Catholic Church under Papal supremacy at the Council of Florence in 1439, the Roman Church made determined and persistent efforts to win over the Eastern Orthodox Christian peoples to Uniatism, and that, after the subsequent Protestant revolt in the West against the Roman Church, Western Catholics and Protestants competed with each other for trying to gain the Eastern Orthodox peoples' allegiance, or, short of that, at least their support and sympathy. In this context it has also been noted that the Eastern Orthodox clergy and their flocks were remarkably successful in resisting this early modern religious pressure from the West, in spite of the Eastern Orthodox Christian World's relative weakness, both cultural and political, in this age. The competitive Western pressure in the field of religion did, however, have an incidental linguistic effect in the Greek-speaking part of Eastern Orthodox Christendom. So long as the competition lasted, it worked in favour of the $\delta\eta\mu o\tau\iota\kappa\dot\eta$. This incidental encouragement of the use of the $\delta\eta\mu o\tau\iota\kappa\dot\eta$ was temporary, but it was important nevertheless, since the liturgy of the Graecophone Eastern Orthodox Church had been the principal agency for the perpetuation of the use of the Attic $\kappa o\iota\nu\dot\eta$.

The Protestants were, of course, advocates, on principle, of translating the Bible and the liturgy into the living vernacular languages; and, among Eastern Orthodox clerics who came into contact with Protestants, this Protestant stand on the language question had an appreciable influence. It influenced the majority who rejected Protestant theology, as well as the small minority—which included, however, such eminent men as Cyril Loúkaris and Mêtrophánês Kritópoulos—who were attracted by Protestantism in some degree.

The Patriarch Jeremías II (*fungebatur* 1572-9, 1580-4, 1586-95) was not won over to an acceptance of the Protestant position by his friendly correspondence, started on Crusius' initiative, with the theologians of the Protestant German University of Tübingen,[376] but he did attempt, though this without success, to give ecclesiastical currency to the living

---

[375] In Chapter IX (i), pp. 166–79.
[376] See Vakalópoulos, op. cit., vol. ii, part ii, pp. 196–201.

form of the Greek language.[377] Cyril Loúkaris' cousin and patron, Melétios Pêghás of Candia (1549–1601), who became Patriarch of Alexandria in 1590 and was temporarily the *epitêrêtês* of the Patriarchate of Constantinople in 1597, preached in the δημοτική and had his work, *Orthódhoxos Dhidhaskalía*, translated from the κοινή into a simpler form of Greek, though his theological stand was anti-Western (i.e. anti-Uniate in his case).[378]

As for Cyril Loúkaris himself, he wrote in the δημοτική,[379] and he took the initiative in having the New Testament translated into Modern Greek by Máximos of Gallipoli and published, in 1638, at Geneva.[380] Loúkaris' protégé and agent, Metrophánês Kritópoulos, who was sent by Loúkaris to England in 1617 in response to an invitation from George Abbott, the Archbishop of Canterbury,[381] and who afterwards travelled widely in Protestant countries in the years 1623–7,[382] wrote a grammar of the δημοτική, though Metrophánês wanted, not to promote the living Greek language, but to rehabilitate the dead Hellenic form of it.[383]

The Roman Catholic Church stood, in principle, for the maintenance of the use of Latin as its liturgical language, but, at least as early as Charlemagne's time, Western preachers had begun to address their congregations in the living language of their time and place, and, even on the question of the liturgical language, the decisions of the Council of Florence had been liberal. Uniates were allowed to continue to celebrate the liturgy in their own historic liturgical languages, so long as they acknowledged the Pope's jurisdictional supremacy and conformed to Roman Catholic theology.

Thus, when the Jesuits set out to convert the Greek Orthodox Christians, there was no obstacle, in the regulations of their own Church, to their preaching and teaching in the δημοτική, and they were quick to perceive that the use of the δημοτική would give them an opening for missionary work among the adherents of a church which, like the Roman Church of the Latin rite, insisted on celebrating the liturgy in a 'dead language'. Accordingly the Jesuit missionaries in Greek Orthodox Christendom learned the δημοτική, preached in it, and published grammars of it.[384] A particularly popular Jesuit missionary was the French Father François Richard (1612–73), who opened a school on the island of Santoríni and used a Χριστιανικὴ Διδασκαλία, written in demotic Greek and printed in France.[385]

---

[377] Ibid., p. 195.
[378] Ibid., pp. 437–47.
[379] Ibid., pp. 449–51.
[380] See above, p. 137 with n. 3.
[381] Vakalópoulos, op. cit., vol. ii, part ii, p. 452; Runciman, op. cit., pp. 268–9 and 294–5.
[382] Vakalópoulos, op. cit., vol. ii, part ii, pp. 458 and 466.
[383] Ibid., p. 468.   [384] Ibid., pp. 393, 397, 416, 432–3.   [385] Ibid., p. 416.

The Jesuit missionaries' example was followed by Greeks. The Cretan Orthodox bishop of Kýthera (Cerigo), Máximos Marghoúnios, who hoped to bring about a reconciliation between the Orthodox and the Roman Church, dedicated to the Patriarch of Constantinople, Jeremías II, and published at Venice in 1607, a translation into demotic of the work of Saint John τῆς Κλίμακος. He also translated an anthology of *synaxária* (there were six editions of this translation in the seventeenth century), as well as some abridgements of lives of saints.[386]

The promotion of the use of the living Greek language in the sixteenth and seventeenth centuries, in consequence of the rivalry in the Levant between the Catholic and Protestant factions of Western Christendom, was a prelude to a new development in the eighteenth century. The victory of Russia in the Russo-Turkish war of 1768–74, and the terms of the peace treaty of Küçük Kainarca, made it evident that the Ottoman Empire's days were numbered. The Ottoman Greeks—who, by this date, included all non-expatriate Greeks except the Greek subjects of Venice in the Ionian Islands—could now look forward with some assurance to regaining the political independence that had not been enjoyed by any Greeks anywhere since 1461. If part, at any rate, of the Greek people was going to be able to re-establish a Greek state under Greek rule in the near future, what form of the Greek language was to be the medium of this coming Greek state's administration, legislation, and system of education? And in what form of Greek were this state's citizens to write their letters and to compose their literature? If the Modern Greeks' linguistic and literary heritage from the Hellenic Greeks had not still been potent, this question would not have presented itself. The Modern Greeks would have taken it as a matter of course that, in the future independent Greek state, their living mother tongue, in the contemporary phase of its development, would be the language in which they would write and read, as well as talk, in the transaction of public business and in private intercourse.

The hold of the living language on the Greek people's hearts and minds was manifest. In 1703, Efthýmios Pendaghiótes, one of the five surviving monks of the monastery of the Saviour, had written, in unsophisticated, and therefore unadulterated, contemporary colloquial Greek a chronicle of the history of the little Rumeliot maritime city-state Ghalaxeídhi,[387] on the north shore of the Corinthian Gulf. The author's sources were partly the local records and partly a local folk-memory that had gone some way towards transmuting history into legend. The folk-poetry in the living language had reached, in the course

---

[386] Vakalópoulos, op. cit., vol. ii, part ii, p. 436.

[387] Pendaghiótês, Efthýmios, Χρονικὸν τοῦ Γαλαξειδίου, ed. by Valetas, G. (Athens 1944). First published by Sathas, K. N. (Athens 1865).

of the eighteenth century, the highest pitch of excellence so far attained in its long history. It had developed a distinctive style and a repertory of themes that were congenial to the people's temperament. The sophisticated poetry in the living language which had come to flower in Crete had lived on in the hearts of the people in Crete, and had been carried from there to other Greek lands, after the development of this Cretan Greek literature had been cut short by the Ottoman conquest of its native island. The 'Thoúrios' ('war-song' or 'battle-hymn') composed in the living language (ἡ δημοτικὴ γλῶσσα) by Rhêghas Velestinlês in 1796 spread like wildfire wherever Greek was spoken. As a work of literary art, it is mediocre by comparison with the seventeenth-century Cretan literature and with the folk-songs, but it gave expression to the Greek people's reawakened political aspirations in a language that every Greek could understand and could sing.

It was natural that, in the blueprint for an 'Hellenic Republic' which Rhêghas printed in 1797, he should prescribe, as he did, that the *dhêmotikê* was to be his imaginary future state's official language.[388] It was fantastic to suppose that the non-Greek-speaking majority of the population of Rhêghas' grandiose 'Hellenic Republic' would be willing to accept demotic Greek, or any other form of Greek, as a common official language. But demotic Greek was the natural official language for the homogeneous national state which was the form of polity in which the Greeks actually regained their political independence in the event. Rhêgas' declaration in favour of demotic Greek was, in fact, the only point in his blueprint that, so far from being Utopian, was sensible and practical.

Yet, though Rhêghas was not alone in his advocacy of the *dhêmotikê*, he was in a minority. There was a party which held that the only language worthy of a politically independent Greek people was the Attic dialect of Hellenic Greek, purged of the 'impurities' that had sullied it when it had become the common (κοινή) language of the expanded Hellenic World of the age inaugurated by Alexander the Great. This linguistic programme was, of course, as chimaerical as Rhêghas' political programme, and it, too, was espoused only by a minority of the educated Greeks who discussed the 'language question' in and after the last quarter of the eighteenth century. A majority followed the lead of the expatriate Smyrniot Greek Adhamándios Koraês (1748–1833), who advocated what, from his standpoint, was a middle way.[389]

Koraês rejected both the dream of reinstating Hellenic Greek[390] and a

---

[388] See above, pp. 223-4.

[389] For Koraês' exposition of his 'middle way', see Thereianós, D., op. cit., vol. ii, pp. 218-19, 220, 222, 232, 249.

[390] This had been the dream of Alexander Mavrokordháto (1636?-1707), the Western-educated Dragoman of the Porte (see Bien, op. cit., p. 20; Politis, op. cit., pp. 12, 74, 76).

readiness to acquiesce in writing and speaking 'like the hewers of wood and drawers of water' (ὡς γράφουσι καὶ λαλοῦσιν οἱ ξυλοφόροι καὶ ὑδροφόροι).[391] His intention was to arrive at a compromise.[392] He had the common sense to perceive and declare that it was impossible to raise the Hellenic Greek language from the dead.[393] He recognized that colloquial modern Greek is the language 'which we have imbibed with our mother's milk',[394] and that it was senseless to despise this 'pedestrian' (πεδή) language.[395] But he was willing to take colloquial Modern Greek, in preference to Attic Greek, as his linguistic basis only because he believed that 'the language, though it has been barbarized, is capable of being given a beautifying-treatment' (ἡ γλῶσσα, ἂν καὶ βαρβαρωθεῖσα, δυνατὸν εἶναι νὰ καλλωπισθῇ).[396] Modern Greek writers of Greek 'have not studied the extent to which the language is susceptible of being Hellenized' (μέχρι πόσου εἶναι δεκτικὴ Ἑλληνισμοῦ).[397] Koraês' proposed 'middle course' was to Hellenize the Modern Greek language up to the limit; and, in this process of rectifying the 'barbarized' living language, the only limit, in his view, was the point at which the language would become obscure (ἀσαφής) and exotic (παράξενος).[398] In fact, Koraês' programme was to go as far towards Hellenizing Modern Greek as he could go without putting the poor tormented language out of action.[399] Yet this programme drew on him bitter attacks from the spokesman of the uncompromising Hellenists, Panayiotákês Kodhrikás,[400] who, like Alexander Mavrokordháto, was content with nothing short of the resurrection of Attic Greek.

It is impossible to imagine a comparable 'language question' arising in Italy on the eve of the Risorgimento, yet all but one of the circumstances that gave rise to this Greek controversy have Italian parallels. The Greeks had been humiliated from 1204 to 1821, the Italians from 1494 to 1815. At the Congress of Vienna, Metternich had dismissed the Italian people's aspirations for political independence and

---

[391] Thereianós, op. cit., pp. 218-19. This passage and the one next quoted are to be found in Koraês' Prolegomena to his edition of Heliodorus, published in 1804.

[392] See Bien, op. cit., pp. 53-4; Politis, op. cit., pp. 80-1.

[393] Koraês, cited by Thereianós, in op. cit., vol. ii, p. 232.

[394] Ibid., p. 220.

[395] Ibid., p. 224.

[396] Ibid., p. 223.

[397] Ibid., p. 219.

[398] Ibid., p. 221.

[399] Koraês went beyond this limit in his revised (i.e. re-archaized) version of Maximos' translation of the New Testament, which Koraês published in 1810. In answer to an enquiry from the British and Foreign Bible Society, J. F. Usko, a German resident in Smyrna, whose wife was a Smyrniot Greek, reported, in a memorandum dated 6 November 1811, that Koraês' language was 'so difficult to readers who have not learned the Ancient Greek that it cannot be supposed to be generally understood by all the Greeks' (see Bien, op. cit., pp. 59-62).

[400] The controversy between Kodhrikás and Koraês is recorded in detail by Thereianós in op. cit., vol. ii, pp. 217 and 283-352.

unity in the provocative dictum that 'Italy' was merely 'a geographical expression'. The Greeks had been overawed by a linguistic and literary heritage from the past; the Italians had a similar heritage in the Latin language and literature. The Tuscan language was derived from Latin, as Modern Greek was from Attic Greek. Latin was familiar to Roman Catholic Italians, as the Attic *koine* was to Eastern Orthodox Greeks, in virtue of being the liturgical language of their church. Latin was also a staple subject of higher education for Italians, as Hellenic Greek was for Modern Greeks. It might perhaps be contended that the gulf between Latin and Tuscan was wider than the gulf between Hellenic Greek and Modern Greek; yet, in both cases alike, the gulf was so wide that the dead 'classical' language from which the modern living language was derived had to be learnt as a foreign language by the moderns who spoke the living language as their mother tongue.[401]

The difference between the respective situations of the Italians and the Modern Greeks at the turn of the eighteenth and nineteenth centuries was that, by that date, the Italians had created for themselves a literature in Tuscan that could bear comparison with the literature in Latin, whereas the Byzantine and Modern Greeks had been so thoroughly cowed by the Hellenic Greek language and literature that they had produced nothing to match this in their own tongue. There has been no 'language question' for the modern Italians because, five centuries before the Risorgimento, the question had been asked by Dante and had been given by him a magisterial answer in the *Divina Commedia*. Dante had played with the idea of writing his masterpiece in quantitative unrhymed Latin hexameters; he had actually written it in accentual rhyming Tuscan verse. Dante had accepted Virgil as his guide through Hell and Purgatory, but on the threshold of Paradise he had exchanged him for Beatrice.

If the Byzantine Greeks had produced a Dante, and not just a Pródhromos, the controversy between Kodhrikás and Koraês could not have arisen. The question at issue between them would have been settled conclusively in advance, and have been settled in favour of neither of them. Koraês defeated Kodhrikás quickly and easily, though Kodhrikás had on his side the Greek Orthodox Church;[402] but we have not yet seen the end of the tussle between two rival forms of Modern Greek. The pedantically denatured form of it, fathered by Koraês, which its advocates call euphemistically 'the purist form' ($\dot{\eta}$ $\kappa\alpha\theta\alpha\rho\epsilon\acute{\upsilon}o\upsilon\sigma\alpha$), is still

---

[401] Both Modern Greek and Tuscan had developed on the lines followed by all modern languages that are derivatives of the Indo-European *Ursprache*. They had gone some way towards replacing built-in inflexions by detached prepositions and auxiliary verbs.

[402] The Ecumenical Patriarch Gregory V addressed to Kodhrikás a letter, denouncing Koraês' programme, in 1820 (the year before the Patriarch was put to death by the Ottoman Government). See Thereianós, op. cit., vol. ii, p. 345.

contesting the legitimacy of a more natural form, the so-called popular form (ἡ δημοτική). The Modern Greeks are still waiting for a Greek Dante to come to judgement.

Koraês has been ill-served by the unfortunate success of his programme. Kodhrikás' programme was so impracticable that it presented no threat to the living Modern Greek language. Koraês' programme was practicable enough actually to be put into practice, and Koraês himself might have been rueful if he could have foreseen the lamentable consequences of his triumph. On at least two points of cardinal importance, Koraês' observations about the nature of language were true and pertinent.

Koraês saw that, when a language becomes the vehicle for a literature, besides being a medium for intercourse in everyday life, the written form of the language is not, and cannot ever be, identical with the spoken form.

> It seems probable that the language that Plato and Isocrates wrote was not identical with the language spoken by [contemporary] Athenian seamen. . . . Conversely, it seems probable that Plato and Isocrates spoke in a language that was intelligible even for seamen.[403]

This finding of Koraês' will be endorsed by anyone who has ever been set the laborious task of transforming a tape-record of his own spoken words into a script for sending to press. He finds that the syntax and vocabulary that he has used for communicating orally with listeners have to be recast radically for presentation in print to the eyes of readers. The style that is natural and practical for talking is too informal and too diffuse to be submitted to a reader's eye; but if the script, as edited for the reader, were then to be recorded on tape orally for a listener, the scribal style might seem stilted and pedantic. The difference between the two styles that are appropriate for the ear and for the eye respectively is appreciable even when the writer is identical with the speaker and when he is speaking in his mother tongue. The difference is accentuated when this language has become the vehicle of a complicated and sophisticated culture and when the speaker–writer himself has received a higher education that has set its imprint on his style of writing but has not denatured his spontaneous idiom when he is talking.

When a culture is becoming more sophisticated and more complicated, the vocabulary of the language or languages in which this culture is conveyed must be constantly expanding. The English language, for instance, has borrowed French words and idioms at every stage of its development from 1066 till the present day. It has also, like French and other Western languages, borrowed or invented Latin and Greek words

---

[403] A letter of Koraês', dated 1 May 1805, quoted by Thereianós in ibid., p. 226.

for new things, new techniques, and new ideas. The Germans, unlike most other West European peoples, have tried to coin the equivalent of these exotic neologisms in native German words. 'Radio', for example, has been neatly Germanized as '*Rundfunk*'; yet German, too, has found itself constrained to admit into its vocabulary, *more Anglico*, a number of untranslated Latin, Greek, and even French words.

This problem of gathering materials and discovering techniques for enlarging a language's vocabulary becomes more pressing when the speakers of the language in question transfer their allegiance from one culture to another. The problem becomes acute when the alien culture that is being adopted is more complex and more subtle than the cultural migrants' native culture. The Modern Greeks have been confronted by this problem ever since the seventeenth century, when, reversing their previous aloof and hostile attitude towards the Western civilization, they decided to adopt it.

By that time, Eastern Orthodox Christendom and Western Christendom had been estranged from each other for about 1,200 years, and, during that span of time, the West, which had originally been the Hellenic Greek civilization's pupil, had gone its own way and had eventually forged ahead of the Byzantine and Modern Greeks into fields of activity and experience which, so far, the Greeks had not explored. By the seventeenth century, Westernization demanded an 'acculturation' that was arduous even for Greeks who were highly cultivated in terms of Hellenic pre-Christian and patristic Christian literature. *A fortiori*, the cultural gulf that had to be crossed was formidably wide for Ottoman Greek peasants; and the Greek War of Independence brought to the fore peasants whose cultural horizon had previously been confined to their traditional folk-culture. The mother tongue of these peasants was a genuine colloquial Modern Greek that was innocent of Koraês' 'beautifying-treatment' (καλλωπισμός). Yet, as soon as these ex-peasants stepped out of their ancestral environment to become generals and politicians in a Western-style Greek national state, their mother tongue inevitably changed, in their mouths and on their pen points, now that they were having to transact business in a strange new world.

This inevitable change of language in response to changes in the speaker's or writer's circumstances is illustrated by the language of Makriyiánnês' *Memoirs* (Ἀπομνημονεύματα).[404] Makriyiánnês began to write his *Memoirs* in 1829[405] when he was about thirty-two years old and was already a prominent participant in the public life of the nascent

[404] Makriyiánnês, Ioánnês, Ἀρχεῖον, ed. by Vlakhoyiánnês, I. (Athens 1907, 2 vols.; 2nd edn., Athens 1947). The first edition is the one that is quoted in the present work. For Makriyiánnês' career, see the present work, pp. 210–11.

[405] See Vlakhoyiánnês' Introduction to the *Memoirs* in Makriyiánnês, op. cit., ed. cit., vol. ii, on p. 39 of the Introduction.

Greek national state. He had not been prompted by anyone else to record his experiences; he did this spontaneously.[406] He did not dictate; he wrote with his own hand;[407] he wrote the language that he spoke;[408] his language, as he wrote it, was almost uniform[409] over the long period—1829 to 1850[410]—during which he was writing; he wrote without any affectation; it would never have occurred to Makriyiánnês to 'Hellenize' his language deliberately, in Koraês' manner; and yet Makriyiánnês' demotic is not the language that he would have written if the War of Independence had not happened to carry him out of the traditional private life of a Rumeliot peasant into novel public affairs in a national—indeed, an international—arena.

This extreme change in the field and in the scale of Makriyiánnês' experiences in the course of his eventful life is reflected in his vocabulary. He could not describe his experiences without enlarging his vocabulary to match. He enlarged it by introducing words already coined by his more sophisticated Greek contemporaries for denoting institutions and ideas of Western origin. In adopting these, for him, exotic words, Makriyiánnês assimilated them unselfconsciously to his demotic mother tongue;[411] yet, even in their 'naturalized' form, they have made the demotic Greek of the general and the politician a different demotic from the original language of the Rumeliot peasant lad that Makriyiánnês had once been.

In the published works of other uneducated or semi-educated participants in the War of Independence, the authors' demotic mother tongue has been modified deliberately, and in some cases drastically, either by the authors themselves, under the influence of previously published works written in the 'purist' (καθαρεύουσα) version of Modern Greek, or else by their purist-minded amanuenses or editors. In Theodore Kolokotrónês' *Reminiscences*, which were dictated by him in 1836 and were published in 1851,[412] there are sophisticated words and phrases that may have been introduced either by Kolokotrónês himself

---

[406] Makriyiánnês, op. cit., vol. ii, p. 26.

[407] Ibid., pp. 32–3.

[408] Ibid., pp. 33 and 43.

[409] Ibid., p. 31.

[410] He wrote his Próloghos to his *Memoirs* in 1850 (ibid., pp. 42–3).

[411] See ibid., pp. 29–32. Τὸ γνησίως φθογγολογικὸν στοιχεῖον τῆς δημοτικῆς κυριαρχεῖ παρὰ τῷ Μακρυγιάννῃ, ὅπερ εἶναι τεκμήριον ὄχι μόνον ὅτι τὸ γλωσσικὸν αὐτοῦ αἴσθημα ἦτο σταθερὸν καὶ δυσνίκητον, ἀλλ' ἐξ ἀντιθέτου καὶ ἡ γλωσσοπλαστικὴ καὶ ἀφομοιωτικὴ τούτου δύναμις μεγάλη, διαρκὴς καὶ δραστικωτάτη. "Ὅθεν πᾶσαν ἐκ τῆς λογίας λεξιν ἀφομοιοῖ πρὸς τοὺς νόμους τοὺς φθογγολογικοὺς τῆς δημοτικῆς (ibid., p. 31). Makriyiánnês' unselfconscious handling of the Modern Greek languages was the converse of Koraês' self-conscious handling of it. Koraês deliberately 'Hellenized' the *dhêmotikê*; Makriyiánnês 'Demoticized' spontaneously the Hellenic vocabulary that his experiences constrained him to add to his ancestral repertory of demotic Greek.

[412] Kolokotrónês, Th., Διήγησις συμβάντων τῆς Ἑλληνικῆς φυλῆς 1770–1836 (Athens 1889–1901, 2 vols.).

or by his amanuensis G. Tertsétês.[413] In Photákos Khrysanthópoulos' *Memoirs*[414] it is possible to trace the progressive 'Hellenization' of the author's more or less genuinely demotic original language.[415]

It is in the nature of language to be changing all the time in the processes of communication from mouth to ear and of transmission from one generation to another. The penalty for 'freezing' a language in some particular one of its successive transient forms is to turn it into a dead language. The always necessary practical business of communication will then be carried on in a language that, because it is living, will be foreign to the dead language that it will have superseded, except, perhaps, for liturgical and academic purposes. The penalty for 'denaturing' a living language, as Modern Greek has been 'denatured' by being forced into the pseudo-Hellenic mould of the *katharévousa*, is the relegation of this unnatural form of the language to formal uses. The *raison d'être* of human speech is to serve as a means of communication, and, if a language is artificially manipulated, its capacity for performing its function is impaired in proportion to the lengths to which the manipulation is carried.

A language changes autonomously, regardless of the wills of the human beings who speak it and write it, and it is more volatile in the mouth than on paper. By the close of the eighteenth century, the Modern Greek language was already at least twelve centuries old; during that span of time it had been changing[416]—and this all the more vigorously because, so far, it had been used only fitfully and grudgingly as a vehicle for sophisticated literature. It was bound to change more rapidly and more radically when it became the language of a Western-style Greek national state whose citizens were committed to adopting the modern form of Western civilization. In these revolutionary circumstances, the further development of the Modern Greek language could have been left to look after itself, as is demonstrated by the spontaneous evolution of it that can be observed in Makriyiánnês' *Memoirs*. Koraês' deliberate manipulation of his and Makriyiánnês' common mother tongue was uncalled-for and was foredoomed to failure.

Koraês himself recognized, in his controversy with the Atticists, that it was both unjustifiable and futile to attempt to dictate to a people how it should speak and write its own language.

The language is one of the most inalienable possessions of the nation. This

---

[413] See Vlakoyiánnês, in Makriyiánnês, op. cit., ed. cit., pp. 23–6.

[414] Khrysanthópoulos, Ph., Ἀπομνημονεύματα (Athens 1899, 2 vols.).

[415] See Vlakhoyiánnês, in Makriyiánnês, op. cit., ed. cit., pp. 16–23.

[416] For the evolution of the Modern Greek language, see Browning, op. cit., and also Dawkins in Baynes and Moss, *Byzantium*, pp. 252–67.

possession is shared by all members of the nation on a footing of what I would call democratic equality. No man, however highly cultivated (σοφός) he may consider himself to be, either possesses or can assume the right to dictate to the nation: 'this is how I wish you to speak and to write.' . . . The nation's intellectuals (οἱ λόγιοι ἄνδρες τοῦ ἔθνους) are naturally the legislators of the language that the nation speaks, but (I repeat) language is a field in which legislation has to be democratic. The reformation of the language is the intellectuals' prerogative, but the language is a possession, and a sacred one, of the whole nation. So innovation must be conducted with prudence and without forcing the pace.[417]

Moreover, Koraês was aware of the indomitable autonomy that is of the essence of human speech. A tyrant's power over his subjects has only one limitation. So long as he leaves a victim alive,

he cannot change this victim's language. The victim speaks his own language at home, and this accompanies him in exile. Time alone is empowered to change the languages of the nations, as it changes the nations themselves. If anyone tries to change the language prematurely by force, he is exposing himself to the censure that the unhappy Haimon uttered in his retort to his tyrannical father.[418]

Koraês understood that a language takes its own time to evolve. In a letter written on 26 March 1805,[419] he wrote:

It is ridiculous to be polemical and dogmatic about something that is not going to be decided till the year 1950—the date at which, according to my reckoning, the first good [Modern Greek] comedy or tragedy will be staged in a Greek (γραικικόν) theatre.

In the passage cited above from an essay written in 1804, Koraês confesses that, in pointing out that it is both illegitimate and futile to attempt to dragoon a language, he is laying himself open to the charge of contradicting his own doctrine. Indeed he is doing so, and his inconsistency with himself raises the question: what was it that moved him, against his own better judgement, to play the martinet in the linguistic field, in which, as he recognizes, this approach is out of place?

Koraês and the other sophisticated Greeks of his generation were moved by a crushing sense of inferiority in face of their Hellenic linguistic and literary heritage. This sense of inferiority had revealed itself, as far back in time as the Age of Augustus, in the emergence of neo-Atticism. The post-classical Greeks felt themselves to be inferior to their

---

[417] Koraês in his Prolegomena to his edition of Heliodorus, published in 1804. The quotation is taken from Thereianós, op. cit., vol. ii, pp. 221–2.

[418] Koraês, in ibid. The reference is to the dialogue between Haimon and Kreon in Sophocles' *Antigone*, lines 635–765—in particular, perhaps, to line 737.

[419] Quoted in ibid., p. 224.

overwhelmingly glorious 'classical' ancestors in so far as they were different from them. The *epigoni* did not venture to imagine that they might be different from their ancestors and at the same time might be equal to them in spiritual stature in some original way of their own. The only way in which they could imagine themselves regaining equality was by regaining identity.

This was, of course, a Psyche's task. 'Can a man . . . enter the second time into his mother's womb, and be born?'[420] The Modern Greek Hellenizers' subconscious awareness of the impracticability of their enterprise accounts for the acrimony with which the 'language question' has been debated. Koraês was furiously denounced as a traitor by Kodhrikás and other ultra-Hellenists[422] who were cherishing the dream of making Modern Greek peasants talk the Attic Greek of Isocrates. On the premise that was the common faith of Koraês and Kodhrikás, Kodhrikás' denunciation of Koraês was justifiable. This premise was the erroneous belief that some particular phase in the evolution of a language is the perfect form of the language, and that the inevitable departure from this particular transient form is, not the natural and wholesome change that it really is, but a corruption that is deplorable and that can be, and ought to be, rectified. This linguistic fantasy generates an ethical one. The 'corruption' of a language is thought to indicate a moral debasement of the speakers of the language. If they have corrupted their linguistic heritage, they must have corrupted the whole of their way of life. 'A nation is not entitled to be called enlightened till it has carried its language to the point of perfection.'[422] Conversely, 'the corruption of language is a disease that is related to the corruption of morals.'[423]

By Koraês' time, Greeks who had been educated in the Hellenic Greek language and literature had been inhibited for seventeen centuries from recognizing the potentialities of their own living language as a vehicle for literature. In so far as these potentialities had been made to bear fruit, this had been done by Greeks who had not had an Hellenic education, and who had consequently escaped the blinding and paralysing effects of this. These culturally uninhibited Modern Greeks had been either uneducated peasants or intellectuals whose education had been, not Hellenic, but Western. The peasants had created a fine folk-literature; the Western-educated intellectuals had

---

[420] John 3: 4.

[421] e.g. P. Soútsos in a book published in 1853 with the title Νέα σχολὴ τοῦ γραφομένου λόγου (see Bien, op. cit., pp. 65–8; Politis, op. cit., pp. 134–41) and Kóndos, K. S., in his Γλωστικὰι παρατηρήσεις, published in 1882 (see Bien, op. cit., pp. 68–71; Politis, op. cit., pp. 170–1).

[422] Koraês in his Prolegomena to his edition of Heliodorus, quoted by Thereianós, op. cit., vol. ii, pp. 220–1.

[423] Koraês in a letter of 6 August 1804, cited ibid., p. 222.

created the sophisticated demotic Greek literature of seventeenth-century Crete. This was virtually a branch of Western literature, though it had a distinctive Greek quality of its own which was comparable to the distinctive qualities of the branches of Western literature in each of the polyglot Western civilization's native local languages.

When the Greek people as a whole decided that they were going to adopt the Western civilization, and when, about 200 years later, the establishment of an independent Greek national state gave the Greeks a new stimulus and a more ample opportunity, it could be predicted that, if a new Modern Greek literature did come to birth, its relation to the contemporary literature of the Western World would be like that of the seventeenth-century Cretan Modern Greek literature. It could also be predicted that the pioneers would, once again, be poets, not savants or clerics.

In the history of the emancipation of the Western languages and literature from Latin, the poets had taken the lead. Poets had dared to write epic poetry in the living French language of the day at as early a date in Western history as the twelfth century; Western savants had not dared to assert their intellectual equality with 'the Ancients' until the seventeenth century, when Western philosophy and science made their belated declaration of independence. In the field of religion, the Bible and the liturgy were translated into the living vernaculars in the sixteenth century in those parts of Western Christendom in which Protestantism prevailed; but in the Roman Catholic Church it is only in our own day that Latin has lost its traditional prerogative of being the obligatory language for the celebration of the Mass.

This story has repeated itself in the history of the Modern Greek language. The creators of the folk-poetry and of the sophisticated Westernizing poetry in the Modern Greek language belonged to markedly different social and cultural milieux, but they had one all-important thing in common. Poetry, not prose, was their medium of literary expression. Fortunately for the Modern Greek language and literature, there appeared, in the next generation to that of Koraês and Kodhrikás, a great Greek poet, Dhionýsios Solomós[424] (1798–1857),[425] the illegitimate son of a Westernized Zantiot Greek nobleman, whose family were migrants from Crete,[426] and an uneducated Zantiot servant-girl, and who thus combined in his own person the Modern Greek language's two sources of poetic inspiration—the native Greek peasantry and the exotic Western World.

[424] Besides Solomós' own poetry, see Jenkins, R. H. J., *Dionysius Solomós* (Cambridge 1940). See also Politis, op. cit., pp. 113–23.

[425] Solomós was a near contemporary of Makriyiánnês (1797?–1864).

[426] Jenkins, op. cit., p. 2.

Of course, Solomós could not have been the great poet that he was if he had not had an inborn genius, but his genius was given its opportunity to fructify by a combination of fortunate circumstances: his parentage, his birthplace, and his education. These circumstances saved Solomós, as his contemporary Makriyiánnês was saved by the piquantly different circumstances of his life, from being overawed by the Modern Greeks' Hellenic heritage. This heritage meant nothing to Solomós' mother; she was uneducated. It meant nothing to his father; he was Westernized. It meant nothing to Solomós himself; for his spiritual home was Italy. He was educated there for ten years on end (1808–18), first at Venice, then at Cremona, then at the university of Padua,[427] where so many eminent Modern Greeks of previous generations had received a Western education already. Solomós gained in Italy something more than education in the formal sense. He made friends and he became a liberal.

It is true that in the Ionian Islands under the Venetian regime the nobility, as well as the peasantry, had continued to adhere to the Orthodox Church. Yet, though the Ionian Islands had remained Eastern Orthodox Christian in their ecclesiastical allegiance, they had become an integral part of the Western World in their culture,[428] and, by Solomós' generation, Western culture had become secularized. In that generation the Ionian Islanders were the only Greeks who were still under Western rule. By the year 1818, when Solomós came home again to Zante from Italy,[429] the Ionian Islands had become a British protectorate, and Solomós lived under a British regime for the rest of his life. He did not fight in the War of Independence, and he did not migrate to the independent Greek national state that was established in 1829–32.[430]

After his return to Zante in 1818 Solomós joined an Italianate literary circle there whose members extemporized sonnets in Italian as a parlour-game,[431] and when, in 1822, he was adjured by a Mesolongiot insurgent, Spiridhión Trikoúpês,[432] to become the Dante of a Greek Parnassus, his answer was: 'I don't know Greek.' Solomós meant that he

---

[427] Ibid., pp. 15–27.

[428] The Peloponnesian *klepht* Theodore Kolokotrónês, dictating his *Memoirs* in 1836, said— apropos of his finding asylum on Zante in 1806, when the Ottoman authorities had made his native Pelopónnêsos too hot to hold him—that in 1806 'Zante seemed as far away as the ends of the Earth do now. What America is to us now—that is pretty well what Zante was to them [i.e. the Ottoman Greeks in 1806]. When they went to Zante, they called it "going to the Western World" ("*Phrangiá*")' (Kolokotrónês, op. cit., vol. i, p. 49).

[429] Jenkins, op. cit., p. 30.

[430] Koraês did not migrate to Greece either, nor did Jean Psichari (1854–1929), the foremost nineteenth-century academic advocate of the *dhêmotikê*. Psichari and Koraês both preferred to remain Parisians, and Kaváphês remained an Alexandrian.

[431] Jenkins, op. cit., pp. 31–2.

[432] See Trikoúpês' own account of his visit to Solomós in 1822, in ibid., p. 54.

did not know Hellenic Greek[433]—the hallowed language of the pre-Christian Greek literature, the Greek Christian Fathers, and the Greek Orthodox Christian liturgy. The Zantiot Solomós' Rumeliot visitor retorted: 'The language which you imbibed with your mother's milk is Greek.'

The words are Koraês', in a work of his that had been published in 1804.[434] Possibly Trikoúpês was consciously quoting Koraês to Solomós. These words of Koraês' contradict Koraês' own doctrine; and Trikoúpês had no use for the *katharévousa*. In any case, Trikoúpês' shot went home. Solomós now started to compose, in his mother's artless Greek, sophisticated poetry in contemporary Western metres in the contemporary Western manner and on contemporary Western themes.[435] Solomós was the first poet, writing in Modern Greek, to win a place on a Parnassus that was Greek yet was Western too. He was the first of a series of Modern Greek poets[436] who have made their mark in the wide world, beyond the relatively narrow bounds of the geographical area within which Modern Greek is spoken today. They have distinguished themselves because, like Western poets since the twelfth century, they have written in the living language of their time and place and have experienced and expressed their own generation's concerns—its joys and griefs, its hopes and fears.

Modern Greek poets, like Western poets, have, of course, drawn inspiration from Hellenic Greek literature and history, but, also like Modern Western poets, they have confronted the Hellenes on equal terms. They have not felt, and have been eminent enough, in their own right, to have no cause to feel, the crushing sense of inferiority that overwhelmed Koraês. The nineteenth-century and twentieth-century Greek poets have looked at their Hellenic Greek predecessors with the bold eyes of modern men.

Kaváphês, for example, was a member of the Greek community in Alexandria who spent his life in his native city. Kaváphês was intrigued by Alexandria's Late Hellenic Greek past, and this period of Hellenic history, the thousand years running from the fourth century B.C. to the seventh century of the Christian Era, gave him his cue for some of his

---

[433] See Jenkins, op. cit., pp. 63–5.

[434] See above, pp. 251–2 with n. 391.

[435] Solomós method of composing a poem in Modern Greek was inauspicious. See Jenkins, op. cit., pp. 97–8. He first made notes in Italian, then translated these Italian notes into an expanded Greek prose text, and then worked his Greek prose into Greek verse in some Western metre. To produce great poetry by this process was a *tour de force* which gives the measure of Solomós' genius. Solomós relapsed in his old age into writing in Italian, which, for him, had never ceased to be the natural linguistic medium for literary work.

[436] Some of the most eminent of Solomós' successors, so far, are Kostês Palamás (1859–1943), Constantine Kaváphês (1868–1933), Ángelos Sikelianós (1884–1951), Níkos Kazandzákês (1885–1957), George Seférês (1900–1971).

most subtle—and also most ironical—poems. The Hellenic Greeks of that age aroused Kaváphês' interest, not because he revered them as paragons, but because he recognized in them the counterparts of modern men such as the poet was himself—men who, beneath the mask of a refined civilization, were subject to the frailties that are common to human nature at all times and places.[437] As for Kazandzákês, he had the audacity between 1925 and 1938 to compose in Modern Greek, and in a verse of his own that is neither the traditional Modern Greek 'metropolitan' fifteen-syllable line nor the Homeric hexameter, an epilogue to the *Odyssey* which runs to 33,333 lines—that is, nearly three times as many as the 12,110 lines of the *Odyssey* itself.[438]

These Greek poets who have arisen since Koraês' day have been changing the Modern Greek language gradually. Koraês himself[439] recognized that the evolution of a language must be the work of time, and that it is both unwarrantable and futile for a self-appointed 'linguistic legislator' to attempt to force the pace. Yet Koraês could not resist the temptation to promulgate the instantaneous and arbitrary legislation that, on principle, he deprecated. Koraês' offence against his own principles was rewarded with an undeserved success, because the sense of inferiority, and the consequent lack of self-confidence, which goaded Koraês into Hellenizing Modern Greek up to the limit, were shared by a majority of his Hellenically educated Greek contemporaries and their successors. The eminent Greek poets who have made their appearance since Koraês' day have altered the living Greek language in the course of a century and a half as much as Koraês altered it within a single industriously spent lifetime. But their objective has been different from Koraês', and so, therefore, has been their poetry's effect on their mother tongue.

Koraês' objective was to make Modern Greek approximate to Hellenic Greek as closely as Modern Greek could be constrained to fit into this arbitrarily applied Hellenic mould. The poets' objective has been to develop Modern Greek into an adequate instrument for writers who are addressing themselves to modern-minded readers. The product of Koraês' 'linguistic legislation' has been the 'purist' (*katharévousa*)

---

[437] Kaváphês' self-confidence set him free to make the Greek language serve his purposes. 'His language is the most bizarre and arbitrary mixture of *Katharevousa*, demotic Byzantine, and ancient Greek. . . . Yet this linguistic hodge-podge is precisely equivalent to what he is trying to say' (Bien, op. cit., pp. 221–2). This appreciation of Kaváphês vocabulary and syntax will be endorsed by other admirers of Kaváphês' poetry.

[438] Bien, op. cit., pp. 220–3, justly contrasts Kazandzákês' language in his *Odyssey* with Kaváphês' language in his poems. The subject of Kazandzákês' *Odyssey*, too, is sophisticated, but the language is studiously and learnedly—in fact, pedantically—'folksy'. His ultra-colloquial language eventually found an appropriate subject in the novels that he began to write in 1941 (see ibid., pp. 225 and 228).

[439] See the passages quoted above on p. 258.

version of Modern Greek. The product of the poets' spontaneous creative work has been a development of Modern Greek that is 'demotic' but is at the same time sophisticated in a different way from Koraês' product. The poets' Greek is 'demotic' in the sense that it is the living language of the contemporary Greek-speaking public; it is sophisticated in the sense that it is capable of conveying the feelings and thoughts of cultivated members of the modern society with which the poets' readers, as well as the poets themselves, have cast in their lot.

If Solomós and Makriyiánnês had not been forestalled by Koraês, the direction given by them to the evolution of the Modern Greek language might have been followed by the Greek people unanimously. If history had taken this happier course, the Greeks would have spared themselves the controversy over the 'language question' which, in spite of the poets' creative intervention, has been grinding along by now for two centuries without having yet been settled conclusively. So long as this controversy is maintained, it will continue to obstruct the natural evolution of the language and to restrict the realization of its potentialities as a vehicle for literature.

Both the language and the literature have suffered from the excesses of the extreme wings of the two contending parties and from the confusion of mind that has been produced by the contest itself and by the fluctuations in the fortunes of this linguistic civil war. These fluctuations are registered in regulations and counter-regulations, introduced by successive governments that have differed in their linguistic ideologies, for the use or disuse or reuse of one or other of the competing forms of the language as the obligatory medium of instruction in the public schools. Koraês' *katharévousa* was made the obligatory language for education in the Kingdom of Greece by laws enacted in 1834 and 1836. Fortunately for the flowering of the Modern Greek language and literature, these laws did not bind the Greek population of the Ionian Islands till the union of the Ionian Islands with the Kingdom in 1864.[440] During the fifty years 1917–67 the demotic form of the language was the subject, as well as the medium, of instruction in the lower forms of schools, with three short intervals during which the *katharévousa* was reinstated. Since the military coup of 21 April 1967, the use of demotic in the schools has once again been banned completely.[441] For schoolchildren, the arbitrary infusion of politics into education has been bewildering, and for adults, too, the proliferation of different versions of their mother tongue has been an impediment.

[440] See Bien, op. cit., pp. 63 and 92.
[441] Browning, op. cit., p. 111; Politis, op. cit., p. 13, referring to the emergency law 129 of 1969 and the constitution of 1968. Professor Browning has now drawn my attention to the fact that the Papadhópoulos regime was eventually constrained, by intractable linguistic facts, to reintroduce demotic as the medium of instruction in the lowest forms.

A Greek newspaper—before April 1967—was linguistically a most interesting document. Official proclamations, public announcements, texts of laws, etc. were in katharévousa. Editorial matter, literary criticism and the like were in literary demotic. The news pages were in various varieties of the mixed language, the more technical sections, e.g. financial news, inclining towards katharévousa, the sports pages affecting a more demotic tone.[442]

The Chamber of Deputies until its dissolution in 1967 conducted its business in purist Greek. The few interventions in demotic made by General Sarafis, the former resistance leader, are said to have been electrifying in their effect.[443]

From 1822, when Solomós wrote his first poem in Greek,[444] till the seizure of power in Greece by a junta of military officers in 1967, the *dhêmotikê* was, on the whole, gaining ground from the *katharévousa*,[445] and, in the process, it was of course changing, just because it was meeting the Greek people's developing linguistic needs with increasing success over a widening field. Since 1967 the *katharévousa* has been reimposed by an arbitrary regime. Whatever the near future may have in store, we may guess, with some assurance, that, sooner or later, the pedants will be defeated by the poets. This guess seems reasonable because the 'language question' has a psychological origin, and the controversy over it is likely to be resolved, not by fiats issued by dictators on the plane of politics, but by the psychological experience of the Greek people; and the human psyche, like human speech, goes its own way and defies attempts to direct it.

If the opposition were exclusively political, no doubt it would be overcome quickly; but the dictators have been supported by the ecclesiastics and by the snobs. In Greece it is illegal to publish any translation of the Christian Scriptures into Modern Greek without previous authorization by the Holy Synod at Athens. When Pallis published his translation of the Gospels into demotic Modern Greek in 1901, there was a riot.[446] The rioters were not clerics, and they were not animated by religious zeal. They were socially ambitious plebeians who

---

[442] Ibid., p. 112. The labels here used by Browning are A. Mirambel's.

[443] Ibid., p. 118 n. 8. Unfortunately for the Modern Greeks, they have no current foreign lingua franca which could be used to obviate the imposition on them of one or other of the controversial versions of their own mother tongue. In the Hungarian parliament, Latin was the language in which business was conducted till 1846. This use of Latin, so long as it lasted, saved the Hungarian people from having to face the issue of the respective statuses of Magyar, German, Slovak, Serbo-Croat, and Roumanian.

[444] Τὴν εἶδα τὴν ξανθούλα.

[445] For instance, prose literature in Modern Greek was permanently deflected away from the *katharévousa* towards the *dhêmotikê* by the publication, in 1888, of J. Psichari's *Τό ταξίδι μου*. Psichari did some harm to his own cause by going to provocative extremes (see Browning, op. cit., pp. 109–11); but this was perhaps the unavoidable price of the vitality that won for *Τό ταξίδι μου* its instant revolutionary effect, and that still gives a feeling of exhilaration to the present-day reader.

[446] See above, p. 137.

had been conditioned to believe that the mastery and use of the *katharévousa* was the indispensable talisman for achieving mundane success.[447]

The *katharévousa* is a product of the Modern Greeks' mistrust of themselves in the face of Hellenic predecessors for whom they have felt themselves to be no match. The development of the *dhêmotikê* in the works of the eminent Modern Greek poets is the fruit of a confident belief that the Modern Greeks can confront the Hellenic Greeks as their equals and can respond successfully to the challenge—which the Hellenic Greeks never had to face—of having to win a footing for themselves in the formidable modern world.

The poets have anticipated most of the rest of their fellow Greeks in being animated by this confidence, but, if we take a retrospective glance at the last 200 years of the history of the Greek people as a whole, we shall see that the poets' confidence has come to be shared in increasing measure by a growing number of their compatriots. In the course of these last two centuries, the Greeks have engaged in the life of the modern world in a number of fields with signal success. Their world-wide activity in commerce and shipping has been noted in a previous chapter. They have also been pioneers in the study of the problem of urbanism—a world-wide problem that has recently taken the world by surprise. Today the world-centre for the study of urbanism is Athens, and this is appropriate, for present-day Athens is one of the most rapidly growing cities in the modern world, and consequently the problem of urbanism, in its many facets, can be studied in the life there on the spot.[448]

Koraês had speculated that the first good Greek comedy or tragedy would be staged in a Greek theatre in the year 1950.[449] No doubt, in Koraês' estimation, the best plays that ever had been, or ever could be, staged anywhere in any language were those staged in the Dionysiac theatre at Athens in the fifth century B.C. Koraês would have been thrilled if it could have been foretold to him that, in the third quarter of the twentieth century, these inimitable plays—Aristophanes' comedies and the tragedies of Aeschylus, Sophocles, and Euripides—would be played, once again, in the theatre at Athens, and in the theatres at Epídhavros and Dodona and Thásos too.

If Koraês could have foreseen this, would he have concluded that he himself had been, after all, too cautious? Would he have conceded that Kodhrikás' apparently fantastic dream had been a correct anticipation

---

[447] See Bien, op. cit., pp. 141, 144, 160, 165; Politis, op. cit., pp. 173 and 207.

[448] The Greek initiator of this study, Constantine Doxiadis, has broadened its scope to include the whole subject of human settlements in all its numerous interrelated aspects, and he has coined, from the vocabulary of Hellenic Greek, a new name—'Ekistics' ($Οἰκιστική$)—to describe this new nodal point for the concentration and synthesis of the many branches of the study of human affairs.

[449] See the passage quoted above, p. 258.

of a future reality? After the Greek people's recovery of their political independence, was it truly going to take them only half a dozen generations to transcend Koraês' purified form of Modern Greek and to speak and understand unadulterated Attic? What would Koraês have said when it was broken to him that Attic Greek would still be an unintelligible foreign language for those Greeks who, in the 1970s, would be flocking into the Hellenic theatres in their thousands to see and hear the dramas of the fifth-century-B.C. Athenian playwrights? When Koraês learnt that these sacrosanct Hellenic plays would be performed in translation—and this not even into his own *katharévousa*, but into the language of the χυδαῖοι—Koraês would certainly have been both shocked and astonished. He would have been shocked by such impiety and have been astonished at such audacity, and he would not have believed his ears if he had then been told that, by the 1970s, the χυδαϊσμός of the vulgar tongue would have been refined by a series of poets—one of whom was, in 1804, already six years old—into a language that would be capable of expressing all the feelings and thoughts of both 'classical' Athens and the 'Enlightened Europe' of the modern age.

Koraês would have been incredulous. Yet in 1974 it could be foreseen that, thanks to the creative work of six generations of poets, the Modern Greek language would eventually be reunified. When the living language has grown into an organ that can express fully everything that a modern man needs to say or to write, it will fill the whole field and will push the superfluous *katharévousa* out into limbo.

X

CONCLUSION

IN this book, we have looked at four heritages that have been received by Greeks from Greek predecessors at successive stages of the Greek people's history. This history is a long one. It can reasonably be held to have begun at the beginning of the Neolithic Age in Greece, about 4,000 years before the arrival in Greece of the first contingent of Greek-speakers.[1] Reckoning even only from the probable date, either just before or just after the beginning of the second millennium B.C., at which Greek-speakers first established themselves in continental European Greece, Greek history has already been in the making for about 4,000 years, and no end to it is yet in sight. In 1974 the future of the whole human race may be in doubt, but the Greeks have as much or as little chance of surviving as the other peoples of the present-day world. In any case, the Greeks' history, within the time-span of its first 8,000 or first 4,000 years, provides evidence for the effect of heritages from the past on a people's efforts, at later stages, to cope with the current problems of the day.

This is a subject of general interest, for every people's life is affected, at every stage of its history, by its image of its past—and this whether the image is or is not an accurate reflection of the authentic historical facts. Few, however, of the peoples that possess distinctive identities today have had as long a history as the Greeks, if we interpret history as meaning, not simply chronological duration of existence, but a continuity of identity which has never ceased to be recognized and to be remembered.

Four thousand years of Greek history have produced four Greek heritages, each of which has had an effect on the life of the Greeks in later stages of their history. The Hellenic Greeks received a heritage from the Mycenaean Greeks, the Byzantine Greeks received one from the Hellenic Greeks, the Modern Greeks have received one heritage from the Byzantines and a second from the Hellenes.

If we compare the respective effects of these heritages with each other, we are likely to conclude that the influence of the past is most beneficent

[1] See above, p. 10.

when the memory of the past is faint and when the veneration for it is temperate. This was the Hellenic Greeks' relation to their Mycenaean heritage, and the Hellenes found in this heritage of theirs the inspiration for creating a great original Hellenic work of art, the Homeric epic poetry, which was the first instalment of a magnificent Hellenic literature. By contrast, the Byzantine Greeks' knowledge of their Hellenic predecessors' language and literature was so ample, and their veneration for these Hellenic treasures was so intense, that they were almost completely inhibited from attempting to create a Greek literature in their own living language, which was Modern Greek at an early stage of this language's development. As for the Byzantine Greeks' Modern Greek successors, they have had to cope with both a Byzantine and an Hellenic heritage, and both these heritages of theirs have been will-o'-the-wisps. The Modern Greeks' Byzantine heritage lured them into imagining the 'Great Idea' and into attempting to translate this dream into a reality. Their Hellenic heritage has plagued the Modern Greeks with the 'language question'.

In looking at the Greeks' successes and failures at different stages of their history, we have found that they have been beset, not only by heritages from their own past, but by the impacts of contemporary non-Greek societies. In the seventeenth century B.C. the Mycenaean Greeks encountered the Minoans; in the second century B.C. the Hellenic Greeks encountered the Jews; in the second millennium of the Christian Era, the Byzantine Greeks and their Modern Greek successors have encountered the Western civilization.

The Mycenaean Greeks adopted the Minoans' style of art, but they then gradually infused into it some of the spirit of their own previous native art. They also adopted the Minoans' bureaucratic system of administration, but apparently they did not succeed in establishing on the mainland the peace and security that appear to have been attained in Crete. The capitals of some of the Mycenaean states (e.g. Mycenae, Tiryns, Gla, but not Pylos) were eventually fortified, whereas the capitals of the Minoan states were open cities—even Mállia, which lay on a plain within a stone's-throw of the Cretan coast.

The Hellenic Greeks did not adopt Judaism, but they became converts to a Helleno-Judaic religion, Christianity. There is an Hellenic ingredient in Christianity, but the Judaic ingredient in it is dominant. Indeed, Christianity is so strongly Judaic that conversion to it brought with it, for the Greeks, a change of civilization. In becoming Christians, the Hellenes turned into Byzantines.

The Byzantine Greeks were under increasing pressure from Western Christendom from the eleventh century until the rise of the Ottoman Empire in the fourteenth and fifteenth centuries. The Byzantine Greeks accepted political subjection to the 'Osmanlis as being, in their estimation, a lesser evil than ecclesiastical subjection to the Roman See. In the seventeenth century—the century in which the West began to secularize its way of life—the Modern Greeks abandoned the Byzantine tradition of hostility towards the West, and, after that, they were attracted towards two new objectives: political liberation from Ottoman rule and cultural Westernization. It has been noted that the Modern Greeks' increasing success in finding a place for themselves in the Western World has given them the confidence to assert their spiritual independence of both their Hellenic and their Byzantine heritage.

This, however, will not be the end of the story of the Modern Greeks' encounter with the Western civilization. Since the seventeenth century the Western civilization in its secular modern form has become a world-wide civilization that has been adopted not only by the Greeks but also by most of the other originally non-Western peoples. However, at the very time when the Western civilization has been captivating the whole world it has been showing signs of spiritual sickness. It is not yet clear how serious this sickness is, but it is already certain that the whole world is now implicated in the West's future fortunes, whatever these may prove to be. Thus the Modern Greek people's future seems likely to be determined by the common future of a Modern world that has now been united on a global scale within an originally Western framework.

APPENDICES

Chapter II. Appendix
The Post-Mycenaean Dark Age[1]

THE Hellenic, Byzantine, and Modern ages of Greek history have each been demarcated from its predecessor by a partial break of historical continuity. The sharpest of the three breaks was the first, and this was followed by the Hellenic Age, in which the Greeks were more successful than they were in the foregoing Mycenaean Age and than they have been either in the subsequent Byzantine Age or in the Modern Age so far. This correlation between the degree of the break with the past and the degree of the ensuing age's success seems unlikely to be fortuitous, but it cannot be taken for granted, without investigation, that the relation is one of cause and effect. The break between the Mycenaean and the Hellenic Age, which is manifest to us, seems not to have been apparent to the Hellenes. Moreover, modern students of Greek history have not seen eye to eye with each other in assessing the relative importance of the various factors by which the post-Mycenaean break was produced.

For the Hellenes, the Mycenaean Age was not a distinct chapter of Greek history; it was just a prelude to their own Hellenic chapter. For the author or authors of the *Iliad* and the *Odyssey*, it was a glamorous heroic Age;[2] for Hesiod, who probably lived and wrote at the close of the eighth or at the opening of the seventh century B.C., there had been a progressive deterioration of the conditions of life in his world from a primaeval golden age to the iron age into which Hesiod himself had been born—though, to our eyes, it looks as if, in Hesiod's time, life in Greece, so far from being at its nadir, was bursting, once again, into flower.[3] Thucydides' picture of the course of Greek history is the inverse of Hesiod's inasmuch as Thucydides sees it as having been, not steadily

---

[1] The chronological span of the post-Mycenaean Dark Age can be equated with the whole of the period of illiteracy in the Greek World between the oblivion of the 'Linear B' syllabic script at some date in the twelfth century B.C. and the adoption and adaptation of the Phoenician alphabetic script at some date in the eighth century B.C. Thus defined, the post-Mycenaean Dark Age has a time-span of at least four centuries, and probably runs to four and a half centuries. This is the span covered by Snodgrass in *The Dark Age of Greece*. On the other hand Desborough, in *The Greek Dark Ages* (e.g. on pp. 11 and 489) limits the span of the Dark Age to the period *c.* 1125/1100 B.C.—*circa* 900 B.C. This is the period covered by the sub-Mycenaean Age and the subsequent Protogeometric Age, together, in those parts of the Greek World which were the first to change over from the Mycenaean (*alias* Late Helladic) III style to the sub-Mycenaean style, and were also the first to change over from the Protogeometric style to the Early Geometric.

[2] See above, p. 28 with n. 14.

[3] For Hesiod's conception of his own age and of its antecedents, see Desborough, *The Greek Dark Ages*, p. 322.

degenerating, but gradually progressing;[4] but Thucydides agrees with Hesiod, as against all modern students of Greek history, in seeing the curve as a continuous trend in one direction—ascending for Thucydides, descending for Hesiod—and not as an undulation in the shape of crest-trough-crest.[5] In fact, these varying Hellenic Greek interpretations of the Hellenes' dim recollection of the Mycenaean Age agree in virtually annexing the Mycenaean chapter of Greek history to their own Hellenic chapter.[6] For them, the Mycenaean chapter is not a distinct and separate historical episode.

Though this is the common Hellenic view of the Mycenaean Age, it is unconvincing to modern students of Greek history because it is incompatible with their knowledge of the Hellenes' antecedents. This knowledge is much greater than the Hellenes' knowledge ever was, thanks to the discoveries made by modern archaeologists within the past hundred years. We see, with convincing clarity, both the crest of the Mycenaean wave and the subsequent post-Mycenaean and pre-Hellenic trough. Against the background of a knowledge of the zenith of the Mycenaean Age—a knowledge that we possess, but that the Hellenes did not—we can discern the features of the post-Mycenaean trough: depopulation,[7] loss of skills and arts (for instance, loss of literacy), impoverishment, isolation, and perhaps also an aggravation of insecurity.[8] The Greek World was dark, in the particular sense of being illiterate, for at least 450 years (*circa* 1200–750 B.C.). There has been no break in literacy in subsequent Greek history since the Hellenic Greeks' adoption of the Phoenician alphabet at some date before the end of the eighth century B.C.

Modern students of Greek history have, however, disagreed with each other in their assessment of the relative importance that they have attributed to the several causes that, between them, may have produced the post-Mycenaean Dark Age. Each of the three major breaks in Greek history has been accompanied—and, no doubt, has been also partly caused—by a *Völkerwanderung*. The collapse of the Byzantine Greek civilization between A.D. 1182 and A.D. 1453 was accompanied by a movement of Turkish-speaking pastoral nomads (*yürüks*) out of the Eurasian steppe into Asia Minor and, from there, into the Balkan Peninsula. There was also a less massive contemporary movement into southern continental Greece of Albanian-speaking shepherds and peasants from Albania. The collapse of the Hellenic civilization was accompanied by a movement of Slavonic-speaking barbarian peasants into the heart of continental European Greece, as far southward as the Pelopónnêsos. The collapse of the Mycenaean civilization was accompanied, or was followed, by a movement that resembled the subsequent Slav migration inasmuch as, in this case too, the migrants were barbarian peasants, not nomads. However, the post-Mycenaean *Völkerwanderung* differed from its post-Hellenic counterpart in three important points.

Though these earlier peasant migrants likewise came in from the north, there

[4] See Thucydides, Book I, chapters 1–21, and Desborough, *The Last Mycenaeans*, pp. 322–3.

[5] See Snodgrass, op. cit., pp. 1, 7–8, 10, 19.

[6] For this, see also the present work, pp. 35–6.

[7] For this, see the present Appendix, pp. 281–2 with nn. 54–6.

[8] For this list of symptoms, see Snodgrass, op. cit., p. 2.

is no evidence that their previous habitat was so remote. They did not come in from somewhere north of the Danube; their starting-point appears to have been Êpeiros, Akarnania, and the interior of Aetolia—a region that lay only just beyond the north-west frontier of the Mycenaean World. Secondly, the mother tongue of at least the great majority of these migrants was not a non-Greek language;[9] it was the North-West-Greek/Doric dialect of Greek; and it is now thought that, before the post-Mycenaean Dark Age, the Greek dialects had not yet become so decidedly differentiated from each other as they were in the ensuing Hellenic Age until the Attic *koine* established—or re-established— linguistic uniformity in the Greek-speaking world by putting other dialects out of currency, as the 'Linear B' *koine* seems to have done in the Mycenaean Age, for the writing of administrative documents, at any rate. Thirdly, these North-West-Greek-speakers were perhaps almost encircled by outposts of the Mycenaean civilization before they themselves migrated south-eastwards into the Mycenaean World. The neighbouring islands, Ithaca and Kephallênía, were included, according to the Homeric tradition, in one of the kingdoms of the Mycenaean World, and there is some slight archaeological confirmation of this tradition. There have been a few finds there of objects of an earlier date than Late Helladic III C.[10] There were Mycenaean beach-heads at Pleuron and Kalydon (i.e. in Aetolia proper), and possibly also along the coasts of Akarnania and Êpeiros, and, in the interior of Êpeiros, at Kalbaki near Yánnina[11]—and thus also near Dodona, which, in the *Iliad*,[12] is represented as having been held sacred by Achilles.

Thus the pre-migration habitat of the North-West-Greek-speakers was exposed to the radiation of influences from the Mycenaean World, and it is credible that a tincture of the Mycenaean civilization may have overlaid and partially obliterated the previous local native culture, as, in the subsequent Hellenic Age, this same outlying north-western part of Greece acquired a tincture of the Hellenic civilization that had come to full flower round the shores of the Aegean. If this tentative reconstruction of the North-West-Greek-speaking migrants' previous cultural history is convincing, it will seem likely that the post-Mycenaean *Völkerwanderung* had a less disruptive effect than the post-Hellenic and post-Byzantine *Völkerwanderungen* had. In the post-Mycenaean case the incoming barbarians, unlike their later counterparts the Slavs and the Turkish *yürüks* and the Albanians, were linguistically, and perhaps also to some

[9] There are indications, in traditions current in the Hellenic Age, that part, at least, of the region vacated by the North-West-Greek-speaking migrants in Êpeiros, together with some enclaves of territory in Aetolia, was occupied by Illyrian-speakers who eventually became Greek-speakers. There are also indications that some Thracian-speakers penetrated still further into Greece in the course of the post-Mycenaean *Völkerwanderung*. (See Toynbee, A. J., *Some Problems of Greek History* (London 1969), pp. 97–8 and 105–17.) The finds, with Macedonian affinities, at Marmariani and at Rhakhmani, in north-eastern Thessaly, are perhaps pieces of archaeological evidence for a southward thrust of Thracian-speakers. For these finds, see Desborough, *The Last Mycenaeans*, pp. 22, 133, 137–8, 250, 255; *eundem, The Greek Dark Ages*, pp. 213–15 and 346; Snodgrass, op. cit., pp. 236, 330, 406–7.

[10] See Desborough, *The Last Mycenaeans*, pp. 103–11; *eundem, The Greek Dark Ages*, p. 85.

[11] See Desborough, *The Last Mycenaeans*, p. 102; *eundem, The Greek Dark Ages*, pp. 85–6; Snodgrass, op. cit., pp. 102–3.

[12] *Iliad*, Book XVI, lines 233–5.

extent culturally, akin to the heirs of the broken-down civilization on whose domain they were intruding.

At the same time it is manifest, as has been noted already, that the post-Mycenaean break of historical continuity was more radical than the post-Hellenic and post-Byzantine breaks were. There must have been some special feature of the post-Mycenaean break that would account for the greater direness of its effect; and some modern scholars have guessed—though this guess is contrary to the *a priori* probability—that the cause of the direness of the post-Mycenaean break was the barbarousness and brutality of the North-West-Greek-speaking intruders. The following verdicts are recent:

> Even though fine things were rubbed out by the Dorians . . . on the whole it was well for Europe that the slate was wiped clean.[13]
>
> In the fact that the Dorians did end the Mycenaean Age lies their significance. Greek[14] civilization could never have arisen if that disruption had not occurred and had not shaken the old conventions.[15]

This explanation of the unparalleled thoroughness of the post-Mycenaean break is not only improbable *a priori*; it has now been flatly contradicted by the findings of archaeology, and it is not borne out by the Hellenic tradition. In this, the North-West-Greek/Doric-speakers' migration is not presented as having been the epoch-making event that some modern scholars have taken it to be.[16]

However, the Hellenes are partly responsible for these modern scholars' evident exaggeration of the post-Mycenaean *Völkerwanderung's* disruptive effects. In the Hellenic World in the fifth century B.C., the rivalry, and eventual conflict, between the two most powerful Hellenic city-states of that age was translated into racial terms as a confrontation between 'Dorians' and 'Ionians',[17] on the ground that the Athenians spoke a variety of the Ionic dialect, whereas the Spartans and some of their most bitterly anti-Athenian allies, e.g. the Corinthians and the Aeginetans, spoke varieties of the Doric dialect. In reality, these linguistic facts had been culturally and politically irrelevant until political capital was made of them in the fifth century B.C. The post-Dark-Age boundaries between dialect-areas had never been barriers to the transmission of thought, of visual art, or of styles of poetry.[18] Nor were

---

[13] Dow, in Kirk, op. cit., p. 165.

[14] This equation of the word 'Greek' *sans phrase* with the Hellenic chapter of Greek history gives the measure of the degree to which Hellenism has dominated the view, taken by posterity, of Greek history as a whole. For many historians, the non-Hellenic chapters of this history do not count.

[15] Starr, op. cit., pp. 73-4.

[16] This is pointed out by Snodgrass, op. cit., pp. 19-20.

[17] This, too, is pointed out by Snodgrass, op. cit., pp. 303-4 and 385-6. Examples of this fifth-century-B.C. racial interpretation of the dialect map of the Greek language in the Hellenic Age are the alleged colloquy between the Athenian priestess of the Parthenon on the acropolis of Athens and the Spartan King Cleomenes I (Herodotus, Book V, chapter 72) and Thucydides' constant interpretation of differences of dialect as being tantamount to racial differences. The most extreme case is the passage (Book VII, chapters 57-8) in which he notes that, in the struggle for Syracuse in 414-413 B.C., there were contingents of Ionic-speakers and Doric-speakers in both camps. In his view, this meant that neither camp was racially homogeneous (οὐδὲ κατ᾽ ἀλλήλων κατὰ συγγένειαν στάντες).

[18] See Snodgrass, op. cit., pp. 304 and 385.

fifth-century-B.C. Sparta and Athens fair samples of the Doric-speaking and Ionic-speaking areas as a whole.[19] Both the fifth-century-B.C. super-powers had become highly peculiar and unrepresentative; yet the dramatic contrast between their temperaments and their ways of life in the fifth century B.C.[20] was now erroneously interpreted as being a contrast between 'Dorians' and 'Ionians' in general, and this imaginary contrast was read back, in retrospect, with an ideological *arrière pensée*, into the relations between 'Dorians' and 'Ionians' since the beginning of these dialects' differentiation from each other. By implication, the grimness of the Spartan spirit since Sparta's eighth-century-B.C. conquests and her consequent seventh-century-B.C. adoption of the 'Osmanli-like militaristic 'Lycurgan' *agogê* was attributed to all Doric-speakers at the time of their original migration into the Mycenaean World, and these migrants were debited falsely with a barbaric brutality for which there was no authentic evidence dating from that remote and undocumented age.

This fifth-century-B.C. ideological misrepresentation of past Hellenic history partly accounts for, and discounts, the exaggeration, by some modern scholars, of the post-Mycenaean North-West-Greek-speaking migrants' role in causing the undisputedly extreme break of historical continuity between the Mycenaean and the Hellenic Age of Greek history. If the extremeness of the break is not attributable to the *Völkerwanderung*, some other, more convincing, explanation has to be found. What light does the evidence throw on the *Völkerwanderung*'s date, character, course, extent, and historical effect? And does the evidence bring to light other causes of the manifest break of historical continuity?

We possess four different kinds of evidence: the material products of the inhabitants of the Greek World in the post-Mycenaean Dark Age that have been disinterred by modern archaeologists, the dialect-map of the Hellenic World that can be reconstructed from inscriptions, the social structure of certain Hellenic Greek communities that is described in trustworthy Hellenic literary sources, and—fourth and last—the Hellenic traditions about the history of the pre-Hellenic Dark Age.

Among these four different kinds of evidence, the archaeological evidence must be given credence in cases in which it conflicts with evidence of other kinds.[21] The archaeological evidence has serious limitations.[22] In a case—which is the actual case of the post-Mycenaean Dark Age—in which the society under investigation is illiterate, the archaeological evidence is dumb. For instance, it cannot inform us about a community's political structure; and, though it is more informative about social life, its information in this field is not proportionate to the realities. In Greece, we have retrieved far more numerous

---

[19] For instance, Doric-speaking Syracuse, and Sparta's own overseas colony, Doric-speaking Tarentum, were less like Sparta than they were like Athens in their way of life. The Doric dialect was not automatically accompanied by the Lycurgan *agogê*.

[20] The classic exposition of this contrast is made in the speech put into Pericles' mouth by Thucydides in Book II, chapters 35–46.

[21] This point is made by Desborough in *The Last Mycenaeans*, pp. 255 and 257, and in *The Greek Dark Ages*, pp. 321–5; and by Snodgrass in op. cit., p. 296.

[22] These are signalled by Desborough in *The Last Mycenaeans*, on p. 257, and (apropos of the continuity of the cult of Hyakinthos at Amyklai) in *The Greek Dark Ages*, pp. 280 and 283.

utensils and architectural structures belonging to the sepulchres of the dead than those belonging to the habitations of the living;[23] textiles have perished, leaving only indirect traces in the form of brooches and pins; these and other metallic objects are relatively scarce; and the most numerous surviving objects are potsherds.

Pottery, even in the form of intact earthenware vessels, is an imperfect index of the character and development of an entire culture. The physical durability of potsherds is greater than their cultural significance.[24] Yet the evidence provided by material objects, including potsherds, is instructive. Just because the material relics of an illiterate society are dumb, they cannot deliberately deceive us, though their mute testimony may, of course, be misinterpreted by us. Moreover, pottery is an invaluable indicator of relative chronology—and of absolute chronology too, if the potsherds discarded by an illiterate culture are found in association with products of a literate culture that can be dated. In all cultures the shapes, decorations, and fabrics of earthenware vessels change frequently, in response to developments of technique and to changes of fashion. The stratification of successive styles of pottery thus enables us to construct a chronological chart of the history of a culture's material facet, and the evidence of each successive stratum is contemporary evidence.

This contemporaneity of the archaeological evidence is its sovereign virtue. Tradition cannot challenge its credibility if and when tradition is discordant with it, and the superiority of the archaeological to the traditional evidence is especially decisive for an illiterate age in which the tradition has had to be handed down orally for at least 450 years before a script in which it can be put in writing has come into use.[25] Oral transmission is notoriously inaccurate, except for the transmission of magical or religious formulae which are believed to forfeit their efficacy if the recital of them is not word-perfect.

The map of the geographical distribution of the Greek dialects in the Hellenic Age is much better evidence than the traditions about the post-Mycenaean *Völkerwanderung* that survived into the Hellenic Age or were fabricated in it. In so far as the Hellenic-Age dialect-map is based on inscriptional evidence, it has archaeological credentials that are as good as those provided by the material relics of the pre-Hellenic Dark Age. The weakness of the inscriptional evidence is the lateness of its date. The earliest Greek alphabetic inscriptions are no older than the late eighth century B.C., and, though inscriptions of probable eighth-century date are fairly widespread,[26] there are many parts of the Hellenic Greek World in which the inscriptions so far found are few and are in some cases as much as five centuries later in date. This is a grave limitation on the value of the evidence of Hellenic-Age dialect-inscriptions for dating the post-Mycenaean *Völkerwanderung* and for charting its geographical course.

Language is as changeable as pottery styles are. The post-Mycenaean

---

[23] See Snodgrass, op. cit., pp. 24 and 141.

[24] This point is made by Desborough, *The Last Mycenaeans*, p. 257, and by Snodgrass, op. cit., pp. 28 and 393.

[25] See Desborough, *The Last Mycenaeans*, p. 255, and *The Greek Dark Ages*, pp. 321-5.

[26] See the list of their locations in Snodgrass, op. cit., p. 421.

Völkerwanderung itself is now thought to have accelerated and accentuated the differentiation of the Greek dialects from each other. Their relations with each other, as attested by even the earliest alphabetic Greek inscriptions, may be considerably different from what their relations had been in the pre-*Völkerwanderung* Age. Moreover, communities can change their language, and this is particularly easy when it is merely a question of exchanging one dialect for another dialect of the same language. In the Hellenic Age, Attic Greek had probably begun to become a lingua franca before the fall of the First Athenian Empire in 404 B.C., and the supplanting of other Greek dialects by the Attic *koine* went with a run after King Philip II of Macedon had adopted Attic as his administrative language and after Alexander had annexed the former domain of the Persian Empire to the Hellenic World.

On a smaller scale, there had probably been changes in the Hellenic World's dialect-map at earlier stages in the Hellenic chapter of Greek history. For instance, by the date of the earliest inscriptions and literary works in the Ionic dialect, this dialect was being spoken, with local variations, throughout Ionia, as well as in the Cyclades, Euboea, and (with a more sharply pronounced local idiosyncracy) in Attica. Yet, according to tradition, as preserved, in three separate versions, by Herodotus,[27] Strabo,[28] and Pausanias,[29] each of the Asian Ionian city-states was founded by the coalescence of a number of parties of settlers, hailing from different parts of European Greece, and some of these parties came from non-Ionic-speaking districts. Many of the details of this tradition are suspect of being fabrications for purposes of political propaganda.[30] But there is no reason for doubting the general statement, which is common to all accounts, that the original settlers were speakers of a number of different dialects of Greek, and this statement implies that the exclusive currency of the Ionic dialect in Ionia in and after the eighth century B.C. was a development that was subsequent to the settlement.

If this is the truth, Ionia became homogeneously Ionic-speaking, not as a result of having been colonized exclusively by Ionic-speaking settlers, but as a result of the non-Ionic-speaking settlers' or their descendants', having voluntarily adopted the dialect of their Ionic-speaking fellow-settlers. If the dialect-map thus simplified and consolidated itself in the course of the Hellenic Age in Ionia, the same thing may have happened more or less contemporaneously in other regions of the Greek-speaking World. It thus appears that the post-*Völkerwanderung* distribution of dialects may have been produced, not exclusively by migrations of populations, but partly by changes of dialect, or even perhaps changes of language, on the part of populations that remained stationary in their ancestral homes. In so far as the Hellenic-Age dialect-map was produced by the second of these two processes, it is not an accurate indicator of the history of the antecedent *Völkerwanderung*.

Nevertheless, the Hellenic-Age dialect-map does reveal the general lines of

---

[27] Herodotus, Book I, chapters 146–8.

[28] Strabo, Book XIV, chapters 1 and 3 (C. 632) for Teos and Khios, and 15 (C. 637) for Samos.

[29] Pausanias, Book VII, chapters 2–4.

[30] The evidence has been assembled and sifted by M. B. Sakellariou in *La migration grecque en Ionie* (Athens 1958).

the *Völkerwanderung's* movement. It shows us that, at some date, migrants from North-West Greece pushed their way south-eastwards as far as the Dodecanese and some beach-heads at the south-west corner of continental Asia Minor. It also shows that this migration of North-West-Greek-speakers split up the former domains of the speakers of North-East (*alias* Aeolic) Greek and of South (*alias* Arcado-Cyprian and Ionic) Greek. The South-Greek dialect's original domain was presumably the Pelopónnêsos, Central Greece as far westward as Phokis inclusive, and Euboea; the North-East-Greek dialect's original domain was presumably Thessaly. The North-West-Greek-speaking migrants evidently drove some of the Peloponnesian South-Greek-speakers overseas to Cyprus and penned the remainder of them up in Arcadia. They drove some of the South-Greek-speakers in Central Greece overseas into Ionia, and expedited the differentiation of the Ionic variety of South Greek from the Arcado-Cyprian variety. In the third place they drove some of the North-East-Greek (Aeolic) speakers out of Thessaly into Boeotia, while others were eventually driven overseas into the Asian Aiolis.

The Hellenic-Age evidence that is most at variance with the Dark-Age archaeological evidence is at the same time more intractable than the evidence presented by the Hellenic-Age dialect-map and the Hellenic-Age tradition. This intractable evidence is the well-attested Hellenic-Age structure of society in Crete and in Thessaly. This resembles the contemporary structure in the southern part of the Pelopónnêsos. In all three regions alike, we find a dominant minority holding down a majority that has been reduced to serfdom. We know that, in the south of the Pelopónnêsos, this structure had been produced by the Spartan city-state's conquest of Amyklai, Helos, and Messenia in the course of the second half of the eighth century B.C. Here the structure had nothing to do with either the post-Mycenaean *Völkerwanderung* or the Hellenic-Age dialect-map. It was wholly the result of well-attested military and political action by a particular Hellenic city-state. But we have no similar evidence for the date at which the ruling caste in the Cretan city-states and in Thessaly established its dominance, or for the means that it employed. In these two regions there is no Dark-Age or post-Dark-Age archaeological evidence, except possibly at one site in north-western Thessaly, for conquests of the kind that Sparta is known to have made in the eighth century B.C.[31]

If we examine the Dark-Age archaeological evidence, do we find that the North-West-Greek-speaking migrants have left any material traces of their arrival? It used to be thought that it was they who had brought with them the funerary rite of cremation as a substitute for inhumation, the use of iron as a

---

[31] For the non-correspondence of the Dark-Age archaeological evidence with the Hellenic tradition in the case of Thessaly, see Desborough, *The Last Mycenaeans*, p. 250; Snodgrass, op. cit., p. 312. The destruction of the Mycenaean palace at Iolkos at some date before the close of the twelfth century (see Desborough, *The Greek Dark Ages*, pp. 24 and 100) is not very likely to have been the work of invaders from the north-west. On the other hand, some of the contents of Dark-Age graves at Exalophos (Hexalophos), 8 miles to the west of Trikkala, in the Hellenic-Age Thessalian tetrarchy Histiaiotis, have affinities with the Dark-Age culture of Êpeiros, and these finds suggest that the north-west corner, at any rate, of Thessaly, may have been occupied at this date by the Thessaloi who eventually became dominant in Thessaly as a whole (see Desborough, *The Greek Dark Ages*, pp. 98, 206, 339–40).

substitute for bronze, and the Protogeometric style of decorating pottery. It now appears that the rite of cremation was already being practised on the Anatolian plateau by *circa* 1600 B.C. and in Troy VI before 1300 B.C., and that it probably spread from Asia Minor westwards.[32] In continental European Greece, Athens, which was never occupied by the North-West-Greek-speaking migrants, was one of the earliest places in which the rite of cremation was adopted.[33] In the Kerameikos cemetery at Athens, 106 out of 109 sub-Mycenaean graves are inhumations, but 51 out of 57 Protogeometric graves are cremations, and, in the Early Geometric Age at Athens, cremation was practised exclusively.[34] Athens (Kerameikos) and Salamis were also, in the twelfth century B.C., pioneers in 'the whole-hearted adoption . . . of the principle of single burial' instead of the Mycenaean practice of multiple burial in family vaults.[35] The technology of iron-working seems to have been introduced into Greece from Cyprus in the eleventh century B.C.[36] If we date the beginning of the Iron Age at the time when iron was substituted for bronze as the metal for artifacts intended for practical uses, the Iron Age begins in Greece contemporaneously with, or only slightly later than, the beginning of the Protogeometric Age, and, for both these two innovations, as well as for cremation, the pioneer community in continental European Greece was Athens.[37]

Desborough once held that the North-West-Greek-speaking migrants have left a material trace of their arrival and settlement in the shape of cist-tombs and pithos-burials.[38] Snodgrass has disputed this former thesis of Desborough's. He maintains 'that the cist-tomb and its associated forms of single burial, so far from being an indication of a new wave of settlers supervening on the ruins of the Mycenaean civilization, are merely a resurgent phenomenon of pre-Mycenaean Greece which had never been wholly dormant even in Mycenaean times'.[39] On this question, Desborough's most recent conclusions are more tentative than his original findings.[40]

Thus there is not any undisputed direct archaeological evidence for the arrival and settlement of North-West-Greek-speaking intruders in the Mycenaean World at the time of the destruction of the Mycenaean palaces *circa*

---

[32] Snodgrass, op. cit., p. 189; Desborough, *The Last Mycenaeans*, pp. 71 and 157.

[33] Snodgrass points out, in op. cit., p. 146, that a change in funerary rites does not necessarily imply a change of population or of religion. It may be due merely to a change of fashion. As examples of this, he cites the alternating vogues of inhumation and cremation in Roman society, and the increase of the vogue for cremation in Britain from 1.7 per cent of funerals in 1935 to 52.4 per cent in 1968.

[34] Snodgrass, op. cit., p. 144. The archaeological evidence gives Desborough the impression that at Athens, during and after the second half of the eleventh century B.C., 'the society as a whole took on a rather regimented character' (*The Greek Dark Ages*, p. 158; cp. pp. 139 and 292). This is, indeed, what is to be expected if at Athens, in contrast to all other seats of the Mycenaean civilization, the Mycenaean authoritarian regime survived without a break of continuity, but in a temporary state of siege.

[35] Snodgrass, op. cit., pp. 147 and 177; Desborough, *The Greek Dark Ages*, pp. 268-77.

[36] Snodgrass, op. cit., pp. 229-30; Desborough, *The Last Mycenaeans*, p. 25.

[37] Snodgrass, op. cit., pp. 222 and 229.

[38] See Desborough, *The Last Mycenaeans*, General Index, p. 287, s.v. New settlers—(non-Mycenaeans).

[39] Snodgrass, op. cit., p. 184. See the whole of pp. 177-86 and 314-17.

[40] See Desborough, *The Greek Dark Ages*, p. 270.

1200 B.C.[41] The destruction at this date was so widespread that it seems more likely to have been caused by invaders coming from abroad than by fratricidal warfare among the Mycenaeans themselves.[42] But Desborough and Snodgrass are in agreement with each other in holding that, if the destruction *circa* 1200 B.C. was in truth the work of invaders, there is 'no sign whatever'[43] of the invaders having settled in the districts that had been devastated by them and had been evacuated by Mycenaean refugees. 'What remains is . . . purely Mycenaean'.[44] 'Nowhere do we find destruction at this time followed immediately by the signs of a new cultural element.'[45] If the invaders did settle in the Mycenaean World after they had devastated it, they must either have brought with them a culture that was indistinguishable from the Mycenaean culture or must have adopted the culture of their Mycenaean victims.[46] Alternative possibilities are that the invaders withdrew with their loot to their homeland in the north-west or that they pushed on further afield in quest of further loot in the Levant—that they were, in fact, the 'Sea Peoples', or a contingent of these, whose unsuccessful assault in Egypt has been recorded by Ramses III.

On the other hand there is some substantial indirect evidence for the lodgment in the Mycenaean World of invaders at this date. There is, first of all, the transition from the Late Helladic III B to the Late Helladic III C style of pottery, which can be dated between 1230 B.C. and 1185 B.C.[47] This change in pottery-style was contemporaneous with the destruction of the majority of the Mycenaean palaces. There is also the archaeological evidence for movements of refugees, and these must have been fleeing from, or have been evicted by, newcomers. The places where this evidence has been found are at the western end of the Peloponnesian Akhaïa (the part to the west of Mount Panakhaïkós, not the strip along the southern shore of the Corinthian Gulf),[48] the adjacent islands of Kephallênía and Ithaca, Eastern Attica (Perati), Lefkandi in Euboea, Áyios Ioánnês in Kynouría, Embório on the south coast of Khios, Cyprus, and Tarsós.[49] The evidence for the movements of refugees consists of

[41] Professor Browning points out that, likewise, there is no archaeological evidence for the arrival and settlement of Slavonic-speaking intruders in the Pelopónnêsos at the close of the Hellenic Age of Greek history. This reminds me of my own naïve surprise, when I visited Spoleto in 1911, at finding that there was no archaeological evidence there for the arrival and settlement of German-speaking Lombards. Apparently it is unusual for barbarian invaders of civilized regions to leave unquestionable material traces of their presence.

[42] Desborough, *The Greek Dark Ages*, p. 22.

[43] Ibid., p. 21.

[44] Ibid. Professor Browning comments: 'It seems to me that the problems are a bit like those of Dark-Age England, where it is now clear that there was a survival of Roman institutions of a kind until the late sixth century, in spite of English victories about the middle of the fifth, and that the real break with the past comes around 600.'

[45] Snodgrass, op. cit., pp. 311–12.

[46] Ibid., p. 312.

[47] For the evidence, see Desborough, *The Last Mycenaeans*, p. 240; Snodgrass, op. cit., pp. 107–9.

[48] Desborough, *The Last Mycenaeans*, p. 227. The same district was occupied by refugees from the Slav *Völkerwanderung* in the early seventh century of the Christian Era, as is attested by the place-names Ano Akhaïa and Kato Akhaïa.

[49] For this list, see Snodgrass, op. cit., p. 311, and compare Desborough, *The Greek Dark Ages*, pp. 20–3. For the western end of Akhaïa, see Vermeule, op. cit., p. 270; Desborough, *The Last Mycenaeans*, pp. 9, 35, 103–9. For Eastern Attica, see ibid., pp. 35, 112, 115; Snodgrass, op. cit.,

finds of pottery of the Late Helladic III C style, i.e. the style that replaced the Late Helladic III B style after the destruction of the majority of the Mycenaean palaces, and which dates this destruction *circa* 1200 B.C. In Cyprus the evidence of pottery is supplemented by the sudden appearance of Mycenaean-type chamber-tombs.[50] During the Late Helladic III C period, there seem to have been two migrations of Mycenaean refugees to Cyprus,[51] one immediately after the widespread destruction of Mycenaean palaces *circa* 1200B.C., and a second after the destruction of the Granary at Mycenae *circa* 1150 B.C. or later. In the areas where the settlement of Mycenaean refugees is indicated by finds of Late Helladic III C pottery, this is in nearly all cases strikingly more abundant than pottery of the antecedent Late Helladic III B type. This suggests that, after the major catastrophe in the Mycenaean World *circa* 1200 B.C., there was an actual increase of population in the districts which then became reception-areas for refugees.[52] Embório was a new settlement. This was the first place, and the Late Helladic III C period was the earliest date, at which the Mycenaeans won a foothold on the island of Khios.[53]

Besides the indirect evidence in the shape of movements of refugees, there is negative evidence, in the shape of depopulation, for the impact of intruders from North-West Greece on the Mycenaean World.[54] Laconia and Messenia were not merely depopulated; apparently these two districts remained derelict, and perhaps almost uninhabited, for about two centuries.[55] Elis, too was

pp. 40, 110, 147–8, 312, 317, 326. For Cyprus, see Desborough, *The Last Mycenaeans*, pp. 24–5, 28, 229, 236; Snodgrass, op. cit., pp. 29, 314, 316, 365. For Tarsós, see Desborough, pp. 205–6, 222, 236; Snodgrass, op. cit., pp. 311, 324.

[50] See Desborough, *The Last Mycenaeans*, p. 25.

[51] See ibid., pp. 25 and 236; *eundem*, *The Greek Dark Ages*, pp. 20, 24, 49, 51; Snodgrass, op. cit., p. 365.

[52] See Desborough, *The Last Mycenaeans*, p. 35; Snodgrass, op. cit., p. 29.

[53] Ibid.

[54] See Desborough, *The Last Mycenaeans*, General Index, *s.v.* Depopulation at end of Late Helladic III B and during Late Helladic III C. Desborough guesses, in *The Greek Dark Ages*, p. 18, that, by 1100 B.C., the population of the Mycenaean World had shrunk to one tenth of what it had been in 1200 B.C. In ibid., pp. 19–20, Desborough gives the following figures for the fall in the number of known occupied sites as between the thirteenth and the twelfth century B.C.: in the south-western Pelopónnêsos, a fall from about 150 to 14 (see also ibid., p. 84); in Laconia from 30 to 7; in the Argolid and Corinthia from 44 to 14; in Attica from 24 to 12; in Boeotia from 27 to 3: in Phokis and Lokris from 19 to 5. In the whole of Greece and the Aegean basin, there are fewer than 30 Dark-Age settlements (ibid., p. 261; cp. p. 263). Snodgrass's figures, in op. cit., p. 364, for the number of so far known inhabited sites in the Greek World in the Dark Age is 320 for the thirteenth century B.C., 130 for the twelfth century B.C., and 40 for the eleventh century B.C. Nearly 200 Early Helladic sites and nearly 250 Middle Helladic sites have been found (Snodgrass, op. cit., p. 367). This extreme degree of depopulation would be easier to account for if it were proven that the effect of the ravages of fratricidal warfare and barbarian invasion was reinforced by a simultaneous change of climate. Ellsworth Huntington, the pioneer student of the effect of climatic changes on human history, was so much in advance of his time that his findings were rejected by a majority of contemporary students of human affairs. Evidence for the effect of climatic changes on Greek history has now been presented by Rhys Carpenter in *Discontinuity in Greek Civilization* (Cambridge 1966). While the present book was being written, climatic change was producing catastrophic effects in the Sahil (i.e. the belt of savannah country between the former southern edge of the Sahara and the northern edge of the African tropical rain forest).

[55] See Desborough, *The Last Mycenaeans*, pp. 34–5, 97, 251; *eundem*, *The Greek Dark Ages*, pp. 240–1, 255–6; Snodgrass, op. cit., pp. 29–30, 130–1.

depopulated,[56] and so was Western Attica in contrast to Eastern Attica. However, in Western Attica, the acropolis of Athens never fell, and the depopulation of the countryside here was perhaps not so extreme, and was certainly not so long protracted, as it was in the southern part of the Pelopónnêsos.

The movements of refugees into some areas and the depopulation of other areas and the widespread destruction of palaces, with the contemporaneous change of pottery-style, give us indications not only for dating at least the first wave of the *Völkerwanderung* from North-West Greece, but also for charting this first wave's course. The fortification of most of the Mycenaean palaces (with the conspicuous exception of Ano Englianos, which is presumably Pylos) in the fourteenth century B.C.[57] may have been a precaution against attack, not by barbarians from beyond the pale, but by one Mycenaean kingdom against another. The destruction of Thebes in the Late Helladic IIIA period (late fourteenth-century B.C.), for which there is archaeological evidence,[58] may have been the work of the Kingdom of Mycenae, as it is said to have been in the Hellenic tradition. The destruction of Troy VIIa about half-way through the thirteenth century B.C.,[59] which the archaeological evidence also attests, may have been the work of an expeditionary force, consisting of contingents supplied by a number of Mycenaean kingdoms under the leadership of a war-lord who may have been chosen *ad hoc* or may have been the permanent suzerain of all the states in the Mycenaean World. However, an expectation of an attack by barbarians from the north-west is perhaps indicated by the great size of the areas enclosed within the *enceintes* of the Mycenaean fortified towns to the north-west of Attica.[60] These must have been designed as cities of refuge for the surrounding population, with its flocks and herds, and not solely as defences for the permanent residents.[61] Moreover, the construction of a wall across the Isthmus of Corinth in the Late Helladic IIIB period (the second half of the thirteenth century B.C.),[62] indicates that at that date, as in 480 B.C. and again in the fourteenth and fifteenth centuries of the Christian Era, the Peloponnesians were expecting an attack overland via Central Greece.

In spite of the lack of positive evidence for the arrival of migrants from North-Western Greece, the movement of refugees into some areas, the depopulation of other areas, the widespread simultaneous destruction or abandonment of Mycenaean palaces and settlements *circa* 1200 B.C., and the transition from the Late Helladic IIIB to the Late Helladic IIIC style of pottery at about the same date, cannot be accounted for, as the earlier destruction of Thebes can be, by the hypothesis that this was the work of fratricidal warfare between Mycenaean kingdoms. At this date 'Krisa in Phokis, Gla in Boeotia, Zygouries in Corinthia, Mycenae and Tiryns in the Argolid, the Menelaïon site in Laconia, Pylos and

---

[56] Desborough, *The Last Mycenaeans*, p. 97.

[57] See above, p. 17.

[58] See Desborough, *The Last Mycenaeans*, p. 12; cp. Snodgrass, op. cit., p. 12.

[59] For the date, see above, p. 20.

[60] See Desborough, *The Last Mycenaeans*, pp. 30 and 221.

[61] Similarly capacious *enceintes* are also characteristic of the Hellenic-Age fortifications of towns in North-Western Greece.

[62] See Desborough, *The Last Mycenaeans*, pp. 30, 85, 221; Snodgrass, op. cit., p. 311.

Nichoria in Messenia, all suffered very serious damage, and, of these sites, only Mycenae seems subsequently to have been occupied in any strength.'[63] At the same date the Mycenaeans abandoned Eutresis in Boeotia, possibly some minor sites in Western Attica, Berbati and Prosymna in the Argolid, as well as some minor settlements there too, and probably a considerable number of sites in Laconia and Messenia.[64] This must have been the work of barbarian invaders from somewhere beyond the bounds of the Mycenaean World. The Mycenaeans may have exposed themselves to being overthrown by outsiders through having weakened themselves by engaging in fratricidal wars and in overseas expeditions, but they cannot all have overthrown each other simultaneously. Simultaneous mutual destruction was not yet feasible in the pre-atomic age.

By what route did the North-West-Greek-speaking invaders make their way, *circa* 1200 B.C., into the Pelopónnêsos? If the devastation and depopulation of Messenia and Laconia at this date was their doing, they can hardly have reached these objectives overland; for, in the Hellenic Age, North-West-Greek-speaking Messenia was still insulated from North-West-Greek-speaking Elis by Arcadian-speaking Triphylia, and the North-West-Greek-speaking Eurotas basin from the North-West-Greek-speaking Argolid by Kynouria—a South-Greek-speaking district that had only gradually taken to speaking Doric,[65] and that, at Áyios Ioánnês, had provided an asylum for Mycenaean refugees, according to the evidence of archaeology.[66] Yet Desborough points out[67] that one stream of Mycenaean refugees fleeing from the invasion made for Western Akhaïa and for Kephallênía and Ithaca—asylums that were right athwart what would have been the route of a sea-borne invasion of the southern Pelopónnêsos from North-West Greece. On Ithaca there was continous occupation through the Late Helladic III C period into the Protogeometric period.[68]

This seems to rule the sea-route out, and perhaps the likeliest possibility is that *circa* 1200 B.C. the invaders of the Pelopónnêsos took the route that was taken by the Slav invaders eighteen centuries later and that is followed by the present-day automobile road from Yánnina to Athens. This overland route runs down the west side of Central Greece, crosses by water the narrow mouth of the Corinthian Gulf, from Andírrhion to Rhíon, and then runs along the southern shore of the Gulf to Corinth itself,[69] from where the traveller can head either southwards for the Argolid or eastwards for Attica.[70] The invaders who

---

[63] Desborough, *The Last Mycenaeans*, p. 221.

[64] Ibid.

[65] See Herodotus, Book VIII, chapter 73.

[66] See above, p. 280.

[67] In *The Last Mycenaeans*, p. 223.

[68] Snodgrass, op. cit., pp. 84-5 and 331; Desborough, *The Last Mycenaeans*, pp. 109 and 110.

[69] The North-West-Greek-speaking migrants' Slav successors seem never to have taken either Corinth or Argos. On the other hand, they occupied Arcadia, which their twelfth-century-B.C. predecessors failed to penetrate.

[70] Desborough, in *The Last Mycenaeans*, p. 224, brings the invaders of the Mycenaean World from North-West Greece by the alternative overland route through Central Greece as far as Boeotia; from there over the Isthmus to the Argolid; and from the Argolid to Laconia and Messenia. But the Mycenaean refugees' asylum at Áyios Ioánnês lies athwart the land-route from the Argolid to the Eurotas basin, and, though, along the alternative passable route through Central Greece, Krisa

took this route *circa* 1200 B.C. seem to have invaded and partly depopulated Western Attica, though they failed to take the acropolis of Athens. We may assume that they were more eager to take Mycenae, which was the more lucrative of their two possible prizes. We may also assume that, after taking Mycenae, they settled in the Argolid, in spite of their having left there no direct traces of their arrival at this date. In the third place, there are archaeological indications that, for the time being, they did not take to the sea. The cultural uniformity, which had displayed itself throughout the whole of the Mycenaean World in the Late Helladic III B period, was maintained, after the transition to the Late Helladic III C style, in the Aegean basin from Eastern Attica (Perati) through the islands to Miletus inclusive. This continuing uniformity of culture in this south-eastern quarter of the Mycenaean World shows that peaceful maritime trade was still being carried on there after the catastrophe that had befallen continental European Greece *circa* 1200 B.C.[71] Crete, too, was left in peace at this time.[72]

These archaeologically attested facts present some substantial indirect evidence for an overland invasion of the Mycenaean World from the north-west *circa* 1200 B.C., and this raises several puzzling questions. What was the relation between this invasion of the Argolid and perhaps also Attica *circa* 1200 B.C. and the repulse, in the eighth year of Ramses III's reign—a year which most Egyptologists now equate with 1191 B.C.[73]—of the invasion of Egypt by the 'Sea Peoples' who had borne down upon Egypt in a simultaneous advance by sea along the Syrian coast and overland through Syria itself? Where was the rendezvous from which this coalition of various peoples launched its operations? And who was it that contemporaneously devastated and depopulated Laconia, Messenia, and Elis—Peloponnesian districts that were sealed off,[74] by archaeologically attested asylums of Mycenaean refugees, from attack by the overland invaders of the Argolid from North-Western Greece?

and Gla were destroyed, Eutresis was abandoned, and Western Attica was partially depopulated, finds of potsherds of the Late Helladic III C period indicate that Mycenaean Delphi, perhaps one or two other sites in Phokis, the remnant of Mycenaean Thebes, Perakhóra on the Isthmus, and Korákou in Corinthia all survived. Moreover, the acropolis of Athens never fell, and the South-Greek dialect, in its Ionic differentiation, survived in the whole of Attica and in Euboea. If the main thrust of the invasion had been through Central Greece, the Ionic dialect would hardly have been able to retain the foothold that it did succeed in retaining in continental European Greece. Euboea is virtually part of the mainland, and the Mycenaean refugee settlement at Lefkandi was close to the Euripus, a strait that is narrower than the mouth of the Corinthian Gulf. The invaders' principal objective was presumably Mycenae, the richest of all the fortified palaces of the Mycenaean World, and the shortest and easiest route from North-West Greece to Mycenae—and, for that matter, to Athens as well, as the Modern Greek road-builders have found—traverses the mouth of the Corinthian Gulf and then runs along the Gulf's southern shore.

However, the argument presented in this footnote is contested by Professor Browning in the following comment: 'Surely a Mycenaean defensive position could be turned. In the Slav invasions, many a fortified place was by-passed. Sardica remained a Byzantine island—probably with a brief interruption—till the end of the ninth century.'

[71] See Desborough, *The Last Mycenaeans*, pp. 222 and 228–30; *eundem*, *The Greek Dark Ages*, p. 24; Snodgrass, op. cit., p. 312.

[72] Desborough, *The Last Mycenaeans*, p. 229.

[73] See Snodgrass, op. cit., p. 109.

[74] But see Professor Browning's comment in n. 70, above.

The Egyptian record of the assault on Egypt in the eighth year of Ramses III's reign[75] states that this movement started because 'the Northerners were disturbed in their isles'; this implies that the isles were the starting-point of the wave of migration that broke upon the Nile Delta and was repulsed from there; the isles in question can hardly have been any other than those of the Aegean Archipelago; yet the archaeological evidence testifies that this region remained at peace at the time of both the destruction of the Mycenaean palaces on the mainland of Greece and the 'Sea Peoples'' invasion of Egypt. However, these two contemporaneous migrations—one in continental Greece and the other in the Levant—must surely have had some connection both with each other and with the simultaneous overthrow of the Hittite Empire and eviction of a number of refugee Hittite and Luvian communities from Asia Minor into Northern Syria—whether this third upheaval was the work of the 'Sea Peoples' or was caused by the *Völkerwanderung* of the Phrygians from South-Eastern Europe, across the Hellespont (the Dardanelles) into Asia Minor. These three movements must surely all have been parts of a single great convulsion.

Desborough[76] has proposed a convincing explanation of the immunity of the Aegean islands at this time. He conjectures that the Mycenaeans who were ejected from continental Greece eastwards by the overland invasion of the Mycenaean World from North-West Greece may have formed part of the host of the Sea Peoples, and that the Mycenaeans' occupation of Embório[77] on Khios and of Tarsós[78] in Cilicia and their first occupation of Cyprus may have been incidents in the advance of the 'Sea Peoples' round the shores of the Eastern Mediterranean. The Egyptian record mentions the 'Sea Peoples'' devastation, *en route*, of places whose Egyptian renderings have been identified as representing Arzawa, which was somewhere in the west of Asia Minor, and Alasiya, which is believed to have been Cyprus itself. If 'the isles' provided the whole host of the 'Sea Peoples' with a rendezvous and a jumping-off ground, and if the Mycenaean refugees there took part, themselves, in a joint expedition into the Levant, this might explain how 'the isles' came to be spared. This does not explain, however, the devastation and dereliction of Laconia, Messenia, and Elis. These districts must have been ravaged by raiders from the sea, but we do not know who these were or whence they came. This is a mystery that is not elucidated either by modern archaeological explorations on the spot or by contemporary Egyptian records.

The repulse of the 'Sea Peoples'' assault on Egypt in the eighth year of Ramses III's reign was the end of the *Völkerwanderung* as far as Egypt and Syria were concerned. The foiled 'Sea Peoples' settled down along the coast of Palestine. The infiltration of the Libyans into Egypt did not take place till about two centuries later. In the Aegean and Cyprus there were further commotions and destructions, but not on the scale of those *circa* 1200 B.C.[79] *Circa* 1150 in the Argolid, the Granary at Mycenae was burnt, but even Mycenae

---

[75] See Desborough, *The Last Mycenaeans*, pp. 237–9.
[76] Ibid.
[77] Ibid., pp. 158–9.
[78] Ibid., pp. 205–6.
[79] See ibid., pp. 231–3; Snodgrass, op. cit., pp. 313–14.

itself was not yet entirely deserted, and on this occasion Argos and Asine seem to have escaped unscathed.[80] Contemporaneously the Mycenaean palace (but not the town) was destroyed at Iolkos in Thessaly, and so were the Mycenaean refugee settlements at Lefkandi in Euboea and at Embório on Khios, and the Mycenaean beach-head at Miletus. At this time, too, the second wave of Mycenaean migrants broke upon Cyprus. There was also perhaps some violent intrusion into Crete.[81]

Was this further bout of destruction and eviction the work of invaders from beyond the confines of the Mycenaean World? And, if there was a twelfth-century second wave of invaders, did these, like their predecessors *circa* 1200 B.C., come from the north-west, and did they, unlike those previous invaders, leave positive material evidence of their arrival and lodgement? Desborough has given cautious and tentative affirmative answers to both these questions.[82] He finds this positive evidence in the distinctive features of the sub-Mycenaean culture (*circa* 1125–1050 B.C.) which was 'confined to a fairly compact area of central mainland Greece—West Attica and the Argolid, Boeotia, Corinthia and Elis.'[83] The sub-Mycenaean culture in this area was homogeneous.[84] It expanded into the Central Aegean, and across the Aegean to Miletus, when the Mycenaean culture faded out in this maritime region, where it had survived the destruction of the Mycenaean palaces on the mainland of Greece *circa* 1200 B.C. The sub-Mycenaean culture also spread to Lefkandi, in Euboea, and to Theotókou in the Thessalian Magnesia.[85]

The sub-Mycenaean culture has been labelled as such in terms of its pottery-style, which might be classed as being a degenerate sequel to Mycenaean III C, in contrast to the subsequent revolutionary new departure represented by Protogeometric. However, the label 'sub-Mycenaean' proves to be a misnomer when all the non-ceramic elements in this culture are also taken into consideration,[86] and Desborough holds that the so-called sub-Mycenaean culture—notwithstanding the Mycenaean affinities of its pottery—broke radically with the Mycenaean past of the region in which it established itself. The sub-Mycenaean settlers abandoned the earlier Mycenaean settlement sites; they chose different sites of their own; they were not shy of locating their burial grounds above and within the former Mycenaean settlement areas; they changed over from multiple burial to individual burial; and their long dress-pins and arched *fibulae* indicate that they abandoned the Mycenaean style of dress.[87] Thus, according to Desborough, the sub-Mycenaean culture was a new one, 'almost surrounded for some time by Mycenaean communities which held fast to an earlier civilization.'[88]

---

[80] Snodgrass, op. cit., p. 29.

[81] See Desborough, *The Last Mycenaeans*, pp. 235–6; *eundem, The Greek Dark Ages*, pp. 51, 58, 114.

[82] See ibid., especially Chapter 5, 'The Origins of the Sub-Mycenaean Culture, on pp. 106–11. See also Snodgrass, op. cit., pp. 28–40.

[83] *The Greek Dark Ages*, p. 269. In *The Last Mycenaeans*, pp. 17–20, Desborough had defined the area of sub-Mycenaean as being limited to West Attica (i.e. to Athens and Salamis).

[84] *The Greek Dark Ages*, p. 75.   [85] Ibid., pp. 78–82.

[86] See Snodgrass, op. cit., p. 33.

[87] Desborough, *The Greek Dark Ages*, p. 107. Cp. ibid. pp. 69 and 76.

[88] Ibid., p. 106.

If the bearers of the sub-Mycenaean civilization were, as Desborough holds, a new swarm of invaders from the north-west, was it they who introduced the North-West-Greek/Doric dialect of Greek into Central Greece and into the northern Pelopónnêsos? Desborough does not suggest this, yet this conjecture would not be incompatible either with the Dark-Age archaeological evidence or with the Hellenic-Age tradition.

After this second, less violent, convulsion, Greece and the Aegean islands and Cyprus seem to have settled down for a time. The cemeteries in Western Akhaïa and on Kephallênía indicate that the refugees there were undisturbed for at least two or three generations.[89] In the Argolid the Mycenaeans may have survived for nearly three generations.[90] If the archaeological evidence for this still holds good, it it not incompatible with the possibility that North-West-Greek-speaking intruders may have settled here, side by side with the survivors of the Mycenaean population, since the catastrophe *circa* 1200 B.C. or at any rate since the beginning of the sub-Mycenaean Age. In the twelfth century B.C., Thessaly was at peace, and so was Crete on the whole.[91] At any rate, in Crete, Minoan religious and funerary practices survived.[92] Here the sub-Minoan Age lasted for 200 years, and perhaps for nearly 300 years in some out-of-the-way places.[93] Sub-Minoan Crete was both advanced and independent in its metallurgy,[94] and it was also relatively prosperous.[95] Indeed, in the Greek World as a whole, from the convulsion circa 1150 B.C. onwards throughout the rest of the Dark Age, there is no further trace of foreign invasion, and, till almost the end of the eighth century B.C., there is hardly any trace of the violent destruction of a settlement.[96]

By this latter date, of course, the Hellenic city-states had been organized, and during the half millennium beginning in the eighth century B.C. these states were chronically at war with each other, until peace was imposed on them by

[89] Desborough, *The Last Mycenaeans*, p. 226; *idem, The Greek Dark Ages*, pp. 20, 88, 91.

[90] Desborough, *The Last Mycenaeans*, p. 231.

[91] Snodgrass, op. cit., p. 30.

[92] Desborough, *The Last Mycenaeans*, pp. 181, 189, 190, 193.

[93] Snodgrass, op. cit., pp. 41–2 and 79. See also Desborough, *The Greek Dark Ages*, pp. 112–29.

[94] Snodgrass, op. cit., p. 250.

[95] Ibid., p. 251.

[96] Ibid., pp. 297–8, 324, and 364. The siting of Dark-Age settlements indicates 'a quick return to relatively peaceful conditions' (Desborough, *The Greek Dark Ages*, p. 265). Most Dark-Age settlements were near though not actually on, the former Mycenaean sites (ibid., pp. 261 and 264), and, contrary to Thucydides's belief (see Thucydides, Book I, chapter 7), most of them, except in Attica, were coastal yet were also unfortified (ibid., p. 264). The diffusion of pottery wares and styles suggests that there was peaceful trade (ibid., p. 292). The exceptional region is Crete; for here, notwithstanding the continuing survival of the Minoan civilization, new settlements, in highly defensible positions, were founded *c.* 1150 B.C. at Karphi and Kastri and Vrokastro (ibid., p. 114). The altitude of Karphi is 4,000 feet (see ibid., pp. 114 and 120–9, with the striking panoramic photograph on pp. 122–3). However, Karphi was abandoned early in the tenth century B.C. at the latest (ibid., p. 235). There are few weapons in sub-Mycenaean graves at Athens (ibid., p. 67) and none of the Dark-Age period in the southern Pelopónnêsos, except for Laconia (ibid., p. 256). In this point, too, Dark-Age Crete is exceptional. Here weapons (all of iron) are plentiful (ibid., pp. 231–2), though, as between the Dark-Age settlements in Crete, 'intercommunication was apparently both easy and frequent' (ibid., pp. 238–9; cp. p. 312). Is this an indication that, in Cretan society in the Dark Age, there was already a dominant minority that had reduced the majority of the population to serfdom and was holding the serfs down by force of arms?

the Roman conquest. Yet the first city-wall of Smyrna, which was built about half-way through the ninth century, has no contemporary counterpart in European Greece;[97] and the exceptionally early date of this city-wall may be evidence of unusual affluence rather than of unusual insecurity; for the date of the wall is about a century later than the date of the settlement itself, and the persistence here of a native monochrome pottery, side by side with a Protogeometric pottery that was presumably either imported, or manufactured on the spot, by the Greek settlers, 'suggests that there was a fusion between native and immigrant elements.'[98]

The apparent relative peacefulness of the Greek World for four centuries running from *circa* 1150 B.C. may not be an illusion; for, in this age, the Greeks did not have the means, the skill, or the organization for making war that had been possessed previously by the Mycenaean kingdoms and that was acquired subsequently by the Hellenic city-states. We must, however, also allow for the difference in the nature of the evidence for Greek history before and after the eighth century B.C. Our evidence for the Dark Age is exclusively archaeological, and it is non-documentary. From the later decades of the eighth century B.C. onwards, the archaeological evidence includes inscriptions and is supplemented by literary records; and, though the literary records, unlike the inscriptions and the remains of buildings and utensils, are to a large extent non-contemporary, much of the information that they provide is more or less trustworthy, and this literary information throws light on fields of activity for which the material evidence is uninformative—though it has the virtue of being contemporary with the events of which it is a relic. If we possessed trustworthy literary records about the Dark Age, we should probably find that it was a less peaceful age than its material remains suggest that it was.

In the absence of informative evidence, we may guess that the repeopling of Laconia and Messenia was coeval with the appearance of Protogeometric pottery there; that this was coeval with the spread of the Doric dialect there; and that the Doric-speaking settlers in these two Peloponnesian districts came in by sea, and not across the adjoining districts to the north in which the Arcadian dialect continued to be spoken. The Doric dialect must in any case have been conveyed by sea to the islands on which it was eventually spoken—for instance, to Thera (Santoríni), Melos, Crete, and the Dodecanese. But the archaeological evidence does not tell us whether the Doric dialect's eventual propagation overseas beyond the Argolid was due to its being peacefully adopted or to its being imposed by conquest. Nor does the archaeological evidence provide any clue to the process by which the population of Crete, and of Thessaly too, came to consist of a dominant minority of masters ruling over a subject minority of serfs.

For the dating of the imposition of this social structure on Thessaly, one possible indication is the absence of any evidence, older than the eighth century B.C., for the presence of a Greek population on Lesbos and in the continental Asian Aiolis.[99] The Asian Aeolic-speaking Greeks seem likely to have been

---

[97] Snodgrass, op. cit., p. 298.

[98] Desborough, *The Greek Dark Ages*, p. 183.

[99] See p. 38 n. 1. If in truth the Greek colonization of the Asian Aiolis began as much as three centuries later than the colonization of the Asian Ionia, this is, at first sight, surprising. It would be

refugees from an invasion of Thessaly that made a linguistic mark on the Thessalian variety of the Aeolic dialect in the shape of an infusion into it of elements of North-West Greek. If it is the truth that the Asian Aiolis was not colonized till the eighth century B.C., this suggests that the expansion of North-West-Greek-speaking conquerors of western Thessaly eastwards from Histiai-otis and Thessaliotis into Pelasgiotis and Phthiotis may have been no earlier than that. If so, the conquest of the two eastern Thessalian tetrarchies by the Thessaloi and the Histiaioi will have been approximately contemporary with the Spartans' conquest of Amyklai, Helos, and Messenia.

The lack of any direct archaeological traces of the irruption of North-West-Greek-speaking invaders into the Mycenaean World until, at earliest, the beginning of the sub-Mycenaean Age is as impressive as the conspicuousness of the archaeological evidence for the survival of the Mycenaean population and culture after the presumable date, *circa* 1200 B.C., of the first wave of the *Völkerwanderung*. 'The most remarkable quality of this Mycenaean twilight epoch is shown to be its persistence and forcefulness.'[100] Evidently the *Völker-wanderung* was neither the occasion nor the principal cause of the break of cultural continuity between the Mycenaean and the Hellenic chapter of Greek history. The archaeological evidence shows that the break was not the immediate sequel to the Mycenaean kingdoms' collapse, but it also shows that the break, when it did eventually come, was very sharp. The symptoms of it, as has already been noted,[101] are the cutting of communications, the loss of skills, impoverishment, and depopulation.

The cutting of internal communications in the Mycenaean World is made manifest by the dramatic contrast between the uniformity of culture in the Late Helladic III B period and its diversification in and after Late Helladic III C. 'Such uniformity in a sophisticated culture has not been known before or since in Greek lands.'[102] On the other hand, the Dark Age was an age of regionalism.[103] The maintenance of communications after the catastrophe *circa* 1200 B.C. in an area extending from Eastern Attica to the Dodecanese was short-lived. This area, too, was engulfed in the post-Mycenaean chaos. 'In Mycenaean [i.e. L.H.] III C pottery, we have the signs of a significant new phenomenon, a variegated style with different local manifestations.'[104] More-over, the replacement of uniformity by variety, besides displaying itself geographically, can be observed in the time-dimension as well.

---

explained if, on Lesbos, there was a local pre-Greek power that was stronger than the pre-Greek population of the adjacent region, to the south, that became Ionia. If Mytilênê means 'the city of Muwattalliš', this may indicate that the Hittite emperor of that name had planted a military colony there after the overthrow of the Arzawan Empire by Muwattalliš's predecessor, Mursiliš. A Motylos is credited by Stephanos of Byzantium, s.v. 'Samylia', with the foundation of a city at the south-west corner of Asia Minor. A Hittite garrison at Mytilênê might have survived the *Völkerwanderung* in the twelfth century B.C. which destroyed the Hittite Empire itself.

[100] Snodgrass, op. cit., p. 28. See also Desborough, *The Greek Dark Ages*, pp. 20 and 106.

[101] See above, p. 275.

[102] Desborough, *The Last Mycenaeans*, p. 242. Cp. ibid., pp. 1, 166, 219, and also Snodgrass, op. cit., p. 25.

[103] Ibid., pp. 24–5 and 97.

[104] Ibid., p. 30.

In Attica the Late Helladic III and sub-Mycenaean styles of pottery were replaced by the Protogeometric style as early as *circa* 1050 B.C.; on Ithaca the same change did not take place till *circa* 950 B.C.; in the other regions of the diversified Greek World of the Dark Age, the change occurred at different dates within the time-span of about a century between the Attic and the Ithacan extreme.[105] Athens was the principal centre at which the Protogeometric style was created, and from which it was diffused.[106] 'The Attic school retained its pre-eminence for much of the Geometric period.'[107] The diffusion of the Protogeometric style from Athens seems to have been rapid.[108] At Argos city, where Protogeometric makes its appearance earlier than at other sites in the Argolid, the imitation of the Attic Protogeometric was 'close and direct.'[109] Yet, to the west of a line running north-west and south-east from the Pindus Range, west of Delphi, to Cape Malea, the local Protogeometric styles cannot be traced to Attic influence.[110] One of the places here in question is Ithaca,[111] where, as in Attica, there was an exceptional degree of continuity of occupation.[112] Moreover, though Attica took the lead, to the east of the line above-mentioned, in introducing the Protogeometric style of pottery, and though she also took the lead in the substitution of iron for bronze,[113] the Argolid, which followed Attica's lead in both these fields, did not follow suit to Attica in the field of funerary practice. The Argolid did not take to cremation.[114] Nor, in this field, is Attic influence discernible anywhere after *circa* 1100 B.C.[115]

Snodgrass points out[116] that, in the Dark Age, there was a 'dichotomy between certain relatively advanced, active, and accessible regions, and the rest' of the Greek World, and that, for the most part, the advanced regions moved in step with each other in their adoption of cultural innovations. Yet, in the Geometric period, regional styles still continued to be distinctive.[117] This local diversity was, of course, accentuated by the political fission of the Hellenic Greek World into a mosaic of city-states, each of which was obsessively self-centred.

The *leitmotiv* of Greek history in the Hellenic Age is the obstinate resistance of the city-states to the unification, at all levels, that was made imperative by the economic revolution of the seventh and sixth centuries B.C., which replaced autarky by interdependence on the economic plane. Hellenic Greek particularism was overcome, only gradually and piecemeal, by the dissemination of the Homeric poems, by the adoption of their language, metre, and style by poets whose native dialects were not Ionic, by the inauguration of the pan-Hellenic recurrent festivals, by the spread of the Attic *koine* at the expense of other dialects, by the development of a common system of higher education and of a corresponding conception of culture, and, eventually, on the political plane too, by the reduction of the once sovereign city-states to the subordinate status

---

[105] See Snodgrass's illuminating chronological/regional chart of Dark-Age pottery-styles in op. cit., on pp. 134–5. See also Desborough, *The Greek Dark Ages*, p. 289.

[106] Snodgrass, op. cit., pp. 32–3 and 47–8.

[107] Ibid., p. 48.

[108] Ibid., p. 44.

[109] Ibid., p. 57.

[110] Ibid., p. 84.

[111] Ibid., p. 85.

[112] See above, p. 283.

[113] Snodgrass, op. cit., p. 237.

[114] Ibid., p. 153.

[115] Ibid., p. 190.

[116] In ibid., p. 374.

[117] Ibid., p. 261.

of municipalities functioning as cells of the Roman Imperial body politic. Yet even in the second century of the Christian era the cumulative effect of these unifying forces had hardly raised the Hellenic Greek World to the degree of uniformity that the Mycenaean Greek World had attained by the time, *circa* 1200 B.C., when it had been overtaken by an unretrieved catastrophe.

The internal disruption that the Greek World suffered at the transition from Late Helladic III B to Late Helladic III C persisted longer than its simultaneous isolation from the domains of adjacent non-Greek civilizations. The index here is the substitution, in the Greek World, of iron for bronze as the normal material for utilitarian metallic implements.[118] Iron is not tougher than a bronze that has a 10 per cent content of tin,[119] and, in the Greek climate, iron rusts more readily than bronze.[120] Thus iron was not superior to bronze intrinsically; it was merely more accessible for smiths in the Greek World in an age in which communications with non-Greek civilizations were in suspense; for iron ores are widely distributed within the Greek World itself,[121] whereas copper, or ready-made bronze, would have had to be imported from Cyprus, and the tin-component of the bronze might have had to be fetched from still farther afield. When iron predominates over bronze as the material for metallic implements, we may guess that the iron-work is home-made, not imported.[122] The finds in the Kerameikos cemetery at Athens show that here the elimination of the use of bronze reached its maximum during the middle Protogeometric period. In this period, iron was used at Athens almost exclusively, and the same pattern of metallurgical development can be discerned at the same date in the Argolid.[123] But in both regions there was a recrudescence of the use of bronze in the late Protogeometric and early Geometric periods,[124] and this can be taken as being evidence that, by that time, communications between the Aegean basin and Cyprus were improving.

The second of the symptoms of the sharpness of the break between the Mycenaean and the Hellenic chapter of Greek history is the loss of skills. The most striking illustration of this is the loss of literacy for about 450 years as a result of the permanent oblivion of the 'Linear B' script. The art of masonry was also lost except here and there—e.g. at Iolkos, on Naxos, and, above all, in Crete, for instance in the refugee settlement at Karphi.[125] Razors did not outlast the extinction of the Mycenaean civilization.[126] Shaving is not one of the necessities of masculine life; nor, for either sex, are shaped, sewn, and buttoned clothes, which, in the Dark Age, were replaced by a one-piece *peplos*, as is testified by the presence of pins in Dark-Age graves.[127] A more serious regression into inefficiency and discomfort was the apparent loss of the technique for producing artificial light. 'Objects which are recognisable as lamps, either by shape or by traces of use, are altogether missing from Greece

---

[118] Ibid., p. 229; Desborough, *The Greek Dark Ages*, pp. 314–18.

[119] Snodgrass, op. cit., pp. 215–16.

[120] Ibid., p. 216.

[121] Ibid., p. 231.

[122] Ibid., p. 222.

[123] Ibid., p. 233.

[124] Ibid., pp. 233 and 237–8.

[125] See Desborough, *The Last Mycenaeans*, pp. 29–32; *eundem*, *The Greek Dark Ages*, p. 120; Snodgrass, op. cit., pp. 368–73.

[126] Desborough, *The Last Mycenaeans*, p. 59.

[127] Snodgrass, op. cit., p. 394.

between the Mycenaean [i.e. L.H.] III C period and the later stages of Protogeometric'.[128]

Conversely, the appearance of new skills is symptomatic of the rise of the new Hellenic civilization among the old Mycenaean civilization's débris. Both the technique of iron-working (probably invented in Asia Minor) and the device of combining the use of the multiple brush with the use of the compass for decorating Protogeometric and Geometric pottery[129] seem to have been acquired by Greece from Cyprus[130] before the temporary cutting of communications between them. Iron-working requires technical processes that are not required for producing bronze.[131] The crowning evidence that a new civilization had come to birth is, of course, the adoption and adaptation of the Phoenician alphabet in the eighth century B.C. for writing Greek.

Loss of technical skill is indirect evidence for the impoverishment that is attested directly by, among other things,[132] the almost complete absence of objects made of gold and silver in the Kerameikos cemetery for about a century.[133] Interruption of the continuity of the occupation of sites is indirect evidence for depopulation.[134] 'The population of Greek lands in the eleventh century B.C. was lower than it had been for a thousand years . . .; it was probably never so low at any later time in antiquity.'[135] A decline of population of this degree cannot be fully accounted for by mass emigration, and Snodgrass concludes convincingly that it must have been the consequence of some great economic disaster.[136] The reoccupation of deserted sites in European Greece began, in some cases, before 1000 B.C.[137] In the eighth century B.C. there was a 'population explosion' in the Greek World,[138] and this seems to have continued till the second century B.C.

Conspicuous examples of breaks in the continuity of settlement are, as has already been noted, the *interregna* in Laconia, Messenia,[139] and Elis. Other cases are those of Aigina[140] and Gla.[141] Western Attica, too, was depopulated, but the acropolis of Athens never fell, and both in Western Attica and on Salamis the recovery was rapid.[142] In Western Akhaïa there was a complete break after the abandonment of the cemeteries of the Mycenaean refugees in this district.[143]

---

[128] Snodgrass, op. cit., p. 394.

[129] For this combination, which makes its appearance both at Athens and in Cyprus at the beginning of the Protogeometric Age, see Desborough *The Last Mycenaeans*, p. 262, and Snodgrass, op. cit., pp. 47 and 328. The use of a faster wheel and the co-ordination of the decoration of a pot with the pot's shape were further Protogeometric innovations.

[130] Snodgrass, op. cit., p. 328; Desborough, *The Greek Dark Ages*, pp. 43 and 340–1.

[131] See Snodgrass, op. cit., pp. 214, 216, 230.

[132] See ibid., pp. 380–5 and 388 for details.

[133] Ibid., pp. 261–2; Desborough, *The Greek Dark Ages*, p. 313.

[134] For figures of the fall in the number of inhabited sites, see p. 281, footnote 54.

[135] Snodgrass, op. cit., p. 367.

[136] Ibid., p. 365. The migration to the west coast of Asia Minor did not begin, at the earliest, much before 1000 B.C. (ibid., p. 373), and, by that date, the reoccupation of sites in European Greece had already begun (ibid., p. 364).

[137] Ibid.

[138] Ibid., p. 367. Cp. ibid., pp. 268, 337, 421.

[139] For the break at Nikhoria in Messenia, see Desborough, *The Last Mycenaeans*, pp. 95–6.

[140] Ibid., p. 119.   [141] Ibid., p. 121.   [142] Ibid., p. 116.

[143] Ibid., p. 101; Desborough, *The Greek Dark Ages*, pp. 92–4.

The most impressive breaks, however, are those, not in the continuity of settlements, but in the continuity of holy places and of the forms of religious installations and rites. In the field of religion, there is only a minimum of continuity between the Minoan and the Mycenaean civilization, and again between the Mycenaean and the Hellenic.

The Minoan-type domestic shrine, of Late Helladic III C date, in the Mycenaean palace and Asine in the Argolid[144] is unique in Mycenaean-Age Greece, and so is the Hellenic-type temple, containing life-size terracotta images of gods, also of Late Helladic III C date, at Ayía Eirênê on the Island of Keos.[145] Snodgrass[146] gives a list of non-sacred Bronze-Age sites which, after a break of continuity, attracted temples and sanctuaries in the Hellenic Age, through the prestige of their antiquity, which was deemed to be a warrant of holiness. He also gives a shorter list of Bronze-Age holy places whose former sacredness meant nothing to the Hellenic-Age reoccupants. Among the exceptional Mycenaean-Age holy places which retained their holiness through the Dark Age into the Hellenic Age are the sanctuary near Epidauros that, in the Hellenic Age, was dedicated to Apollo Maleatis;[147] Eleusis (though here there was a break between the Late Helladic III C period and the sixth century B.C.);[148] Delphi (enigmatic);[149] Delos (doubtful);[150] Amyklai (probable);[151] the Dictaean Cave in Crete (certain, but, in the Dark Age, Crete was a world of its own).[152] It is significant that at Olympia, which became the locus of the greatest of the four pan-Hellenic recurrent festivals, there are traces of pre-Hellenic habitation but there is no trace of a pre-Hellenic ceremonial past.[153]

The sharpness of the break of cultural continuity is clear. At the same time, it is also clear that the Hellenic civilization, which arose after the break, originated in a region where the break had been relatively short and moderate. The acropolis of Athens had not been one of the major Mycenaean palace-fortresses, but it was the only one of them that never fell, and Attica as a whole was relatively fortunate. Eastern Attica escaped unscathed; Western Attica, though ravaged and depopulated, was quickly liberated and repeopled. In the Dark Age the Argolid, which had been the heart of the Mycenaean World, and which had therefore been the barbarian invaders' main objective, took second place to Athens in the enterprise of creating a new Greek civilization.

We may perhaps guess that the Mycenaean civilization's downfall was mainly the work of the Mycenaean 'establishment' itself and not of invaders

[144] Desborough, *The Last Mycenaeans*, p. 42; *idem, The Greek Dark Ages*, p. 285.

[145] Desborough, *The Last Mycenaeans*, p. 44; *idem, The Greek Dark Ages*, pp. 160 and 280–1; Snodgrass, op. cit., p. 395.

[146] In op. cit., p. 398. Cp. Desborough, *The Greek Dark Ages*, pp. 278–81.

[147] Desborough, *The Last Mycenaeans*, pp. 42–3. Cp. Snodgrass, op. cit., p. 395.

[148] Desborough, op. cit., p. 43.   [149] Ibid., pp. 43–4.   [150] Ibid., pp. 44–6.

[151] See Snodgrass, op. cit., pp. 88 and 131; he expresses greater doubt on p. 395. Desborough, *The Greek Dark Ages*, pp. 280 and 283, points out that, in the archaeological evidence, there is a break in continuity, but that the reality in the continuity of the cult of Hyakinthos here is attested by the Hellenic literary evidence.

[152] For evidence of continuity of cult at the Dictaean Cave and elsewhere in Crete, see Snodgrass, op. cit., pp. 275 and 402; Desborough, *The Greek Dark Ages*, pp. 128, 284, 286.

[153] See Snodgrass, op. cit., pp. 276 and 397. Desborough is less categorical in *The Greek Dark Ages*, pp. 84 and 281.

from outside. The structure of Mycenaean society was highly artificial. The ruling class was probably a small minority; its culture was sophisticated and exotic; its system of administration was elaborately bureaucratic. This civilization seems unlikely to have struck deep roots among the subject majority of the population. The ruling class's position would therefore probably have been precarious in any case; and it became untenable when the Mycenaean kingdoms sapped their own strength, such as it was, by making war against each other and by engaging in exhausting expeditions overseas. The catastrophe of *circa* 1200 B.C. was the nemesis of these previous suicidal acts. The Mycenaean civilization, which was the earliest of the successive Greek civilizations, was also the least potent of them. It is not surprising that the Hellenes' memory of their Mycenaean predecessors was faint and unoppressive by comparison with the burdensomeness of the post-Hellenic Greeks' memory of the Hellenes.

Chapter VI. Appendix I

Poúplios' Graeco-Syrian Monastery

THE text of chapter 5 (*Πούπλιος*) of Theodórêtos' *Religiosa Historia* will be found in Migne, *Patrologia Graeca*, vol. lxxxii, cols. 1351–7. The details, given in this passage, of the amicable relations between Greek-speaking and Syriac-speaking Eastern Orthodox Christians in and after the fourth century are so interesting that they deserve fuller consideration than it has been possible to give to them in the text of chapter VI of the present work on p. 87. The following references are to the text in Migne, *Patrologia Graeca*.

Poúplios (Publius), the founder of this monastic establishment, which was a distance of about 30 stadia from Zévghma, originally recruited Greek-speaking monks only, and he housed them in separate cells. On advice, he then brought them together under a single roof.[1]

These exercises and exertions of Poúplios' fellow Greek-speakers in chanting the praises of God in Greek inspired in the speakers of the local language, too, an eagerness to lead this way of life. Some of these got together and begged to be admitted into Poúplios' community and to share in his holy instruction. Poúplios welcomed their request . . . and built a second mansion to house his Syriac-speaking postulants, side by side with his mansion for Greek-speaking monks. He then built a church, and instructed the two communities to meet there at the beginning and end of the day, in order to offer, together, to God, their morning and evening chant in two separate choirs, each monk chanting in his own language, sending up their song to Heaven alternately. This way of life has survived there down to the present day.'[2]

When Poúplios died, separate superiors, one Greek-speaking and the other Syriac-speaking, were appointed to take over the government of the twin communities. Down to the date of Theodórêtos' visit, these pairs of superiors had co-operated with each other amicably and loyally to maintain the pair of choirs and the rest of the founder Poúplios' arrangements.[3]

---

[1] Cols. 1351–4.

[2] Cols. 1353–4. Οὕτω τῶν ὁμογλώττων γυμναζομένων τε καὶ ἀγωνιζομένων, καὶ Ἑλλάδι φωνῇ τὸν Θεὸν ἀνυμνούντων, ἔλαβεν ἔρως ταυτησὶ τῆς πολιτείας καὶ τοὺς τῷ ἐγχωρίῳ κεχρημένους φωνῇ· καὶ συνδραμόντες τινὲς ἱκέτευον καὶ τῆς ἀγέλης γενέσθαι καὶ τῆς ἱερᾶς αὐτοῦ διδασκαλίας μεταλαχεῖν. ἐδέξατο δὲ τὴν αἴτησιν . . . καὶ παρ' ἐκεῖνο τὸ καταγώγιον ἕτερον οἰκοδομήσας ἐκεῖ τούτους διάγειν ἐκέλευε· νεών τινα θεῖον κατασκευάσας, εἰς ὅν καὶ τούτους κἀκείνους συνιέναι προσέταξεν ἀρχομένης τε καὶ ληγούσης ἡμέρας, ἵνα καὶ τὴν ἑσπερινὴν καὶ τὴν ἑωθινὴν ὑμνῳδίαν κοινῇ προσφέρωσι τῷ Θεῷ, διχῇ μὲν διῃρημένοι καὶ τῇ οἰκείᾳ ἕκαστος κεχρημένος φωνῇ, ἐκ διαδοχῆς δὲ τὴν ᾠδὴν ἀναπέμποντες. Διέμεινε δὲ μέχρι καὶ τήμερον τόδε τῆς πολιτείας τὸ εἶδος.

[3] Cols. 1355–6.

Chapter VI. Appendix II

Victimized Patriarchs

THE list of victimized Patriarchs is impressive, and their courage is admirable, even though some of them, like some of the pre-Constantinian martyrs, invited persecution by being provocatively intransigent.

The list is headed by Athanasius, the famous Patriarch of Alexandria, who was deposed and deported by both Constantine I and Constantius II for refusing to readmit Arius to communion after Arius had recanted. The first of the victimized Patriarchs of Constantinople was Saint John Chrysostom. He was deported first in 403, and finally in 404, for having publicly censured the conduct of the Imperial 'establishment', including the Empress Evdhoxía. The Patriarch Yermanós I was deposed in 730 for standing out against Iconoclasm (Leo III's attempt to depose Pope Gregory II had ended in a fiasco). The Patriarch Nikêphóros I, the famous chronicler, was deposed in 815 for standing out against the revocation of the acts of the anti-Iconoclast council of 787. The Patriarch John VII was deposed in 843 for standing out against the reinstatement of the *eikóns*.

The Patriarch Ighnátios was deposed in 858 for having publicly censured the conduct of the Caesar Várdhas. Phótios was deposed in 867 by Basil I for having discountenanced Basil's murdering of Várdhas and of Michael III. Phótios refused to give Basil communion.[1] Phótios was reinstated in 877, but he was deposed again in 886 by Leo VI. The Patriarch Nikólaos I was deposed in 907 by Leo VI for having barred the Emperor out of the Ayía Sophía at Christmas 906 and at Epiphany 907, when Leo had got himself legally married for the fourth time by a compliant priest.

The Patriarch Arsénios was deposed in 1264 by Michael VIII. Arsénios had excommunicated Michael in 1261 for having blinded his co-Emperor John IV, and he had then opposed Michael's plan to re-unite the Constantinopolitan with the Roman Church at the price of acknowledging the Papacy's ecclesiastical supremacy. After Michael had carried out this intention in 1274, he deposed Arsénios' second successor, Joseph I, who had absolved Michael for his murder of the Emperor John IV on humiliating terms,[2] for refusing to accept union with the Roman Church. In 1275 Michael appointed to the Patriarchate John XI Vékkos, who did accept the union; but the popular opposition to the union was so strong that, when Michael VIII died in 1282, his successor deposed the Patriarch John XI as a gesture of appeasement.

A Patriarch of Constantinople did occasionally make a stand against an Emperor with impunity. In 969 the Patriarch Polýefktos imposed on John Dzimiskês, the murderer of the Emperor Nikêphóros II, three onerous

---

[1] Leo Grammaticus, p. 254 Bonn; Georgius Monachus Continuatus, p. 841 Bonn.
[2] See Runciman, *The Great Church in Captivity*, p. 68.

conditions that the murderer had to fulfil in order to induce the Patriarch to recognize him and to crown him as his victim's successor. In 1054 the Patriarch Michael I Keroulários put his Patriarchate out of communion with the Roman See at a moment when the Imperial Government particularly needed the Pope's political co-operation against the Normans. On this occasion, Michael Keroulários thwarted the Imperial Goverment's policy with impunity. He kept his seat on the patriarchal throne till 1058, when he came into collision with the Emperor Isaac I Komnenós. He refused to abdicate, and was saved from deposition thanks to being overtaken opportunely by death.

Keroulários' term of office (1043–58) was contemporaneous with the reign of the Emperor Constantine IX (1042–55). In this reign the East Roman gold coin (*nómisma*) was debased from 24 to 18 carats,[3] and this was one of the earliest palpable symptoms of the Empire's decline. The middle decades of the eleventh century were also the turning-point in the Empire's relations with the Church.[4] From that time on, the balance of power inclined more and more decisively in the Church's favour. For instance, when, in 1369, the Emperor John V recognized the supremacy of the Roman See, this was merely a personal act. The reigning Patriarch of Constantinople, Philótheos, declared against union and campaigned against it, with impunity, throughout Orthodox Christendom, both inside and outside the dominions of the Emperor who was Philótheos' political sovereign.[5]

---

[3] Hussey, *The Byzantine World*, p. 51, cited in Chapter IX (i) above, p. 168.
[4] Ibid., pp. 48–9.
[5] Ibid., pp. 80–1.

Chapter VIII. Appendix

George Yemistós Plêthon's Totalitarian Hellenism

GEORGE YEMISTÓS PLÊTHON's role in the Modern Greeks' appropriation of their heritage from the Hellenic Greeks has been noticed already in Chapter VIII. But Plêthon's ideas, aims, and expectations need to be considered in greater detail, because he carried Byzantine and Modern Greek neo-Hellenism to its logical conclusion, and because this totalitarianism is a *reductio ad absurdum*, yet also, surprisingly, a posthumous vindication, of the Hellenists' ideology.

The project of replacing Eastern Orthodox Christianity by pre-Christian Hellenic philosophy and religion was chimerical in Plêthon's own day. It was advocated as a recipe for giving the Greek people a new inspiration[1] in an age in which the Byzantine Greek civilization had manifestly gone bankrupt. But to seek salvation in Hellenism for Byzantinism's failure was unrealistic. Eastern Orthodox Christianity and the East Roman Imperial regime had been the Byzantine Greek civilization's twin foundations; and, of the two, the religious foundation had proved to be a more efficacious help in time of trouble during the crisis through which the Greek World had passed in the seventh century of the Christian Era. In Plêthon's lifetime (*circa* A.D. 1360–1452) the Greek World was in grievous trouble once again. The East Roman Imperial regime was, by then, in its last agonies, and the Greeks had therefore become almost wholly dependent, for their survival as a community with a distinctive identity of its own, on the maintenance of the Greek branch of the Eastern Orthodox Church.

This Greek Church, as well as the Empire, had fallen into adversity. The number of its adherents had been depleted by conversions to Islam, and the Church itself was under pressure to sacrifice its ecclesiastical independence in the hope—a forlorn hope[2]—that, at the price of recognizing the supremacy of the Papal See, the Greeks would be able to purchase their Western co-religionists' military assistance against the 'Osmanlis. Yet the Eastern Orthodox Church, even in this plight, was a tower of strength for the Greek people by comparison with a 'fancy religion' that was not even a genuine re-suscitation of the Greeks' pre-Christian religious past.[3]

---

[1] '*L'effort de Pléthon pour arriver par la philosophie à une nouvelle forme de civilisation*'—C. Alexandre in his edition of Plêthon's *Nómoi* (Paris 1858; reprint Amsterdam 1966), Notice Préliminaire, p. lxxvii.

[2] George Skholários (subsequently the Pādishāh Mehmet II's Ecumenical Patriarch Yennádhios) points out this out in his letter πρὸς πλήθωνα, ἐπὶ τῇ πρὸς τὸ ὑπὲρ Λατίνων βιβλίον αὐτοῦ ἀπαντήσει, ἢ κατὰ Ἑλλήνων, printed in Plêthon, *Nómoi*, ed. cit., pp. 313–69, as Appendix IX. Here Skholários denounces the Unionists for betraying Orthodoxy in vain—ὠνούμενοι τὴν ἐκ τῶν ἐχθρῶν σωτηρίαν ἐκ τῶν μήτε δυναμένων μήτε βουλομένων ἴσως ταύτην παρέχειν, ἀλλα γράμμασι μόνοις ἀντὶ τῶν ἔργων καὶ κεναῖς ἐλπίσι ψυχαγωγούντων ἡμῶν το μικρόψυχον (op. cit., p. 358).

[3] Skholários, who by this date had become the Ecumenical Patriarch Yennádhios, points out, in his letter to Joseph the Exarch, that Plêthon had no first-hand information about the doctrines of the pre-Christian religious worthies, historical or mythical, whom Plêthon cites as his authorities.

The revival of an ancient native philosophy and religion, and deposition of an interloping alien religion, is not inherently impossible. It was impracticable for the Byzantine and Modern Greeks, but it was achieved successfully by the Chinese. In China the Mahayana form of Buddhism seemed, from the fourth to the ninth century of the Christian Era, to be supplanting the Chinese people's pre-Buddhist philosophy and religion as effectively as the Greek people's pre-Christian philosophy and religion has actually been supplanted by Eastern Orthodox Christianity (now being supplanted, in its turn, by modern Western rationalism). Yet, in China, neo-Confucianism did eventually depose the Mahayana from a supremacy that had appeared to have become impregnable. Neo-Confucianism achieved this success in an age in which the Chinese World, like the contemporary Greek World, was being progressively subjugated by alien military invaders. One of the means by which neo-Confucianism got the better of the Mahayana was its unavowed but transparent plagiarism of Buddhist thought. However, Plêthon likewise plagiarized from Christianity, yet did not win any comparable success from the same manoeuvre.

This difference in the fortunes of neo-Hellenism and neo-Confucianism can be accounted for. In the first place, the Chinese body social was much bigger and tougher than the Greek. It could, and did, survive a rain of blows without disintegrating. It was consolidated by a civil service, recruited from a well-educated land-owning social class, which had held together and had also managed, even when it was at its nadir, to keep some hold over the public administration. In the second place, Confucianism, and the rites and myths associated with it, could be represented as being more rational than the intrusive Buddhism against which Confucianism was reasserting itself. The Mahayana was ascetic and fantastic. It had legions of monks and nuns, hosts of Bodhisattvas, and aeons of cosmic cycles. The mythical figures of Confucianism were utilitarian culture-heroes, and its rites were sober safeguards of social order and decorum. Christianity, like the Mahayana, is vulnerable to modern Western rationalism. Its tenets, likewise, can be dismissed as being extravagant and unverifiable. On the other hand, they can be represented—as Yennádhios finds easy in his letter to Joseph the Exarch[4]—as being more rational than Plato's flights of imagination, and, *a fortiori*, more rational than the myths and rites of popular Hellenic Greek religion.

Thus neo-Hellenism was at a disadvantage by comparison with neo-Confucianism, and, in Plêthon's hands, it was also handicapped by its expositor's personal temperament. Plêthon lived in an imaginary private world of his own, in which the facts of life did not intervene to moderate two weaknesses in Plêthon's character, namely unwarrantable self-assurance and unrealistic pedantry. These were grave weaknesses, and they were more than doubly grave in combination. At Florence, during the Council of Union in 1439, George of Trebizond heard Plêthon say (so this witness declares) that, within a few years, the World would be converted to one single religion; and, when George of Trebizond asked Plêthon whether he meant Christianity or

See the Greek text of this letter of Yennádhios' in Appendix XIX to C. Alexandre's edition of the surviving fragments of Plêthon's *Nómoi*, pp. 412–42. The reference here is to p. 423.

[4] e.g. in loc. cit., on pp. 429–31 and in numerous other passages of this letter of Yennádhios'.

Islam, Plêthon replied (so George of Trebizond reports) that he meant neither of these religions, but one that was identical with paganism (*gentilitate*)—i.e. with Plêthon's own version of neo-Hellenism.[5]

Yennádhios, in apostrophizing Plêthon in his letter to Joseph the Exarch, starts by asking Plêthon: 'Whom do you expect to convert?'[6] In a later passage of the same letter,[7] Yennádhios notes that Plêthon, in his *Nómoi*, prescribes the death-penalty for anyone who takes objection to Plêthon's enactments.[8] Yennádhios points out that, in this, Plêthon takes after ($\delta\mu o\iota\omega\theta\epsilon\iota s$) Muhammad.[9] Actually, the death-penalty as the punishment for unbelief is less likely to have been borrowed from Islam by Plêthon[10] than to have been copied by him from Plato's *Laws*, but Plêthon's approval of polygamy[11] may indeed have been inspired by Islam, as Yennádhios asserts that it was,[12] and so also may have been Plêthon's combination of fatalism[13] with a logically incongruous belief in God's providence.[14] Before his migration from Constantinople, which had probably become too hot to hold him,[15] to his permanent asylum in the autonomous East Roman Despotate of the Morea, Plêthon had spent some time at Adrianople, which at that date was the capital of the Ottoman Empire.

Yennádhios taxes Plêthon[16] with taking after Muhammad, not only in enacting the death-penalty for unbelief and in approving of polygamy, but in his legislation about war, sacrifices, food, drink, prayers, and much besides, 'but, above all, in the objective of the whole enterprise'. Yennádhios notes that Muhammad has the advantage over Plêthon in the two most important points of all. Muhammad was a monotheist, and he did not embark on his audacious venture till he had acquired sufficient political and military power for putting his ambitious plans into effect.

By comparison with Muhammad, Plêthon was, in truth, an unpractical visionary. It has been noted already[17] that Plêthon felt confident that the Greece of his day would be able to repel the Ottoman Empire, because the

---

[5] George of Trebizond, *Comparatio Platonis et Aristotelis*, last chapter but one. The passage is quoted in the original Latin by Alexandre in his edition of Plêthon's *Nómoi*, Notice Préliminaire, p. xvi n. 1.

[6] Loc. cit., p. 421.

[7] Ibid., pp. 437–8.

[8] Plêthon: *Nómoi*, Book III, chapter xxxi, $\Pi\epsilon\rho\iota$ $\Delta\iota\kappa\hat\omega\nu$, p. 126 in ed. cit.: $\eta\nu$ $\tau\iota s$ $\pi\alpha\rho\grave\alpha$ $\tau\grave\alpha s$ $\dot\eta\mu\epsilon\tau\epsilon\rho\alpha s$ $\tau\alpha\dot\nu\tau\alpha s$ $\delta\delta\xi\alpha s$ $\sigma o\phi\iota\zeta\delta\mu\epsilon\nu o s$ $\dot\alpha\lambda\hat\omega$, $\zeta\hat\omega\nu$ $\kappa\alpha\grave\iota$ $o\dot\upsilon\tau o s$ $\kappa\epsilon\kappa\alpha\dot\upsilon\sigma\epsilon\tau\alpha\iota$.

[9] Yennádhios refers to Muhammad by the periphrasis: $\tau\hat\omega$ $\tau\grave\eta\nu$ $\pi\rho o\phi\eta\tau\hat\omega\nu$ $\kappa\grave\alpha\iota$ $\nu o\mu o\theta\epsilon\tau\hat\omega\nu$ $\dot\alpha\rho\pi\alpha\sigma\alpha\nu\tau\iota$ $\tau\dot\alpha\zeta\iota\nu$, $\pi\alpha\rho\alpha\chi\omega\rho\eta\sigma\epsilon\iota$ $\Theta\epsilon o\hat\upsilon$ (ibid., p. 438).

[10] For Jews and Christians who submitted to becoming subjects of the Islamic state, the Qur'anic penalty is, not death, but a surtax.

[11] Table of Contents of his *Nómoi*, Book III, chapter xvi.

[12] Yennádhios, Letter to Joseph the Exarch, in loc. cit., p. 438.

[13] See Masai, op. cit., pp. 98, 187–200, 201–2.

[14] Plêthon accuses the Unionists of disbelieving in God's providence, and he sees in this the explanation of God's aggrandizement of the 'Osmanlis at the Greeks' expense. $\Delta\hat\eta\lambda o\iota$ $\gamma\dot\alpha\rho$ $\epsilon\dot\iota\sigma\iota\nu$ $o\iota$ $\pi o\lambda\lambda o\grave\iota$ $\dot\epsilon\kappa\epsilon\dot\iota\nu\omega\nu$ [sc. the 'Osmanlis] $\tau\grave\eta\nu$ $\tau o\hat\upsilon$ $\tau\grave o\nu$ $\Theta\epsilon\grave o\nu$ $\tau\hat\omega\nu$ $\dot\alpha\nu\theta\rho\omega\pi\dot\iota\nu\omega\nu$ $\pi\rho o\nu o\epsilon\hat\iota\nu$ $\delta\delta\xi\alpha\nu$ $\pi o\lambda\grave\upsilon$ $\tau\hat\omega\nu$ $\dot\eta\mu\epsilon\tau\epsilon\rho\alpha s$ $\beta\epsilon\beta\alpha\iota o\tau\epsilon\rho\alpha\nu$ $\dot\epsilon\chi o\nu\tau\epsilon s$ $\dot\epsilon\nu$ $\tau\alpha\hat\iota s$ $\psi\upsilon\chi\alpha\hat\iota s$. ($\Pi\lambda\dot\eta\theta\omega\nu o s$ $\pi\rho\grave o s$ $\tau\grave o$ $\dot\upsilon\pi\grave\epsilon\rho$ $\tau o\hat\upsilon$ $\Lambda\alpha\tau\iota\nu\iota\kappa o\hat\upsilon$ $\delta\delta\gamma\mu\alpha\tau o s$ $\beta\iota\beta\lambda\dot\iota o\nu$ in Plêthon, *Nómoi*, ed. cit., pp. 300–11, on p. 310).

[15] See Chapter VIII, on p. 159.

[16] Ibid.

[17] In Chapter VIII, on p. 158.

Persian Empire had been successfully repelled by the Greece of the fifth century B.C. In a memorial, written in A.D. 1418, on the affairs of the Pelopónnêsos,[18] Plêthon counsels the Emperor Manuel II and his son the Despot Theodore II to rejuvenate the principality by reforming its administrative organization and its social structure on Hellenic lines; but the Hellenic constitution that Plêthon recommends is not one that had ever been an historical reality. It is not, for instance, the constitution of the Achaean Confederation, which had embraced the whole of the Pelopónnêsos for amost half a century ending in 146 B.C. Plêthon's source is the academic blueprint for an ideal Hellenic city-state which is set out by Plato in *The Republic* and in *The Laws*.[19]

Plêthon's greatest folly was to expatiate on his high-handedly revised version of the Hellenic pantheon, and to compose a set of prayers and hymns for a neo-Hellenic liturgical year. Here he was anticipating Comte's prescriptions for the nineteenth-century Positivist Church's 'Religion of Humanity'. Plêthon apes Eastern Orthodoxy as solemnly as Comte apes Western Catholicism. In Plêthon's *Nómoi*, these frills are as provocative as they are superfluous.

Plêthon was circumspect enough to withhold from publication his exposition of the mythological and liturgical elements of his neo-Hellenism.[20] The only chapters of his *Nómoi* that he appears to have published[21] are those on Fate[22] and on the Calendar.[23] During his lifetime he appears not to have divulged the whole of his doctrine—except, perhaps, verbally to one or two converts. For instance, Michael Apostólês, in a letter to Plêthon himself,[24] boasts of having been Plêthon's accomplice, while, in two letters addressed to John Argyró-poulos,[25] Apostólês ostentatiously invokes the Hellenic pantheon and associates Plêthon with himself as being a fellow true believer. The anonymous author of an indignant protest against the burning of Plêthon's *Nómoi* by Yennádhios after Plêthon's death likewise knew, and much admired, what Plêthon had written in that book περὶ Ἑλληνικῆς θρησκείας κὰ θεολογίας.[26] On the other hand, if Ierónymos Kharitónymos[27] and Gregory the monk[28] had been aware of the lengths to which Plêthon had carried his repudiation of Christianity, they would hardly have been able to praise Plêthon's life's work and to lament his death with a whole-heartedness that is manifestly sincere; for, in the elegies of these two admirers of Plêthon, there is internal evidence that both of them were believing Christians.[29]

---

18 See Alexandre in op. cit., p. ix; Vakalópoulos, A. E., Ἱστορία τοῦ νέου Ἑλληνισμοῦ vol. i, pp. 173-80; and the present work, p. 160.

19 See above, p. 160.

20 See ibid.

21 See Alexandre in op. cit., pp. xc-xciii.

22 Book II, chapter vi, Περὶ Εἱμαρμένης, printed in Alexandre's edition on pp. 64-79.

23 Book I, chapter xxi, fragments printed in ibid., pp. 58-63.

24 Plêthon, *Nómoi*, ed. cit., Appendix X, pp. 370-1.

25 Ibid., Appendices XI and XII, pp. 372-5.

26 See ibid., Appendix XVIII, pp. 408-11, on p. 410.

27 Ὑμνῳδία τῷ σοφωτάτῳ διδασκάλῳ κυρίῳ Γεωργίῳ τῷ Γεμιστῷ· ibid., Appendix XIII, pp. 375-86.

28 Μονῳδία τῷ σοφῷ διδασκάλῳ Γεωργίῳ τῷ Γεμιστῷ· ibid., Appendix XIV, pp. 387-403.

29 For instance, Kharitónymos writes (ibid., p. 381) τοῦ παρ' ἡμῖν Μαθουσάλα, with the implication that the Hellenic μακρόβιοι, Tithonós and Arganthónios, with whom he couples

Vêssaríon and Skholários were also, both alike, believing Christians, and both were, besides, clerics who rose to eminent, and highly responsible, posts in the ecclesiastical hierarchy. Vêssaríon came to be first an Eastern Orthodox archbishop and then a Roman cardinal; Skholários came to be the Ecumenical Patriarch Yennádhios II. Both these ecclesiastical statesmen were as fully aware as Michael Apostólês was of Plêthon's repudiation of Christianity. Their forbearance towards Plêthon is remarkable. Skholários had an inducement. Plêthon, like Skholários, had eventually declared himself against union with the Roman Church; and Plêthon's prestige in the contemporary Greek World, as a stylist in Hellenic Greek and as a connoisseur of Hellenic philosophy, was so great that an Eastern Orthodox anti-Unionist could not afford to alienate such a potent ally.[30] This consideration partly accounts for Skholários' tactful handling of Plêthon during Plêthon's lifetime. Vêssaríon's tenderness towards Plêthon is even more remarkable; for Vêssaríon had come down on the opposite side to Plêthon and to Skholários in the Greeks' domestic controversy over the pros and cons of Union; and an apostate is apt to feel bitterness against ex-coreligionists who have put him to shame by refusing to follow his example. Yet Vêssaríon's eulogies of Plêthon after Plêthon's death are among the most enthusiastic of those that are on record.

Though Plêthon had refrained from publishing more than a couple of chapters of his *Nómoi* that were relatively uncontroversial,[31] he had shown his hand in conversation at Florence in 1439[32] and also in three published tracts: *A Clarification of the Obscurities in Zoroaster's Dicta*,[33] *Points of Difference between Aristotle and Plato*,[34] and *Animadversions on the Tract supporting the Latin Dogma* [concerning the Procession of the Holy Spirit].[35] In the last of these three pieces, Plêthon maintains that the Latin dogma, according to which the Spirit proceeds from the Son as well as from the Father, is based on an axiom that is congenial to 'the Hellenic theology' but is utterly at variance with Christian theology.[36] In this piece, Plêthon has gratuitously inserted a digression setting

Methuselah, were aliens. As for Gregory the monk, he declares naïvely that, for him 'the sacred truth' [of Christianity] is paramount (ibid., pp. 389–90), and the climax of his eulogy of Plêthon, after he has put him on a par with Plato, Thucydides, and Xenophon, is to raise him to a par with the Christian Fathers Saint Basil, Saint John Chrysostom, and Saint Gregory of Nazianzós (ibid., p. 392). Kharitónymos praises Plêthon (ibid., pp. 377–8) for shining at the Council of Florence and for confuting Aristotle (ibid., p. 378). Gregory the monk praises him for confuting the Romans [i.e. the Latins] (ibid., p. 389).

[30] See Skholários' letter to Plêthon ἐπὶ τῇ πρὸς τὸ ὑπὲρ Λατίνων βιβλίον αὐτοῦ ἀπαντήσει in Plêthon, *Nómoi*, ed. cit., Appendix IX, pp. 313–69. οὐ γὰρ μικρὸν ἡ σὴ ψῆφος δυναται (pp. 319–20); ἴσως νῦν ἡ σὴ βιάσεται ψῆφος (p. 358). ἄλλως δὲ χρήσιμος ὁ ἀνήρ (ibid., Appendix IV, Skholários' letter to Mark the Metropolitan of Ephesos, pp. 288–91, on p. 289).

[31] See p. 300, with nn. 15–17.

[32] See pp. 299–300.

[33] Extracts in *Nómoi*, ed. cit., Appendix II, pp. 274–81.

[34] Extracts in ibid., Appendix III, pp. 281–8.

[35] Text in ibid., Appendix VII, pp. 300–11. The tract that Plêthon is here combating is probably not John Argyrópoulos', but one that has not been preserved. This hypothetical lost tract may have been written by Vêssaríon and been published by him anonymously (see Alexandre in Plêthon, *Nómoi*, ed. cit., p. xxviii n. 1.)

[36] Ibid., p. 300. The axiom here formulated by Plêthon is that a difference of faculties (δυνάμεις) involves a difference of essences (οὐσίαις).

out, in short compass, his own version of Hellenic polytheism which he was perhaps already elaborating by then in his unpublished *Nómoi*. In his *Animadversions* Plêthon is ostensibly just reporting what the doctrine of 'the Hellenic theology' is, without explicitly endorsing it; but he makes it clear that, in his opinion, 'the Hellenic theology' is logically self-consistent and that the Christian theology is not, and it is easy to read between the lines that Plêthon's version of 'the Hellenic theology' is in truth the creed in which Plêthon himself believes.

Skholários (by this time a monk and Ecumenical Patriarch under the name Yennádhios) records, in his letter to Joseph the Exarch about his having burnt Plêthon's *Nómoi* after Plêthon's death,[37] that he (Skholários) had already become aware, first in the Pelopónnêsos[38] and afterwards in Italy,[39] that Plêthon had been engaged over a number of years in writing a book of the kind that the *Nómoi* has proved to be now that this magnum opus of Plêthon's has eventually come into Yennádhios' hands since Plêthon's death. Skholários had previously declared, in his letter to Mark the Metropolitan of Ephesos, enclosing a copy of Skholários' reply to Plêthon's *Points of Difference between Aristotle and Plato*,[40] his conviction that 'time will show' that Plêthon's champions and Skholários's critics are mistaken. Plêthon *has* witten a pagan book, and Skholários' motive is *not* malice; his conscience compels him to combat Plêthon's religious errors which he, Skholários, has correctly divined. In both his letter to Mark of Ephesos and in his subsequent letter to Joseph the Exarch, Skholários-Yennádhios states[41] that the reason for his having written a reply to Plêthon's *Points of Difference* is that he had perceived that Plêthon's ostensible attack on Aristotle on Plato's behalf was really a covert attack on Christianity. Hellenic paganism, as interpreted by Plêthon, was Skholários-Yennádhios' own real target.[42]

This was, in fact, the line taken by Skholários in his discreet reply to Plêthon's *Animadversions on the Tract supporting the Latin Dogma*. In this piece, as in his letters to Mark and to Joseph, Skholários dismisses the disputes over the respective merits of Plato and Aristotle as being of only secondary importance.[43] This rejoinder of Skholários' to Plêthon has the alternative title *Against the Hellenes*, and this indicates what is Skholários' true objective. However, in attacking Hellenic paganism as interpreted by Plêthon, Skholários takes care to avoid implying that Plêthon himself believes in these pagan doctrines, just as Plêthon, in the tract to which Skholários is here replying, had taken care to avoid implying that these doctrines are his (Plêthon's) own.

Skholários merely notes that, in the opinion of some unnamed Christian high authorities, 'if people were now, after mankind's enlightenment by Christ, to

---

[37] Plêthon, *Nómoi*, ed. cit., loc. cit., on pp. 412–13.

[38] Perhaps in the suite of the East Roman Emperor John VIII, who visited the Pelopónnêsos in 1428 and there consulted Plêthon on the question of Union (Alexandre in ibid., pp. xii and xiv).

[39] At Florence in 1439, Skholários had already recorded his awareness of Plêthon's indiscretions in Italy in his (Skholários') reply to Plêthon's *Points of Difference* (see Plêthon, *Nómoi*, ed. cit., Appendix V, p. 292).

[40] Ibid., Appendix IV, pp. 288–91, on p. 289.

[41] See ibid., pp. 289 and 413.   [42] Ibid.

[43] Ibid., pp. 289, 315, 318, 413. On p. 289 he calls such disputes *jeux d'esprit* (παιγνία).

revive the rotten nonsense-tales of the Hellenes (τὰ σαπρὰ ῾Ελλήνων ἀνανεοῖεν λ̣ηρήματα), they would be wallowing in falsehood'.[44] So far from accusing Plêthon of being guilty of this offence, Skholários says to him: 'In exposing this nonsense of the Hellenes, you have given me no small pleasure; and what you have done will not, I guess, be labour lost. People who did not know about this nonsense might have been led astray by somebody, but now, thanks to your exposition, these potential victims of deceit will learn and will condemn.'[45] 'We [Eastern Orthodox Christians] have been in a bad way for many years by now.'[46] For instance, 'people who have been convicted of having caught the plague of Hellenic paganism are permitted to live and to receive honour and to corrupt their neighbours, whereas they ought to be condemned to suffer the extreme penalty. Worst of all, they have the audacity to hold forth about the divine doctrines [of Christianity].'[47] Skholários' ironical tactfulness is masterly.

Plêthon's prime merit in both Skholários' and Vêssaríon's eyes, was, rightly, Plêthon's virtuousness and personal attractiveness. Skholários, in the letter to Mark of Ephesos in which he denounces Plêthon's neo-Hellenic paganism, writes[48] that, 'in point of morals, Plêthon could serve as an example for members of the rising generation who are genuine aspirants to virtue'. Vêssaríon, in a letter to Nikólaos Sekoundínos,[49] enclosing copies of his letter of condolence to Plêthon's two sons[50] and of his two epitaphs on Plêthon in Hellenic elegiac verse,[51] extols Plêthon's character and concludes: 'I admire him, to tell the truth, more than anyone else whom I have ever met and have conversed with, so far.'[52]

Plêthon's naïve admirer the monk Gregory, who ascribes to his hero the entire gamut of virtues, notes[53] that, in controversy, Plêthon was never the first to start a quarrel. This may be true, but Plêthon has left evidence against himself that he could be quarrelsome in taking up the gauntlet. In his reply to Skholários' reply to his (Plêthon's) *Points of Difference between Aristotle and Plato*, Plêthon writes with a rudeness that constrasts unfavourably with the courtesy of Skholários' reply, at a later stage in the exchange of tracts between him and Plêthon, to Plêthon's provocative *Animadversions on the Tract supporting the Latin Dogma.* However, Plêthon's rudeness to Skholários is a minor blemish in a character which, on the whole, was admirable according to the testimony of contemporaries, including Skholários-Yennádhios himself, who knew Plêthon personally.

However, Plêthon's probity might not have availed to shield him if it had not been seconded by his reputation as a stylist and a scholar. The contemporary testimony to Plêthon's literary and scholarly eminence is unanimous. 'He is an unsurpassed stylist.'[54] 'I constantly admire in you, besides your other qualities, your erudition and your style' (ὅσα εἰς σοφίαν καὶ την τῶν λόγων ἐστὶ τέχνην).[55]

---

[44] Plêthon, *Nómoi*, ed. cit., Appendix IV, p. 324.
[46] Ibid., p. 361.
[48] Ibid., p. 289.
[50] Ibid., Appendix XV, pp. 404–5.
[52] Ibid., p. 408.
[54] Skholários, ibid., p. 289.

[45] Ibid., p. 325.
[47] Ibid., p. 362.
[49] Ibid., Appendix XVII, pp. 407–8.
[51] Ibid., Appendix XVI, p. 406.
[53] Ibid., p. 395.

[55] Skholários, ibid., p. 314. 'Erudition', rather than 'wisdom', is the meaning of the Hellenic Greek word σοφία when used by an Hellenically educated Byzantine Greek.

The participants in the Council of Florence 'admired, beyond words, Plêthon's erudition and character and eloquence'.[56] 'The erudite Yemistós.'[57] 'He has become a great glory for all Ellás' (μέγα κλέος Ἑλλάδι πάσῃ γέγονεν).[58] 'The most translucent and illustrious ornament of the most unfortunate Hellenes.'[59]

This last encomium from an uncritical admirer was shown by Skholários-Yennádhios to be double-edged. 'We lamented our people's disaster, their shame, their disgrace; and, as if our misfortunes were not grievous enough already, they had to be aggravated by this: the treasures of the Hellenic culture were finally bequeathed to one solitary old man; and all that he got from his Hellenic studies was a shameful mental derangement. His aberrations are not those of a sane mind.'[60] 'He was a painstaking stylist in the classical manner' (εὐφραδίας δὲ ἐπεμελήθη μὲν καλῶς τῆς ἀρχαίας), but the work in which he employed his good style was utterly impious and demented.[61]

Skholários-Yennádhios' admiration for Plêthon's literary style and erudition was shared by his and Plêthon's Unionist contemporary Vêssaríon and by all the rest of the dwindling band of Hellenically educated Greeks of that generation. Skholários, too, like Vêssaríon and like Plêthon himself, not only wrote exclusively in the dead Attic *koine*, but took pains to write the *koine* with as near an approach to classical correctness as he could attain. The approval and prestige that Plêthon had acquired by his laborious Hellenic style and erudition accounts for Skholários-Yennádhios' apologies for his opposition to Plêthon. He is on the defensive even in his letters on the subject to Mark of Ephesos and to Joseph the Exarch, though both these clerics were at one with Skholários-Yennádhios in condemning Plêthon's neo-Hellenic paganism. Indeed, the Patriarch, in burning Plêthon's *Nómoi*, had anticipated a suggestion from the Exarch that reached the Patriarch after the deed had been done.[62] But the Patriarch had to defend his own action even against himself; for his admiration for Plêthon, though rueful, was sincere. Skholários' Hellenic pedantry was at war with his Christian conscience.

For an educated Graecophone Eastern Orthodox Christian, it was obligatory to ape the classical Hellenic Greek writers' language and style, but it was no less obligatory to ignore the ideas and beliefs that were conveyed in classical Hellenic Greek literature. The correct attitude for a Greek Orthodox Christian is explained lucidly by Yennádhios in the arraignment of Plêthon that is embodied in the Patriarch's letter to the Exarch.

Why did you [i.e. Plêthon] give your allegiance to doctrines that are rotten and fugitive, and that have been confuted from many angles, till they have lost all hold on human souls? Do you imagine that the Hellenic literature has been preserved solely for your benefit? Our forefathers saved this literature for two reasons: for the sake of the language, and as evidence for exposing the misguidedness of Hellenism as a foil against which the purity of the Christian theology would shine out. They were confident that no one would be so simple-minded as to embrace Hellenic paganism instead of condemning it.

[56] Kharitónymos, in *Nómoi*, ed. cit., p. 377.
[57] Vêssaríon, ibid., p. 404.
[58] Vêssaríon, ibid., p. 405.
[59] Gregory the monk, ibid., p. 389.
[60] Skholários-Yennádhios to Joseph the Exarch, ibid., p. 420.
[61] Skholários-Yennádhios, ibid., p. 442.
[62] See ibid., p. 412.

In other words, the correct Byzantine Greek attitude towards Hellenic Greek literature was to draw a rigid distinction between its verbal form and its intellectual substance.[63] This distinction is absurd, but, by Skholários' time, it had been in vogue continuously for about eighteen centuries. It can be traced back to the academic Athenian stylist Isocrates, Plato's contemporary, in whose generation the Hellenic civilization had passed its zenith. This is one of the maladies that killed the Hellenic Greek culture and blighted its Byzantine Greek successor. The absurdity was extreme,[64] but the punishment for taking seriously the matter of Hellenism, as well as its form, was condign. Phótios in the ninth century, Psellós in the eleventh century, and Plêthon in the fifteenth century all came under suspicion and all suffered in various degrees for their intellectual honesty.

Skholários questions Plêthon's intellectual ability. 'He has no conception of dialectical method.'[65] 'The presentation of the topics of his *Nómoi* is chaotic.'[66] He is wilfully ignorant of Christian theology.[67] These strictures may be justified. Skholários was competent to pass judgement. He was well versed in Eastern Orthodox theology, and he had clarified this theology's deliberate avoidance of precision by tempering it with an infusion of Western neo-Aristotelian logic. Plêthon may have been intellectually second-rate; this was not incompatible with erudition or with literary style of the kinds that a cultivated minority of the Byzantine Greeks admired. But it required no great intellectual acumen to perceive that the conventional Byzantine dichotomy between the form and the matter of the Hellenic Greek literature was preposterous. What was required was the probity that would disapprove of this preposterous convention, and the courage that would break with it; and these were virtues that Plêthon possessed in sufficient measure for getting himself into serious trouble on that account.

Skholários' sincerity is no more open to doubt than Plêthon's is. Skholários was a believing Christian. When asked, on the eve of the Ottoman conquest of Constantinople, what his nationality was, he replied, according to his own account: 'I do not call myself a Hellene because I do not believe as the Hellenes believed. I might call myself a Byzantine because I was born at Byzantium. But

[63] Professor Browning observes that John Ítalos had been condemned specifically on the charge of having paid attention to the content and not just the form of classical Greek literature. Michael Psellós had been accused of having committed the same offence.

[64] I know what I am talking about here from personal experience; for I myself had a Byzantine-like education in England from 1899 to 1911. From as early an age as I can remember, I was brought up to take it for granted that the tenets of Christianity (of the Anglican Protestant denomination) were true and binding. At the age of ten, I began to learn the Hellenic form of the Greek language; by the age of fifteen, I was reading Hellenic Greek literature widely. By the age of nineteen I was studying the philosophy of Plato and Aristotle. It was assumed by my parents and teachers that my Christianity and my Hellenism were to be insulated from each other in separate water-tight mental compartments. I was to become proficient in writing pseudo-Attic Greek prose and verse and in understanding the Hellenic Greek poets' and philosophers' meaning, but I was not to take the Hellenic *Weltanschauung* seriously. I found this impossible. I did take Hellenism seriously, and consequently I lost my incompatible Christian faith. Like Plêthon, I should have suffered for divulging my paganism if I had happened to be born one or two generations earlier than I was.

[65] Skholários to Mark, in Plêthon, *Nómoi*, ed. cit., p. 290.

[66] Skholários to Joseph, ibid., p. 416.

[67] Ibid., p. 424.

I prefer simply to call myself a Christian.'[68] Though he eventually became a leading anti-Unionist, he declared, as a Christian, that 'the Latins are the most godly (εὐσεβεστέροις) of all peoples, next to us' [Eastern Orthodox Christians].[69] He is manifestly sincere in protesting that he was driven, first to oppose Plêthon in controversy, and finally to burn Plêthon's *Nómoi*, by the dictates of his own Christian conscience; that he had no other motive; and that he acted most reluctantly.

Why was Skholários so rigid in his confrontation with Plêthon, who was his fellow anti-Unionist, when the Unionist Vêssaríon was so indulgent to Plêthon? Skholários held positions of great public responsibility in Greek Orthodox Christendom. In John VIII's reign he was καθολικὸς [i.e. general] κρίτης τῶν Ῥωμαίων, καθολικὸς [i.e. general] σεκρετάριος τοῦ Βασιλέως, and διδάσκαλος [i.e. lay reader in theology].[70] In Mehmet II's reign, he was the first Ottoman Ecumenical Patriarch. Skholários was a conscientious public servant. He did not shirk painful tasks.

However, in his indictment of Plêthon there is at least one inconsistency. When he asks his dead antagonist rhetorically: 'Whom were you expecting to convert?'[71] the unwritten but inevitable answer to this question is: 'Nobody, except perhaps a few of the frankest and boldest members of the fast-dwindling band of Hellenically educated Greek intellectuals.' This is the truth; but, in a supplementary denunciation of 'the atheists or determinists' (ἀθέων ἢ αὐτοματιστῶν),[72] Yennádhios says that, in opposing Plêthon, he was concerned primarily, not with Plêthon himself, but with 'the present uneducatedness (ἀμαθίας) of the majority of the nation—a nation which, in the past and until recently, was the most highly cultivated (σοφωτάτῳ) in the World.' Yennádhios avers that this lack of education might have put the more simple souls in jeopardy. They might have been beguiled by Plêthon's undeserved reputation for erudition (σοφίας).[73] Actually, lack of education was, and always is, a protection from 'dangerous thought'. The controversy over Christianity versus Hellenic paganism, masked as a controversy over Aristotle versus Plato, would have been 'Greek' (i.e. unintelligible Hellenic Greek) to the uneducated majority of Yennádhios' and Plêthon's Greek contemporaries. The advantage of having an uneducated flock became apparent to Yennádhios' successors in the government of the Ecumenical Patriarchate when the then at last increasing number of Greek intellectuals was exposed to the eighteenth-century Western 'Enlightenment', carried far and wide in the blast of the French Revolution.[74]

As for Vêssaríon's indulgence to Plêthon, it is evident that Vêssaríon

---

[68] Skholários-Yennádhios, 'Against the Jews', in *Oeuvres complètes* (ed. by Petit, L.; Sidérides, X. A.; and Jugie, M.: (Paris, 1928–36), 8 vols.), vol. iii, p. 252, quoted by Runciman, *The Great Church in Captivity*, p. 121, and cited in the present work, p. 161 n. 21.

[69] Letter to Joseph, in Plêthon, *Nómoi*, ed. cit., Appendix IX, p. 360.

[70] See Alexandre in Plêthon, *Nómoi*, ed. cit., Notice Préliminaire, p. xxiii with n. 3, and p. xxiv with nn. 1 and 2. Alexandre cites the authorities for these titles.

[71] Skholários-Yennádhios to Joseph, ibid., Appendix XIX, p. 421, cited already on p. 300.

[72] Ibid., Appendix XX, pp. 441–3.

[73] Ibid., p. 441–2; and see above, p. 304 n. 55.

[74] See Chapter VII, p. 143 n. 20, and Chapter IX, p. 176.

continued to feel affection for Plêthon as his instructor in the highly-prized art of writing the *koine* in a classical style. Plêthon's anti-Unionism did not vex Vêssaríon when Vêssaríon had taken his own decision to join the Roman Church and had been rewarded by being made a cardinal. Nor was Plêthon's neo-Hellenic paganism Vêssaríon's concern after Vêssaríon had seceded from the Constantinopolitan to the Roman Patriarchate. If Plêthon was any Patriarch's ecclesiastical subject, his ecclesiastical sovereign was the Ecumenical Patriarch, not the Pope.

Moreover, in pre-Reformation Renaissance Italy, the bulkhead insulating the form of Hellenism from the matter of it was temporarily shifted to allow pagan Hellenic literary conceits—and perhaps serious pagan beliefs, too, *sub rosa*—to count as being innocuous and permissible formalities. Vêssaríon could write to Plêthon's sons with impunity from latitudinarian pre-Reformation Papal Rome that their dead father was on his way to join the Olympian gods in their mystic Bacchanalian song and dance (τὸν μυστικὸν τοῖς 'Ολυμπίοις θεοῖς συγχορεύσοντα ἴακχον)[75] and that, *if* one were to accept the Pythagorean and Platonic doctrine of an endless series of metempsychoses, one would be bound to conclude that Plato's soul had been re-incarnated in Plêthon's body.[76] Vêssaríon the cardinal had a licence in a temporarily care-free Rome that was denied to Skholários, the ex-East Roman Imperial civil servant turned monk in a beleaguered Constantinople, pending his elevation to the Ecumenical Patriarchate by Mehmet the Conqueror.

Each of these three eminent fifteenth-century Greeks had his own recipe for salvaging his compatriots from the shipwreck of the Byzantine civilization. Skholários-Yennádhios' solution for the common problem was to preserve the ecclesiastical independence of the Eastern Orthodox churches at the price of political subjection to the 'Osmanlis for the whole of the Eastern Orthodox Christian World except for Russia. Vêssaríon's solution was to unite Eastern Orthodox Christendom with Western Christendom at the price of ecclesiastical subjection to the Roman See and reception of Roman theological doctrine. Plêthon's solution was to rejuvenate Greek society by a thorough-going revival of the Hellenic Greek civilization. He was not willing to limit the practice of Hellenism to the puerile conceit of writing the Attic *koine* in the classical style; he wanted to revive Hellenic philosophy, to put into effect the Hellenic philosophers' blueprints for political and social institutions, and to re-animate the beliefs and rites of the pre-Christian Hellenic Greek religion.

Of these three recipes, Skholários-Yennádhios' was the most practical for dealing with the immediate crisis in the Greek people's fortunes. Skholários came to the conclusion[77]—in which he had been anticipated by Plêthon[78]—that an ecclesiastical and theological capitulation to the Roman See would win for the Greeks from the Westerners only perfunctory verbal, not effective military, support against the 'Osmanlis. The rejection of Union secured for the

---

[75] Plêthon, *Nómoi*, ed. cit., Appendix XV, p. 404.

[76] Ibid., pp. 404–5.

[77] See p. 298 n. 2.

[78] See Plêthon, *Nómoi*, ed. cit., Appendix VII, pp. 309–11. Hereafter, in this Appendix—except where stated—all references are to Alexandre's edition of Plêthon's *Nómoi*.

Greek Eastern Orthodox Church, as represented by the Ecumenical Patriarchate, not merely its ecclesiastical independence but the re-establishment of
its ecclesiastical dominion over the Bulgarian and Serbian churches and also
a large measure of civil, as well as ecclesiastical, authority over a semi-
autonomous *Rum milleti* into which the Ottoman Government rounded up all
Eastern Orthodox Christians, non-Greek as well as Greek who fell under
Ottoman rule. The weak point in Skholários-Yennádhios' recipe was that the
Ottoman regime and the Islamic civilization had only two more centuries to
run before they, in their turn, would suffer the shipwreck that had overtaken
the East Roman Empire and the Byzantine civilization by Yennádhios' own
day. Before the close of the seventeenth century, Eastern Orthodox Christendom was once again exposed to the impact of Western 'dangerous thought', this
time in the form, not of the *filioque*, but of a dynamic secular 'Enlightenment',
culminating in the infectious 'Ideas of the French Revolution'.

Vêssaríon must have reckoned that, in opting for Union, he was launching
himself on 'the wave of the future'. It is true that, in Vêssaríon's and
Yennádhios' and Plêthon's generation, Renaissance Italy still had half a
century of power and wealth and cultural predominance ahead of her before
she was to be dwarfed and subjugated by the Transalpine and Transmarine
backwoods of Western Christendom; the Roman Church still had a century of
ecclesiastical sovereignty ahead of it before its domain was to be reduced in
northern Europe by the secession of the Protestants as drastically as the
Ecumenical Patriarchate's domain had already been reduced in Asia Minor by
mass-conversions there of ex-Eastern Orthodox Christians to Islam. The
Western World as a whole, of which Vêssaríon had become a naturalized
citizen in virtue of having become a Uniate, had five centuries of power ahead
of it; but by 1974 it was already apparent that the days of the Western
minority's supremacy in the World were numbered. The Western wave to
which Vêssaríon had committed himself was not endowed with the power of
perpetual motion.

Was there, and is there, any future for the fifteenth-century Greek World's
third alternative recourse, namely the adoption of Plêthon's version of the pre-
Christian Hellenic religion?

Plêthon himself and Skholários fell into the identical error of supposing that
Hellenism and Christianity were mutually exclusive. Actually Christianity,
which had started as a sectarian form of Judaism, had transformed itself into an
independent religion and had captured the Graeco-Roman World by taking on
board a multiple cargo of Hellenism. Christian theology had been built with
Greek philosophy; Christian mysticism had been inspired by Neoplatonism;
and, most important of all, Graeco-Roman popular religion had been taken up
bodily into Christianity with a mere change of nomenclature. When a local
Hellenic or pre-Hellenic *daimon* or hero was christened with the name of a local
Christian saint or martyr, the unsophisticated majority of the population had
been able to continue to practise their traditional rites and to celebrate their
traditional festivals without being required to make any painful or disconcerting breaks with the familiar and congenial past. Pre-Christian Hellenic
religion was already deeply embedded in the fifteenth-century Eastern

Orthodox Christian liturgy and in the para-Christian popular practices that the ecclesiastical authorities prudently tolerated. Plêthon's solemn Hellenic parody of the Christian liturgy had no more chance of supplanting the official and unofficial practices of the contemporary Eastern Orthodox Church than Comte's similar lucubrations had of supplanting nineteenth-century Roman Catholic practices in the Western World. The Christian ecclesiastical authorities would have agreed with Plêthon that the masses are not fit to be allowed to have the last word in matters of doctrine;[79] but they would have been secretly amused and reassured by Plêthon's lack of worldly wisdom in failing to provide realistically for the satisfaction of the masses' psychological needs.

When Plêthon set out his would-be neo-Hellenic religion in his *Nómoi*, his aim was to make a sharp and shocking break with Christianity. He did reassert some tenets of some Hellenic philosophers that were incompatible with the Christian belief in a god who is credited with being the omnipotent creator of the Universe. Plêthon was a determinist,[80] and he had to exercise all his verbal dexterity in order to reconcile his determinism with his belief in the power and the benevolence of his gods,[81] particularly his supreme god Zeus.[82] Plêthon also held that the Universe has had no beginning and will have no end,[83] and this tenet, too, was incompatible with the Christian belief in a creator god. Closely associated with Plêthon's doctrine of the infinity of the Universe in the time-dimension was his doctrine of the everlastingness of human souls, and his consequent doctrine—taken from Plato and from Plato's master, Pythagoras—that human souls are re-incarnated an infinite number of times.[84] Skholários-Yennádhios complains that Plêthon's doctrine of never-ceasing reincarnation denies to human souls the possibility of ever coming to rest in Heaven.[85] In the next sentence, he complains of Plêthon's un-Christian approval of polygamy.

These are genuine pre-Christian and un-Christian features of Plêthon's system; but there are other points in which Plêthon's would-be sensational religious revolution was actually limited to the trivial field of nomenclature. For instance, there is a multitude of gods,[86] and this flaunting of the word 'gods' in the plural is meant to shock; yet what is there in a name? The Church had long since anticipated Plêthon in catering for the needs of the unsophisticated majority of its adherents by providing them with a multitude of saints and martyrs and by diffracting the monolithic One God of Judaism into the Christian Trinity.

Plêthon, too, has his Trinity, and Christianity's three persons show through Plêthon's Hellenic masks. The First Person of Plêthon's Trinity is Zeus, but this is a Zeus who, unlike the Zeus of an unexpurgated Hellenic mythology, is

---

[79] Book I, chapter 2, p. 28.

[80] See Book II, chapter 6, Περὶ Εἱμαρμένης, pp. 64–79.

[81] See I, 5, p. 44, and II, 6, p. 64.

[82] See II, 6, p. 64, and *Epinomis*, pp. 242–5.

[83] II, 27: Περὶ τῆς τοῦ παντὸς ἀϊδιότητος, pp. 82–3.

[84] II, 22: Περὶ ἀθανασίας ψυχῆς τῆς ανθρωπίνης, pp. 78–9. cp. III, 34, p. 198; *Epinomis*, pp. 250–3 and 258–61; *Résumé of the doctrines of Zoroaster and Plato*, pp. 266–7.

[85] Letter to Joseph, p. 439.

[86] Table of Contents, Book II, chapter 7.

unbegotten[87] and does not beget by sexual procreation in the medium of matter (ὕλης).[88] If any god had sexual relations, these would be incestuous, and this is unthinkable.[89] Zeus does not have sexual relations with Hera—who, in Plêthon's pantheon, is Zeus's eldest daughter,[90] not his sister. Nor does Zeus have such relations with any other divinity.[91]

Poseidon—who, for Plêthon, is Zeus's eldest son, not his brother—is singled out from all other gods to be the Second Person. Poseidon is 'the great, begotten by Zeus as the eldest and best of his offspring, the best possible and the most perfect of Zeus' works.'[92] Poseidon is subject to Zeus alone, and is in command of all the other gods[93] as Zeus' deputy.[94] Plêthon's Poseidon is repeatedly given prominence.[95] The Christian Son of the Father shows through the Poseidonian mask unmistakably.

Plêthon's Third Person of the Trinity is Hera. Whereas Poseidon causes and produces form, Hera does the same for matter.[96] Her δύναμις is not on a par with Poseidon's.[97] Hera is the senior representative of the female principle—the principle that provides matter and nourishment for all created beings.[98] Hera is, in fact, the Great Mother, and Plêthon, in assigning the third place in the Trinity to a mother goddess, reproduces the real Christian Trinity under his Hellenic masks; for the real Third Person of the Christian Trinity is Mary, not the Holy Spirit. The official Third Person of the Christian Trinity has always been relatively dim. The Christian Church has never adopted Joachim of Fiore's glorification of the 'Age of the Spirit' as a climax in which the preceding Ages of the Son and the Father are to culminate.

The roles of Zeus and Poseidon as the First and the Second Person of Plêthon's Trinity are reaffirmed emphatically in the *Epinomis*[99] and in the *Résumé of the Doctrines of Zoroaster and Plato*,[100] which are Plêthon's creeds. Hera's role as the Third Person is affirmed no less clearly in Plêthon's *Afternoon Allocution to the Gods, Number One*.[101]

Plêthon also imitates Christianity in making the Godhead both plural and singular. His 'Prayer to the One God'[102] is so unadulteratedly monotheistic that it might have been written by Muhammad or by Cleanthes.

Plêthon has done to Zeus and the other Homeric gods what the Hellenic philosophers did to them and what the Israelite and Jewish prophets and their successors the Pharisees did to Yahweh. He has made them ethical and benevolent. 'The gods are not the causes of evil.'[103] Even the *daimones* are not wicked.[104] The gods live in perfect harmony with each other, in perfect filial

---

[87] Ἀγένητον: I, 5, p. 46.
[88] III, 15, p. 92.
[89] Ibid.
[90] III, 34, p. 134.
[91] III, 15, p. 118.
[92] I, 5, p. 46.
[93] Ibid., p. 48.
[94] Ibid., p. 56.
[95] e.g. on pp. 82 (II, 26); 92, 104 and 116 (III, 15); 134, 154, 156-8, 174 (III, 34); 204-6 and 218 (hymns); 240 (III, 43, *Epinomis*).
[96] III, 15, p. 106.
[97] Ibid., p. 104.
[98] Ibid., p. 106.
[99] pp. 240-61.
[100] pp. 262-9.
[101] III, 34: Εἰς Θεοὺς Προσρήσεις, pp. 132-203; Δειλινῶν ἐς Θεοὺς Προσρήσεων πρώτη, pp. 156-65, on p. 158.
[102] pp. 273-4.
[103] Table of Contents, Book II, chapter 5. Text on p. 44.
[104] Table of Contents, Book II, chapter 19.

obedience to their father and creator, Zeus.[105] This idyllic vision bears no relation to the satirically humorous Homeric picture of everyday life on Olympus. Moreover, if the gods are sexually continent, are in harmony with each other, and never do harm to human beings, what becomes of the plots of Euripides' plays *Ion, Hippolytus,* and *The Bacchae*? No wonder that Plêthon has no use for the poets, and that he refers his hypothetical converts for guidance to the lawgivers and the philosophers.[106]

Plêthon's code for human morals is puritanical likewise. His horror of homosexuality, for which he prescribes the death-penalty,[107] is strikingly un-Hellenic. It is, in truth, an uneradicated Christian aversion which is part of Christianity's heritage from Judaism. Plêthon's incongruous anti-Hellenism on this issue contrasts with Kaváphês' practice and theory five centuries later. Kaváphês was not a linguistic or stylistic Hellenist. He was too great a poet to be capable of being a pedant. He wrote in his native living Modern Greek in an inimitable style of his own. Kaváphês was a Hellenist in the sense that he had a power of empathy—quite beyond Plêthon's ken—which enabled him to enter into the feelings and thoughts of his Greek predecessors, Hellenic and Byzantine too. Kaváphês condoned in himself a practice about which his own feelings were ambivalent by reminding himself that he was being true to the Hellenic tradition. Plato would have been indulgent to Kaváphês; Plêthon would have given Kaváphês short shrift. In Plêthon's eyes, Kaváphês' sexual offence would have been aggravated by his writing of poetry—and this in the vulgar tongue, which, in Plêthon's judgement, was a symptom of decadence, not an instrument for the expression of an abiding vitality.

Then was Skholários in the right when he dismissed Plêthon's version of pre-Christian Hellenic religion as being an inept and misguided revival of 'the Hellenes' rotten nonsense'?[108] Was it true that Plêthon has no prospect of winning any converts[109] for his fantasy? Till the 1960s, most Western Christians, and most Western ex-Christian rationalists too, would have endorsed Yennádhios' judgement. The rationalists would have added that Yennádhios' own religion was as fantastic and as irrelevant to the realities of life as the Plêthonian 'fancy religion' that Yennádhios was condemning. In 1974, ex-Christians might still believe that Yennádhios' and Plêthon's religions were, both alike, untrue, but no one could still believe that they were academic. By 1974 it had become apparent that the conflict between these two religions raised an issue in which the destiny of mankind was at stake. This issue was concerned with the relation between Man and his habitat in the terrestrial biosphere: that thin film of soil, water, and air, enveloping the planet Earth, within which, alone, life is feasible.

Christianity has inherited from Judaism the belief in, and the worship of, a solitary transcendent god who is deemed to have created the Universe, including Man, and to have licensed Man to exploit the whole of the non-human residue of Nature. God's supposed warrant to Man is set out in the

---

[105] I, 5, p. 50.　　　　　　　　　　　　　　　　　[106] I, 2, pp. 26-37.
[107] III, 31, *Περὶ Δικῶν*, p. 124.
[108] Skholários' reply to Plêthon's *Animadversions*, quoted already on pp. 303-4.
[109] Skholários-Yennádhios to Joseph the Exarch, quoted already on pp. 300 and 307.

twenty-eighth verse of the first chapter of the Book of Genesis: *Be fruitful and multiply and replenish the Earth and subdue it and have dominion.* Yahweh was evicting all the other gods and was inciting Man to appropriate for himself those other gods' vacated dominions.

> From haunted spring and dale
> Edgèd with poplar pale,
> The parting genius is with sighing sent.[110]

Yahweh's directive to Man was innocuous so long as Man was so helpless that he lay at non-human Nature's mercy. However, since the beginning of the Upper Palaeolithic Age, perhaps about 70,000/40,000 years ago, the balance of power has been changing in Man's favour. It has been changing at an accelerating rate, and, since the beginning of the Industrial Revolution, about 200 years ago, the acceleration has gone with a run. By 1974 the balance had been completely reversed, and Man had just awoken to the ironic and alarming truth that his victory over non-human Nature threatened him with self-destruction. Triumphant human technology had reduced the human death-rate while increasing the death-rate of most other forms of life; it had consumed irreplaceable natural resources; and it had polluted the exiguous biosphere. This suicidal triumph of technology was the fruit of Judaic monotheism; for this religion had drained the divinity out of Nature and had thereby exposed non-human Nature to be exploited by human greed, to mankind's own undoing, under licence from a hypothetical, unique, transcendent, omnipotent god.

The antidote to monotheism is a polytheism which recognizes that non-human Nature is divine and that consequently she has divine rights which Man violates at his peril. The worship of the divine powers inherent in non-human Nature is the earliest form of human religion of which a record has survived. This religion was relevant to the realities of life in the Lower Palaeolithic Age; it has become relevant again to the realities of life in A.D. 1974. As the balance of power between Man and non-human Nature changed, the gods who had originally stood for awesome natural forces were prostituted to stand for unethical organizations of collective human power in the forms of states, before these gods were driven right off into Limbo by Yahweh in Christendom and in Dār-al-Islām.

Plêthon had the nerve to re-evoke these banished gods. Moreover, in his high-handed treatment of the Hellenic mythology that he adored, he had the insight to cleanse the gods of their sinister 'politicization' and to present them in their authentic original role as symbols of the divinity inherent in non-human Nature.[111] In fact, Plêthon re-consecrated non-human Nature, and thereby re-imposed on human greed the primaeval curb of awe. At a date half-way through the fifteenth century of the Christian Era, this curb was still superfluous. Three-quarters of the way through the twentieth century, the astonishing advance of human technology in the meantime had made the Plêthonian resuscitation of this primaeval curb into the last possible sheet-anchor for a generation of mankind that was now threatening to wreck, no

---

[110] Milton: *Ode on the Morning of Christ's Nativity.*
[111] See III, 34, Ἐις Θεοὺς Προσρήσεις, pp. 132–203, especially pp. 158–60 and 164–6.

longer just some single local civilization, but human life itself. By 1974 'the rotten nonsense of the Hellenes'—i.e. the original religion of all mankind—had become, for the living generation, a serious alternative to self-inflicted genocide. At Florence in 1439, Plêthon predicted that, 'within a few years', neither Christianity nor Islam but Plêthon's version of the pre-Christian Hellenic religion would become the universal religion of mankind.[112] 'Few' is a relative word. On the time-scale of human history, a span of 535 years is as brief as the twinkling of an eye. In 1974, Plêthon's prediction no longer sounded as extravagant as it must have sounded in 1439 to George of Trebizond.

Then are we, in our day, to put down mighty Yahweh from his seat and re-exalt a *thiasos* of more ancient divinites: great Pan (an older 'Lord'), and perhaps Priapus, and Shiva-Dionysos too, as well as their less scandalous colleagues Demeter and Athena? What, reinstate the cloven hoof and the lingam? The Plêthonian renaissance of pre-Christian and pre-Muslim nature-worship may turn out to be as shocking for twentieth-century Western rationalists as it was for the fifteenth-century Ecumenical Patriarch Yennádhios.

Yet nature-worship has never been extirpated in India or in Eastern Asia, and these two regions, together, are the habitat of much more than half the human race. A god's power is demonstrated by his ability to take vengeance on human beings who dispute it. This is how Dionysos made Pentheus aware of who and what he was. In our day Mother Earth has begun to demonstrate to modern Man that he cannot violate her realm, the biosphere, with impunity. Yahweh may have licensed Man to subdue the Great Mother; but Yahweh's directive does not excuse, in this goddess's eyes, the impious liberties that Yahweh's licensee, Adam, has been taking with her. Between gods, as between human sovereign states, force is the *ultima ratio*. In the present conflict between the chthonic gods and the thunderer from Sinai, do ex-Christian rationalists feel confident that Yahweh will prevail? If we are in doubt, it will be rash to dismiss, as 'the rotten nonsense of the Hellenes', a religion that was already immemorially old before Judaism and Christianity and Islam were heard of.

[112] See above, pp. 299–300.

BIBLIOGRAPHY

Chapters II, II Appendix, III, IV

Blegen, C. W., *Troy and the Trojans* (London 1963), Thames & Hudson.

Bowra, C. M., 'The Meaning of a Heroic Age', in Kirk, *The Language and Background of Homer* (q.v.), pp. 22–48.

Burn, A. R., *The Lyric Age of Greece* (London 1960), Arnold.

Chadwick, J., 'The Greek Dialects and Greek Prehistory', in Kirk, op. cit. pp. 106–18.

——'Mycenaean Elements in the Homeric Dialect', in Kirk, op. cit. pp. 119–25.

Crossland, R. A., and Birchett, A. [eds.], *Bronze Age Migrations in the Aegean: Archaeological and Linguistic Problems in Greek History* (London 1974), Duckworth.

Desborough, V. R. d'A., *The Greek Dark Ages* (London 1972), Benn.

——*The Last Mycenaeans and their Successors: An Archaeological Survey c. 1200–c. 1000 B.C.* (Oxford 1966), Clarendon Press.

Dodds, E. R., 'Homer', in Kirk, op. cit. pp. 1–21.

Dow, S., 'The Greeks in the Bronze Age', in Kirk, op. cit. pp. 140–73.

Finley, M. I., 'Homer and Mycenae: Property and Tenure', in Kirk, op. cit. pp. 191–217.

Forsdyke, J., *Greece before Homer: Ancient Chronology and Mythology* (London 1956), Parrish.

Hood, Sinclair, *The Minoans* (London 1971), Thames & Hudson.

Hope Simpson, R. and Lazenby, J. F., *The Catalogue of Ships in Homer's Iliad* (Oxford 1970), Clarendon Press.

Kirk, G. S. [ed.], *The Language and Background of Homer: Some Recent Studies and Controversies* (Cambridge 1964), Heffers.

——'Objective Dating Criteria in Homer', in ibid., pp. 174–90.

Page, D. L., *History and the Homeric Iliad* (Berkeley and Los Angeles 1959), University of California Press.

Parry, Milman, *The Making of Homeric Verse: Collected Papers* (Oxford 1971), Clarendon Press.

Risch, E., 'Die Gliederung der griechischen Dialekte in neuer Zeit', in Kirk, op. cit. pp. 90–105.

Sakellariou, M. B., *La migration grecque en Ionie* (Athens 1958).

Schachermeyr, F., *Die ältesten Kulturen Griechenlands* (Stuttgart 1955), Kohlhammer.

——*Die minoische Kultur des alten Kreta* (Stuttgart 1964), Kohlhammer.

Snodgrass, A. M., *The Dark Age of Greece* (Edinburgh 1971), University Press.

Starr, C. G., *The Origins of Greek Civilization* (New York 1961), Knopf.

Taylour, *Lord* William, *The Mycenaeans* (London 1964), Thames & Hudson.

Vermeule, E., *Greece in the Bronze Age* (Chicago and London 1964), Chicago University Press.

Webster, T. B. L., *From Mycenae to Homer* (London 1958), Methuen.

Weinberg, S. S., 'The Stone Age in the Aegean', in *Cambridge Ancient History*, vol. i, 3rd edn., pp. 557–618 (Cambridge 1970), University Press.

Chapters V, VI, VII, and VIII Appendix

Anastos, M. V., 'Iconoclasm and Imperial Rule, 717-842', in *Cambridge Medieval History*, vol. iv, 2nd edn., part i, pp. 61-104.

Anonymus, *Τὸ Χρονικόν τοῦ Μορέως*, (i) ed. by J. Schmitt (London 1904), Methuen; (ii) ed. by P. Kalonaros (Athens 1940), Dhêmêtrákos.

——*Βασιλείον Διγενοῦς 'Ακρίτουλόγοι ὀκτώ*, ed., with translation, introduction, and commentary, by J. Mavrokordato (Oxford 1956), Clarendon Press.

Baynes, N. H., *Byzantine Studies and Other Essays* (London 1955), Athlone Press.

——and Moss, H. St. L. B. [eds.], *Byzantium* (Oxford 1948), Clarendon Press.

Beck, H.-G., *Geschichte der byzantinischen Volksliteratur* (Munich 1971), Beck.

Brown, P., 'The Rise and Function of the Holy Man in Late Antiquity', in *Journal of Roman Studies*, vol. lxi (1971), pp. 80-101.

Browning, R., *Medieval and Modern Greek* (London 1969), Hutchinson.

Cambridge Medieval History, vol. iv, *The Byzantine Empire*, 2nd edn. (Cambridge, part i 1966, part ii 1967), University Press.

Cameron, A., *Porphyrius the Charioteer* (Oxford 1973), University Press.

Dawkins, R. M., 'The Greek Language in the Byzantine Period', in Baynes and Moss, op. cit. pp. 252-67.

Delehaye, H., 'Byzantine Monasticism', in Baynes and Moss, op. cit. pp. 136-65.

Dhoúkas, *Historia Byzantina*, ed. by I. Bekker (Bonn 1834), Weber.

Dölger, F., 'Byzantine Literature', in *Cambridge Medieval History*, vol. iv, 2nd edn., part ii, pp. 207-63.

Dvornik, F., *Byzantine Missions among the Slavs* (New Brunswick 1970), Rutgers University Press.

——*The Slavs: Their Early History and Civilization* (Boston 1956), American Academy of Arts and Sciences.

Every, G., *The Byzantine Patriarchate, 451-1204* (London 1947), S.P.C.K.

Grabar, A., 'Byzantine Architecture and Art', in *Cambridge Medieval History*, vol. iv, 2nd edn., part ii, pp. 307-53.

Grégoire, H., 'The Byzantine Church', in Baynes and Moss, op. cit. pp. 86-135.

Haussig, H. W., *A History of Byzantine Civilization* (London 1971), Thames & Hudson.

Herman, E., 'The Secular Church', in *Cambridge Medieval History*, vol. iv, 2nd edn., part ii, pp. 105-33.

Hussey, J. M., *The Byzantine World* (London 1957), Hutchinson.

——and Hart, T. A., 'Byzantine Theological Speculation and Spirituality', in *Cambridge Medieval History*, vol. iv, 2nd edn., part ii, pp. 185-205.

Kandakouzênós, John, *Historiae*, ed. by L. Schopen (Bonn 1828-32), Weber, 3 vols.

Khalkokondýlês, Laónikos, *Historiae*, ed. by I. Bekker (Bonn 1843), Weber.

Kritóvoulos Imvriótês, *Ξυγγραφὴ 'Ιστοριῶν* in Ch. Müller, *Fragmenta Historicorum Graecorum*, vol. v (Paris 1883), pp. 40-161; *History of Mehmed the Conqueror*, English translation by C. T. Riggs (Princeton 1954), University Press.

Krumbacher, K., *Geschichte der byzantinischen litteratur (527-1453)*, 2nd edn. (Munich 1897), Beck.

l'Orange, H. P., and Nordhagen, P. J., *Mosaics* (London 1966), Methuen.

Makhairas, *Chronicle*, ed. by R. M. Dawkins (Oxford 1932), Clarendon Press, 2 vols.

Marshall, F. H., 'Byzantine Literature', in Baynes and Moss, op. cit. pp. 221-51.

Masai, F., *Pléthon et le platonisme de Mistra* (Paris 1956), Les Belles Lettres.

Meyendorff, *Baron*, and Baynes, N. H., 'The Byzantine Inheritance in Russia', in Baynes and Moss, op. cit. pp. 369-91.

Mêtsákês, K., *Βυζαντινὴ ὑμνογραφία* (Thessaloníkê 1971), *Πατριαρχικὸν Ἴδρυμα Πατερικῶν Μελετῶν*.

Moravcsik, Gy., 'Hungary and Byzantium in the Middle Ages', in *Cambridge Medieval History*, vol. iv, 2nd edn., part i, pp. 567–92.

Obolensky, D., *The Byzantine Commonwealth* (London 1971), Weidenfeld & Nicolson.

Phrantzês (Sphrandzês), George, Χρονικόν, ed. by I. Bekker (Bonn 1938) Weber; ed. by Vasile Grecu (Bucharest 1966).

Plêthon, Yemistos, Νόμων συγγραφῆς τὰ σωζόμενα: *Traité des Lois*, ed. by C. Alexandre, tr. by A. Pellisier (Paris 1858; reprint Amsterdam 1966), Hakkert.

Runciman, S., *The Great Church in Captivity* (Cambridge 1968), University Press.

——*A History of the Crusades*, vol. i (Cambridge 1951), University Press.

——*A History of the First Bulgarian Empire* (London 1930), Bell.

——*The Last Byzantine Renaissance* (Cambridge 1970), University Press.

Toynbee, A. J., 'The Modern West and the Main Body of Orthodox Christendom', with Annexes I and II, in *A Study of History*, vol. viii, pp. 150–98 and 679–83 (London 1954), Oxford University Press.

Trypanis, C. A. [ed.], *Medieval and Modern Greek Poetry: An Anthology* (Oxford 1951), Clarendon Press.

Vakalópoulos (Bakalópoulos), A. E., 'Die Frage der Glaubwürdigkeit der Leichenrede auf L. Notarás von Johannes Moschos', in *Byzantinische Zeitschrift* (1959), pp. 13–21.

——Ἱστοριά τοῦ νέου Ἑλληνισμοῦ: Thessaloníkê, vol. i (1961); vol. ii, part i (1964); vol. iii (i.e. vol. ii, part ii) (1968). Vol. i, English translation, *Origins of the Greek Nation: The Byzantine Period, 1204–1461* (New Brunswick 1970), Rutgers University Press.

Vasmer, M., *Die Slaven in Griechenland* (Berlin 1941), de Gruyter.

Vlasto, A. P., *The Entry of the Slavs into Christendom* (Cambridge 1970), University Press.

Vryonis Jr., Sp., *The Decline of Medieval Hellenism in Asia Minor and the Process of Islamization from the Eleventh through the Fifteenth Century* (Berkeley, Los Angeles, and London 1971), University of California Press.

Wellesz, E., 'Byzantine Music and Liturgy', in *Cambridge Medieval History*, vol. iv, 2nd edn., part ii, pp. 135–60.

Zachariä von Lingenthal, C. E. [ed.], *Jus Graeco-Romanum*, Pars III, *Novellae, Constitutiones* (Leipzig 1857), Weigel; reprinted in Zepos, J. and P. [eds.], *Jus Graeco-Romanum*, vol. i (Athens 1931).

Chapters VIII and IX (i)-(iii)

Amandos, K., *Anékdhota éngrapha perì Rhêga Velestinlê* (Athens 1930).

Anthimos, Patriarch of Jerusalem, Ἡ διδασκαλία πατρική (Istanbul 1798); English translation by Richard Clogg in *Middle Eastern Studies*, vol. v (1969), pp. 102–8.

Aravandinos, Sp. P., Ἱστορία τοῦ Ἀλῆ Πασᾶ τοῦ Τεπελενλῆ (Athens 1895), Kousoulínou.

Argenti, P. P., *Chius Vincta (1566–1912)* (Cambridge 1941), University Press.

——*The Expedition of Colonel Fabvier to Chios* (London 1933), Lane.

——*The Expedition of the Florentines to Chios* [1595] (London 1934), Lane.

——*The Massacres of Chios described in Contemporary Diplomatic Documents* (London 1932), Lane.

——*The Occupation of Chios by the Venetians, 1694* (London 1935), Lane.

Babinger, F., *Mehmed der Eroberer und Seine Zeit* (Munich 1953), Bruckmann.

Beaujour, F., *Tableau du commerce de la Grèce* (Paris 1800), Renouard, 2 vols.

Bótzaris, N., *Visions Balkaniques dans la préparation de la révolution grecque (1789–1820)* (Geneva 1962), Droz; (Paris 1962), Minard.

Boulter, V. M., 'The Exchange of Populations between Greece and Turkey', in *Survey of International Affairs, 1925*, vol. ii, pp. 257–99 (London 1928), Oxford University Press.

Camariano, N., *Alexandre Mavrocordato le Grand Drogman: activité diplomatique* (*1673-1704*) (Thessaloníkê 1970), Institute for Balkan Studies.

Campbell, J., and Sherrard, P., *Modern Greece* (London 1968), Benn.

Clarke, E. D., *Travels in Various Countries of Europe, Asia, and Africa*, part ii, section iii, pp. 281 and 285-8 [Ambelákia, 23-4 December 1801] (London 1816), Cadell and Davies.

Clogg, R., 'Two Accounts of the Academy of Ayvalík (Kydonies) in 1818-1819' [William Jowett, May 1818; Charles Williamson, 1819], in *Revue des Études Sud-Est Européennes*, Tome X (1972), no. 4, pp. 633-67.

——'The "Dhidhaskalía Patriki" (1798): an Orthodox Reaction to French Revolutionary Propaganda', in *Middle Eastern Studies*, vol. v (1969), pp. 87-115.

Clogg, R. [ed.], *The Struggle for Greek Independence* (London 1973), Macmillan.

Crusius, (Kraus), M., *Turcograeciae libri Octo* (Basel 1584).

Dakin, D., *The Greek Struggle for Independence 1821-1833* (London 1973), Batsford.

—— *The Unification of Greece, 1770-1923* (London 1972), Benn.

Daskalakis, A., *Rhigas Velestinlis* (Paris 1937).

David, C. E., dispatch dated 14 June 1824, enclosing 'Mémoire sur Scio', printed in Argenti, *The Massacres of Chios* (q.v.), pp. 52-95.

Davison, R. H., *Reform in the Ottoman Empire, 1856-1876* (Princeton 1963), University Press.

Dhêmêtrios-Apostolakis, I., Κυδωνιακὴ Μελεταὶ καὶ Παραλλισμοί, vol. i, Τὰ πρὸ τῆς κεταστροφῆς (Kydhonies 1914), "Ο Ἥλιος" Press.

d'Ohsson, I. M., *Tableau général de l'Empire Ottoman* (Paris 1788-1824), Didot, 7 vols.

Finlay, G., *A History of Greece from its Conquest by the Romans to the Present Time: B.C. 146- A.D. 1864*, ed. by H. F. Tozer, vols. v-vii (Oxford 1877), Clarendon Press.

Gerlach, S., *Tagebuch* (Frankfurt am Main 1674).

Gibb, H. A. R. and Bowen, H., *Islamic Society and the West*, London: vol. i, part i (1950); vol. i, part ii (1957), Oxford University Press.

Hadrovics, I., *L'Eglise serbe sous la domination turque* (Paris 1947), Presses Universitaires de France.

Hofmann, G., 'Patriarch Kyrillos Loúkaris: Einfluss Abendländischer Schriften auf seine Predikten', in *Orientalia Christiana Periodica*, vol. 7 (1921), pp. 250-65.

Inalcik, H., 'The Policy of Mehmed II towards the Greek Population of Istanbul and the Byzantine Buildings of the City', in *Dumbarton Oaks Papers*, Numbers Twenty-three and Twenty-four (1969-70), pp. 229-50.

Khrysanthópoulos, Photákos, Ἀπομνημονεύματα (Athens 1899), Sakellários, 2 vols.

Kolokotrónês, Th., Ἀπομνημονεύματα: Διήγησις συμβάντων τῆς Ἑλληνικῆς φυλῆς 1770-1836 (Athens 1901), Estía.

Koraês, A., Ἀπάνθισμα Ἐπιστολῶν, ed. by I. Rhotas (Athens 1839), Rhállês.

——Ἐπιστολαί (Athens 1885-6), Perrhes, 3 vols. (vol. iii in two parts).

—— *Mémoire sur l'état actuel de la civilisation dans la Grèce* (Paris 1803; Greek translation in Thereíanos, Ἀδαμάντιος κοραῆς (q.v.), vol. iii, Annex 4, pp. μζ'-πβ'.

League of Nations, *Greek Refugee Settlement* (II Economic and Financial, 1926, ii, 32).

Makriyiánnês, I., Ἀρχεῖον (Athens 1907), Vlastos, 2 vols.

Manéssês, A. J., 'L'activité et les projets politiques d'un patriote grec dans les Balkans vers la fin du XVIIIᵉ siècle', in *Balkan Studies*, vol. iii (1962).

Pandazópoulos, N. I., *Rhêgas Velestinlês* (Thessaloníkê 1964).

Prokesch-Osten, A. Freiherr von, *Geschichte des Abfalls der Griechen vom türkischen Reiche im Jahre 1821 und der Gründung des hellenischen Königreiches aus diplomatischen Standpunkte* (Vienna 1853-76), 6 vols.; vols. i-iii published by Braumüller; vol. vi by Gerold.

Rhêghas Velestinlês, Ἅπαντα, ed. by L. I. Vranoúsês (Athens 1968), Νεοέλληνες Κλασσικοι.

Rhêghas Velestinlês, *Les Oeuvres*, ed. by A. Daskalakis (Paris 1937).

Sakellários, M. V., Ἡ Πελοπόννησος κατὰ τὴν δευτέραν Τουρκοκρατίαν (*1715-1821*) (Athens 1939), Byzantinisch-neugriechischen Jahrbücher.

Sakkárês, G., Ἱστορία τῶν κυδωνιῶν (Athens 1920), Vitsikounákês.

Skholários, G. (Yennádhios II, Patriarch of Constantinople), Ἅπαντα (*Oeuvres Complètes*) (Paris [?]), 3 vols.

Thereíanos, D., Ἀδαμάντιος Κοραῆς (Trieste 1889-90), Economo, 3 vols.

Tsakonas, D., *Geist und Gesellschaft in Griechenland* (Bonn 1965), Bouvier.

Vlakhoyiánnês, G., Κλέφτες τοῦ Μοριᾶ (Athens 1935).

Vranoussês, L. I., *Rhêgas* (Athens 1953), Vasikê Vivliothêkê.

Vryonis, Jr., Sp., 'The Byzantine Legacy and Ottoman Forms', in *Dumbarton Oaks Papers*, Numbers Twenty-three and Twenty-four (1969-70), pp. 251-308.

Wittek, P., *The Rise of the Ottoman Empire* (London 1938), Royal Asiatic Society.

Woodhouse, C. M., *Capodistria* (London 1974), University Press.

—— *The Greek War of Independence: its Historical Setting* (London 1952), Hutchinson.

Chapter IX (iv)

Bien, P., *Kazantzakis and the Linguistic Revolution in Greek Literature* (Princeton 1972), University Press.

Browning, R., *Medieval and Modern Greek* (London 1969), Hutchinson.

Dawkins, R. M., 'The Greek Language in the Byzantine Period', in Baynes and Moss, op. cit., pp. 252-67.

Dhêmaras, K. Th.: Ὁ Κοραῆς καὶ ἡ ἐποχή του (Athens 1953), Actos.

Fauriel, C., *Chants Populaires de la Grèce Moderne* (Paris 1824-5), Didot, 2 vols.

Henderson, G. P., *The Revival of Greek Thought, 1620-1830* (Edinburgh 1971), Scottish Academic Press.

Jenkins, R. H. J., *Dionysius Solomós* (Cambridge 1940), University Press.

Kaváphês, K. P., Ἀνέκδοτα Ποιήματα (*1882-1923*) (Athens 1968), Ikaros.

—— Ποιήματα (*1896-1918*) (Athens 1963), Ikaros.

—— Ποιήματα (*1919-1933*) (Athens 1963), Ikaros.

Khadzidhákis, G. N., *Einleitung in die neugriechische Grammatik* (Leipzig 1892).

—— Μελέτη ἐπὶ τῆς Νέας Ἑλληνικῆς, ἢ Βάσανος τοῦ ἐλέγκου τοῦ ψευδοαττικισμοῦ (Athens 1884).

—— Μεσαιωνικὰ καὶ Νέα Ἑλληνικά (Athens 1905-7), 2 vols.

—— Σύντομος Ἱστορία τῆς Ἑλληνικῆς Γλωσσης (Athens 1915).

Koraês, A., *Vios Adhamandíou Koraê synghrapheis parà tou idhíou* (Paris 1833); reprinted in Dhêmaras, Ὁ Κοραῆς καὶ ἡ ἐποχή του, pp. 240-50.

Máximos of Gallipoli [translator], Ἡ καινὴ Διαθήκη . . . Δίγλωσσος (Geneva 1638).

Palamás, K., Ἅπαντα (Athens 1960-), 16 vols.

Pallis, A. A. [translator], Ἡ Νέα Διαθήκη . . . μεταφρασμένη (Liverpool 1902), 'Liverpool Bookseller'; reprinted 1910.

Passow, A. [ed.], *Carmina Popularia Graeciae Recentioris* (Leipzig 1860), Teubner.

Pendaghiótês, E., Χρονικὸν τοῦ Γαλαξειδίου, ed. by G. Valetas (Athens 1944), Ikaros.

Pernot, H. [ed.], *Recueil de textes en grec usuel* (Paris 1918), Garnier.

Petrópoulos, D. [ed.], Ἑλληνικα δημοτικὰ τραγούδια (Athens 1958), Βασικὴ Βιβλιοθήκη, 2 vols.

Politis (Polítês), L., *A History of Modern Greek Literature* (Oxford 1973), Clarendon Press.

—— Ἱστορια τῆς νέας ἑλληνικῆς λογοτεχνίας, 2nd edn. (Thessaloníkê 1969).

—— ὁ Σολωμὸς στὰ γράμματα τοῦ (Athens 1956).

Polítês, N. G., Ἐκλογαὶ ἀπὸ τὰ τραγούδια τοῦ ἑλληνικοῦ λαοῦ (Athens 1914), Estía; 6th edn. 1969.

——Μελέται περὶ τοῦ βίου καὶ τῆς γλώσσης τοῦ ἑλληνικοῦ λαοῦ (Athens 1904), Sakellários, 2 parts.

——Ποιητικὴ Ἀνθολογία (Athens 1964–7), Galaxias, 7 vols.

Psichari, J. (Psykhárês, I.), *Essais de grammaire historique néo-grecque* (Paris 1886–9), 2 vols.

——Τὸ ταξίδι μου, *1888*, ed. by A. Ányelos (Athens 1971), Ἑρμῆς.

Sephérês, G., Ποιήματα, 5th edn. (Athens 1964), Ikaros.

Solomós, Dh., Ἅπαντα, ed. by L. Polítês (Athens 1948–60), Ikaros, 2 vols. and Appendix.

Thumb, A., *Handbuch der neugriechischen Volkssprache*, 2nd edn. (Strassburg 1910), Trübner.

Trypanis, C. A. [ed.], *Medieval and Modern Greek Poetry* (Oxford 1951), Clarendon Press.

INDEX

324

Index

Dhiyenês Akrîtas (epic), 126
Dhosítheos, Patriarch of Jerusalem, 152, 154, 176
Dhoúkas, 130 n. 133
Dictaean Cave (Crete), 293
Dio Chrysostom, 139
Diocletian, Emperor , 88
Dionysius the Areopagite, 101
Dionysius II, Despot of Sicily, 160
Dionysos (god), 42-3, 64, 69, 314
Dniepr Cossacks, 175
Dodecanese, 38, 233, 242, 288
Dodona, 273
dogma (Byzantine), 82, 85-6, 99
Don Cossacks, 142, 175
Dorian invasion, 23, 274
Doric dialect, 23 n. 94, 49-50, 274-5, 288
Doxiadis, Constantine, 266 n. 448
Dragoman of the Fleet, 148-9, 153
Dragoman of the Porte, 148-9, 153
Drakhmáni (Elateia; Central Greece), 10-11
Druz Christians, 198
Ducatus Romanus, 117 n. 106
Ducetius (of Sikel), 40

East Roman Empire: modern Greeks seek to revive ('Great Idea'), 5, 140-1, 215, 218-19, 221, 228, 234; effect on Byzantines, 73, 80-1, 85, 89, 113, 119-22; and city-states, 74; decline, 113, 118, 121, 215, 229; effect on Eastern Orthodox Church, 113-19; and peasantry, 119, 211; taxation and finance, 119-21; economy, 120-1, 139; extinction, 120, 122; territory, 121, 234; relations with Bulgaria, 121 2; Greek predominance, 136; and Ottomans, 136-7, 153, 181-2; Greeks' claim to, 155-6; successor states, 156, 227; eleventh-century revival and reverses, 167-8, 197, 215; recognition of Papal supremacy, 168; relations with West, 166-71. *See also* Byzantine Greeks, Eastern Orthodox Church, and Rome
Eastern Orthodox Church: dogma and theology, 82, 85-6, 99; marriage laws, 85, 106; and transubstantiation, 86; monasticism, 86-7, 102-5, 236; and state, 87; liturgy, 87, 90, 96, 98-100, 106, 112 n. 95, 125, 135, 137, 248; expansion and conversions to, 90-5, 98, 109, 111; linguistic liberality, 90-1, 93, 97-9, 134-5, 154; submits to Ottomans, 94, 141-2, 144-5, 148, 150-1, 154, 177-8, 183-4, 198, 309; development of, 95-7; use of Greek language, 95-9, 134-5, 137, 245, 248-9; mysticism in, 101-2; and laity, 105-7; mockery in, 106; clergy in, 106-7; and schism, 108, 110 n. 90; ecclesiastical juris-

diction, 108-11, 116-18, 142; reconciliation with Rome, 108 n. 87; government, 110-11, 115; relations with East Roman Empire, 113-19; and fragmentation, 115-16; and neo-Hellenism, 160-2, 298-9; and papal authority, 162, 168, 177, 220, 248, 270, 296-7; and relations with West, 163, 166-9, 171-9, 220, 248, 309; endows higher education, 170; and Protestantism, 171-3; hostility to philosophy, 171 n. 28; influence of Roman theology on, 175-7, 220; and secularizing/rationalizing movement, 176-8; and 'Enlightenment', 177-8, 309; conversions to Islam from, 183, 313; in Greek national state, 235; supports autocephaly, 235-6. *See also* Byzantine Greeks, Christianity, and Roman Catholic Church
Echmiazin, Katholikos of, 142
'economy' (*oikonomia*), 82-5
Ecumenical Patriarchate, 107, 111, 143 n. 21, 145, 216, 220, 235, 307, 309
Efsévios (Eusebius) of Kaisárea, 128
Efstathios, Archbishop of Thessaloníkê, 104, 130 n. 138
Egypt: civilization, 2, 7; Mycenaean trade with, 15, 37; attacks on, 20-1, 284-5; Greek rule in, 44; religious independence, 44, 94; sculpture, 57; revolt against Persia, 66; Athens and, 66; Greek language in, 136; Ottomans conquer, 142; Greek settlers in, 186; decline, 199
eikóns, 78-9, 84, 100, 102, 112, 116-17, 296. *See also* iconoclasm
Eirênê, Empress, 55, 116
'Ekistics', 266 n. 448
Elefsís, 244
Eleusis, 64, 68 9, 293
Elis, 69, 281, 283-5, 292
Elisaius, 159 n. 9
'Ellás', Rhêgas' map of, 222-3
Embório (Khios), 38 n. 1, 280-1, 285-6
Emperors (Byzantine), status of, 83-4, 115-16, 118
England, *see* Britain
English language, 123-5
'Enlightened Europe', 233, 309
Êpeiros, 23 n. 94, 156, 170 n. 22, 203 n. 215, 218, 230, 273
Ephesus, 61 n. 53, 70, 102 n. 58, 108 n. 88
Ephorus, 128
Epicurus, 71, 80 n. 10
Epidaurus, 293
epigoni, 28, 45-6, 259
Erotókritos (epic), 247
Ethiopia, 166
Etruscans, 55, 59-60
Euboea, 277-8
Euripides, 266, 312